£24·95

Combinatorial
Search

Wiley–Teubner Series in Computer Science

Editorial Board

Combinatorial Search

Martin Aigner
Fachbereich Mathematik
Freie Universitat Berlin
West Germany

B. G. TEUBNER
Stuttgart

JOHN WILEY & SONS
Chichester · New York · Brisbane · Toronto · Singapore

CIP-Titelaufnahme der Deutschen Bibliothek

Aigner, Martin:
Combinatorial search / Martin Aigner. – Stuttgart : Teubner :
Chichester : Wiley, 1988
  (Wiley–Teubner series in computer science)

  ISBN 3–519–02109–9 (Teubner) Gb.

  ISBN 0–471–92142–4 (Wiley) Gb.

British Library Cataloguing in Publication Data available

Printed and bound in Great Britain by the Bath Press, Avon

Preface

In the past few decades many papers have appeared under the general heading "search", both in pure and applied mathematics. No doubt, the rise of high-speed computers and the analysis of algorithms greatly contributed to this rapid development. The origin of search theory and its first great result was Shannon's work on the entropy of experiments and his noiseless coding theorem. However, until the sixties the connection between coding and search was not well understood: The average time needed to locate an unknown object equals the average length of an optimal code which, in turn, is roughly the information or uncertainty encountered at the start of the search. Initially, sorting problems provided the paradigm for combinatorial search. Since then, several other questions have been studied successfully from this point of view, such as problems on graphs, posets, geometrical configurations, and many more.

The purpose of this book is to give an introduction to the basic ideas (Chapter 1) and present a collection of the most interesting instances of search problems (Chapters 2-6). At the beginning the scope of combinatorial search is spelled out (roughly meaning that all tests of the search process are error-free). The arrangement of chapters 2-6 allows the reader to use them almost independently and to combine chapter 1 and some of the subsequent sections into an introduction to search theory. Every section is followed by a set of exercises. An asterisk indicates that this exercise is particularly helpful or interesting, with a solution appearing at the end of the book. Every chapter is concluded by a list of unsolved problems and a guide to further reading. The references are by no means exhaustive or representative; usually they have been included because they were used in one way or another in the preparation of the text. Books are marked by an asterisk. As to the problems, I would be grateful to learn of any solution or suggestion by the reader.

I was introduced to combinatorial search during a series of lectures given by the late A. Renyi and G. Katona at the University of North Carolina at Chapel Hill in 1969. Thanks to them I have taken a keen interest in the subject ever since. Special thanks are due to T. Andreae, D. Grieser and E. Triesch who read all or part of the manuscript; to M. Barrett for her competent type-setting done in LaTeX; and to P. Spuhler of Teubner-Verlag for the pleasant cooperation on the project.

It is my hope that I have been able to record some important developments that search theory has seen in recent years while retaining its origins as an intuitively appealing mathematical pleasure.

Berlin,
May 1988

M. Aigner

Contents

Chapter 1

Basic Results

In practically every field of human activity we encounter problems which require that we search for an unknown object. This may be a search in the literal sense of the word, e.g. the search for a faulty part in a mechanical device which caused it to malfunction, or for the exact place in a datafile where a certain piece of information is stored. It may also be a search of a vaguer manner like the search for the meaning of a cryptical message or for the basic principles of a complex system. Most of these problems have one thing in common: The aim is to find the unknown object in as short a time or with as little cost as possible.

As is the case with any part of applied mathematics, our first task is then to formulate a reasonable model for a general search process and develop methods for the solution of concrete problems. This shall be the content of the present chapter.

1.1 The Model

Let us start with a few examples, thereby gaining some first insights into common features and also characteristic differences of various search problems.

Example 1.1. Weighings. Perhaps the oldest and certainly most widely known problem concerns the search for a counterfeit coin. In a set of n coins there is precisely one fake coin, say, heavier than the rest. We want to identify the counterfeit coin with as few weighings as possible using an equal arms balance. A variant is: Suppose there are some good coins whose common weight is known and also some heavier coins whose common weight is also known. Determine the counterfeit coins by using a spring scale.

Example 1.2. Group tests. It is feared that a contagious desease has infected parts of a given population. In order to identify the sick, a blood sample is drawn from every single person. Instead of evaluating all samples (which may be too costly), some samples are poured together, and the mixture is then analyzed. In this way we learn whether the group tested contains at least one sick member or is overall healthy. By judiciously choosing the groups, the sick subpopulation is isolated.

Example 1.3. Sorting. We are given an ordered list of items (say records or words, ordered alphabetically), and an additional item. The task is to bring the new item into its proper place using as few comparisons as possible.

Example 1.4. Twenty questions. This is a game known in variants all over the world. Somebody leaves the room. The other players agree on a certain subject (or a person or almost anything). Upon returning the player is required to determine this subject by asking only yes-no questions, winning if he learns the answer with at most 20 queries.

In all these examples we are given a ground-set containing the unknown element or elements, and we are faced with the task to identify these elements by performing certain tests.

Definitions. Let S be a non-empty set, called the *search domain*, $x^* \in S$, and let $\mathcal{F}$ be a family of functions on S, called the *test family*. We choose a function $f_1 \in \mathcal{F}$ and receive as answer the value $f_1(x^*)$. With this information we choose again a function $f_2 \in \mathcal{F}$ and get back the value $f_2(x^*)$, and so on. A (successful) *search algorithm* $\mathcal{A}$ consists in the choice of functions $f_1, f_2, f_3, \ldots \in \mathcal{F}$ such that the values $f_1(x^*), f_2(x^*), f_3(x^*), \ldots$ determine x^* uniquely. We tacitly assume that at least one such sequence always exists. The pair $(S, \mathcal{F})$ is called a *search process*.

Let us emphasize again that the choice of the k-th test function $f_k \in \mathcal{F}$ will, in general, depend on the values $f_1(x^*), f_2(x^*), \ldots, f_{k-1}(x^*)$ previously obtained. Although we will often use the sequential notation $\mathcal{A} = (f_1, f_2, f_3, \ldots)$ for a search algorithm, we mean the "dynamic" interpretation of $\mathcal{A}$ in the above sense.

Example 1.5. Let us analyze the sorting problem of Example 1.3 for a small case. The elements $y_1 < y_2 < y_3 < y_4$ are given, and z is a new element which is to be brought into its right place. The search domain is $S = \{0, 1, 2, 3, 4\}$ where $i \in S$ means that $y_i < z < y_{i+1}$ with $0 \in S$ meaning that $z < y_1$ is at the top of the list and $4 \in S$ that $y_4 < z$, i.e. z is at the bottom of the list. We have four test functions f_j corresponding to y_j at our disposal, $j = 1, \ldots, 4$. If we compare z and y_j then either $z > y_j$ which means that the unknown place x^* is one of $j, j + 1, \ldots, 4$, or $z < y_j$ which implies that x^* is one of $0, 1, \ldots, j - 1$. Hence the test functions f_j are completely described by

$$f_j(i) = \begin{cases} 1 & \text{if } i \geq j \\ 0 & \text{if } i < j \end{cases} \quad (j = 1, \ldots, 4),$$

meaning $f_j(x^*) = 1$ if $y_j < z$ and $f_j(x^*) = 0$ if $z < y_j$.

A possible algorithm $\mathcal{A}$ is the following:

Test 1: $y_3 : z$, i.e. f_3 is the first test function.
    If $f_3(x^*) = 1$, i.e. $y_3 < z$, then
        Test 2: f_4
            if $f_4(x^*) = 1$, then $x^* = 4$, i.e. $y_4 < z$ $-$ stop.
            if $f_4(x^*) = 0$, then $x^* = 3$, i.e. $y_3 < z < y_4$ $-$ stop.

    If $f_3(x^*) = 0$, i.e. $z < y_3$, then
        Test 2: f_2
            if $f_2(x^*) = 1$, then $x^* = 2$, i.e. $y_2 < z < y_3$ $-$ stop.
            if $f_2(x^*) = 0$, then

        Test 3: f_1
            if $f_1(x^*) = 1$, then $x^* = 1$, i.e. $y_1 < z < y_2$ $-$ stop
            if $f_1(x^*) = 0$, then $x^* = 0$, i.e. $z < y_1$ $-$ stop.

We see that this algorithm determines x^* with at most 3 tests and needs $\frac{1}{5}(3 \cdot 2 + 2 \cdot 3) = \frac{12}{5}$ tests on the average. To represent $\mathcal{A}$ we use the following tree-diagram, where the round nodes show the candidates for x^* that are still possible at this stage of the algorithm, and the end-nodes depict the uniquely determined elements of S at the end.

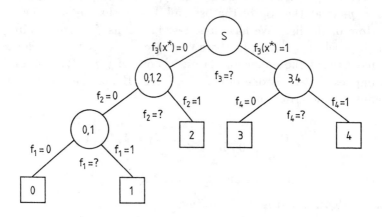

Figure 1.1

Search processes $(S, \mathcal{F})$ can be classified according to a variety of different features. Let us briefly discuss some of the most important types.

A. **Cardinality of S.** If S is finite or denumerable, then we speak of *discrete processes*, otherwise of *continuous processes* (e.g. determination of a certain real number in $[0, 1]$).

B. An a priori probability distribution $\underline{p}$ may be given on S, i.e. $x^* \in S$ is the unknown element with probability $p(x^*)$. In example 1.2 one can imagine that the probability of a certain person or subpopulation being infected depends on location or social status or the like. The case when no probabilities are given may also be treated in this general setting, by assuming uniform distribution (as in example 1.5).

C. We may classify the processes according to the family $\mathcal{F}$ of admissible test functions. In example 1.5 we are only permitted functions which attain 2 values and even among these we may use only a few, depending on the linear structure of S.

D. A very important distinction concerns the nature of the algorithms $\mathcal{A}$. An algorithm $\mathcal{A}$ is called *sequential* if the choice of f_k depends on the values $f_1(x^*), \ldots, f_{k-1}(x^*)$ obtained until then (as in example 1.5). If the functions $f_1, f_2, \ldots$ are fixed beforehand, then $\mathcal{A}$ is called *predetermined*. In some books one finds the terms dynamic and static, or adaptive and non-adaptive. Since predetermined algorithms can obviously be regarded as special cases of sequential algorithms they will, in general, take longer than the best sequential algorithms. On the other hand, if the data needed for sequential algorithms exceed the available space, predetermined algorithms may well be called for.

F.. The final two distinctions concern the global nature of our search processes. So far, we have been required to identify the unknown element x^* with certainty. For very large problems, however, we may be content with determining x^* "almost" certainly, say with probability $\geq 1 - \varepsilon$. We then speak of *probabilistic algorithms*. Another variant is that we stop the algorithm once we know that x^* is in a "small" subset. In this case we speak of *approximate algorithms*. For example, in the real number search we may be satisfied to determine x^* up to an error $\delta > 0$, i.e. we stop when we know that x^* is in an interval of length $\leq \delta$.

F. Lastly, we classify search processes according to their overall aim. The problem at hand may call for minimizing the length of successful algorithms considering all possibilities for x^*; this is called a *worst-case problem*. Or we may be interested in minimizing the average length (given a certain a priori distribution). We then speak of an *average-case problem*. Again, the tests may have different costs and we may be required to look for algorithms of minimal cost, or a combination of time and cost (so-called trade-off problems).

After this general overview it is time to spell out the precise scope of combinatorial search treated in this book. Without further mention, we will always make the following assumptions:

1. The search domain S is finite; the cardinality of S will mostly be denoted by $|S| = n$.

2. The test family $\mathcal{F}$ is finite. Since every function $f \in \mathcal{F}$ attains only finitely many values, we may assume without loss of generality that $f(S) \subseteq \{0, 1, \ldots, q-1\}$ for all $f \in \mathcal{F}$, where $q \geq 2$.

3. We are only interested in algorithms that determine the unknown element with certainty.

The most important and, at any rate, best understood case arises for $q = 2$, i.e. when there are always at most two answers to a test query, as in the game of 20 questions. We then call $(S, \mathcal{F})$ a *binary search process*. It is clear that for $q = 2$ a test function $f \in \mathcal{F}$ is determined by the set $A = \{x \in S : f(x) = 1\}$, with $f(x^*) = 1$ or 0 according to whether $x^* \in A$ or $x^* \notin A$. Hence $\mathcal{F}$ may be identified with a family $\mathfrak{A} \subseteq 2^S$, and every algorithm $\mathcal{A}$ with a sequence of sets $A_1, A_2, \ldots$ in $\mathfrak{A}$. We will frequently make use of this correspondence.

Exercises 1.1.

1*. Suppose 9 coins are given one of which is heavier. Show that it is possible to detect the counterfeit coin with 2 weighings using an equal arms balance. Show that 3 weighings suffice for 27 coins. Generalize to $n = 3^k$.

2. A variant: Suppose it is not known in advance whether the false coin is heavier or lighter than the good coins. How many weighings are now needed for $n = 3^k$?

3*. Find an algorithm which sorts four coins of different weight (according to weight) using weight comparisons of single coins only. What if some coins may have the same weight?

4. As in the previous exercise assume that the n coins have different weights. Find the heaviest coin using $n - 1$ single-coin comparisons. Is this best possible? What about the average case, assuming that all coins are equally likely to be heaviest?

5*. As in example 1.2 assume there are 10 persons some of whom may be sick (or all may be healthy). If we test a subset A, then $f(A) = 1$ means that A contains a sick person; if $f(A) = 0$ then all are healthy. By testing one person after the other we certainly identify the sick using 10 tests. Can you do better?

6. Show that the algorithm given in example 1.5 is best possible for both the worst-case and the average-case problem.

7. Develop predetermined algorithms for the counterfeit problem for $n = 9, 27$, or general 3^k.

8*. Suppose we are given a group of mn people arranged in an $m \times n$-grid. You are required to find an unknown person X^* in the grid by asking questions of the form: Is X^* in the i-th row? Is X^* in the j-th column? How many questions do you need? Try a small example first.

9. Consider as in example 1.5, $y_1 < \ldots < y_{15}$ and a new element z which is to be sorted in. Construct an approximate algorithm of length 3 which determines the correct place of z up to an error of 1 place.

1.2 Search Processes and Trees

Consider a search process $(S, \mathcal{F})$ satisfying the assumptions given at the end of the last section.

Definition. $(S, \mathcal{F})$ is called an (n, q)-*process*, if $\mid S \mid = n \geq 1$ and $f(S) \subseteq \{0, 1, \ldots, q-1\}$, $q \geq 2$, for all $f \in \mathcal{F}$.

Suppose we are given a successful algorithm $\mathcal{A} = \{f_1, f_2, \ldots\}$. The values $f_1(x^*), f_2(x^*), \ldots, f_{\ell(x^*)}(x^*)$ determine $x^* \in S$ uniquely where $\ell(x^*)$ will, in general, depend on x^*.

Definition. The number $\ell(x^*)$ is called the (search) *length* for x^* in $\mathcal{A}$, and $L(\mathcal{A}) = \max_{x^* \in S} \ell(x^*)$ the *length* of $\mathcal{A}$. If we have a probability distribution $\underline{p} = (p(x^*) : x^* \in S)$ on S, (i.e. $p(x^*) \geq 0$ for all $x \in S$ and $\sum_{x^* \in S} p(x^*) = 1$), then $\overline{L}(\mathcal{A}; \underline{p}) = \sum_{x^* \in S} p(x^*)\ell(x^*)$ is called the *average length* of $\mathcal{A}$ (relative to $\underline{p}$). If a distribution is not explicitly given, then the uniform distribution on S is assumed, whence in this case $\overline{L}(\mathcal{A}) = \frac{1}{n} \sum_{x^* \in S} \ell(x^*)$.

We can now formulate the two main problems:

Let $(S, \mathcal{F})$ be an (n, q)-search process with distribution $\underline{p} = (p(x^*) : x^* \in S)$:

(L) *Determine* $L(S, \mathcal{F}) := \min_{\mathcal{A}} L(\mathcal{A})$.

$(\overline{L})$ *Determine* $\overline{L}(S, \mathcal{F}; \underline{p}) := \min_{\mathcal{A}} \overline{L}(\mathcal{A}; \underline{p})$.

$L(S, \mathcal{F})$ is termed the *worst-case cost* or *worst-case complexity* of the search process $(S, \mathcal{F})$, $\overline{L}(S, \mathcal{F}; \underline{p})$ the *average cost*. Any algorithm $\mathcal{A}$ with

$L(\mathcal{A}) = L(S, \mathcal{F})$ or $\overline{L}(\mathcal{A}; \underline{p}) = \overline{L}(S, \mathcal{F}; \underline{p})$ is called an (L)-*optimal* or $(\overline{L})$-*optimal* algorithm, respectively. Note that the problems (L) and $(\overline{L})$ are well- defined since there are obviously only a finite number of reasonable algorithms under the given assumptions.

Our first goal is to describe all possible algorithms for $(S, \mathcal{F})$. Let $\mathcal{A} = \{f_1, f_2, \ldots\}$ be any algorithm. After the tests $f_1, f_2, \ldots, f_k$ we have the following information: The unknown element x^* belongs to the set $S_k(x^*)$ of all $x \in S$ for which $f_1(x) = f_1(x^*), \ldots, f_k(x) = f_k(x^*)$. Hence,

$$S = S_0(x^*) \supseteq S_1(x^*) \supseteq \ldots \supseteq S_{\ell(x^*)}(x^*) = \{x^*\}$$

by the definition of $\ell(x^*)$. More generally, we set

$$S(e_1, \ldots, e_k) = \{x \in S : f_1(x) = e_1, \ldots, f_k(x) = e_k\}$$
$$\text{for } e_1, \ldots, e_k \in \{0, 1, \ldots, q - 1\}.$$

$S(e_1, \ldots, e_k)$ is then the set of elements $x \in S$ that are still candidates for the unknown object x^* when the outcomes of the first k tests were $e_1, \ldots, e_k$. Hence, S together with all non-empty sets $S(e_1, \ldots, e_k)$ for $k = 1, 2, \ldots$ completely describe the algorithm $\mathcal{A}$.

As in example 1.5 of the last section, we associate with every non-empty set $S(e_1, \ldots, e_k)$ a node and join $S(e_1, \ldots, e_k)$ with every non-empty successor-set $S(e_1, \ldots, e_k, e)$, $e \in \{0, 1, \ldots, q - 1\}$. The sets $S(e_1, \ldots, e_k, e)$ clearly partition $S(e_1, \ldots, e_k)$ into at most q blocks. The end-nodes correspond bijectively to the sets $S_{\ell(x^*)}(x^*) = \{x^*\}$. Let us now formalize this tree structure.

Definition. A *directed graph* G consists of a pair (V, K) of finite sets with $K \subseteq V^2$. The elements of V are called *nodes* (or *vertices*), those of K *edges* (or *arrows*). We say that the edge $e = (u, v) \in K$ *leads* from u to v, in symbols $u \to v$. A *path* in G is a sequence $v_0 \to v_1 \to \ldots \to v_k$ with $v_i \neq v_j$ for all $i \neq j$. A path $v_0 \to \ldots \to v_k$ together with $v_k \to v_0$ is called a *directed cycle* in G. Now we call $T = (V, K)$ a *rooted tree* if T has no directed cycle and if there is a distinguished node r, the *root* of T, such that for every node $v \neq r$ there is precisely one path $r \to v_1 \to v_2 \to \ldots \to v$ leading from the root to v.

If $u \to v$, then u is called the *predecessor* or *father* of v, and v a *successor* or *son* of u. It follows from the definition that any node $\neq r$ has a unique predecessor. The node $v \in V$ is an *end-node* or *leaf* of T, if no edge leads out from v, i.e. there is no edge (v, w); otherwise v is called an *inner node*.

We usually denote the collection of leaves and inner nodes by $E(T)$ and $I(T)$, respectively, distinguishing them in a picture by boxes (for $E(T)$) and circles (for $I(T)$). The *length* $\ell(v)$ of a node v is the length (= number of edges) of the unique path from r to v, where by definition $\ell(r) = 0$. The *length of the tree* is the number

$$L(T) = \max_{v \in V} \ell(v).$$

Example 1.6. The tree in figure 1.2 has 22 nodes, 12 of them being leaves and 10 inner nodes. The length of the tree is 4.

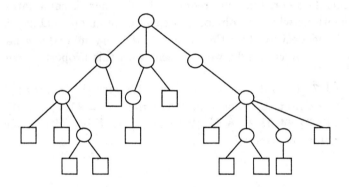

Figure 1.2

To connect this general concept with our previous discussion we give the following definition.

Definition. The rooted tree T is called an (n, q)-*tree* if T possesses precisely n leaves and if there are at most q successors to every inner node. T is a *regular* (n, q)-tree if any inner node has precisely q successors.

The tree in figure 1.2 is a $(12,4)$-tree whereas the tree in figure 1.1 is a regular $(5,2)$-tree. If $q = 2$, then we speak of a *binary tree* and, in general, without specifying n of a *q-ary tree*. As in the figure we usually draw trees from top to bottom whence we may omit the arrows. Since, in this chapter at least, we are always dealing with rooted trees, we will just speak of trees.

Let $\mathcal{A} = \{f_1, f_2, \ldots\}$ be an algorithm for the (n,q)-search process $(S, \mathcal{F})$. By associating the root to S and nodes to all non-empty sets $S(e_1, \ldots, e_k)$, we obtain an (n,q)-tree T whose leaves $\boxed{x^*}$ correspond bijectively to the elements $x^* \in S$. Furthermore, the length $\ell(x^*)$ of x^* in $\mathcal{A}$ equals precisely the length $\ell\boxed{x^*}$ in T, whence $L(\mathcal{A}) = L(T)$. T is termed the *decision tree* corresponding to $\mathcal{A}$. We see further that an inner node $v \leftrightarrow S(e_1, \ldots, e_k)$ can be uniquely recovered from the leaves $E(T)$ since v corresponds precisely to the subset of those x^* for which a path from v to x^* exists.

Definition. An algorithm $\mathcal{A}$ of an (n,q)-process is called *irreducible*, if always $S(e_1, \ldots, e_k) \underset{\neq}{\supseteq} S(e_1, \ldots, e_k, e)$ holds, and *regular*, if all sets $S(e_1, \ldots, e_k, e)$ are non-empty, $e = 0, 1, \ldots, q - 1$, whenever $|S(e_1, \ldots, e_k)| \geq 2$.

An irreducible algorithm thus reduces the number of candidates at every stage, something which we obviously expect from an optimal algorithm. For the associated decision tree this means that every inner node has at least two successors. Accordingly, we call trees with this property *irreducible*.

Example 1.7. Let T be the tree of figure 1.3 with the leaves as given. The inner nodes are from top to bottom, left to right: $S = \{1, 2, \ldots, 10\}, \{1, 2, 3\}, \{4, \ldots, 9\}, \{2, 3\}, \{4, 5\}, \{7, 8, 9\}, \{2, 3\}$ and $\{4\}$. T is a (10,3)-tree which is neither regular nor irreducible.

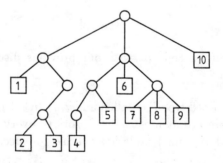

Figure 1.3

In summary: To every algorithm $\mathcal{A}$ of an (n,q)-process there corresponds a *unique* (n,q)-tree T, the decision tree of $\mathcal{A}$. Irreducible algorithms correspond to irreducible trees, regular algorithms to regular trees.

Conversely, to any (n, q)-tree T there exists an algorithm $\mathcal{A}$ for *some* (n, q)-search process $(S, \mathcal{F})$ whose decision tree is precisely T. To see this we just label the leaves of T with the elements of S and the edges leading out from an inner node with $\{0, 1, \ldots, q - 1\}$ in some manner. If we then define $f_k : S \to \{0, 1, \ldots, q - 1\}$, $k = 1, \ldots, L(T)$, by

$$f_k(x^*) = \begin{cases} j & \text{if } k \leq \ell(x^*) \text{ and the } k\text{-th edge} \\ & \text{in the path from } r \text{ to } x^* \text{ is labeled } j \\ 0 & \text{if } k > \ell(x^*), \end{cases}$$

we obtain an algorithm whose decision tree is precisely T.

Example 1.8. Let $S = \{1, 2, \ldots, 10\}$. The figure shows one possible correspondence $T \longrightarrow \mathcal{A}$.

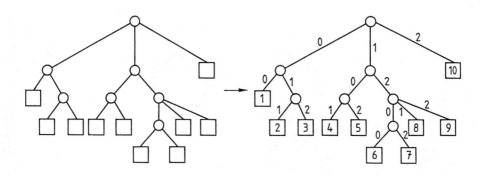

Figure 1.4

We obtain $f_1(1) = f_1(2) = f_1(3) = 0$, $f_1(4) = \ldots = f_1(9) = 1$, $f_1(10) = 2$; $f_2(1) = f_2(4) = f_2(5) = f_2(10) = 0$, $f_2(2) = f_2(3) = 1$, $f_2(6) = f_2(7) = f_2(8) = f_2(9) = 2$, etc..

Notice that the algorithm $\mathcal{A}$ thus defined is *predetermined*. Hence every tree corresponds to a predetermined algorithm. $\mathcal{A}$ is dependent on x^* in the sense that $\mathcal{A}$ stops after $\ell(x^*)$ tests, since x^* is then determined.

It should be clear from our discussion that, in general, many algorithms correspond to a given tree, owing to the freedom we have in labeling the leaves and the edges. It is therefore a fundamental question, *what the trees look like*, that correspond to a given process $(S, \mathcal{F})$. At any rate, if *all* test functions are permitted, i.e. $\mathcal{F} = \{0, 1, \ldots, q-1\}^S$, then any tree is possible, whence we may regard our problems (L) and $(\overline{L})$ as problems on (n, q)-trees. This will be the subject of sections 4 and 5.

Example 1.9. The simplest search process $(S, \mathcal{F}_0)$ is the *element-for-element search*. Let $S = \{x_1, \ldots, x_n\}$ and suppose $\mathcal{F}_0$ consists of all functions f_i, $i = 1, \ldots, n$ with

$$f_i(x^*) = \begin{cases} 1 & \text{if } x^* = x_i \\ 0 & \text{otherwise.} \end{cases}$$

Any algorithm $\mathcal{A}$ consists then in a permutation of a subset of the f_i's. It is obvious that in this case $L(S, \mathcal{F}_0) = n - 1$. If we are given a probability distribution p on S, we number the elements such that $p(x_1) \geq p(x_2) \geq \ldots \geq p(x_n)$. An optimal $(\overline{L})$-algorithm is equally obviously given by $\{f_1, \ldots, f_{n-1}\}$. Figure 1.5 shows the corresponding decision tree.

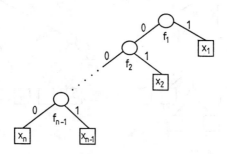

Figure 1.5

We conclude that $\overline{L}(S, \mathcal{F}_0; p) = \sum_{i=1}^{n-1} ip_i + (n-1)p_n$. If p is the uniform distribution, then $\overline{L}(S, \mathcal{F}_0) = \frac{n+1}{2} - \frac{1}{n}$.

Exercises 1.2.

1. Construct decision trees for some or all of the exercises of section 1.

2. Consider the element-for-element search in example 1.9 with probabilities $p_1 \geq p_2 \geq \ldots \geq p_n$. Compute $\overline{L}(\mathcal{A}; p)$ for every one of the $n!$ algorithms $\mathcal{A}_{i_1, \ldots, i_{n-1}} = \{f_{i_1}, \ldots, f_{i_{n-1}}\}$.

3*. Suppose $|S| = 7$ and consider the binary process $(S, \mathfrak{A}_{\leq 2})$ where $\mathfrak{A}_{\leq 2} = \{A \subseteq S : |A| \leq 2\}$. Develop algorithms for this process and describe the optimal $(7,2)$-trees that occur. What is $L(S, \mathfrak{A}_{\leq 2})$ and $\overline{L}(S, \mathfrak{A}_{\leq 2})$ assuming uniform distribution?

4*. Discuss the worst-case cost of $(S, \mathfrak{A}_{\leq 2})$ of the previous exercise when only predetermined algorithms are permitted.

5. Show that an optimal algorithm for a process $(S, \mathcal{F})$ is always irreducible, for both the worst-case and average-case.

6. There are several ways to arrange the nodes of a tree in a natural order, e.g. top-to-bottom, left-to-right. Discuss some other plausible orderings.

7*. A challenging problem. Two (n, q)-trees with leaves labeled $1, \ldots, n$ are called *isomorphic* if there exists a bijection ϕ of the node-sets which maps edges $u \to v$ precisely onto edges $\phi u \to \phi v$ (so, in particular, the root onto the root), with $\phi i = i$ for all end-nodes. Determine the number $t(n)$ of non-isomorphic regular binary trees. (Answer: $t(n) = 1.3.5 \ldots (2n - 3)$, $n \geq 2$.)

8. Show that the number of edges in a tree is always one less than the number of nodes.

1.3   Search Processes and Codes

There is another very useful way to represent algorithms $\mathcal{A}$ of an (n, q)-search process $(S, \mathcal{F})$. Let $A = \{0, 1, \ldots, q - 1\}$. For every $x^* \in S$, we consider the sequence $f_1(x^*), f_2(x^*), \ldots, f_{\ell(x^*)}(x^*)$ which uniquely determines x^*. This sequence is a vector $w(x^*) \in A^{\ell(x^*)}$, which we call the *codeword* of x^* (with respect to $\mathcal{A}$). The *code* corresponding to $\mathcal{A}$ is then the collection of all codewords $w(x^*)$, $x^* \in S$.

Let us give a general definition of what we mean by a code.

Definition. Let A be a set. We set $A^* = \bigcup\limits_{i=0}^{\infty} A^i$ and call the elements of A^* *words* over the alphabet A. By convention, A^o consists of the empty word. A *code* C over the *alphabet* A is just a subset of A^*. C is called an

$(n, q) - code$ if $\mid A \mid = q$ and $\mid C \mid = n$. If $w \in C$ and $w \in A^\ell$, then $\ell = \ell(w)$ is the *length* of the codeword w, and $L(C) = \max\limits_{w \in C} \ell(w)$ is the *length* of C.

Hence, to any algorithm $\mathcal{A}$ of an (n, q)-process $(S, \mathcal{F})$ there corresponds a unique (n, q)-code $C = \{w(x^*) : x^* \in S\} \subseteq A^*$, called the *search code* of $\mathcal{A}$. The mapping $x^* \mapsto w(x^*)$ is a bijection between S and C with $\ell(x^*) = \ell(w(x^*))$ for all $x^* \in S$.

Example 1.10. Consider the algorithm in Figure 1.4. Here $S = \{1, 2, \ldots, 10\}$ and we have the correspondence $S \longleftrightarrow C$:

1	$\longleftrightarrow$	00	6	$\longleftrightarrow$	1200
2		011	7		1202
3		012	8		121
4		101	9		122
5		102	10		2

Search codes C possess the following important property. If $v \neq w \in C$, then v is not an initial segment of w, and vice versa. In other words, if $v = (e_1, \ldots, e_s)$ and $w = (e'_1, \ldots, e'_t)$ with $s \leq t$, then we do not have $e_1 = e'_1, e_2 = e'_2, \ldots, e_s = e'_s$. To see this, suppose v corresponds to $x^* \in S$ and w to $y^* \in S$. By the definition of $v = (f_1(x^*), f_2(x^*), \ldots, f_{\ell(x^*)}(x^*))$, $w = (f_1(y^*), \ldots, f_{\ell(y^*)}(y^*))$, $s = \ell(x^*)$ and $t = \ell(y^*)$, the equalities $f_1(x^*) = f_1(y^*), \ldots, f_{\ell(x^*)}(x^*) = f_{\ell(x^*)}(y^*)$ imply that $\{x^*, y^*\} \subseteq S_{\ell(x^*)}(x^*)$ which means that x^* would not be uniquely determined.

Codes with this property are called *prefix codes*. So we see that the search code of any algorithm $\mathcal{A}$ is a prefix code. But the converse is also true. To every (n, q)-prefix code C over the alphabet $A = \{0, 1, \ldots, q - 1\}$ there exists an algorithm $\mathcal{A}$ of some (n, q)-search process $(S, \mathcal{F})$ whose search code is precisely C. We just take any bijection $x^* \in S \leftrightarrow w(x^*) \in C$ and define the functions $f_k : S \to \{0, 1, \ldots, q - 1\}$ by

$$f_k(x^*) = \begin{cases} j & \text{if } k \leq \ell(w(x^*)) \text{ and } j \text{ is the} \\ & \quad k\text{-th letter of } w(x^*) \\ 0 & \text{if } k > \ell(w(x^*)). \end{cases}$$

Example 1.11. Let $S = \{1, 2, 3, 4, 5\}$, $A = \{0, 1, 2\}$ and $C = \{0102, 022, 1201, 101, 2010\}$. Figure 1.6 shows an algorithm (in tree representation) whose search code is C.

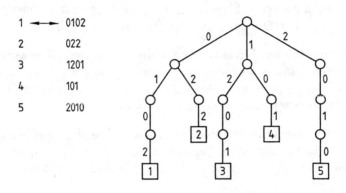

Figure 1.6

As in the last section, we see that the algorithm constructed in this way is actually *predetermined*. Hence we conclude that to every (n, q)-prefix code C there exists a predetermined algorithm of some (n, q)-process. Again, the central question is, which codes correspond to algorithms of a given test family $\mathcal{F}$. If $\mathcal{F} = \{0, 1, \ldots, q - 1\}^S$, then all prefix codes are possible, and our (L)- and $(\overline{L})$-problems reduce to problems on codes.

The unique correspondence: prefix code $C \longrightarrow$ tree T should now be clear. The nodes of T are all initial segments of the words in C (including the empty segment), and we connect two such segments $I \longrightarrow J$ if I is an initial segment of J and J contains precisely one more letter than I.

We now have three desciptions of an algorithm $\mathcal{A}$: a) as a sequence of functions, b) as a code, c) as a tree. The code and the tree do not reflect the possible sequential character of $\mathcal{A}$ anymore (apart from the number of tests needed to identify x^*), and the tree does not distinguish between the function values, but only tells whether these values are distinct or not.

Exercises 1.3.

1. Construct the search codes of some or all of the exercises in section 1.

2. Define the terms irreducible and regular for a search code.

3*. Let $\mathcal{A}$ be a regular algorithm of an (n, q)-search process. Show that the associated code C has the following property: Whenever a letter is removed from a codeword of C, then the resulting code fails to have the prefix property. Show, conversely, that for binary codes this latter property characterizes regularity (but not for $q \geq 3$).

4. Consider the first 100 numbers $S = \{0, 1, 2, \ldots, 99\}$. The usual decimal representation is obviously not a prefix code over $\{0, 1, \ldots, 9\}$. Find an (L)-optimal prefix code of S over $\{0, 1, \ldots, 9\}$ and an $(\overline{L})$-optimal prefix code assuming uniform distribution.

5. Consider again the weighing problem with one of n coins being heavier. What do the corresponding search codes look like? Is every $(n, 3)$-prefix code also search code of some weighing algorithm?

6*. Consider the distribution $\underline{p} = (p_1, \ldots, p_n)$ for a binary process and assume $p_i + p_j > p_k$ for all i, j, k. Show that the lengths of two codewords in an $(\overline{L})$-optimal code differ by at most one.

7. The ordering $y_1 < y_2 < y_3 < y_4 < y_5$ is given, and z is a new element to be sorted in. Suppose the probability distribution is $p(y_1 < z < y_2) = p(y_2 < z < y_3) = p(y_5 < z) = \frac{1}{10}$, $p(z < y_1) = p(y_4 < z < y_5) = \frac{1}{5}$ and $p(y_3 < z < y_4) = \frac{3}{10}$. Find an $(\overline{L})$-optimal search code.

8*. This exercise discusses an important property enjoyed by prefix codes. Let S and the alphabet A be given. Any injective mapping $\kappa : S \longrightarrow A^*$ is called a *coding* of S over A. We extend κ to a mapping κ^* from $S^* \longrightarrow A^*$ by setting $\kappa^*(x_{i_1} \ldots x_{i_s}) = \kappa(x_{i_1}) \ldots \kappa(x_{i_s})$ for $x_{i_1}, \ldots, x_{i_s} \in S$. Thus κ^* is what is usually called juxtaposition. Example: $S = \{x_1, x_2, x_3\}$, $A = \{0, 1\}$, $\kappa(x_1) = 0$, $\kappa(x_2) = 1$, $\kappa(x_3) = 01$, then $\kappa^*(x_1 x_2) = \kappa^*(x_3) = 01$, $\kappa^*(x_2 x_3) = 101$. κ is a coding but suffers from an obvious deficiency. If the receiver reads the message 01, then he does not know whether $x_1 x_2$ or x_3 was sent. Hence we call $C = \kappa(S)$ *uniquely decodable* if $\kappa^* : S^* \longrightarrow A^*$ is injective as well. Prove: C is a prefix code iff C is uniquely decodable and whenever $v \in C$ is a prefix of $w \in C^*$ then $w = vv'$ with $v' \in C^*$.

1.4 Search Processes With All Tests Admitted: Worst Case

When an (n,q)-search process $(S, \mathcal{F})$ admits all possible test functions, i.e. $\mathcal{F} = \{0,\ldots,q-1\}^S$, then, as explained in the previous sections, we may confine our attention to prefix codes or trees. To solve the main problems of section 1, it is easiest to consider trees. Denote by $T(n,q)$ the class of (n,q)-trees.

Proposition 1.1. *Let $T \in T(n,q)$ and denote by $I = I(T)$ the set of inner nodes. Then*

i) $|I| \geq \lceil \frac{n-1}{q-1} \rceil$,

ii) T *is regular iff* $|I| = \frac{n-1}{q-1}$. *In particular, for a regular tree we must have* $q - 1 \mid n - 1$,

Conversely, to every pair (n,q) with $n \geq 1$, $q \geq 2$, there exists an (n,q)-tree with $|I| = \lceil \frac{n-1}{q-1} \rceil$, and hence a regular (n,q)-tree with $|I| = \frac{n-1}{q-1}$ if $q - 1 \mid n - 1$.

Proof. Let $T \in T(n,q)$. There is precisely one edge leading into every node except the root. On the other hand, there are at most q edges leading away from every inner node, thus

$$n + |I| - 1 \leq |I| \, q,$$

from which i) and ii) follow. For the converse, we use induction on $k = \lceil \frac{n-1}{q-1} \rceil$. For $k = 0$, i.e. $n = 1$, the trivial tree $\square$ (just consisting of the root) will do, and for $k = 1$ the tree consisting of the root and $n \leq q$ successor end-nodes. Now let $k \geq 2$ and $n - 1 = k(q - 1) - r$, $0 \leq r < q - 1$. Then $n - q = (k - 1)(q - 1) - r$ and by the induction hypothesis there exists an $(n - q + 1, q)$-tree T' with $|I(T')| = k - 1$. Choosing an arbitrary leaf of T' and making the replacement,

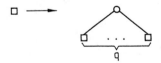

we obtain a tree $T \in T(n,q)$ with $|I(T)| = k = \lceil \frac{n-1}{q-1} \rceil$. $\square$

Example 1.12. There is an especially important type of (n,q)-trees with $|I| = \lceil \frac{n-1}{q-1} \rceil$ which warrants detailed discussion. Let $T \in \mathcal{T}(n,q)$ with E the set of leaves, and $L(T) = L$. The k-*level* $S_k(T)$ of T is defined as the set of nodes of length k, i.e. $S_k(T) = \{v \in V : \ell(v) = k\}$, $k = 0, 1, \ldots, L$. The tree T is called *complete* iff

  i) $v \in S_k$, $k \le L - 2 \Rightarrow v$ has precisely q successors.

 ii) T has the maximal number of leaves on S_{L-1} which are possible under
     i). (Note that i) implies $E \subseteq S_{L-1} \cup S_L$.)

For $L = 0$ the conditions are trivially satisfied. Hence we may assume $L \ge 1$. Because of i), we have $|S_k(T)| = q^k$ for $k = 0, 1, \ldots, L-1$. Let S_{L-1} contain a leaves and thus $b = q^{L-1} - a$ inner nodes, where $b > 0$ by the assumption $L(T) = L$. From $qb \ge n - a$, we infer

$$(q-1)b \ge n - a - b = n - q^{L-1},$$

and thus

$$b \ge \lceil \frac{n - q^{L-1}}{q-1} \rceil.$$

The minimal possible number for b is therefore $b = \lceil \frac{n-q^{L-1}}{q-1} \rceil$ whence the maximal possible number for a is $a = \lfloor \frac{q^L - n}{q-1} \rfloor$. We conclude $|I| = \sum_{k=0}^{L-2} q^k + b = \frac{q^{L-1}-1}{q-1} + \lceil \frac{n-q^{L-1}}{q-1} \rceil = \lceil \frac{n-1}{q-1} \rceil$. Because of $b > 0$ and $a \ge 0$ we further see that $q^{L-1} < n \le q^L$, i.e. $L = \lceil \log_q n \rceil$, which means that L is uniquely determined by i) and ii). In summary, any complete (n,q)-tree T has length $L(T) = \lceil \log_q n \rceil$, $\lfloor \frac{q^L - n}{q-1} \rfloor$ leaves on level S_{L-1} and $\lceil \frac{nq - q^L}{q-1} \rceil$ leaves on level S_L.

Example 1.13. Figure 1.7 shows two complete $(13,3)$-trees.

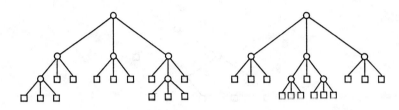

Figure 1.7

We now solve the worst-case problem for (n, q)-trees. We use the short notation $L(n, q) := \min\{L(T) : T \in \mathcal{T}(n, q)\}$.

Theorem 1.2. *Let $n \geq 1$, $q \geq 2$. Then*

$$L(n, q) = \lceil \log_q n \rceil,$$

where $\log_q n$ is the logarithm to the basis q.

Proof. Let $T \in \mathcal{T}(n, q)$ with $L(T) = L$. Since there are at most q successors to every inner node, we see by induction that for the k-level $S_k(T)$

$$|S_k(T)| \leq q^k \qquad (k = 0, 1, \ldots, L).$$

If v is an end-node of T with $\ell(v) < L$, then we replace v by an inner node v'_0 and attach to v'_0 a string of descendent nodes $v'_1, v'_2, \ldots, v'_{L-\ell}$ with $\ell(v'_i) = \ell(v) + i$, where $v'_{L-\ell}$ is an end-node again. In this way, we obtain a new tree $T' \in \mathcal{T}(n, q)$ with $E(T') \subseteq S_L(T')$. By our inequality above, we conclude $n = |E(T)| = |E'(T)| \leq q^L$ and thus $L \geq \lceil \log_q n \rceil$, since L is an integer. The complete trees of example 1.12 show that this bound can actually be attained. $\square$

Remark. The complete trees are, in general, not the only examples of (L)-optimal trees. Figure 1.8 shows an (L)-optimal $(5,2)$-tree which is plainly not complete.

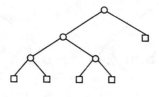

Figure 1.8

As every (n, q)-process $(S, \mathcal{F})$ for arbitrary test families $\mathcal{F}$ can be represented as a decision tree, we see that $\lceil \log_q n \rceil$ is a *lower bound* for the worst-case cost of any such process.

Corollary 1.3. *Let $(S, \mathcal{F})$ be any (n, q)-process. Then*

$$L(S, \mathcal{F}) \geq \lceil \log_q n \rceil.$$

The lower bound in Corollary 1.3 is usually called the *information-theoretic bound* for the process $(S, \mathcal{F})$. The reason is the following. One of the central problems in information theory is to find a reasonable measure for the *information content $H(S)$* of an event S which has, say, n possible outcomes. Let us make the following experiment: Suppose person B knows the outcome of S, whereas person A does not. How many questions must A ask in order to establish the outcome of S with certainty? (The questions correspond, of course, to the test family $\mathcal{F}$.) The number of questions necessary is then a first rough measure for $H(S)$. The more questions A has to ask, the higher $H(S)$ will be. Since the first question has at most q answers, the number of possible outcomes after the query is at least $\frac{n}{q}$ in the worst case. Similarly, after two questions, the number of possible outcomes is at least $\frac{n}{q^2}$, and so on. Since after L questions, A knows the outcome with certainty, we must have $1 \geq \frac{n}{q^L}$ or $L \geq \lceil \log_q n \rceil$. Note that this reasoning provides another proof of **1.3**. We will return to this information-theoretic viewpoint later on.

Example 1.14. Consider the weighing problem in example 1.1. We have n coins one of which is heavier. We are required to find the counterfeit coin x^* by weighings with an equal arms balance. The search domain S consists of the n coins, and the tests f have three possible outcomes since the false coin may be on the left-hand or right-hand side or it may be in the remaining set not considered by f. Corollary 1.3 tells us that at least $\lceil \log_3 n \rceil$ weighings are needed. Since not all tests are permitted (the left- and right-hand sides must always contain the same number of coins) it is not immediately clear whether $\lceil \log_3 n \rceil$ weighings will actually suffice. The reader can easily convince himself that there are indeed successful weighing algorithms using only $\lceil \log_3 n \rceil$ tests, or he may wait until chapter 2 where this topic will be treated in depth.

Exercises 1.4.

1*. Let $T \in \mathcal{T}(n, 2)$ be regular. Prove $e(T) = i(T) + 2(n - 1)$ where $e(T) = \sum_{v \in E} \ell(v)$, $i(T) = \sum_{v \in I} \ell(v)$.

2. Which irreducible trees $T \in \mathcal{T}(n, q)$ achieve $\max\{L(T) : T \in \mathcal{T}(n, q)$ irreducible$\}$? Which achieve $\max\{\overline{L}(T)\}$?

3. Consider the sorting problem. We are given n elements which are ordered according to an unknown linear order. S is therefore the set of all $n!$ orderings, and we are required to determine the proper order by making comparisons $a : b$, where as answer we receive $a < b$ or $b < a$. Compute the information-theoretic lower bound $\lceil \log n! \rceil$ for $n \leq 10$, and find algorithms achieving this bound for $n \leq 6$.

4*. Recall the grid problem in exercise 1.1.8 and suppose you are allowed questions of the form: Is X^* in rows I or columns J? for $I \subseteq \{1, \ldots m\}$, $J \subseteq \{1, \ldots, n\}$. Construct an algorithm whose length exceeds the information-theoretic bound by at most 1.

5. Give an immediate answer to exercise 1.1.5 by using Corollary 1.3.

6*. Solve the weighing problem in example 1.1.1 with one counterfeit coin by constructing an algorithm of length $\lceil \log_3 n \rceil$.

1.5 Search Processes With All Tests Admitted: Average Case

We turn to the $(\overline{L})$-problem for (n, q)-processes $(S, \mathcal{F})$ when $\mathcal{F} = \{0, 1, \ldots, q - 1\}^S$. Again we consider the class of $\mathcal{T}(n, q)$ of (n, q)-trees. The following inequality is of central importance.

Proposition 1.4. (Kraft's inequality)

i) Let $T \in T(n,q)$ and let $\ell_1,\ldots\ell_n$ be the lengths of the leaves of T. Then $\sum_{i=1}^{n} q^{-\ell_i} \leq 1$ with equality iff T is regular.

ii) Suppose $\ell_1,\ldots,\ell_n \in I\!N_0$ satisfy $\sum_{i=1}^{n} q^{-\ell_i} \leq 1$. Then there exists an (n,q)-tree whose leaves have precisely the lengths $\ell_1,\ldots,\ell_n$.

Proof. To prove i), we note first that an arbitrary (n,q)-tree T can be transformed into a regular (n',q)-tree T' with $n' \geq n$ by attaching leaves to "non-saturated" inner nodes of T. Since the sum $\sum q^{-\ell_i}$ will increase by this process, it suffices to show $\sum q^{-\ell_i} = 1$ for regular (n,q)-trees T. We use induction on $k = \frac{n-1}{q-1}$ (see Proposition 1.1). For $k = 0$, i.e. $n = 1$, we have $T = \square$ and $q^{-0} = 1$. Now assume $k \geq 1$. We replace in T an end-configuration

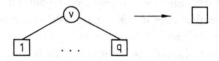

where we assume that the inner node v has length $\ell - 1$ and the successors are the leaves $1,\ldots,q$. The new tree T' is a regular $(n - q + 1, q)$-tree and hence satisfies the equality in the proposition by the induction hypothesis. We conclude for the original tree T

$$\underbrace{\sum_{i=1}^{n} q^{-\ell_i}}_{T} = \sum_{i=q+1}^{n} q^{-\ell_i} + q \cdot q^{-\ell} = \underbrace{\sum_{i=q+1}^{n} q^{-\ell_i} + q^{-(\ell-1)} = 1}_{T'}.$$

Let, conversely $\ell_1,\ldots,\ell_n \in I\!N_0$ with $\sum_{i=1}^{n} q^{-\ell_i} \leq 1$ be given. Set $w_k := \mid \{i : \ell_i = k\} \mid$, $k = 0, 1, \ldots, L = \max_i \ell_i$, i.e. w_k is the number of leaves of length k in the tree T to be constructed. The condition of the proposition reads for the w_k's

$$\sum_{k=0}^{L} w_k q^{-k} \leq 1,$$

or equivalently

(1.1) $$w_0 q^L + w_1 q^{L-1} + \ldots + w_{L-1} q + w_L \leq q^L.$$

We construct T inductively. If $w_0 = 1$, then $L = 0$ by (1.1), i.e. $T = \square$. Suppose we have already constructed the tree down to level S_k. Consider the k-th level S_k. If we had constructed the complete tree (with q successors each time) we would obtain q^k nodes on S_k. However, we have already designated w_i nodes on S_i to be leaves ($i = 1, \ldots, k-1$). Hence on S_k, the nodes below these end-nodes are not available anymore, and we conclude that on S_k we have $q^k - \sum_{i=0}^{k} w_i q^{k-i}$ inner nodes at our disposal. (1.1) implies

$$w_{k+1} q^{L-k-1} \leq q^L - \sum_{i=0}^{k} w_i q^{L-i},$$

i.e.

$$w_{k+1} \leq q^{k+1} - \sum_{i=0}^{k} w_i q^{k+1-i} = q\left(q^k - \sum_{i=0}^{k} w_i q^{k-i}\right).$$

We conclude that all w_{k+1} leaves on level S_{k+1} can be reached from inner nodes on S_k, and the proof is complete. $\square$

Example 1.15. To illustrate the foregoing construction, consider $n = 9$, $q = 3$ and the sequence $\ell_1 = 1$, $\ell_2 = 2$, $\ell_3 = \ell_4 = \ell_5 = \ell_6 = 3$, $\ell_7 = \ell_8 = \ell_9 = 4$. We have $w_0 = 0$, $w_1 = 1$, $w_2 = 1$, $w_3 = 4$, $w_4 = 3$ and $w_1 3^3 + w_2 3^2 + w_3 3 + w_4 = 51 \leq 81 = 3^4$. Figure 1.9 shows the construction of a proper tree where at the last step we suppress all pending branches.

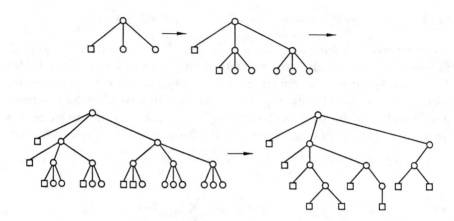

Figure 1.9

Before coming to the main results of this section we review some elementary facts of the logarithm functions. As before, we denote by $\log_a x$ the logarithm to the basis $a > 1$, and by $\ln$ the natural logarithm $\log_e$. The connection between these functions is given by

$$\log_a x = \frac{1}{\ln a}\ln x \qquad (x > 0)$$

and thus

(1.2) $$\log_a x = \frac{1}{\log_b a}\log_b x \qquad (x > 0,\ a, b > 1).$$

This means, that any two logarithms differ just by a constant positive factor. Furthermore

(1.3) $\ln x \leq x - 1$ for all $x > 0$, with equality precisely when $x = 1$.

Lemma 1.5. *Let* $s_1, \ldots, s_n$ *and* $y_1, \ldots, y_n$ *be positive real numbers with* $\sum_{i=1}^{n} s_i \leq \sum_{i=1}^{n} y_i$. *Then*

(1.4) $$\sum_{i=1}^{n} y_i \log_a \frac{y_i}{s_i} \geq 0 \text{ for every } a > 1,$$

with equality precisely when $s_i = y_i$ for all i.

Proof. By (1.2), it suffices to prove (1.4) for the natural logarithm. Considering (1.3), we have

$$\sum y_i \ln \frac{s_i}{y_i} \leq \sum y_i \left(\frac{s_i}{y_i} - 1\right) = \sum s_i - \sum y_i \leq 0,$$

and hence $\sum y_i \ln \frac{y_i}{s_i} \geq 0$. The last assertion follows directly from (1.3) since $\ln \frac{s_i}{y_i} = \frac{s_i}{y_i} - 1$ must hold for all i. $\square$

Let $\underline{p} = (p(x_1), \ldots, p(x_n))$ be a probability distribution on the leaves of (n, q)-trees. The following celebrated theorem by C. Shannon [1948] solves the $(\overline{L})$-problem with an error < 1. Again, we use the shorthand notation $\overline{L}(n, q; \underline{p}) := \min\{\overline{L}(T; \underline{p}) : T \in \mathcal{T}(n, q)\}$.

Theorem 1.6. *Let $n \geq 1$, $q \geq 2$, and $\underline{p} = (p_1, \ldots, p_n)$ a probability distribution on the leaves. Then*

$$-\sum_{i=1}^{n} p_i \log_q p_i \leq \overline{L}(n, q; \underline{p}) < \left(-\sum_{i=1}^{n} p_i \log_q p_i\right) + 1.$$

Proof. Assume $p_i > 0$ for all i. To prove the left-hand inequality we have to show that for any (n, q)-tree T with lengths $\ell_1, \ldots, \ell_n$,

$$\sum_{i=1}^{n} p_i \ell_i \geq -\sum_{i=1}^{n} p_i \log_q p_i$$

holds. Let $T \in \mathcal{T}(n, q)$ with lengths $\ell_1, \ldots, \ell_n$. By Kraft's inequality **1.4**, $\sum_{i=1}^{n} q^{-\ell_i} \leq 1$. Applying **1.5** to the sequence $q^{-\ell_1}, \ldots, q^{-\ell_n}$ and $p_1, \ldots, p_n$, we obtain $\sum p_i \log_q (p_i q^{\ell_i}) \geq 0$, and thus $-\sum p_i \log_q p_i \leq \sum p_i \ell_i$.

For a proof of the strict inequality on the right, define natural numbers ℓ_i by $-\log_q p_i \leq \ell_i < -\log_q p_i + 1$ for all i. Notice that the ℓ_i's are uniquely determined with $\ell_i \geq 0$ because of $0 < p_i \leq 1$. By definition, we have $\frac{1}{p_i} \leq q^{\ell_i}$, i.e. $q^{-\ell_i} \leq p_i$ for all i, and thus

$$\sum_{i=1}^{n} q^{-\ell_i} \leq \sum_{i=1}^{n} p_i = 1.$$

By the second part of Proposition 1.4, we infer the existence of an (n, q)-tree T with lengths $\ell_1, \ldots, \ell_n$, whose average length $\overline{L}(T; \underline{p}) = \sum_{i=1}^{n} p_i \ell_i$ is bounded above by

$$\sum p_i \ell_i < \sum p_i(-\log_q p_i + 1) = \left(-\sum p_i \log_q p_i\right) + 1.$$

We can get rid of the assumption $p_i > 0$ for all i by stipulating $0 . \log_q 0 = 0$. The proof goes then through without restrictions. $\square$

It is common use to represent $-\sum p_i \log_q p_i$ with respect to the basis 2. By (1.2) we have

$$-\sum p_i \log_q p_i = \frac{-\sum p_i \log_2 p_i}{\log_2 q}.$$

Definition.   The expression $H(p_1, \ldots, p_n) := -\sum_{i=1}^{n} p_i \log_2 p_i$ is called the *entropy* of the distribution $(p_1, \ldots, p_n)$.

Hence we may rewrite **1.6** in the form

$$(1.5) \qquad \frac{H(p_1, \ldots, p_n)}{\log_2 q} \leq \overline{L}(n, q; \underline{p}) < \frac{H(p_1, \ldots, p_n)}{\log_2 q} + 1.$$

Analogous to the previous section, **1.6** provides a general lower bound for the $(\overline{L})$-problem.

Corollary 1.7. *Let* $(S, \mathcal{F})$ *be any* (n, q)-*process with probability distribution* $\underline{p} = (p_1, \ldots, p_n)$. *Then*

$$\overline{L}(S, \mathcal{F}; \underline{p}) \geq -\sum_{i=1}^{n} p_i \log_q p_i = \frac{H(p_1, \ldots, p_n)}{\log_2 q}.$$

Let us return once more to the information-theoretic point of view. The entropy is the fundamental measure of information contained in an event S whose outcomes occur with probabilities $p_1, \ldots, p_n$. Why is the average length of an optimal question procedure more apt to be a measure of information than the worst-case? For simplicity, consider $q = 2$. Suppose our experiment S consists in throwing a coin where the probability of heads or

tails is $\frac{1}{2}$ each. We need one throw to decide the outcome. Now, for a second experiment S', assume the coin is rigged; the probability for obtaining
heads is 0.99 and that of tails is 0.01. Again, we need one throw to decide
the outcome, so there is no difference in the worst case. But it is intuitively
clear that in S the outcome is vastly more uncertain than in S', and thus
that the information content $H(S)$ is much greater than $H(S')$. By looking
at the average behavior we have

$$H(S) = -\frac{1}{2}\log_2\frac{1}{2} - \frac{1}{2}\log_2\frac{1}{2} = 1$$

$$H(S') = -0.99\log_2 0.99 - 0.01\log_2 0.01 = 0.0808.$$

Figure 1.10 shows the behavior of $H(p, 1-p) = -p\,\log\,p - (1-p)\log(1-p)$
for $p \in [0,1]$.

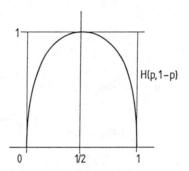

Figure 1.10

By requiring certain natural properties of the information content $H(p_1, \ldots,$
$p_n)$, e.g. $H(p_1, \ldots, p_n)$ should reach a maximum when $\underline{p}$ is the uniform
distribution, it can be readily shown that $H(p_1, \ldots, p_n) = -\sum p_i \log_2 p_i$ is
the *only* function satisfying all these properties (see any of the cited books
on information theory).

Now that we have determined $\overline{L}(n, q; \underline{p})$ up to an error < 1, we tackle the
question as to the precise value of $\overline{L}(n, q; \underline{p})$.
We consider first the uniform distribution $p_1 = \ldots = p_n = \frac{1}{n}$. Theorem 1.6
tells us that

$$\log_q n \le \overline{L}(n, q; \frac{1}{n}, \ldots, \frac{1}{n}) < \log_q n + 1.$$

Let $T \in T(n,q)$ with leaves E. We call the sum $e(T) = \sum_{v \in E} \ell(v)$ the *external length* of T. Hence $e(T) = n\overline{L}(T; \frac{1}{n}, \ldots, \frac{1}{n})$, and our task consists in finding the minimal value of $e(T)$. A moment's thought shows that precisely the complete trees of example 1.12 achieve this minimum. Clearly, any inner node v on level S_{L-1} has at least two successors since otherwise we could just move the unique successor up to v, thereby reducing $e(T)$. Condition i) for complete trees is now obvious, since if there existed an inner node $w \in S_k$, $k \leq L-2$, with less than q successors, then we could move up some leaf of length L to level S_{k+1}, which again reduces $e(T)$. Under the presence of i), condition ii) is now clearly required for optimality. Let us denote the minimal external length by $e(n,q)$. We can easily compute $e(n,q)$ by recalling that any complete (n,q)-tree has $a = \lfloor \frac{q^{L}-n}{q-1} \rfloor$ leaves on level $L-1$ and $n-a$ leaves on level L. Noting that $L = \lceil \log_q n \rceil$, we obtain

$$e(n,q) = a(L-1) + (n-a)L = nL - a = n\lceil \log_q n \rceil - \lfloor \frac{q^L - n}{q-1} \rfloor.$$

Theorem 1.8. *Let $n \geq 2$. Then for $e(n,q) = \min\{e(T) : T \in T(n,q)\}$,*

$$e(n,q) = n\lceil \log_q n \rceil - \lfloor \frac{q^{\lceil \log_q n \rceil} - n}{q-1} \rfloor$$

$$\overline{L}(n,q; \frac{1}{n}, \ldots, \frac{1}{n}) = \lceil \log_q n \rceil - \frac{1}{n} \lfloor \frac{q^{\lceil \log_q n \rceil} - n}{q-1} \rfloor.$$

Let us see how far $\overline{L}(n,q; \frac{1}{n}, \ldots, \frac{1}{n})$ can differ from the lower bound $\log_q n$ established in Theorem 1.6. Set $\lceil \log_q n \rceil = \log_q n + \theta$, $0 \leq \theta < 1$, and $\lfloor \frac{q^L-n}{q-1} \rfloor = \frac{q^L-n}{q-1} - r$, $0 \leq r < 1$. With $L = \lceil \log_q n \rceil = \log_q n + \theta$, we have

$$\begin{aligned}
\overline{L}(n,q; \frac{1}{n}, \ldots, \frac{1}{n}) &= \log_q n + \theta - \frac{1}{n} \frac{q^L}{q-1} + \frac{1}{q-1} + \frac{r}{n} \\
&= \log_q n + \theta - \frac{q^\theta}{q-1} + \frac{1}{q-1} + \frac{r}{n} \\
&= \log_q n + \frac{1}{q-1}(\theta(q-1) - q^\theta + 1) + \frac{r}{n}.
\end{aligned}$$

The function $f(\theta) = \theta(q-1) - q^\theta + 1$ is non-negative in the interval $[0,1]$ and has its maximum at the point θ_0 with $q^{\theta_0} = \frac{q-1}{\ln q}$, i.e. $\theta_0 = \frac{\ln(q-1) - \ln \ln q}{\ln q}$ (see figure 1.11).

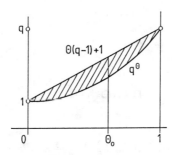

Figure 1.11

Hence we obtain

Corollary 1.9. *For* $n \geq 1$, $q \geq 2$,

$$\log_q n \leq \overline{L}(n,q;\frac{1}{n},\ldots,\frac{1}{n}) \leq \log_q n + \frac{1}{q-1} - \frac{1 + \ln\ln q - \ln(q-1)}{\ln q} + \frac{r}{n},$$

where $\lfloor \frac{q^{\lceil \log_q n \rceil} - n}{q-1} \rfloor = \frac{q^{\lceil \log_q n \rceil} - n}{q-1} - r$, $0 \leq r < 1$.

In particular, for binary trees (when $q = 2$, $r = 0$)

$$\log_2 n \leq \overline{L}(n,2;\frac{1}{n},\ldots,\frac{1}{n}) \leq \log_2 n + (1 - \frac{1 + \ln\ln 2}{\ln 2}) = \log_2 n + 0.086.$$

Example 1.16. Let us consider the weighing problem of example 1.14 for $n = 12$. Here we have $L = \lceil \log_3 12 \rceil = 3$, $q = 3$, and thus

$$e(12,3) = 36 - \lfloor \frac{27 - 12}{2} \rfloor = 29.$$

Any weighing procedure to determine the counterfeit coin must therefore on the average take at least $\frac{1}{12}e(12,3) = \frac{29}{12}$ weighings.

Let us now tackle the general case when an arbitrary distribution $p = (p_1,\ldots,p_n)$ on the leaves is given. Here the complete trees are no longer necessarily ($\overline{L}$)-optimal, as the following example shows.

Example 1.17. Suppose $n = 4$, $q = 2$. Obviously, the only complete (4,2)-tree is

T =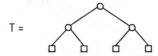

But consider now the distribution $(\frac{3}{6}, \frac{1}{6}, \frac{1}{6}, \frac{1}{6})$. We have $\overline{L}(T) = 2$ whereas for the tree T' with the values

T' =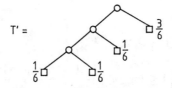

assigned according to the figure, $\overline{L}(T') = \frac{3}{6} + 2\frac{1}{6} + 3(\frac{1}{6} + \frac{1}{6}) = \frac{11}{6} < \overline{L}(T)$. It is plain that T' achieves the minimal value $\overline{L}(4, 2; \frac{3}{6}, \frac{1}{6}, \frac{1}{6}, \frac{1}{6}) = \frac{11}{6}$, and we see in addition that it may well happen that an $(\overline{L})$-optimal tree is not (L)-optimal, and conversely.

We are now going to discuss a famous method due to Huffman [1952] which enables us to construct an $(\overline{L})$-optimal tree for *any* given distribution $p = (p_1, \ldots, p_n)$. Let us relabel the probabilities such that $p_1 \geq p_2 \geq \ldots \geq p_n \geq 0$. Suppose $T \in T(n, q)$ is an $(\overline{L})$-optimal tree with lengths $\ell_1, \ldots, \ell_n$, where ℓ_i corresponds to p_i for all i. Let us analyze T:

i) Set $L = L(T)$ and let $E = \{v_1, \ldots, v_n\}$ be the set of leaves. As for the case of uniform distribution, it is clear that every inner node u of length $k \leq L - 2$ has precisely q successors, and that every inner node on level S_{L-1} has at least 2 successors, i.e. T is irreducible.

ii) $\ell_1 \leq \ell_2 \leq \ldots \leq \ell_n$. Suppose, on the contrary, there exist $i \neq j$ with $p_j > p_j$, $\ell_i > \ell_j$. Interchanging the places of v_i and v_j yields a new tree T' with

$$\overline{L}(T') = \sum_{k \neq i,j} p_k \ell_k + p_i \ell_j + p_j \ell_j = \overline{L}(T) + p_i \ell_j + p_j \ell_i$$

$$-p_i\ell_i - p_j\ell_j = \overline{L}(T) - (p_i - p_j)(\ell_i - \ell_j) < \overline{L}(T),$$

contradicting the minimality of $\overline{L}(T)$.

Let us assume for the moment $q - 1 \mid n - 1$. Then it follows easily from i) that T is regular.

iii) We have $\ell_n = L$ by ii). If $\ell_i = L$, then ii) implies $\ell_j = L$ for all j between i and n. We may thus assume that the q leaves $v_{n-q+1}, \ldots, v_n$ have a common predecessor $u \in S_{L-1}$. Now we make the replacement

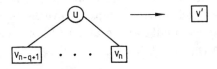

The new tree T' is $(n - q + 1, q)$-regular. By assigning to v' the probability $p = \sum\limits_{i=n-q+1}^{n} p_i$, we conclude

$$
\begin{aligned}
\overline{L}(n - q + 1, q; p_1, \ldots, p_{n-q}, p) &\leq \overline{L}(T'; p_1, \ldots, p_{n-q}, p) \\
&= \overline{L}(T) - pL + p(L - 1) = \overline{L}(T) - p \\
&= \overline{L}(n, q; p_1, \ldots, p_n) - p.
\end{aligned}
$$

iv) Let, conversely, $U' \in \mathcal{T}(n - q + 1, q)$ be an $(\overline{L})$-optimal tree for the distribution $(p_1, \ldots, p_{n-q}, p)$. By our previous discussion, U' is regular. Let w' be a leaf of T' whose probability is p with $\ell(w') = \ell$. We replace

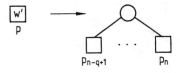

assigning to the new leaves the probabilities $p_{n-q+1}, \ldots, p_n$. The new tree $U \in \mathcal{T}(n, q)$ satisfies

$$
\begin{aligned}
\overline{L}(n, q; p_1, \ldots, p_n) &\leq \overline{L}(U; p_1, \ldots, p_n) = \overline{L}(U') - p\ell + p(\ell + 1) \\
&= \overline{L}(U') + p = \overline{L}(n - q + 1, q; p_1 \ldots, p_{n-q}, p) + p.
\end{aligned}
$$

Taking iii) and iv) together, we conclude

v) $\overline{L}(n, q; p_1, \ldots, p_n) = \overline{L}(n - q + 1, q; p_1, \ldots, p_{n-q}, p) + p.$

This is then the basis for the algorithm. The replacement of the q leaves with the *smallest* probabilities $p_{n-q+1}, \ldots, p_n$ in an $(\overline{L})$-optimal tree T by a new single leaf with probability $p = \sum\limits_{i=n-q+1}^{n} p_i$ leads to an $(\overline{L})$-optimal T' for this new distribution on $n - q + 1$ leaves. In T' we again replace the leaves with the q smallest probabilities by a new leaf, and so on, until we finally arrive at the trivial tree □. Now we unfold the root going all previous steps in reverse direction. Observation iv) ensures that we finally arrive at an $(\overline{L})$-optimal tree for the original distribution $(p_1, \ldots, p_n)$.

vi) If $q - 1 \nmid n - 1$, then we add enough leaves with probability 0 to make T into a regular tree and proceed as before.

Example 1.18. Let $n = 8$, $q = 3$, $p_1 = p_2 = \frac{20}{100}$, $p_3 = \frac{18}{100}$, $p_4 = \frac{17}{100}$, $p_5 = \frac{15}{100}$, $p_6 = \frac{5}{100}$, $p_7 = \frac{3}{100}$, $p_8 = \frac{2}{100}$. Since $q - 1 \nmid n - 1$ we add one leaf with probability $p_9 = 0$. For simplicity, we multiply all probabilities by 100. The "folding" process of the Huffman algorithm looks as follows:

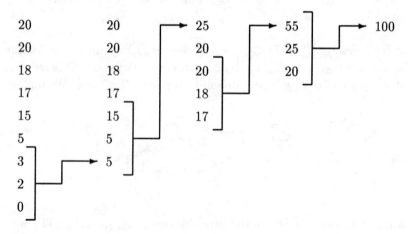

By "unfolding" the trivial tree we obtain:

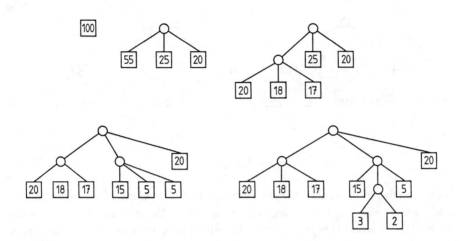

Figure 1.12

The final tree T has $\overline{L}(T;\underline{p}) = 1.85$, which is then the precise value of $\overline{L}(8,3;\underline{p})$. Incidentally, T is again not (L)-optimal since $\lceil \log_3 8 \rceil = 2$.
Note that we have some freedom in unfolding the tree. In our example we could as well have taken the other leaf with probability $\frac{5}{100}$ in the final step. Any tree constructed by this algorithm is called a *Huffman tree* and any associated code a *Huffman code*. Note that not every $(\overline{L})$-optimal tree is necessarily a Huffman tree as the following example shows.

Example 1.19. Consider $n = 6$, $q = 2$ and the distribution $\underline{p} = (0.3, 0.2, 0.15, 0.14, 0.11, 0.1)$. The reader may easily verify that in any Huffman tree the leaves v_1, v_3, v_4 must be in one subtree, and v_2, v_5, v_6 in the other, as in T_1. But, of course, T_2 also achieves the minimum $\overline{L}(6,2;\underline{p}) = 2.5$.

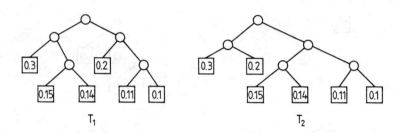

Figure 1.13

Summarizing our results, we see that the i-th codeword of an optimal $(\overline{L})$-code has roughly length $-\log_q p_i$. Thus while there must be a codeword of length at least $\lceil \log_q n \rceil$, some of them might be very short when p_i is large. An optimal code or tree might thus be far from being "balanced", i.e. complete in our terminology.

Our final result shows that the uniform distribution is extremal among all distributions.

Proposition 1.10. *Let $\underline{p} = (p_1 \ldots, p_n)$ be any distribution on an (n, q)-search process with all test functions permitted. Then*

$$\overline{L}(n, q; p_1, \ldots, p_n) \leq \overline{L}(n, q; \frac{1}{n}, \ldots, \frac{1}{n}).$$

Proof. Let $p_1 \geq p_2 \geq \ldots \geq p_n$. We claim that $\sum_{i=1}^{k} p_i \geq \frac{k}{n}$ holds for all $k = 1, \ldots, n$. Suppose, on the contrary, $\sum_{i=1}^{k} p_i < \frac{k}{n}$, $k < n$. Then $p_k = \min(p_1, \ldots, p_k) < \frac{1}{n}$, and thus $p_j < \frac{1}{n}$ for all $j > k$. But this implies $\sum_{j=k+1}^{n} p_j < \frac{n-k}{n}$, and hence $\sum_{i=1}^{n} p_i < 1$, a contradiction. We know from our discussion of the complete trees in example 1.12 that an optimal $(\overline{L})$-tree T for the uniform distribution has $a = \lfloor \frac{q^{\lceil \log_q n \rceil} - n}{q-1} \rfloor$ leaves on level $\lceil \log_q n \rceil - 1$, and $n - a$ leaves on the last level. Associate the a largest probabilities $p_1 \ldots, p_a$ with the leaves on level $\lceil \log_q n \rceil - 1$, and the $n - a$ smallest probabilities with those on level $\lceil \log_q n \rceil$. The average length of T for the distribution $\underline{p}$ is then

$$\overline{L}(T;\underline{p}) = \sum_{i=1}^{a} p_i(\lceil \log_q n \rceil - 1) + \sum_{j=a+1}^{n} p_j \lceil \log_q n \rceil$$

$$= \lceil \log_q n \rceil - \sum_{i=1}^{a} p_i \le \lceil \log_q n \rceil - \frac{a}{n}$$

$$= \lceil \log_q n \rceil - \frac{1}{n} \lfloor \frac{q^{\lceil \log_q n \rceil} - n}{q - 1} \rfloor = \overline{L}(n, q; \frac{1}{n}, \dots, \frac{1}{n})$$

where the last equality follows from Theorem 1.8. We conclude

$$\overline{L}(n, q; \underline{p}) \le \overline{L}(T; \underline{p}) \le \overline{L}(n, q; \frac{1}{n}, \dots, \frac{1}{n}). \qquad \square$$

Remark. The corresponding result $H(p_1, \dots, p_n) \le H(\frac{1}{n}, \dots, \frac{1}{n})$ for the entropy is easily verified using Lemma 1.5. But whereas for the entropy, equality holds precisely for $p_i = \frac{1}{n}$, $i = 1, \dots, n$, it may well happen that for $\overline{L}(n, q; \underline{p})$ the maximum is attained for other distributions as well (see exercise 1.5.10).

From an algorithmic point of view, we have completely settled the ($\overline{L}$)-problem for trees. But what can we say *a priori* about the value $\overline{L}(n, q; \underline{p})$? Unfortunately, very little in general. For a few isolated results the reader may consult the exercises.

Exercises 1.5.

1*. Show that for any distributions $\underline{p} = (p_1, \dots, p_n)$, $\underline{q} = (q_1, \dots, q_n)$,
$$H(p_1, \dots, p_n) \le - \sum_{i=1}^{n} p_i \log_2 q_i$$
with equality iff $p_i = q_i$ for all i.

2. Show that $\overline{L}(n, q; p_1, \dots, p_n) = - \sum_{i=1}^{n} p_i \log_q p_i$ holds precisely when all p_i are of the form $p_i = q^{-\ell_i}$ for some $\ell_i \in I\!N_0$.

3*. Consider the distribution $\underline{p} = (p_1, \dots, p_n)$ with $p_i = \frac{i}{\binom{n+1}{2}}$, $i = 1, \dots, n$, and compute $\overline{L}(n, 2; \underline{p})$.

4. Show for the entropy $H(p_1, \dots, p_n)$:

i) $H(p_1, \ldots, p_n) = 0 \iff p_i = 1$ for some i.

ii) $H(p_1, \ldots, p_n) \leq H(\frac{1}{n}, \ldots, \frac{1}{n}) = \log_2 n$ with equality iff $p_i = \frac{1}{n}$ for all i.

iii) $H(p_1, \ldots, p_n) = H(p_1, \ldots, p_k, s) + sH(p'_{k+1}, \ldots, p'_n)$ where $2 \leq k \leq n-1$ and $s = \sum\limits_{i=k+1}^{n} p_i$, $p'_i = \frac{p_i}{s}$ for $i = k+1, \ldots, n$.

5*. Prove that $h(n,q) = \overline{L}(n, q; \frac{1}{n}, \ldots, \frac{1}{n})$ is increasing in n. More precisely for $q = 2$ we have $h(n,2) + \frac{1}{n} \leq h(n+1, 2)$. When do we have equality?

6. Let $\underline{p} = \frac{1}{100}(30, 20, 15, 14, 11, 10)$ and consider the binary codes C_1, C_2, C_3:

	C_1	C_2	C_3
x_1	01	10	00
x_2	11	01	01
x_3	000	110	100
x_4	100	111	101
x_5	001	000	110
x_6	101	001	111

Show that all three codes are ($\overline{L}$)-optimal. Which of them are Huffman codes?

7*. Suppose the distribution $\underline{p} = (p_1, \ldots, p_n)$ with $p_1 \geq p_2 \geq \ldots \geq p_n$ satisfies $p_{n-1} + p_n \geq p_1$. Show that for a binary process $\overline{L}(n, 2; \underline{p}) = \lceil \log_2 n \rceil - \sum\limits_{i=1}^{s} p_i$, $s = 2^{\lceil \log_2 n \rceil} - n$.

8. We generalize exercise 7. Let $\underline{p} = (p_1, \ldots, p_n)$ with $p_1 \geq \ldots \geq p_n$ be given. We know that any ($\overline{L}$)-optimal binary tree satisfies $\ell_1 \leq \ldots \leq \ell_n$ for the lengths of the leaves. Show that $p_n + kp_{n-1} > p_1$ implies $\ell_n - \ell_1 \leq k$, i.e. the leaves have at most $k+1$ different lengths.

9*. Let $M = (m_{ij})$ be an $n \times n$-doubly stochastic matrix, i.e. all m_{ij}'s are non-negative real numbers and all row-sums $\sum\limits_{j=1}^{n} m_{ij}$ and all column-sums $\sum\limits_{i=1}^{n} m_{ij}$ are equal to 1. Let $\underline{p} = (p_1, \ldots, p_n)$, $\underline{q} = (q_1, \ldots, q_n)$ be two distributions. Show that $\underline{q} = M\underline{p}$ (as a matrix product) implies

$H(p_1 \ldots, p_n) \leq H(q_1, \ldots, q_n)$ and interpret this result. Incidentally the converse is also true (see, e.g., the book by Hardy-Littlewood-Polya [1934]).

10*. Construct an example to show that $\overline{L}(n, q; \underline{p}) = \overline{L}(n, q; \frac{1}{n}, \ldots, \frac{1}{n})$ may hold for non-uniform distributions $\underline{p}$.

11. Generalization of Kraft's inequality. Let C be a uniquely decodable (n, q)-code (see exercise 1.3.8). Then $\sum_{i=1}^{n} q^{-\ell_i} \leq 1$ where $\ell_1, \ldots, \ell_n$ are the word lengths. (MacMillan)

1.6 Alphabetic Search Processes

The remainder of the book is devoted more or less to studying and sometimes solving the (L)- and $(\overline{L})$-problem for various test families $\mathcal{F}$ arising naturally from the topic in question. Weighing and sorting problems are prime examples for this. There is, however, one general property of $\mathcal{F}$ that deserves special treatment.

Recall example 1.5 where our task consisted in bringing a new element z into its proper place of the given linear order $y_1 < y_2 < y_3 < y_4$. The search domain $S = \{0, 1, 2, 3, 4\}$ is linearly ordered, and the four test functions f_j, $j = 1, \ldots, 4$ all share the property that

$$i < i' \Rightarrow f_j(i) \leq f_j(i') \quad (0 \leq i < i' \leq 4),$$

i.e. they all respect the order on S.

Let us generalize this example. Suppose the search domain $S = \{x_1, \ldots, x_n\}$ is linearly ordered, $x_1 < x_2 < \ldots < x_n$. We say that the test function $f : S \rightarrow \{0, 1, \ldots, q-1\}$ is *monotone* if $x_i < x_j$ implies $f(x_i) \leq f(x_j)$ for all $i < j$. Denote by $\mathcal{F}_{mon}$ the set of all monotone functions. It is a well-known fact that $| \mathcal{F}_{mon} | = \left(\begin{array}{c} n + q - 1 \\ n \end{array} \right)$. Hence $\mathcal{F}_{mon}$ will, in general, be much smaller than the whole set of mappings $\{0, 1, \ldots, q-1\}^S$.

Definition. A search process $(S, \mathcal{F})$ with $\mathcal{F} \subseteq \mathcal{F}_{mon}$ is called *alphabetic* (with respect to the linear order on S).

Since in alphabetic search processes the function values are important, it is best to use the code representation of algorithms introduced in section 3. Let $\mathcal{A}$ be an algorithm and let C be the corresponding search code. Suppose $i < j$, and let $w_i, w_j \in C$ be the codewords of x_i, x_j. From the monotony of the test functions we infer that for the first letters in w_i, w_j which are distinct, the one in w_i must be smaller than the one in w_j. This suggests the following definition.

Definition.   Let C be an (n,q)-prefix code over $\{0,1,\ldots,q-1\}$. Let $v = v_1 v_2 \ldots v_s$ and $w = w_1 w_2 \ldots w_t \in C$. We define

$$v \prec w :\Longleftrightarrow v_i < w_i \text{ where } i \text{ is the smallest index with } v_i \neq w_i.$$

The relation $\prec$ is clearly a linear order on C, called the *lexicographic order*. If $S = \{x_1 < x_2 < \ldots < x_n\}$, then the search code $C = \{w_1, \ldots, w_n\}$ is said to be *alphabetic* with respect to $x_1 < \ldots < x_n$ if $w_1 \prec w_2 \prec \ldots \prec w_n$ holds for the corresponding codewords.

Proposition 1.11.   *Let the (n,q)-search process $(S, \mathcal{F}_{mon})$ be given with $S = \{x_1 < x_2 < \ldots < x_n\}$. Every search code C (corresponding to some algorithm) is then alphabetic with respect to $x_1 < \ldots < x_n$. Conversely, let C be a prefix code with lexicographic order $w_1 \prec w_2 \prec \ldots \prec w_n$. Then C is alphabetic search code with respect to some linear order $x_1 < \ldots < x_n$ on S.*

Proof. We have already seen the first part. Consider now the (n,q)-prefix code C with $w_1 \prec w_2 \prec \ldots \prec w_n$. We associate to $x_i \in S$ the codeword w_i, where we set $w_i = w_{i1} w_{i2} \ldots w_{i\ell_i}$, $i = 1, \ldots, n$. Define the function f_1 by

$$f_1(x_i) := w_{i1} \quad (i = 1, \ldots, n).$$

Suppose we have already defined functions $f_1, \ldots, f_k$ (depending on $x^* \in S$). Suppose $f_1(x^*) = e_1, \ldots, f_k(x^*) = e_k$, and $S_k(x^*) = \{x \in S : f_i(x) = e_i, i = 1, \ldots, k\}$. For the words $W_k(x^*) \subseteq C$ corresponding to $S_k(x^*)$, there must exist indices $i \leq j$ with $W_k(x^*) = \{w_i, w_{i+1}, \ldots, w_j\}$ by the definition of $\prec$. If $S_k(x^*) \supsetneq \{x^*\}$, then we define

$$f_{k+1}(x_h) = \begin{cases} w_{h,k+1} & \text{if } i \leq h \leq j \\ 0 & \text{if } h < i \\ q - 1 & \text{if } h > j. \end{cases}$$

All functions defined in this way respect the order $x_1 < x_2 < \ldots < x_n$, and the algorithm determined by the f_k's has precisely C as its search code.
□

To illustrate the second part of the proof, let us look at the following code.

Example 1.20. Let $n = 10$ and $q = 3$, and consider the code $C = \{001, 002, 01, 020, 101, 11, 120, 200, 21, 22\}$. C is lexicographically ordered and we associate $x_i \in S$ to $w_i \in C$. The algorithm constructed in the proposition looks as follows:

$$f_1(x_h) = \begin{cases} 0 & h = 1, \ldots, 4 \\ 1 & h = 5, \ldots, 7 \\ 2 & h = 8, \ldots, 10. \end{cases}$$

If $f_1(x^*) = 0$, then

$$f_2(x_h) = \begin{cases} 0 & h = 1, 2 \\ 1 & h = 3 \\ 2 & h = 4, \ldots, 10. \end{cases} \Rightarrow x^* = x_3$$

If $f_1(x^*) = 1$, then

$$f_2(x_h) = \begin{cases} 0 & h = 1, \ldots, 5 \\ 1 & h = 6 \\ 2 & h = 7, \ldots, 10. \end{cases} \Rightarrow x^* = x_6$$

If $f_1(x^*) = 2$, then

$$f_2(x_h) = \begin{cases} 0 & h = 1, \ldots, 8 \\ 1 & h = 9 & \Rightarrow x^* = x_9 \\ 2 & h = 10 & \Rightarrow x^* = x_{10} \end{cases}$$

If $f_1(x^*) = f_2(x^*) = 0$, then

$$f_3(x_h) = \begin{cases} 1 & h = 1 & \Rightarrow x^* = x_1 \\ 2 & h = 2, \ldots, 10 & \Rightarrow x^* = x_2, \end{cases}$$

and so on.

We note two things. Firstly, it is clear from the construction of the functions in Proposition 1.11 that the choice of f_k will, in general, depend on the unknown element x^*. Hence, we will expect that, in the alphabetic case, predetermined algorithms will take longer than sequential algorithms. We will confirm this fact in section 8. Secondly, we know that every prefix code corresponds to some algorithm. Hence, if we take an (L)-optimal code (of length $\lceil \log_q n \rceil$) with lexicographic order $w_1 \prec w_2 \prec \ldots \prec w_n$, then by the bijection $x_i \longleftrightarrow w_i$ we obtain an admissible algorithm of the same length. The same can clearly be said about the $(\overline{L})$-problem if the distribution is uniform. Hence we have established the following result.

Theorem 1.12. *Let the (n,q)-search process $(S, \mathcal{F}_{mon})$ be given with $S = \{x_1 < x_2 < \ldots < x_n\}$. Then*

   i) $L(S, \mathcal{F}_{mon}) = \lceil \log_q n \rceil$

   ii) $\overline{L}(S, \mathcal{F}_{mon}; \frac{1}{n}, \ldots, \frac{1}{n}) = \overline{L}(n, q; \frac{1}{n}, \ldots, \frac{1}{n}) = \lceil \log_q n \rceil - \frac{1}{n} \lfloor \frac{q^{\lceil \log_q n \rceil} - n}{q - 1} \rfloor.$

When the distribution p is not uniform, then an $(\overline{L})$-optimal code will, in general, depend heavily on the p_i's and thus need not be alphabetic with respect to $x_1 < \ldots < x_n$. There is, however, a beautiful analogue to Theorem 1.6 first proved by Gilbert and Moore [1959].

Theorem 1.13. *Let the (n,q)-search process $(S, \mathcal{F}_{mon})$ be given with $S = \{x_1 < x_2 < \ldots < x_n\}$ and the probability distribution $p = (p_1, \ldots, p_n)$. Then*

$$-\sum_{i=1}^{n} p_i \log_q p_i \leq \overline{L}(S, \mathcal{F}_{mon}; p_1, \ldots, p_n) < \left(-\sum_{i=1}^{n} p_i \log_q p_i\right) + 2.$$

Proof. The lower bound was established in Corollary 1.7. To verify the upper bound we must construct a prefix code C, alphabetic with respect to $x_1 < \ldots < x_n$, whose average length $\overline{L}(C) = \sum_{i=1}^{n} p_i \ell_i$ is less than $-\sum p_i \log_q p_i + 2$. As in the proof of Theorem 1.6, we may confine our-selves to the case when all $p_i > 0$. Let the numbers r_j and ℓ_j be defined by

$$r_j := \sum_{i=1}^{j-1} p_i + \frac{p_j}{q}$$
$$\qquad\qquad (j = 1, \ldots, n).$$
$$\ell_j := \lceil -\log_q p_j \rceil + 1$$

The codeword w_j corresponding to x_j shall consist of the first ℓ_j numbers in the q-ary expansion of r_j. As an example, consider $r_j = 0.145$, $\ell_j = 8$ and $q = 2$. Then $r_j = \frac{1}{2^3} + \frac{1}{2^6} + \frac{1}{2^8} = 0.144531 + r$, $0 < r < \frac{1}{2^8}$ and hence $w_j = 00100101$. Since $r_1 < r_2 < \ldots < r_n$ holds, we certainly have $w_1 \prec w_2 \prec \ldots \prec w_n$, i.e. $C = \{w_1, \ldots, w_n\}$ is alphabetic. It remains to verify the prefix property. Suppose, on the contrary, that w_i is an initial segment of w_j. This means that r_i, r_j have the same numbers in the first ℓ_i positions of their q-ary expansions whence

$$| r_i - r_j | < \frac{1}{q^{\ell_i}} \le \frac{1}{q^{-\log_q p_i + 1}} = \frac{p_i}{q}.$$

On the other hand, we see from the definition of the r_j's that

$$| r_i - r_j | \ge \frac{p_i}{q} + \frac{p_j}{q} > \frac{p_i}{q},$$

a contradiction. To complete our proof, we note that the average length of C is given by

$$\overline{L}(C) = \sum p_i \ell_i = \sum p_i (\lceil -\log_q p_i \rceil + 1) < -\sum p_i \log_q p_i + 2. \qquad \square$$

Two questions come to mind. Can the upper bound be improved? Is there a "Huffman-like" construction of optimal alphabetic codes? Both questions can be answered affirmatively. Slight improvements can be made on the upper bound (see exercise 1.6.4). A famous method due to Hu and Tucker renders optimal codes for any given distribution. The details which are rather involved are again outlined in the exercises.

Exercises 1.6.

1. Verify $| \mathcal{F}_{mon} | = \binom{n + q - 1}{n}$ for given n and q.

2*. Show the following analogue of Kraft's inequality 1.4. If $\sum\limits_{i=1}^{n} q^{-\ell_i} \le \frac{1}{q}$, then a prefix code with word lengths $\ell_1, \ldots, \ell_n$ exists which is alphabetic with respect to $x_1 < \ldots < x_n$.

3. Use the previous exercise to provide an alternative proof of Theorem 1.13.

4. Let $q = 2$. It can be shown that $\overline{L}(S, \mathcal{F}_{mon}; \underline{p}) \leq \sum_{i=1}^{n-1} \max(p_i, p_{i+1}) - p_{\min}$ (where $p_{\min} = \min p_i$). Deduce from this $\overline{L}(S, \mathcal{F}_{mon}; \underline{p}) \leq H(\underline{p}) + 2 - (n+2)p_{\min}$ and $\overline{L}(n, 2; \underline{p}) \leq H(\underline{p}) + 1 - 2p_{\min}$.

5*. This exercise addresses the problem of computing $\max \overline{L}(n, \mathcal{F}_{mon}; \underline{p})$ for $q = 2$. Let $a = 2^{\lceil \log_2 n \rceil} - n$ (as in example 1.12) and prove $\max_{\underline{p}} \overline{L}(n, \mathcal{F}_{mon}; \underline{p}) = \lceil \log_2 n \rceil - \lfloor \frac{a}{2} \rfloor \lfloor \frac{n}{2} \rfloor^{-1}$. (Note that we write max and not sup, i.e. the right-hand side is attained.)

6*. A short description of the Hu-Tucker algorithm for $q = 2$. Suppose we are given probabilities $p_1, \ldots, p_n$.

Step 1. Start with $\boxed{p_1}, \ldots, \boxed{p_n}$ (called the actual sequence). We combine the weights of adjacent nodes p_i, p_j $(i < j)$ into a single interior node with index i containing the weight $p_i + p_j$. The pair (i, j) in the actual sequence we choose is singled out by the following rules:

   i) No end-node occurs between i and j.

   ii) The sum $p_i + p_j$ is minimum among all (i, j) satisfying i).

   iii) The index i is minimum among all (i, j) satisfying i), ii).

   iv) The index j is minimum among all (i, j) satisfying i) to iii).

In this way we construct a rooted tree. Assign the level numbers ℓ_i of this tree to the end-nodes $\boxed{p_1}_{\ell_1}, \ldots, \boxed{p_n}_{\ell_n}$.

Step 2. Discard the internal nodes and start again. The pair (i, j) singled out is determined as follows:

   i') The nodes i, j must be adjacent in the actual sequence.

   ii') The levels ℓ_i, ℓ_j must be maximal.

   iii') The index i must be minimal among all (i, j) satisfying i'), ii').

This procedure always yields an optimal alphabetic tree (see the references).

Construct the optimal alphabetic tree by the Hu-Tucker algorithm for $n = 9$, $p_1 = 8$, $p_2 = 12$, $p_3 = 4$, $p_4 = 30$, $p_5 = 10$, $p_6 = 7$, $p_7 = 13$, $p_8 = 7$, $p_9 = 9$ (probabilities multiplied by 100).

7. Show that the Hu-Tucker algorithm yields complete trees when the distribution is uniform, in accordance with Theorem 1.12.

8*. Compare $\overline{L}(6;\underline{p})$ and $\overline{L}_{mon}(6;\underline{p})$ when $\underline{p} = \frac{1}{12}(2,3,1,1,3,2)$.

1.7 Binary Search Trees

Consider a search process $(S, \mathcal{F}_{mon})$ with $q = 2$. Our example 1.5 was of this kind with the original task being to bring a new element z into its proper place among $y_1 < y_2 < y_3 < y_4$. A moment's thought shows that this sorting situation prevails for all n. Given $y_1 < y_2 < \ldots < y_n$ and a new element z, then the tests $z : y_j$ correspond precisely to the functions $f_j \in \mathcal{F}_{mon}$ where $S = \{0, 1, \ldots, n\}$ is the set of positions with $i \in S$ meaning $y_i < z < y_{i+1}$. Thus the problem of *sorting* z into its proper place among $y_1 < \ldots < y_n$ corresponds precisely to the search process $(S, \mathcal{F}_{mon})$ with $\mid S \mid = n + 1$.

This interpretation as a "sorting in" of z suggests the following generalization, usually called the *data location problem*. Suppose we are given the list $Y = \{y_1 < \ldots < y_n\}$ and a new element z. By comparing z to various y_j's we want to find out whether z appears in the list Y (and if so, locate it), or if not, to determine the right position where it should be sorted in. Our search domain consists therefore of a pair $X \cup Y$, $X = \{x_o, \ldots, x_n\}$, $Y = \{y_1, \ldots, y_n\}$ where y_i means $z = y_i$ and x_j is interpreted as $y_j < z < y_{j+1}$.

Since we now have three possible outcomes to a test: $z < y_j$, $z = y_j$, $z > y_j$, this is a ternary problem. However, as the following example indicates, we can still treat it in a binary fashion.

Example 1.21. Suppose $n = 4$. Let us first compare z with y_2. If $z < y_2$, then we make the test $z : y_1$, while for $z > y_2$ we use $z : y_4$ as next test. In the last case, we might obtain $z < y_4$ whence we ask $z : y_3$. The corresponding decision tree can be set up as follows:

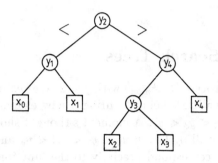

Figure 1.14

We see that the inner nodes correspond to the outcomes y_i with the end-nodes representing the x_j's.

Clearly, the same situation holds for any n. (Recall from **1.1** that a regular binary tree with $n + 1$ end-nodes has n inner nodes.) We should keep in mind, however, that the cost of the outcome y_i is one more that than the length $\ell(y_i)$ in the tree since we have to take the final question $z : y_i$ into account.

Note that any regular binary tree with $n + 1$ leaves corresponds to a data location process by filling in the x_i's and y_j's in an alphabetic way. Thus the worst-case cost $DL(n)$ is simply $\lceil \log_2(n + 1) \rceil$ by **1.2**.

Proposition 1.14. *The worst-case cost for the data location problem is*

$$DL(n) = \lceil \log_2(n + 1) \rceil.$$

Let us now turn to the more rewarding average case. We are given probabilities $p_0, \ldots, p_n$ and $q_1, \ldots, q_n$ with $\sum p_i + \sum q_i = 1$ for the outcomes x_i and y_i, respectively. The average-case cost is denoted by $\overline{DL}(n)$. There are two extremal cases when all $q_j = 0$ or when all $p_i = 0$. The former case corresponds precisely to the situation of the last section (with $q = 2$) with **1.13** and the Hu-Tucker algorithm as main results.

Let us consider for a moment the latter possibility in the uniform case, $q_j = \frac{1}{n}$ for all j. Suppose $n = 5$. The first guess is to compare z with the middle element y_3, but as the following figure shows, this is not an optimal procedure. The first comparison $z : y_2$ (or $z : y_4$ by symmetry) is better.

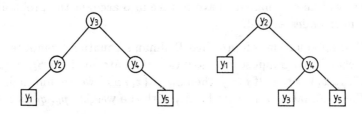

Figure 1.15

The average length of the first algorithm is $\frac{1}{5}(2+2+1+2+2) = \frac{9}{5}$ whereas in the second case we obtain $\frac{1}{5}(1+1+2+2+2) = \frac{8}{5}$, which is clearly the optimal value.

The example shows that the best algorithm will correspond to a complete binary tree T with a total number of n nodes. Since the number of leaves $|E|$ is one more than the number of inner nodes $|I|$, we have $n = 2|E| - 1$, so this is only possible for odd n. For even n we must have one unsaturated inner node. Let $e(T)$ be the external length of T and $i(T)$ the internal length, i.e. $i(T) = \sum_{i \in I} \ell(v)$. It is easily shown that for a regular binary tree T with m leaves, $e(T) = i(T) + 2m - 2$ (see excise 1.4.1). Now suppose n is odd; then $|E| = \frac{n+1}{2}$, $|I| = \frac{n-1}{2}$. By recalling that we have to add 1 to the length of each inner node we obtain

$$\overline{DL}(n) = \frac{1}{n}\left[e(T) + i(T) + \frac{n-1}{2}\right] = \frac{1}{n}\left[2e(T) - \frac{n-1}{2}\right].$$

Formula 1.8 for $e\left(\frac{n+1}{2}, 2\right)$, yields then the following result (the case when n is even is settled by an analogous argument).

Proposition 1.15. *For $n \geq 1$,*

$$\overline{DL}(n; p_i = 0, q_i = \frac{1}{n}) = \lfloor \log_2 n \rfloor + \frac{\lfloor \log_2 n \rfloor}{n} - \frac{2^{\lfloor \log n \rfloor + 1}}{n} + \frac{1}{2} + \begin{cases} \frac{3}{2n} \\ \frac{3}{n} \end{cases}$$

for n odd and even, respectively.

Now we turn to the general case. Any tree corresponding to an algorithm for $\overline{DL}(n; p_0, \ldots, p_n, q_1, \ldots, q_n)$ is called a *binary search tree*. Of course, any tree with $n+1$ leaves and n inner nodes is a possible search tree, by labeling the nodes in the proper alphabetic fashion. But, different from the previous situation, will an optimal tree have to take into account the probabilities q_j for the inner nodes as well.

The following equation, often called Bellman's equation, computes the optimum recursively. Suppose we know that the outcome is in $S_{ij} = \{x_i, y_{i+1}, x_{i+1}, \ldots, y_j, x_j\}$, $i \leq j$. If $i = j$, then $S_{ii} = \{x_i\}$ and we are finished. Denote by c_{ij} the minimal average cost for S_{ij} with the weights p_k, q_k as given, i.e.

$$c_{ij} = \min_T \left\{ \sum_{k=i}^{j} p_k \ell(x_k) + \sum_{k=i+1}^{j} q_k(\ell(y_k) + 1) \right\},$$

where T runs through all trees for the subproblem S_{ij}. Furthermore, set

$$w_{ij} = \sum_{k=i}^{j} p_k + \sum_{k=i+1}^{j} q_k.$$

Proposition 1.16. *For* $0 \leq i \leq j \leq n$,

$$c_{ii} = 0,$$
$$c_{ij} = w_{ij} + \min_{i<k\leq j}(c_{i,k-1} + c_{k,j}) \quad (i < j).$$

Proof. If we compare $z : y_k$, then the cost of the left subtree is $c_{i,k-1}$ while that of the right subtree is c_{kj}. Taking into account the first comparison we have to add w_{ij}. The minimum over all these expressions yields then c_{ij}. $\square$

1.16 suggests the following algorithm. Since $S_{i,i+1} = \{x_i, y_{i+1}, x_{i+1}\}$ we have $c_{i,i+1} = w_{i,i+1}$, $i = 0, \ldots, n-1$. In the next step we make a list of all c_{ij} with $j - i = 2$ using **1.16**, marking an optimal root $z : y_k$ each time. Then we add a list of all c_{ij} with $j - i = 3$ together with the roots, and so on.

Example 1.22. Suppose $n = 4$ with the following list of probabilities (all multiplied by 100).

	0	1	2	3	4
p_i	12	6	16	16	10
q_i		5	15	8	12

	0	1	2	3
$c_{i,i+1}$	23	37	40	38
root	1	2	3	4

	0	1	2
$c_{i,i+2}$	77	98	100
root	2	3	3
$w_{i,i+2}$	54	61	62

	0	1
$c_{i,i+3}$	141	158
root	2	3
$w_{i,i+3}$	78	83

$c_{0,4}$	215
root	3
$w_{0,4}$	100

Retracing all our steps, we arrive at the following optimal tree with average cost 2.15.

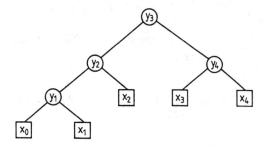

Figure 1.16

Let us, finally, discuss general lower and upper bounds in the spirit of **1.6**. We set $\underline{p} = (p_0, \ldots, p_n; q_1, \ldots, q_n)$ and denote by $H(\underline{p})$ the entropy of the distribution $\underline{p}$. By interpreting our problem as a ternary process with probabilities $x_0, \ldots, x_n, y_1, \ldots, y_n$ we have by (1.5)

$$\frac{H(\underline{p})}{\log_2 3} \le \overline{DL}(n; \underline{p}).$$

But we can do better than that in many cases. First we generalize Kraft's inequality **1.4** to include inner nodes as well.

Proposition 1.17. *Let T be a regular binary tree with $n+1$ leaves $x_0, \ldots, x_n$ and n inner nodes $y_1, \ldots, y_n$. Then*

$$i) \ \sum_{k=0}^{n} 2^{-\ell(x_k)} = 1$$

$ii)$ $\sum_{k=1}^{n} 2^{-\ell(y_k)} \leq \log_2(n+1).$

Proof. i) is just Kraft's equality for regular trees. For the proof of ii) we use induction on n. For $n = 1$, both sides are equal to 1. Suppose the left subtree T_1 contains $\ell - 1$ inner nodes with $n - \ell$ inner nodes in the right subtree T_2, and $\ell(y) = 0$ for the root y. Taking into account that the lengths in the subtrees are one less than in T we obtain by induction

$$\sum_{k=1}^{n} 2^{-\ell(y_k)} \leq \frac{1}{2}\log_2 \ell + \frac{1}{2}\log_2(n - \ell + 1) + 1 = \frac{1}{2}\log_2(\ell(n - \ell + 1)) + 1$$

$$= \frac{1}{2}\log_2((n+1)^2) + \frac{1}{2}\log_2(\frac{\ell}{n+1}\frac{n-\ell+1}{n+1}) + 1.$$

Since $\frac{\ell}{n+1}$ and $\frac{n-\ell+1}{n+1} = 1 - \frac{\ell}{n+1}$ are between 0 and 1 and add up to 1, we infer $\frac{\ell}{n+1} \cdot \frac{n-\ell+1}{n+1} \leq \frac{1}{4}$, and thus

$$\sum_{k=1}^{n} 2^{-\ell(y_k)} \leq \log_2(n+1) - 1 + 1 = \log_2(n+1). \qquad \square$$

Let us use **1.17** to provide a lower bound for $\overline{DL}(n;\underline{p}) - H(\underline{p})$. We have

$$\overline{DL}(n;\underline{p}) - H(\underline{p}) = \sum_{k=0}^{n} p_k(\ell(x_k) + \log_2 p_k) + \sum_{k=1}^{n} q_k(\ell(y_k) + 1 + \log_2 q_k)$$

$$= -\sum_{k=0}^{n} p_k \log_2 \frac{2^{-\ell(x_k)}}{p_k} - \sum_{k=1}^{n} q_k \log_2 \frac{2^{-\ell(y_k)-1}}{q_k}.$$

From (1.3) we infer $\log_2 x \leq (x-1)\log_2 e$ for $x > 0$. For the first summand we therefore obtain by **1.17**(i)

$$-\sum_{k=0}^{n} p_k \log_2 \frac{2^{-\ell(x_k)}}{p_k} \geq -\log_2 e \sum_{k=0}^{n}(2^{-\ell(x_k)} - p_k) = -\log_2 e\left(1 - \sum_{k=0}^{n} p_k\right).$$

Using **1.17**(ii) for the second summand we further have

$$-\sum_{k=1}^{n} q_k \log_2 \frac{2^{-\ell(y_k)-1}}{q_k} = -\sum_{k=1}^{n} q_k \log_2 \frac{2^{-\ell(y_k)-1}}{q_k \frac{1}{2}\log_2(n+1)}$$

$$-\sum_{k=1}^{n} q_k \log_2 \left(\frac{1}{2}\log_2(n+1)\right)$$

$$\geq -\log_2 e \sum_{k=1}^{n} \left(\frac{2^{-\ell(y_k)-1}}{\frac{1}{2}\log_2(n+1)} - q_k\right)$$

$$-(\log_2\log_2(n+1)-1)\sum_{k=1}^{n} q_k$$

$$\geq -\log_2 e \left(1 - \sum_{k=1}^{n} q_k\right)$$

$$-(\log_2\log_2(n+1)-1)\sum_{k=1}^{n} q_k.$$

Taking both inequalities together we thus conclude

$$\overline{DL}(n;\underline{p}) - H(\underline{p}) \geq -\log_2 e - (\log_2\log_2(n+1)-1)\sum_{k=1}^{n} q_k.$$

For a distribution $\underline{p}$ close to the uniform distribution, i.e. $H(\underline{p}) \sim \log_2(2n+1)$, our bound for $\overline{DL}(n;\underline{p})$ is approximately $H(\underline{p}) - \frac{1}{2}\log_2\log_2(n+1)$ and is therefore much better than $\frac{H(\underline{p})}{\log_2 3}$. For small entropies, the latter bound is to be preferred.

To provide an upper bound for $\overline{DL}(n;\underline{p})$ we use an algorithm due to Mehlhorn [1975]. Let us set

$$c(k) = \sum_{i=0}^{k-1} p_i + \frac{p_k}{2} + \sum_{i=1}^{k} q_k \quad (k = 1,\ldots,n).$$

The algorithm chooses the roots y_k of the subtrees in the following way. Suppose we are in the subproblem $S_{ij} = \{x_i, y_{i+1}, x_{i+1}, \ldots, y_j, x_j\}$, then we describe the state of S_{ij} by the pair (w, ℓ), satisfying

i) $w = v2^{-\ell+1}$ where $v \in \{0,1,2,\ldots,2^{\ell-1} - 1\}$ and

ii) $w \leq c(i) \leq c(j) \leq w + 2^{-\ell+1}$.

At the start, when $i = 0, j = n$, we set $w = 0, \ell = 1$ so that i) and ii) are satisfied.

Suppose we are in the subproblem S_{ij}, where we may assume $i < j$ since otherwise $S_{ii} = \{x_i\}$.

Case 1. $i + 1 = j$. Then $S_{ij} = \{x_i, y_{i+1}, x_{i+1}\}$. We choose y_{i+1} as root and are finished after the comparison $z : y_{i+1}$.

Case 2. $i + 1 < j$, $c(i) > w + 2^{-\ell}$. We choose y_{i+1} as root and describe the right subtree on $S_{i+1,j}$ by $(w + 2^{-\ell}, \ell + 1)$. Since $w + 2^{-\ell} = (2v + 1)2^{-\ell}$ with $2v + 1 \in \{0, 1, 2, \ldots, 2^\ell - 1\}$ and $w + 2^{-\ell} < c(i) \leq c(i + 1) \leq c(j) \leq w + 2^{-\ell+1} = (w + 2^{-\ell}) + 2^{-\ell}$, both conditions i) and ii) are satisfied.

Case 3. $i + 1 < j$, $c(j) < w + 2^{-\ell}$. We choose y_j as root and decribe the left subtree on $S_{i,j-1}$ by the pair $(w, \ell + 1)$. Again, both conditions are satisfied.

Case 4. $i + 1 < j$, $c(i) \leq w + 2^{-\ell} \leq c(j)$. We choose the root y_k in such a way that $c(k - 1) \leq w + 2^{-\ell} \leq c(k)$ holds. If $k = i + 1$ or $k = j$, then one of the subtrees is trivial. For $i + 1 < k < j$ we describe the left subtree on $S_{i,k-1}$ by the pair $(w, \ell + 1)$ and the right subtree on $S_{k,j}$ by the pair $(w + 2^{-\ell}, \ell + 1)$. On $S_{i,k-1}$ we have $w = v2^{-\ell+1} = 2v2^{-\ell}$ with $2v \in \{0, 1, \ldots, 2^\ell - 1\}$ and $w \leq c(i) \leq c(k - 1) \leq w + 2^{-\ell}$. Hence i) and ii) are satisfied. A similar argument holds for $S_{k,j}$.

The algorithm constructs therefore a binary search tree T whose cost we now estimate. If y_k is the root of the subproblem S_{ij} with $i < j$, then $\ell(y_k) = \ell - 1$ since we start with $\ell = 1$ and raise the value of ℓ by one at each step of the algorithm. By condition ii) and $i < k \leq j$,

$$2^{-\ell(y_k)} = 2^{-\ell+1} \geq c(j) - c(i) = \sum_{h=i+1}^{j-1} p_h + \frac{1}{2}(p_i + p_j) + \sum_{h=i+1}^{j} q_h \geq q_k,$$

and thus $\ell(y_k) + 1 \leq -\log_2 q_k + 1$.

When the leaf x_m is constructed on, say, the subproblem S_{ij} with parameters (w, ℓ), then by the same reasoning as before $\ell(x_m) = \ell$, and thus with $i \leq m \leq j$

$$2^{-\ell(x_m)+1} = 2^{-\ell+1} \geq \frac{1}{2}p_m, \text{ i.e. } \ell(x_m) \leq -\log_2 p_m + 2.$$

Altogether, we obtain

$$\sum_{m=0}^{n} p_m \ell(x_m) + \sum_{k=1}^{n} q_k(\ell(y_k) + 1) \;\leq\; - \sum_{m=0}^{n} p_m \log_2 p_m + 2 \sum_{m=0}^{n} p_m$$

$$- \sum_{k=1}^{n} q_k \log_2 q_k + \sum_{k=1}^{n} q_k$$

$$= \; H(\underline{p}) + 1 + \sum_{k=0}^{n} p_k.$$

We summarize our findings in the following result.

Theorem 1.18. *Let* $\underline{p} = (p_0, p_1, \ldots, p_n; q_1, \ldots, q_n)$ *be a distribution for the data location problem. Then for the average-case cost* $\overline{DL}(n; \underline{p})$,

$$H(\underline{p}) - \log_2 e - (\log_2 \log_2(n+1) - 1) \sum_{k=1}^{n} q_k \leq \overline{DL}(n; \underline{p}) \leq H(\underline{p}) + 1 + \sum_{k=0}^{n} p_k.$$

Remark. Since the probabilities q_k may all be 0, i.e. $\sum p_k = 1$, we obtain the upper bound of **1.13** again as a special case. In fact, the preceding algorithm was suggested by the method used in the proof of **1.13**.

Example 1.23. The foregoing algorithm does not always provide an optimal search tree. Consider $n = 3$ with the following probabilities:

	0	1	2	3
p_i	$\frac{16}{100}$	$\frac{2}{100}$	$\frac{6}{100}$	$\frac{42}{100}$
q_i		$\frac{16}{100}$	$\frac{14}{100}$	$\frac{4}{100}$

Here we have $c(1) = \frac{33}{100}, c(2) = \frac{51}{100}, c(3) = \frac{79}{100}$. Since $c(1) < \frac{1}{2} < c(2)$, the algorithm of Mehlhorn chooses y_2 as initial root resulting in the left tree of figure 1.17.

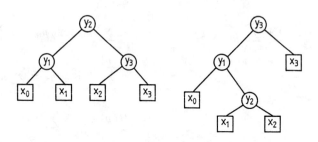

Figure 1.17

The cost of this tree is 1.86, whereas the cost of the optimal tree on the right (constructed by **1.16**) is 1.76.

Exercises 1.7.

1. Complete the proof of Proposition 1.15.

2*. Prove that the bound $\overline{DL}(n;\underline{p}) \le H(\underline{p}) + 1 + \sum_{k=0}^{n} p_k$ is best possible among all bounds of the form $aH(\underline{p}) + b\sum_{k=0}^{n} p_k + c\sum_{k=1}^{n} q_k$.

3. Compute $\overline{DL}(n;\underline{p})$ for example 1.23.

4*. Suppose $p_n = q_n = 0$. Show that an optimal search tree may be

obtained by replacing $\boxed{n-1}$ by $\overset{\displaystyle n}{\underset{\boxed{n-1}\quad\boxed{n}}{\diagup\diagdown}}$ in any optimal

search tree for $(p_0, \ldots, p_{n-1}; q_1, \ldots, q_{n-1})$.

5. Consider the algorithm following Proposition 1.16. Let $r(i,j)$ be the index of the root of the subproblem $S_{i,j}$. Now prove $r(i,j-1) \le r(i,j) \le r(i+1,j)$ for all i,j with $j-i \ge 2$.

6*. Call a binary search tree balanced if for every subtree S_{ij} the root y_k is chosen in such a way that $|w_{i,k-1} - w_{k,j}| = \min_{i<\ell\le j} |w_{i,\ell-1} - w_{\ell,j}|$. Show by example that balanced trees need not be optimal search trees.

7*. Let $c(n) = \max_{\underline{p}} \overline{DL}(n; \underline{p})$. Show that $c(n) = \max_{\underline{p}} \overline{L}_{mon}(n+1, 2; \underline{p})$, i.e. the problems of determining the cost of the "worst" distributions for search trees and alphabetic codes (for $q = 2$) are equivalent.

8*. Call a binary search tree a min − max tree, if for every subtree S_{ij} the root y_k is chosen in the following way. For $i < \ell \le j$ set $m_\ell = \max(w_{i,\ell-1}, w_{\ell,j})$. Now choose k such that $m_k = \min_{i<\ell\le j} m_\ell$. Show by example that min − max trees need not be optimal.

1.8 Predetermined Algorithms

So far, we have exclusively considered sequential algorithms. However, as noted in several places, predetermined algorithms may be just as good as sequential ones especially when all test functions are permitted.

Let us get a clear picture of what a predetermined algorithm looks like. Consider the (n, q)-process $(S, \mathcal{F})$. A predetermined algorithm $\mathcal{A}$ of length, say, L has to put down functions $f_1, \ldots, f_L \in \mathcal{F}$ once and for all. $\mathcal{A}$ may thus be represented in the following *matrix form*. Associate the columns of a matrix $M_{\mathcal{A}}$ with the elements $x_1, \ldots, x_n$ of S and the rows with the functions $f_1, \ldots, f_L$, writing $f_i(x_j)$ in the box indexed by (i, j). $M_{\mathcal{A}}$ is thus an $L \times n$-matrix over $\{0, 1, \ldots, q-1\}$. That $\mathcal{A}$ is a successful algorithm is apparently reflected by the fact that all columns of $M_{\mathcal{A}}$ are *distinct*. The important (if obvious) fact is that the converse is also true. If M is an n-columned matrix whose rows are admissible (according to $\mathcal{F}$) and whose columns are pairwise distinct, then M corresponds to a successful predetermined algorithm for the search process $(S, \mathcal{F})$. Indeed, if we let the functions $f_1, \ldots, f_L$ correspond to the rows, then no matter what the answers to the tests f_i are, at the end the unknown element x^* will be uniquely determined by the pairwise distinctness of the columns of M.

Let us say that the n-columned matrix M over $\{0, 1, \ldots, q-1\}$ is a *search matrix* for the process $(S, \mathcal{F})$ if the columns of M are pairwise distinct and if all rows are sequences $f(x_1), \ldots, f(x_n))$ for some $f \in \mathcal{F}$, $S = \{x_1, \ldots, x_n\}$. Our (L)-problem for predetermined algorithms reduces thus to finding search matrices for $(S, \mathcal{F})$ with a *minimal* number L of rows.

Example 1.24. When $\mathcal{F} = \{0, 1, \ldots, q-1\}^S$, then the only condition on the search matrices M is that the columns be distinct. Since there are q^L

distinct vectors of length $\lceil \log_q n \rceil$ over $\{0, 1, \ldots, q - 1\}$, it follows that any such matrix (with n columns) must satisfy $n \leq q^L$, i.e. $L \geq \lceil \log_q n \rceil$. On the other hand, by taking any $n \leq q^{\lceil \log_q n \rceil}$ distinct columns of length $\lceil \log_q n \rceil$, we obtain a valid search matrix, thereby reaffirming our observation in section 2 that any decision tree corresponds to a predetermined algorithm, and thus that the (L)-problem has the same solution for sequential and predetermined algorithms when all tests are admitted.

As an example, consider $n = 12$, $q = 2$. Any 0,1-matrix with 12 distinct columns and $4 = \lceil \log_2 12 \rceil$ rows will represent a predetermined algorithm; e.g., the following matrix:

$$
\begin{matrix}
0 & 0 & 0 & 0 & 1 & 1 & 1 & 1 & 1 & 1 & 1 & 0 \\
0 & 0 & 0 & 1 & 0 & 1 & 0 & 0 & 1 & 1 & 0 & 1 \\
0 & 0 & 1 & 0 & 0 & 0 & 1 & 0 & 1 & 0 & 1 & 1 \\
0 & 1 & 0 & 0 & 0 & 0 & 0 & 1 & 0 & 1 & 1 & 1
\end{matrix}
$$

Let us denote by $L_{pre}(S, \mathcal{F})$ the worst-case cost of the search process $(S, \mathcal{F})$ when only predetermined algorithms are available. In particular, let $L_{pre}(n, q)$ be the worst-case cost of an (n, q)-process with no restrictions on the functions.

Theorem 1.19. *We have*

  i) $L_{pre}(n, q) = \lceil \log_q n \rceil$

  ii) $L_{pre}(S, \mathcal{F}) \geq \lceil \log_q n \rceil$ *for any (n, q)-process $\mathcal{F}$.*

Let us turn to the average case. Suppose $\mathcal{A}$ is a predetermined algorithm of length L for $(S, \mathcal{F})$ with distribution $\underline{p} = (p_1, \ldots, p_n)$. We again represent $\mathcal{A}$ by its search matrix $M_{\mathcal{A}}$. If the element $x^* \in S$ is uniquely determined after, say, k tests, then we cross out the $L - k$ last entries in the column of $M_{\mathcal{A}}$ corresponding to x^* and replace them by blanks. The resulting *partial* $L \times n$-matrix $M'_{\mathcal{A}}$ has the property that every row corresponds to some vector $(f(x_1), \ldots, f(x_n))$, $f \in \mathcal{F}$ (or can be expanded to such a vector by properly filling in the blanks). Furthermore, no column of $M'_{\mathcal{A}}$ is a prefix of any other column.

It is again immediately clear that any n-columned partial matrix M over $\{0, 1, \ldots, q - 1\}$ with these two properties corresponds to a predetermined algorithm for $(S, \mathcal{F})$. Let us henceforth use the term *search matrix* for this more general situation as well. It will always be clear from the context whether the matrix in question is a partial or a full matrix.

The $(\overline{L})$-problem for predetermined algorithms reduces thus to the construction of search matrices M of column lengths $\ell_1, \ldots, \ell_n$ such that $\overline{L}(M; \underline{p}) = \sum_{i=1}^{n} p_i \ell_i$ is minimal. Note that for the uniform distribution, $\overline{L}(M; \frac{1}{n}, \ldots, \frac{1}{n})$ is precisely $\frac{1}{n}$ times the number of non-blank entries. In analogy to section 5, we denote by $\overline{L}_{pre}(S, \mathcal{F}; \underline{p})$ the average-case cost of $(S, \mathcal{F})$ with distribution $\underline{p}$, with $\overline{L}_{pre}(n, q; \underline{p})$ being the cost when all test functions are admitted. We have noted in section 2 that in the case of no restrictions on the test functions, any tree T or any search code C is possible and corresponds to a predetermined algorithm. A search matrix M associSated with C is simply given by writing the codewords of C as columns. So we note:

Theorem 1.20. *For any probability distribution* $\underline{p}$,

   i) $\overline{L}_{pre}(n, q; \underline{p}) = \overline{L}(n, q; \underline{p})$,

   ii) $\overline{L}_{pre}(S, \mathcal{F}; \underline{p}) \geq - \sum_{i=1}^{n} p_i \log_q p_i$ *for any* (n, q)-*process* $(S, \mathcal{F})$.

The situation changes completely when $\mathcal{F}$ is not the whole set of mappings.

Theorem 1.21. $L_{pre}(S, \mathcal{F}_{mon}) = \lceil \frac{n-1}{q-1} \rceil$ *with ordering* $x_1 < x_2 < \ldots < x_n$.

Proof. Let M be a full search matrix with L rows. By the definition of $\mathcal{F}_{mon}$, all rows of M are monotone words of length n over $\{0 < 1 < \ldots < q - 1\}$. If $\underline{a} = (a_1, \ldots, a_n)$ is a row of M, let us mark the space between a_k and a_{k+1} by a bar if $a_k < a_{k+1}$. For example, if $n = 8$, $q = 4$ we obtain for $\underline{a} = (0, 0, 1, 1, 1, 2, 2, 3)$ the bars $00 \mid 111 \mid 22 \mid 3$.

Hence, in any row of M there are at most $q - 1$ bars. On the other hand, since all columns of M are distinct, there must be a bar somewhere between any two columns k and $k + 1$, for $k = 1, \ldots, n - 1$. We thus conclude

$$n - 1 \leq L(q - 1).$$

A search matrix with precisely $\lceil \frac{n-1}{q-1} \rceil$ rows is easily constructed. Just place the bars in row 1 between columns $1, 2, \ldots, q$, in row 2 between columns $q, q + 1, \ldots, 2q - 1$, and so on, and fill up the rows in a monotone fashion.
□

Example 1.25. Suppose $n = 12$, $q = 4$, thus $\lceil \frac{n-1}{q-1} \rceil = 4$. A search matrix for $\mathcal{F}_{mon}$ is given by

$$
\begin{array}{cccccccccccc}
0 & 1 & 2 & 3 & 3 & 3 & 3 & 3 & 3 & 3 & 3 & 3 \\
0 & 0 & 0 & 0 & 1 & 2 & 3 & 3 & 3 & 3 & 3 & 3 \\
0 & 0 & 0 & 0 & 0 & 0 & 0 & 1 & 2 & 3 & 3 & 3 \\
0 & 0 & 0 & 0 & 0 & 0 & 0 & 0 & 0 & 0 & 1 & 2
\end{array}
$$

Turning to the average case, we can give the precise answer when the elements are uniformly distributed.

Theorem 1.22. Let $(S, \mathcal{F}_{mon})$ be an (n, q)-process with ordering $x_1 < x_2 < \ldots < x_n$.
Then

$$\overline{L}_{pre}(S, \mathcal{F}_{mon}; \frac{1}{n}, \ldots, \frac{1}{n}) = \frac{1}{n}[(q-1)\binom{\lceil \frac{n-1}{q-1}\rceil}{2}) + (n - (q-1)\lceil \frac{n-q}{q-1} \rceil)\lceil \frac{n-1}{q-1} \rceil].$$

Proof. Let M be an L-rowed search matrix for $(S, \mathcal{F}_{mon})$. We complete M to a full search matrix $\overline{M}$ by replacing the blanks in some proper fashion. We know from the previous theorem that $L \geq \lceil \frac{n-1}{q-1} \rceil$. Let us again mark the space between a_k and a_{k+1} of a row $\underline{a} = (a_1, \ldots, a_n)$ be a vertical bar if $a_k < a_{k+1}$. Denote by b_i the row number of the *first* bar appearing between columns i and $i + 1$, for $i = 1, \ldots, n - 1$. A moment's thought shows that the length ℓ_i of the codeword of x_i in M equals $\max(b_{i-1}, b_i)$, $i = 2, \ldots, n-1$ with $\ell_1 = b_1$ and $\ell_n = b_{n-1}$. Thus

$$
\begin{aligned}
\ell_1 &= b_1 \\
\ell_2 &= \max(b_1, b_2) \\
&\;\;\vdots \\
\ell_{n-1} &= \max(b_{n-2}, b_{n-1}) \\
\ell_n &= b_{n-1}.
\end{aligned}
$$

(1.6)

We know that any row contains at most $q - 1$ bars. If there were a row above the last one with less than $q - 1$ first bars, we could reduce $\overline{L}$ by moving up a bar from below that row. By the same reasoning, it follows that $L = \lceil \frac{n-1}{q-1} \rceil$ if M is to be optimal. Hence, we may assume that every row $1, 2, \ldots L - 1$ contains precisely $q - 1$ first bars and that row L contains $(n - 1) - (q - 1)(L - 1)$ such bars. Now we infer from (1.6):

at least $\quad n - (q-1)(L-1) \quad$ lengths ℓ_i are $\geq L$
at least $\quad n - (q-1)(L-1) + (q-1) \quad$ lengths ℓ_i are $\geq L-1$

$\vdots$

It follows that

$$\overline{L}(M) \geq \frac{1}{n}[(n-(q-1)(L-1))L + (q-1)(L-1) + \ldots + (q-1)]$$

$$= \frac{1}{n}[(q-1)\binom{L}{2} + (n-(q-1)(L-1))L],$$

which is precisely the right-hand side of our formula.
By taking $b_1 = \ldots = b_{q-1} = 1$, $b_q = \ldots = b_{2(q-1)} = 2, \ldots$, and filling in the entries in a monotone fashion, we obtain a search matrix M which, by (1.6), satisfies

$$\overline{L}(M) = \frac{1}{n}[(q-1) + \ldots + (L-1)(q-1) + (n-(q-1)(L-1))L],$$

and this completes the proof. $\qquad \square$

Remark. It follows readily from our argument that there are precisely 2^{L-1} optimal search matrices $\left(L = \lceil \frac{n-1}{q-1} \rceil \right)$ apart from a relabeling of the elements of the last row. For example, for $n = 4$, $q = 2$ we obtain the following four optimal search matrices where the last two are mirror images of the first two.

0	1	1	1		0	1	1	1		0	0	0	1		0	0	0	1
	0	1	1			0	0	1			0	0	1			0	1	1
		0	1				0	1				0	1				0	1

For a general distribution, we see again that an optimal search matrix will have $L = \lceil \frac{n-1}{q-1} \rceil$ rows with $q-1$ first bars appearing in the rows $1, 2, \ldots, L-1$. Relation (1.6) in the proof of the preceding theorem also holds; this implies that the search matrix constructed above with $b_1 = \ldots = b_{q-1} = 1$, $b_q = \ldots = b_{2(q-1)} = 2, \ldots$, filling in the entries in a monotone fashion, or its symmetric counterpart with $b_{n-1} = \ldots = b_{n-q+1} = 1$, $b_{n-q} = \ldots = b_{n-2q} = 2, \ldots$, will yield the optimum whenever $p_1 \geq \ldots \geq p_n$ or $p_1 \leq \ldots \leq p_n$ holds, respectively. For general distributions, the problem seems, however, much more difficult. Notice, that any $(\overline{L})$-optimal matrix is also (L)-optimal, in contrast to the sequential case.

Exercises 1.8.

1. Prove the statement in the remark following Theorem 1.22.

2*. Consider the grid problem of exercise 1.4.4. It was proved there that $\lceil \log_2 m + \log_2 n \rceil \leq L \leq \lceil \log_2 m \rceil + \lceil \log_2 n \rceil$. Show for $m = 5$, $n = 3$ that $L = 4$ whereas $L_{pre} = 5$.

3*. Show that for the counterfeit problem (see exercise 1.1.1), $L_{pre} = L$.

4. What can you say about an upper (or lower) bound for $\overline{L}_{pre}(S, \mathcal{F}_{mon}; \underline{p})$ for $q = 2$?

5*. Find a distribution $\underline{p}$ for all $n \geq 2$, $q = 2$, such that $\overline{L}_{pre}(S, \mathcal{F}_{mon}; \underline{p}) > \overline{L}_{pre}(S, \mathcal{F}_{mon}; \frac{1}{n}, \ldots, \frac{1}{n})$.

1.9 Binary Search Processes

The most important and best studied case of search processes arises for $q = 2$. The condition $q - 1 \mid n - 1$ is trivially satisfied and the notions of a process being regular or irreducible coincide. As mentioned in section 1, we may identify a test function $f : S \to \{0, 1\}$ with the set $\mathfrak{A} = \{x \in S : f(x) = 1\}$. We will therefore mostly write $(S, \mathfrak{A})$ to denote binary processes. Every algorithm $\mathcal{A}$ corresponds to a sequence $\mathcal{U} = \{A_1, A_2, \ldots, \}$, where every element $x^* \in S$ is uniquely determined by containment. The corresponding search codes consist of 0,1-words and will accordingly be called *binary codes*. Analogously, the decision trees will be called *binary trees*.

Our main results of sections 4 and 5 are summarized in the following theorem.

Theorem 1.23. *For* $n \geq 1$,

   i) $L(n, 2) = L_{pre}(n, 2) = \lceil \log_2 n \rceil$

   ii) $\overline{L}(n, 2; \frac{1}{n}, \ldots, \frac{1}{n}) = \overline{L}_{pre}(n, 2; \frac{1}{n}, \ldots, \frac{1}{n}) = \lceil \log_2 n \rceil - \frac{1}{n} 2^{\lceil \log_2 n \rceil} + 1$

iii) $H(p_1, \ldots, p_n)$ $\leq$ $\overline{L}(n, 2; \underline{p})$ $=$ $\overline{L}_{pre}(n, 2; \underline{p})$

$\qquad\qquad\qquad\quad \overline{L}(n, 2; \underline{p})$ $<$ $H(p_1, \ldots, p_n) + 1$

$\qquad\qquad\qquad\quad \overline{L}(n, 2; \underline{p})$ $\leq$ $\lceil \log_2 n \rceil - \frac{1}{n} 2^{\lceil \log_2 n \rceil} + 1,$

when the distribution $\underline{p} = (p_1, \ldots, p_n)$ *is given.*
If $(S, \mathfrak{A})$ *is an arbitrary binary search process, then*

iv) $\lceil \log_2 n \rceil \leq L(S, \mathfrak{A}) \leq L_{pre}(S, \mathfrak{A})$

v) $H(p_1, \ldots, p_n) \leq \overline{L}(S, \mathfrak{A}; \underline{p}) \leq \overline{L}_{pre}(S, \mathfrak{A}; \underline{p})$ *for the distribution* $\underline{p} = (p_1, \ldots, p_n)$.

Let the ordering $S = \{x_1 < x_2 < \ldots < x_n\}$ be given. The test family $\mathfrak{A}$ corresponding to $\mathcal{F}_{mon}$ is $\mathfrak{A}_{mon} = \{\emptyset, \{x_n\}, \{x_{n-1}, x_n\}, \ldots, \{x_2, \ldots, x_n\}, S\}$. The theorems of sections 6 and 8 now read:

Theorem 1.24. *Let the binary search process* $(S, \mathfrak{A}_{mon})$ *with* $|S| = n$ *be given. Then*

i) $L(S, \mathfrak{A}_{mon}) = \lceil \log_2 n \rceil, L_{pre}(S, \mathfrak{A}_{mon}) = n - 1$

ii) $\overline{L}(S, \mathfrak{A}_{mon}; \frac{1}{n}, \ldots, \frac{1}{n}) = \lceil \log_2 n \rceil - \frac{1}{n} 2^{\lceil \log_2 n \rceil} + 1,$
$\qquad \overline{L}_{pre}(S, \mathfrak{A}_{mon}; \frac{1}{n}, \ldots, \frac{1}{n}) = \frac{n+1}{2} - \frac{1}{n}.$

Note that for predetermined algorithms we can, by $L_{pre}(S, \mathfrak{A}_{mon}) = n - 1$ and $\overline{L}_{pre}(S, \mathfrak{A}_{mon}; \frac{1}{n}, \ldots, \frac{1}{n}) = \frac{n+1}{2} - \frac{1}{n}$ do no better than the trivial element-for-element search (see example 1.9).

A predetermined algorithm $\mathcal{U} = \{A_1, A_2, \ldots, A_L\}$ is often called a *separating set system* for S since for any $x \neq y \in S$ there exists a set $A_i \in \mathcal{U}$ which contains precisely one of x and y, or, as we say, *separates* x and y. The search matrix $M = (m_{ij})$ corresponding to $\mathcal{U}$ has its rows indexed by the sets of $\mathcal{U}$, its columns by the elements of S with

$$m_{ij} = \begin{cases} 1 & \text{if } x_j \in A_i \\ 0 & \text{if } x_j \notin A_i. \end{cases}$$

Hence M is precisely what is usually called the *incidence matrix* of the family $\mathcal{U} \subseteq 2^S$.

The interpretation of the admissible tests $\mathcal{F}$ as certain families $\mathfrak{A} \subseteq 2^S$ gives rise to a variety of interesting conditions to be imposed on $\mathfrak{A}$. Let us look at two examples.

One natural condition is to consider the test-family $\mathfrak{A}_{\leq k} = \{A \subseteq S : |A| \leq k\}$ of all sets containing at most k elements when, say, the cost of the tests increases with the size of the sets. If $k \geq \frac{n}{2}$, then this imposes no restriction on the sets since with every set we also test its complement.

Proposition 1.25. *Let S be an n-set, $k \leq n$.*

i) $L(S, \mathfrak{A}_{\leq k}) = \lceil \log_2 n \rceil$ *for* $k \geq \frac{n}{2}$,

ii) $L(S, \mathfrak{A}_{\leq k}) = t + \lceil \log_2(n - tk) \rceil$, $t = \lceil \frac{n}{k} \rceil - 2$ *for* $k < \frac{n}{2}$.

Proof. By our remark above, we may assume $k < \frac{n}{2}$. Set $f_k(n) = L(S, \mathfrak{A}_{\leq k})$, $|S| = n$. For fixed k, $f_k(n)$ is increasing as a function of n. To see this, suppose $T \subsetneq S$ and let $\mathcal{U}$ be an optimal algorithm for S of length L. Then $\mathcal{U}'$, consisting of all intersections of the sets in $\mathcal{U}$ with T, is clearly a successful algorithm for T of length $\leq L$. Now suppose A_1 with $|A_1| = \ell \leq k$ is the first test-set in an optimal algorithm for $(S, \mathfrak{A}_{\leq k})$. Considering optimal algorithms within A_1 and $S - A_1$, we arrive at the recursion

$$f_k(n) = 1 + \max(f_k(\ell), f_k(n - \ell)) = 1 + f_k(n - \ell) \geq 1 + f_k(n - k)$$

because of $\ell \leq k < \frac{n}{2} < n - k \leq n - \ell$ and the monotonicity of f_k. Repeating this recursion, we finally obtain

$$f_k(n) \geq 1 + f_k(n-k) \geq 2 + f_k(n-2k) \geq \ldots \geq t + f_k(n-tk) = t + \lceil \log_2(n-tk) \rceil,$$

where t is the smallest number with $k \geq \frac{n-tk}{2}$, i.e. $t = \lceil \frac{n}{k} \rceil - 2$. Hence $L(S, \mathfrak{A}_{\leq k}) \geq t + \lceil \log_2(n - tk) \rceil$.

An algorithm with this many tests is easily constructed. As our first t test-sets we take

$$A_1 = \{x_1, \ldots, x_k\}, A_2 = \{x_{k+1}, \ldots, x_{2k}\}, \ldots, A_t = \{x_{(t-1)k+1}, \ldots, x_{tk}\}.$$

If $x^* \in \bigcup_{i=1}^{t} A_i$, then x^* can be determined using $\lceil \log_2 k \rceil$ further tests since there are no restrictions present. If, on the other hand, x^* is one of $\{x_{tk+1}, \ldots, x_n\}$, then x^* is determined with $\lceil \log_2(n - tk) \rceil$ further tests since $k \geq \frac{n-tk}{2}$. From the definition of t we have $k < \frac{n-(t-1)k}{2}$, i.e. $n - tk > k$, which means that in the worst case our algorithm needs no more than $t + \lceil \log_2(n - tk) \rceil$ tests. $\square$

Example 1.26. Consider $n = 8$, $k = 3$, $S = \{1, 2, \ldots, 8\}$. The algorithm constructed in the proposition has the following decision tree:

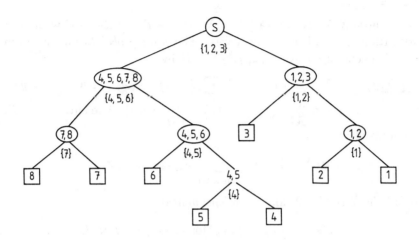

Figure 1.18

Let us turn to the predetermined case. Our task consists in constructing a full search matrix M with a minimal number of rows L, i.e. a 0,1-matrix M all of whose columns are distinct and with all row-sums $\leq k$. Again, for $k \geq \frac{n}{2}$ this poses no restrictions, and we obtain the result $L_{pre}(S, \mathfrak{A}_{\leq k}) = \lceil \log_2 n \rceil$. What about $k < \frac{n}{2}$? Here we make use of the entropy $H(p_1, \ldots, p_n)$ of a distribution. Similar techniques will occur several times throughout the book.

Let us review some elementary facts from probability theory. Let Ω be a finite set with a probability distribution Pr, i.e. Pr is a function from Ω into the non-negative reals $\mathbb{R}^+$ with $\sum_{\omega \in \Omega} Pr(\omega) = 1$. We always think of Ω as endowed with the distribution Pr. A function $X : \Omega \longrightarrow T$ into some finite set $T \subseteq \mathbb{R}$ is called a *random variable*, and we define

$$p(x) = p(X = x) := \sum \{ Pr(\omega) : X(\omega) = x \} \quad (x \in T),$$

setting $p(x) = 0$ if x is not in the image of X. In this way p defines a distribution on T, called the *induced distribution*.

Definition. The *entropy $H(X)$* of the variable $X : \Omega \longrightarrow T$ is defined as the entropy of the distribution $\{p(x) : x \in T\}$, i.e. $H(X) := - \sum_{x \in T} p(x) \log_2 p(x)$ with the convention $0 \cdot \log_2 0 = 0$.

For example, if the distribution is uniform on, say, m values of T, then $H(X) = \log_2 m$.

Now suppose X, Y are two variables $X : \Omega \longrightarrow T, Y : \Omega \longrightarrow U$ with induced distributions p_X and p_Y, respectively. The *joint probability distribution* on $T \times U$ is declared for every $(x, y) \in T \times U$ by

$$p(x, y) := p(X = x \wedge Y = y) = \sum \{ Pr(\omega) : X(\omega) = x \wedge Y(\omega) = y \}.$$

Notice that $p_X(x) = \sum_{y \in U} p(x, y), p_Y(y) = \sum_{x \in T} p(x, y)$. The entropy of (X, Y) is then given by

$$H(X, Y) = - \sum_{(x,y) \in X \times Y} p(x, y) \log_2 p(x, y).$$

We call the variables X and Y *independent* if

$$p(x, y) = p_X(x) p_Y(y) \text{ for all } (x, y) \in T \times U.$$

It is immediately clear how to generalize these concepts to L variables $X_1, \ldots, X_L$. For example, we will call $X_1, \ldots, X_L$ independent if $p(X_1 = x_1 \wedge X_2 = x_2 \wedge \ldots \wedge X_L = x_L) = \prod_{i=1}^{L} p(X_i = x_i)$ holds for all $x_1, \ldots, x_L$. The following result is basic:

Proposition 1.26. *Suppose we are given L random variables $X_1, \ldots, X_L$ with $X_i : \Omega \longrightarrow T : i = 1, \ldots, L$. Then*

$$H(X_1, \ldots, X_L) \le \sum_{i=1}^{L} H(X_i)$$

with equality iff $X_1, \ldots, X_L$ are independent.

Proof. Since $H(X_1, \ldots, X_L) = H((X_1, \ldots, X_{L-1}), X_L)$, it is enough to prove the claim for two variables $X : \Omega \longrightarrow T, Y : \Omega \longrightarrow U$. We have

$$
\begin{aligned}
H(X, Y) &= - \sum_{(x,y)} p(x, y) \log_2 p(x, y), \\
H(X) + H(Y) &= - \sum_{x \in T} p_X(x) \log_2 p_X(x) - \sum_{y \in U} p_Y(y) \log_2 p_Y(y) \\
&= - \sum_{x \in T} \sum_{y \in U} p(x, y) \log_2 p_X(x) - \sum_{x \in T} \sum_{y \in U} p(x, y) \log_2 p_Y(y). \\
&= - \sum_{(x,y)} p(x, y) \log_2 (p_X(x) p_Y(y)).
\end{aligned}
$$

Now we invoke Lemma 1.5 from section 5. Index the elements (x, y) from 1 to $| T \times U |$, and set $y_i = p(x, y)$, $s_i = p_X(x) \cdot p_Y(y)$. Then $\sum y_i = \sum s_i = 1$, and thus

$$\sum_{(x,y)} p(x, y) \log_2 \frac{p(x, y)}{p_X(x) p_Y(y)} \geq 0.$$

We conclude that

$$
\begin{aligned}
H(X, Y) &= -\sum_{(x,y)} p(x, y) \log_2 p(x, y) \\
&\leq -\sum_{(x,y)} p(x, y) \log_2(p_X(x) p_Y(y)) \\
&= H(X) + H(Y),
\end{aligned}
$$

with equality iff $p(x, y) = p_X(x) p_Y(y)$ for all (x, y). $\quad\square$

It is instructive to interpret our result from an information-theoretic point of view. We have previously remarked that $H(X)$ measures the number of questions necessary on the average to determine the outcome of X. Hence, if we want to know about the joint event $(X_1, \ldots, X_L)$ we might use the simple algorithm to determine first X_1, then X_2, and so on. This might not be the best algorithm resulting in the inequality $H(X_1, \ldots, X_L) \leq H(X_1) + \ldots + H(X_L)$. If, however, the events X_i are independent then there is nothing to be learned about X_i by asking about the other events. So in this case we would expect $H(X_1, \ldots, X_L) = \sum H(X_i)$ as verified by our result.

After this short discourse let us apply our findings to the problem at hand. The following result is due to Katona [1966].

Proposition 1.27. *For an n-set S and $k < \frac{n}{2}$,*

$$L_{pre}(S, \mathfrak{A}_{\leq k}) \geq \frac{\log_2 n}{\log_2 e \frac{n}{k}} \cdot \frac{n}{k}.$$

Proof. Let $\mathcal{U} = \{A_1, \ldots, A_L\} \subseteq \mathfrak{A}_{\leq k}$ be a separating set system on $S = \{x_1, \ldots, x_n\}$. We endow S with the uniform distribution $Pr(x_i) = \frac{1}{n}$ for all i. To every $A_i \in \mathcal{U}$ we associate a random variable $X_i : S \longrightarrow \{0, 1\}$ with $X_i(x_j) = 1$ iff $x_j \in A_i$. Thus $(X_i(x_1), \ldots, X_i(x_n))$ is just the incidence vector of A_i. The induced distribution is then given by

$$(1.7) \qquad p_{X_i}(1) = \frac{|A_i|}{n}, \quad p_{X_i}(0) = 1 - \frac{|A_i|}{n} \quad (i = 1, \ldots, L).$$

Let us consider the random vector $(X_1, \ldots, X_L): S \longrightarrow \{0,1\}^L$. The image of $(X_1, \ldots, X_L)$ consists precisely of the n columns of the $L \times n$-incidence matrix of $\mathcal{U}$. Furthermore, since all these columns are distinct, we conclude that the distribution of $(X_1, \ldots, X_L)$ is uniform on n elements. We thus infer from the preceding proposition

$$\log_2 n = H(X_1, \ldots, X_L) \leq \sum_{i=1}^{L} H(X_i).$$

By (1.7), $H(X_i) = -\frac{|A_i|}{n} \log_2 \frac{|A_i|}{n} - \left(1 - \frac{|A_i|}{n}\right) \log_2 \left(1 - \frac{|A_i|}{n}\right)$. We know from section 5 (see figure 1.10) that $H(p, 1 - p)$ is increasing for $p \leq \frac{1}{2}$, whence we see from $\frac{|A_i|}{n} \leq \frac{k}{n} < \frac{1}{2}$ that

$$H(X_i) \leq -\frac{k}{n} \log_2 \frac{k}{n} - (1 - \frac{k}{n}) \log_2(1 - \frac{k}{n})$$

holds for all i. This in turn implies

$$
\begin{aligned}
\log_2 n &\leq L \left[-\frac{k}{n} \log_2 \frac{k}{n} - (1 - \frac{k}{n}) \log_2(1 - \frac{k}{n}) \right] \\
&= L \left[\frac{k}{n} \log_2 \frac{n}{k} + \frac{n-k}{n} \log_2 \frac{n}{n-k} \right] \\
&= L \frac{k}{n} \left[\log_2 \frac{n}{k} + \frac{n-k}{k} \log_2(1 + \frac{k}{n-k}) \right].
\end{aligned}
$$

Now recall from section 5 that $\ln x \leq x - 1$ and thus $\log_2 x \leq (x-1) \log_2 e$ holds for $x > 0$, or equivalently

$$\log_2(1 + x) \leq x \log_2 e \quad \text{for} \quad x > -1.$$

Substituting this into the inequality above, we obtain

$$\log_2 n \leq L \frac{k}{n} \left[\log_2 \frac{n}{k} + \log_2 e \right] = L \frac{k}{n} \log_2 e \frac{n}{k},$$

and thus finally

$$L \geq \frac{\log_2 n}{\log_2 e \frac{n}{k}} \cdot \frac{n}{k}. \qquad \square$$

We state without proof the best known upper bound for L_{pre} due to Wegener [1979]:

Proposition 1.28. *For an n-set S and $k < \frac{n}{2}$,*

$$L_{pre}(S, \mathfrak{A}_{\leq k}) \leq \lceil \frac{\log_2 n}{\log_2 \frac{n}{k}} \rceil \left(\lceil \frac{n}{k} \rceil - 1 \right).$$

It is easily shown that the ratio between the two bounds in **1.28** and **1.27** is $\leq 2(1 + \log_2 e) < 5$ for all n and $k < \frac{n}{2}$; hence both bounds can be considered to be very good. As for the average case, it can be shown that the algorithm constructed in the proof of **1.25** is also $(\overline{L})$-optimal for uniform distribution, thus yielding $\overline{L}(S, \mathfrak{A}_{\leq k}; \frac{1}{n}, \ldots, \frac{1}{n}) \sim \frac{n}{2k} + \log_2 k + C$ for $n \to \infty$ and k fixed. For the predetermined case, it is known that $\overline{L}_{pre}(S, \mathfrak{A}_{\leq k}; \frac{1}{n}, \ldots, \frac{1}{n}) \overset{\sim}{\leq} \frac{n}{k+1} + C(k)$, and the right-hand side is probably the correct growth (see the exercises). For arbitrary distributions, practically nothing is known.

Another interesting condition on a binary search process is obtained by considering only test families $\mathfrak{A}$ with "small intersections". Given k, we require $|A \cap B| \leq k$ for any A, B in an algorithm $\mathcal{U}$. Note that this is a "dynamic" condition on $\mathcal{U}$; in principle all test-sets are allowed.

We confine ourselves to the case $k = 1$. Interestingly enough, we shall see that L and L_{pre} turn out to be the same. Denote by $g(n)$ the worst-case length of sequential algorithms $\mathcal{U}$ under the condition $|A \cap B| \leq 1$ for all $A, B \in \mathcal{U}$ when $|S| = n$. Let us call any such $\mathcal{U} \subseteq 2^S$ a 1-*family*. Notice that we have $g(n) \leq g(n+1) \leq g(n) + 1$. The first inequality is obvious. The second inequality follows by testing the subset $\{x_{n+1}\}$ of an $(n+1)$-set first, and using an optimal algorithm on $\{x_1, \ldots, x_n\}$ if $x^* \neq x_{n+1}$. Hence the function $g(n)$ is completely determined by its "jump-points" $j_0 < j_1 < j_2 < \ldots$ with

$$g(n) = L \iff j_{L-1} < n \leq j_L.$$

Since obviously $g(1) = 0$, $g(2) = 1$, we note $j_0 = 1$.

Lemma 1.29. *We have $j_L = j_{L-1} + L$ for all $L \geq 1$.*

Proof. Suppose we test a k-set A_1 first. If the answer to $x^* \in A_1$ is "yes", then the length of this subtree will be $k - 1$ since any optimal algorithm on A_1 will split off the elements one by one. If, on the other hand, the answer is "no", then the length of this subtree will be $g(n - k)$. We thus arrive at the recursion

$$(1.8) \qquad g(n) = \min_{1 \leq k \leq n-1} \max(k, 1 + g(n - k)).$$

Set $n = j_L$ and suppose k achieves the minimum in (1.8). Then

$$L = g(j_L) = \max(k, 1 + g(j_L - k)),$$

and we conclude $k \leq L$, $1 + g(j_L - L) \leq 1 + g(j_L - k) \leq L$, i.e. $g(j_L - L) \leq L - 1$, which means $j_L - L \leq j_{L-1}$.
Now set $n = j_{L-1} + L$. Then we have by (1.8)

$$g(j_{L-1} + L) \leq \max(L, 1 + g(j_{L-1})) = L$$

i.e. $j_{L-1} + L \leq j_L$, and thus altogether $j_L = j_{L-1} + L$. $\square$

With these preparations we easily obtain the following result due to Sebö [1982].

Proposition 1.30. *For an n-set S and only 1-families admitted,*

$$L(S, \mathfrak{A}) = L_{pre}(S, \mathfrak{A}) = \left\lceil \sqrt{2n - \frac{7}{4}} - \frac{1}{2} \right\rceil.$$

Proof. It follows from $j_0 = 1$ and the Lemma that $j_L = \frac{(L+1)L}{2} + 1$, and hence that

$$L(S, \mathfrak{A}) = g(n) = L \iff \frac{L(L-1)}{2} + 1 < n \leq \frac{(L+1)L}{2} + 1.$$

Solving the inequality on the right we obtain

$$\sqrt{2n - \frac{7}{4}} - \frac{1}{2} \leq g(n) < \sqrt{2n - \frac{7}{4}} + \frac{1}{2},$$

and thus

$$L(S, \mathfrak{A}) = g(n) = \left\lceil \sqrt{2n - \frac{7}{4}} - \frac{1}{2} \right\rceil.$$

Let $A_1(x^*), A_2(x^*), \ldots, A_{g(n)}(x^*)$ be the sets determining x^*, where we set $A_i(x^*) = \emptyset$ if $\ell(x^*) < g(n)$. To prove $L_{pre}(S, \mathfrak{A}) = L(S, \mathfrak{A})$, take a $g(n)$-set A_1 first and consider the disjoint subproblems on A_1 and $S - A_1$, respectively. A_1 can obviously be searched by a predetermined 1-family in $g(n) - 1$ steps and so can $S - A_1$ by induction. Taking the disjoint unions at each step clearly yields a 1-family of size $g(n)$ for S. $\square$

Example 1.27. Consider $S = \{1, 2, \ldots, 10\}$, $g(10) = 4$. An optimal search matrix is given below

$$
\begin{array}{cccccccccc}
1 & 1 & 1 & 1 & 0 & 0 & 0 & 0 & 0 & 0 \\
1 & 0 & 0 & 0 & 1 & 1 & 1 & 0 & 0 & 0 \\
0 & 1 & 0 & 0 & 1 & 0 & 0 & 1 & 1 & 0 \\
0 & 0 & 1 & 0 & 0 & 1 & 0 & 1 & 0 & 0
\end{array}
$$

The average case is again unsettled.

Exercises 1.9.

1*. Suppose we know that in an n-set S, any element is defective independently of the others with equal probability $p > 0$. The goal is to determine the set $X^* \subseteq S$ of defective elements where every test-set A gives the information $A \cap X^* \neq \emptyset$ or $A \cap X^* = \emptyset$ (see example 1.2 and exercise 1.1.5). What is the distribution on the X^*'s ? Discuss L and $\overline{L}$, in particular, show $\overline{L} \geq nH(p, 1 - p)$.

2*. Continuation of exercise 1. Consider $n = 2$. The element-for-element search yields $\overline{L} \leq L = 2$. Show that precisely for $p \geq \frac{3-\sqrt{5}}{2} \sim 0.38$ you can do no better.

3. Continuation of exercise 1. Show that $\overline{L} = n$ ($n \geq 2$) precisely when $p \geq \frac{3-\sqrt{5}}{2}$.

4. Continuation of exercise 1. Suppose $p = \frac{1}{2}$ and we are only allowed $\mathfrak{A}_{mon}$ as test-sets. What is L and $\overline{L}$?

5*. $\mathfrak{A} = \{A_1, \ldots, A_m\} \subseteq 2^S$, $|S| = n$, is called a *completely separating system* if for all $x \neq y \in S$ there exists A_i with $x \in A_i$ and $y \notin A_i$. Show that

$$
\binom{m}{\lceil \frac{m}{2} \rceil} \geq n.
$$

6*. Show that the algorithm in the proof of **1.25** is also optimal in the $(\overline{L})$-case, and compute $\overline{L}(S, \mathfrak{A}_{\leq k})$, when uniform distribution is assumed.

7. Find a good algorithm for $(S, \mathfrak{A}_{\leq k})$ in the predetermined case (see the bound in **1.28**).

8*. Consider the $(\overline{L})$-problem for $(S, \mathfrak{A}_{\leq 2})$ in the predetermined case and uniform distribution. Let $f(n)$ be the total number of entries in an optimal (partial) search matrix M when $|S| = n$. Prove $f(n) = f(n - 3) + 2n$ $(n \geq 4)$ and deduce from this

$$\overline{L} = \frac{n}{3} + 1 - \begin{cases} \frac{1}{n} & n \equiv 0 \pmod 3 \\ \frac{4}{3n} & n \equiv 1,2 \pmod 3. \end{cases}$$

9. Try to generalize **1.30** where only algorithms $\mathcal{U}$ are permitted with $|A \cap B \cap C| \leq 1$ for all $A, B, C \in \mathcal{U}$.

1.10   A Game-Theoretic Point of View

The worst-case problem of a search process $(S, \mathcal{F})$ can also be interpreted as a *search game* between two players A ("Algy") and B ("Strategist"). Player A chooses test functions $f_1, f_2, \ldots \in \mathcal{F}$ and asks B questions of the form: What is $f_i(x^*)$? A wants to determine the unknown x^* with a minimal number of questions. Any sequence $f_1, f_2, \ldots$ determining the unknown $x^* \in S$ is as usual called an *algorithm* $\mathcal{A}$ of player A. Player B, on the other hand, tries to force A to ask as many questions as possible. Any sequence of answers $e_1, e_2, \ldots$ (compatible with $\mathcal{F}$) is called a *strategy* $\mathcal{S}$ of B. The game stops when x^* is determined, and the *length of the game* is the number of questions asked.

Suppose A uses algorithm $\mathcal{A}_0$ and B uses strategy $\mathcal{S}_0$. The length of the resulting game shall be denoted by $L(\mathcal{A}_0, \mathcal{S}_0)$. The worst-case nature is reflected by the fact that when player A forwards algorithm $\mathcal{A}_0$, he must expect B to use a strategy which *maximizes* the number of questions in the presence of $\mathcal{A}_0$. Similarly with B using $\mathcal{S}_0$, A will counter with an algorithm *minimizing* the number of tests under $\mathcal{S}_0$. The following definitions are therefore suggested:

$$L(\mathcal{A}_0) := \max_{\mathcal{S}} L(\mathcal{A}_0, \mathcal{S})$$
$$L(\mathcal{S}_0) := \min_{\mathcal{A}} L(\mathcal{A}, \mathcal{S}_0).$$

$L(\mathcal{A}_0)$ and $L(\mathcal{S}_0)$ are accordingly called the *lengths* of $\mathcal{A}_0$ and $\mathcal{S}_0$, respectively.

Proposition 1.31. *Suppose $(S, \mathcal{F})$ is a search process. Then*

$$\min_{\mathcal{A}} \max_{\mathcal{S}} L(\mathcal{A}, \mathcal{S}) = \max_{\mathcal{S}} \min_{\mathcal{A}} L(\mathcal{A}, \mathcal{S}),$$

or equivalently

$$\min_{\mathcal{A}} L(\mathcal{A}) = \max_{\mathcal{S}} L(\mathcal{S}).$$

The common cardinality is precisely the worst-case cost $L(S, \mathcal{F})$.

Proof. For any fixed $\mathcal{A}_0$ and $\mathcal{S}_0$, we obviously have

$$L(\mathcal{A}_0) = \max_{\mathcal{S}} L(\mathcal{A}_0, \mathcal{S}) \geq \min_{\mathcal{A}} L(\mathcal{A}, \mathcal{S}_0) = L(\mathcal{S}_0),$$

and hence

$$\min_{\mathcal{A}} L(\mathcal{A}) \geq \max_{\mathcal{S}} L(\mathcal{S}).$$

To prove equality, we use induction on n. For $n = 1$, both sides are equal to 0. Suppose $(S, \mathcal{F})$ is an (n, q)-search process. We call an algorithm $\mathcal{A}_0$ *optimal* if $L(\mathcal{A}_0) = \min_{\mathcal{A}} L(\mathcal{A})$; similarly the strategy $\mathcal{S}_0$ is *optimal* if $L(\mathcal{S}_0) = \max_{\mathcal{S}} L(\mathcal{S})$. If f is the first test function of $\mathcal{A}_0$, we denote by $\pi(f) = \{S_0, S_1, \ldots, S_{q-1}\}$ the partition induced by f, i.e. $S_i = \{x \in S : f(x) = i\}$, $i = 0, \ldots, q-1$. We may assume that f attains at least two different values, or in other words, that $S_i \subsetneq S$ for all i. Suppose $\mathcal{A}(S_i)$ is an optimal algorithm for the subprocess $(S_i, \mathcal{F}_i)$ where $\mathcal{F}_i$ is the restriction of $\mathcal{F}$ to S_i. Combining all $\mathcal{A}(S_i)$ and choosing the first test in such a way as to minimize the worst-case length of the subproblem, we apparently obtain an optimal algorithm $\mathcal{A}_0$ for $(S, \mathcal{F})$ with

$$L(\mathcal{A}_0) = 1 + \min_{f}\{\max L(\mathcal{A}(S_i)) : S_i \in \pi(f)\}.$$

Analogously, let $\mathcal{S}(S_i)$ be an optimal strategy for the subprocess $(S_i, \mathcal{F}_i)$. Again by combining all strategies $\mathcal{S}(S_i)$ and choosing the answer to the first question so as to maximize the length of the subproblem, we obtain an optimal strategy $\mathcal{S}_0$ for $(S, \mathcal{F})$ with

$$L(\mathcal{S}_0) = 1 + \min_{f}\{\max L(\mathcal{S}(S_i)) : S_i \in \pi(f)\}.$$

Since all $\mathcal{A}(S_i)$ and $\mathcal{S}(S_i)$ are optimal, we infer by induction $L(\mathcal{A}(S_i)) = L(\mathcal{S}(S_i))$ for all i and f, and thus $L(\mathcal{A}_0) = L(\mathcal{S}_0)$. $\square$

It is apparent from the construction of $\mathcal{A}_0$ and $\mathcal{S}_0$ that

$$L(\mathcal{A}_0) = L(\mathcal{A}_0, \mathcal{S}_0) = L(\mathcal{S}_0).$$

Hence, we can say that the worst-case cost of a search process is the length of the associated search game when both players play optimally. Let us remark that Proposition 1.31 is a special case of the Duality Theorem in Game Theory, where A and B are called the "minimax" and "maximin" player respectively.

The equality $\min_{\mathcal{A}} L(\mathcal{A}) = \max_{\mathcal{S}} L(\mathcal{S})$ can often be fruitfully exploited to provide bounds for $L = L(S, \mathcal{F})$. We have

$$L(\mathcal{S}) \leq L \leq L(\mathcal{A}) \text{ for any } \mathcal{A} \text{ and } \mathcal{S}.$$

Looking at the right inequality, we see that the length $L(\mathcal{A})$ of any algorithm $\mathcal{A}$ provides an *upper bound* for L. Well, this is nothing new. In most problems, however, the real difficulty arises when we try to find lower bounds. Now we can say: The length $L(\mathcal{S})$ of any strategy $\mathcal{S}$ establishes a *lower bound* for L. Quite often, a natural strategy for player B is suggested by the search process, thus leading to a lower bound for L.

Example 1.28. The information-theoretic bound $L(S, \mathcal{F}) \geq \lceil \log_q n \rceil$ for any (n, q)-process $(S, \mathcal{F})$ is trivially established by interpreting $(S, \mathcal{F})$ as a search game. B uses the following strategy S_0: Suppose at a certain stage k, $S_k \subseteq S$ is the set of possible candidates, and f is the next test function. Among the sets $S_{k,i} = \{x \in S_k : f(x) = i\}$, B picks one with maximal cardinality. Hence $\mid S_{k+1} \mid \geq \frac{\mid S_k \mid}{q}$ which immediately implies $1 = \mid S_L \mid \geq \frac{\mid S \mid}{q^L}$, i.e. $L \geq \lceil \log_q n \rceil$. (See the remark after **1.3**, where we have implicitly taken this approach.)

The reader can easily convince himself that the average case-problem $(\overline{L})$ can similarly be interpreted as a search game with a corresponding $\min - \max = \max - \min$ result. The same is, of course, true for the predetermined (L) and $(\overline{L})$-costs, which in terms of the search game means that A plays with "open cards". For B, on the other hand, open play makes no sense since his answers must be consistent with $\mathcal{F}$ and will thus have to depend on the questions asked by A.

To conclude this chapter, we briefly look at a problem closely related with our search process $(S, \mathcal{F})$. Let us again take the game-theoretic approach. So far, the task of player A consisted in identifying the unknown element x^*. We may call this the *identification problem*. Now suppose a subset $S_0 \subseteq S$ is given. A is now required to determine with as few queries as possible whether x^* is in S_0 or not (tacitly assuming, of course, that the family $\mathcal{F}$

contains at least one successful algorithm). This is called the *recognition problem* (relative to S_0). Typically, S_0 is defined by a certain *property* of the elements of S. Player A then wants to verify or recognize whether the unknown object has the given property or not. If $S_0 = \emptyset$ or $S_0 = S$ then no questions need be asked, so we always assume $\emptyset \neq S_0 \neq S$, calling the two other cases *trivial* recognition problems. Player B, of course, tries to force A to ask as many questions as possible. The notions of algorithms and strategies carry over, and a result analogous to Proposition 1.31 can be easily proved.

Thus we may define the worst-case cost $L^{(r)}(S_0, \mathcal{F})$ for any $S_0 \subseteq S$ as the length of the game, provided both players play optimally.

Example 1.29. It is instructive to see some characteristic differences between the new game and the old. Suppose $(S, \mathfrak{A})$ is an $(n, 2)$-process, and denote by $L^{(r)}(S_0, \mathfrak{A})$ the cost of S_0. If $\mathfrak{A} = 2^S$ or, more generally, when $\mathfrak{A}$ contains S_0 or the complement $S - S_0$, then evidently $L^{(r)}(S_0, \mathfrak{A}) = 1$, so this is not interesting. Suppose $2 \leq |S_0| \leq n-2$ and, let $\mathfrak{A}$ consist of all singletons. Then, clearly $L^{(r)}(S_0, \mathfrak{A}) = L^{(r)}(S - S_0, \mathfrak{A}))$, so we may assume $|S_0| \leq \frac{n}{2}$. The element-for-element search yields $L(S_0, \mathfrak{A}) = |S_0| - 1$. On the other hand, by using the simple strategy of saying "no" as long as possible, B forces A to ask at least $|S_0|$ questions, whence $L^{(r)}(S_0, \mathfrak{A}) = \min(|S_0|, n - |S_0|)$.

We will return to this topic in chapter 3 where some very interesting results and methods will be discussed in detail.

Exercises 1.10.

1. Fill in the details of Proposition **1.31** for the average case.

2*. Consider an n-set T and take as search domain $S = 2^T$. The search problem consists in determining whether or not the unknown set X^* is in S_0, for some given $\emptyset \neq S_0 \subseteq S$. Suppose the tests $\mathfrak{A}$ are all questions of the form: Is $x \in X^*$? ($x \in T$). An element-for-element search yields $L^{(r)}(S_0, \mathfrak{A}) \leq n$. Show that $L^{(r)}(S_0, \mathfrak{A}) = n$ if all sets in S_0 have the same cardinality.

3*. Continuation of the previous exercise. Let $n = 2$. Construct a non-trivial family $S_0 \subseteq 2^T$ for which $L^{(r)}(S_0, \mathfrak{A}) = 1$.

4. Discuss $L^{(r)}(S_0, \mathfrak{A}_{\leq 2})$ and, generally, $L^{(r)}(S_0, \mathfrak{A}_{\leq k})$.

5. Similarly, for $L_{pre}^{(r)}(S, \mathfrak{A}_{\leq k})$.

Problems

1. Given a distribution $p = (p_1, \ldots, p_n)$. What can be said about the structure of Huffman trees for p? For which p are all $(\overline{L})$-optimal trees Huffmann trees? (1.5)

2. What more can be said a priori about $\overline{L}(n, q; p)$? Find further classes of distributions p for which $\overline{L}(n, q; p)$ can be computed directly (without using Huffman's procedure)? (1.5)

3. Suppose $p = (p_1, \ldots, p_n)$ with $p_1 \geq p_2 \geq \ldots \geq p_n$ is given, and $\ell_1, \ldots, \ell_n$ are the lengths in an $(\overline{L})$-optimal tree. If $p_1 - p_n = d$, what can be said about $\ell_n - \ell_1$? (1.5)

4. Suppose $p = (p_1 \geq \ldots \geq p_n)$, $p' = (p'_1, \geq \ldots \geq p'_n)$ are two distributions. We set $p' \leq p$ if $\sum_{i=1}^{k} p'_i \leq \sum_{i=1}^{k} p_i$ for all k. Thus $(\frac{1}{n}, \ldots, \frac{1}{n}) \leq p$ for all p (see Proposition 1.10). By exercise 1.5.9, $H(p') \geq H(p)$. Is the same true for $\overline{L}$? Is it true that $(\ell_n - \ell_1)_{p'} \leq (\ell_n - \ell_1)_{p}$? (1.5)

5. Estimate $\overline{L}_{pre}(S, \mathcal{F}_{mon})$ for non-uniform distributions. (1.6)

6. Find better bounds for $\overline{DL}(n; p)$. (1.7)

7. For what distributions p does Mehlhorn's algorithm yield an optimal binary search tree? (1.7)

8. Find better bounds for $L_{pre}(S, \mathfrak{A}_{\leq k})$. (1.9)

9. Estimate $\overline{L}(S, \mathfrak{A}_{\leq k})$ and $\overline{L}_{pre}(S, \mathfrak{A}_{\leq k})$ for uniform or arbitrary distributions. (1.9)

10. Discuss the average case for 1-families. (1.9)

Notes and References

Origin and guide for all our considerations is the yes-no game. This game is known all over the world. In the USA it goes by the name of "twenty questions", whereas e.g. in Hungary a more colorful name is attached to it, Bar Kochba, leader of the last great uprising of Palestinian jews against Rome. The first steps towards the concept of entropy as a measure for the uncertainty of an event were taken by the American engineer Hartley in 1928. His ideas were developped by C. Shannon culminating in his fundamental theorem 1.6 (obtained independently by N. Wiener). Shannon [1948] and Shannon-Weaver [1949] marked the beginning of information theory. Other landmarks are Huffman [1952] on optimal codes, Gilbert-Moore [1959] and Hu-Tucker [1971] treating the alphabetical case. For the early results, the reader may consult Abramson [1963] or Feinstein [1958]. Probably the first mathematically treated problem are the group testing procedures in Dorfman [1943]. With the rise of computer science the main emphasis shifted to the complexity point of view, with worst-case and average-case length as central concepts for the analysis of algorithms. The presentation of the material in this book was greatly influenced by the survey articles Renyi [1969] and Katona [1973].

Abramson N. * [1963], Information Theory and Coding. McGraw-Hill, New York.

Ahlswede R., Wegener I. * [1979], Suchprobleme. B.G. Teubner, Stuttgart.

Aigner M. * [1979], Combinatorial Theory, Springer-Verlag, Berlin.

Bellman R. * [1957], Dynamic Programming. Princeton Univ. Press, Princeton.

Dickson T.I. [1969], On a problem concerning separating systems of a finite set. J. Combinatorial Theory 7, 191-196.

Dorfman R. [1943], The detection of defective members of large populations. Ann.Math.Statist. 14, 436-440.

Feinstein A. * [1958]. Foundations of Information Theory. McGraw-Hill, New York.

Feller W. * [1968], An Introduction to Probability Theory and its Applications. John Wiley & Sons, New York.

Gale D. * [1960], The Theory of Linear Economic Models. McGraw-Hill, New York.

Gilbert E.N., Moore E.F. [1959], Variable-length binary encodings. Bell System. Tech.J. 38, 933-967.

Güttler R., Mehlhorn K., Schneider W. [1980], Binary search trees: Average and worst case behaviour. Elektr. Inf. & Kybernetik 16, 41-61.

Hardy H.H., Littlewood J.E., Polya G. [1934], Inequalities. Cambridge Univ.Press, Cambridge.

Hu T.C., Tucker A.C. [1971], Optimum computer search trees and vari able-length alphabetic codes. SIAM J.Appl.Math. 21, 514-532.

Huffman D.A. [1952], A method for the construction of minimum redundancy codes. Proc. I.R.E. 40, 1098-1101.

Katona G. [1966], On separating systems of a finite set. J. Combinatorial Theory 1, 174-194.

Katona G. [1973], Combinatorial search problems. In: A survey of Combinatorial Theory, North Holland, 285-308.

Kemp, R. * [1984], Fundamentals of the Average Case Analysis of Particular Algorithms. Teubner-Wiley, Stuttgart-New York.

Knuth D. [1971], Optimum binary search trees. Acta Informatica 1, 14-25.

Knuth D. * [1973], The Art of Computer Programming, vol.3, Sorting and Searching. Addison-Wesley, Reading.

Mehlhorn K. [1975], Nearly optimal binary search trees. Acta Informatica 5, 287-295.

Mehlhorn K. [1977], A best possible bound on the weighted path length of optimum binary search trees. SIAM J. Computing 6, 235-239.

Picard C. * [1965], Théorie des Questionnaires. Gauthiers-Villars, Paris.

Renyi A. [1965], On the theory of random search. Bull.Amer.Math. Soc. 71, 809-828.

Renyi A. [1969], Lectures on the theory of search. Univ. North Carolina, Mimeo Series.

Sebö A. [1982], Sequential search using question-sets with bounded intersection. J.Stat.Planning Inference 7, 139-150.

Shannon C.E. [1948], A mathematical theory of communication. Bell System Techn.J. 27, 379-424, 623-657.

Shannon C., Weaver, W. * [1949], The Mathematical Theory of Communication. Univ. Ill. Press, Urbana.

Sobel M. [1960], Group testing to classify efficiently all defectives in a binomial sample. In: Information and Decision Processes, McGraw-Hill, 127-161.

Sobel M. [1968], Binomial and hypergeometric group testing. Studia Sci. Math. Hung. 3, 19-42.

Sterrett A. [1957], On the detection of defective members of large populations. Ann.Math.Stat. 28, 1033-1036.

Ungar P. [1960], The cut-off point for group testing. Comm. Pure Appl. Math. 13, 49-54.

Wegener I. [1979], On separating systems whose elements are sets of at most k elements. Discrete Math. 28, 219-222.

Wong E. [1964], A linear search problem. SIAM Review 6, 168-174.

Zimmerman S. [1959], An optimal search procedure. Amer. Math. Monthly 66, 690-693.

Chapter 2

Weighing Problems

The ancient puzzle of the counterfeit coin served as a prime example in discussing various aspects of search problems in the previous chapter. We will now study several variants in detail. Two natural models come to mind. In the first, the false coin is to be determined using an *equal arms balance*. The scale can only be in balance when there is the same number of coins on either side of the scale. In the second model, we actually *measure the weight*, knowing the weight of the good coins in advance. We will see that these two variants are of an entirely different nature leading each to some very interesting generalizations.

2.1 Balance Scale

Let S be a set of n coins, $n - 1$ of which are "good", while one coin x^* is false, or as we shall say from now on, *defective*. A weighing corresponds to a choice of two disjoint subsets $A, B \subseteq S$ with $| A |=| B |$ where A denotes the coins on the left-hand side and B those on the right-hand side.

Let us first treat the easiest case when we know in advance that the defective coin x^* is, say, heavier. (The case when x^* is lighter is, of course, the same by symmetry.)

Here we conveniently take as our test family $\mathcal{W}$ the set of all functions $f : S \longrightarrow \{1, -1, 0\}$ with

$$f(x^*) = \begin{cases} 1 & \text{if} \quad x^* \in A \\ -1 & \text{if} \quad x^* \in B \\ 0 & \text{if} \quad x^* \in S - (A \cup B). \end{cases}$$

The requirement on f is then $\sum_{x \in S} f(x) = 0$.

S is our search domain and $q = 3$. Corollary 1.3 says that we need at least $\lceil \log_3 n \rceil$ weighings in the worst case. The following result establishes that no more weighings are required, even in the predetermined case.

Theorem 2.1. *For* $\mid S \mid = n \geq 2$,

$$L(S, \mathcal{W}) = L_{pre}(S, \mathcal{W}) = \lceil \log_3 n \rceil.$$

Furthermore, whenever $n \neq 3^L$, $3^L - 2$ *the search matrix can be so chosen that it does not contain the 0-column whereas for* $n = 3^L$ *or* $n = 3^L - 2$ *the 0-column must appear.*

Proof. Since $L_{pre}(S, \mathcal{W}) \geq L(S, \mathcal{W}) \geq \lceil \log_3 n \rceil$, our claim is proved if we can find an $(L \times n)$-search matrix with $L = \lceil \log_3 n \rceil$ rows. That is, we have to construct an $(L \times n)$-matrix M over $\{1, -1, 0\}$ whose columns are distinct and with row-sums equal to 0. Let us call such matrices *admissible*. If the admissible matrix M does not contain the 0-column, then M is said to have the 0-*property*.

Suppose $n = 3^{L-1} + r$, $1 \leq r \leq 2.3^{L-1}$. We use induction on L. For $L = 1$ we have $n \leq 3$ and the result, including the 0-property, is obvious. Let $L \geq 2$. Denote by B_i the $(i \times 3^i)$-matrix whose columns are all distinct $1, -1, 0$-vectors of length i. B_i is obviously admissible. If $n = 3^L$, then clearly B_L is the only admissible $(L \times n)$-matrix (containing the 0-column). If $n = 3^L - 2$, then the only way to obtain an admissible $(L \times n)$-matrix M is to remove a pair of distinct columns $\underline{a}, -\underline{a}$ from B_L. Hence M again contains the 0-column, thus proving our last claim. Let us now assume $n \neq 3^L$, $3^L - 2$, i.e. $r \neq 2.3^{L-1}$, $2.3^{L-1} - 2$.

If n is even, then we remove $\frac{3^L - 1 - n}{2}$ pairs $\underline{a}, -\underline{a}$ and the 0-column from B_L, thus obtaining an admissible search matrix of size $L \times n$. If n is odd, then $n \leq 3^L - 4$. In this case we first remove from B_L the 0-column and the three columns

$$
\begin{array}{ccc}
-1 & 0 & 1 \\
0 & -1 & 1 \\
0 & 0 & 0 \\
\vdots & \vdots & \vdots \\
0 & 0 & 0
\end{array}
$$

Since $n > 3^{L-1} \geq 3$, we have at least $\frac{3^L-4-n}{2}$ pairs of columns $\underline{a}, -\underline{a}$ in the remaining matrix. Removing $\frac{3^L-4-n}{2}$ such pairs yields again an admissible matrix of size $L \times n$.   □

Let us turn to the average case where we assume that all coins are defective with equal probability $\frac{1}{n}$, keeping in mind that it is still exactly one coin that is defective. The lower bound for $\overline{L}(S, W; \frac{1}{n}, \ldots, \frac{1}{n})$ established in this case is (see Theorem 1.8):

$$h(n) = \lceil \log_3 n \rceil - \frac{1}{n} \left\lfloor \frac{3^{\lceil \log_3 n \rceil} - n}{2} \right\rfloor .$$

Perhaps unexpectedly, $h(n)$ can again be achieved using sequential algorithms (except for $n = 6$), and almost when only predetermined algorithms are permitted. Our exposition follows Linial and Tarsi [1982].

Example 2.1. For $n = 6$ we have $h(6) = \frac{11}{6}$. The complete (6,3)-trees are given in figure 2.1 (apart from interchanging the outer subtrees which would obviously give nothing new):

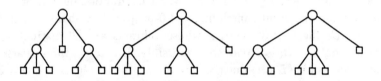

Figure 2.1

Since any tree corresponding to the family W must have an equal number of leaves on the outer trees, we see that none of these trees is possible. The following (6,3)-tree is admissible and obviously optimal, yielding $\overline{L}(6, 3; \frac{1}{6}, \ldots \frac{1}{6}) = 2$.

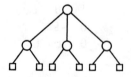

Figure 2.2

We discuss first predetermined algorithms. Set $w(n) = nh(n)$, thus

$$w(n) = n\lceil \log_3 n\rceil - \left\lfloor \frac{3^{\lceil \log_3 n\rceil} - n}{2} \right\rfloor.$$

Suppose M is a search matrix with precisely $w(n)$ non-blank entries. Let us analyze M, where $n = 3^L + r$, $1 \leq r \leq 2.3^L$, $L \geq 0$. We know from Theorem 1.8 and example 1.12 that any $(\overline{L})$-optimal tree has length $L + 1$ and contains a leaves on level L and b leaves on level $L + 1$, where

$$a = \left\lfloor \frac{3^{L+1} - n}{2} \right\rfloor = 3^L - \left\lceil \frac{r}{2} \right\rceil = n - \left\lceil \frac{3r}{2} \right\rceil, \quad b = \left\lceil \frac{3r}{2} \right\rceil.$$

Hence M must have a columns of length L and b columns of length $L + 1$.

Case 1. n odd, $n = 3^L + 2k$, $1 \leq k \leq 3^L$, then $a = 3^L - k = n - 3k$, $b = 3k$, $w(n) = nL + 3k$. Decompose M as in the figure.

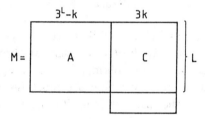

Figure 2.3

By the prefix property, all columns of A are distinct and the columns do not appear in C. Hence any column $\underline{c}$ in C appears precisely three times and is bordered by $1, -1, 0 : \begin{smallmatrix} \underline{c} \\ 1 \end{smallmatrix} \begin{smallmatrix} \underline{c} \\ -1 \end{smallmatrix} \begin{smallmatrix} \underline{c} \\ 0 \end{smallmatrix}$. Thus the sum of row $L + 1$ is certainly 0. Let us denote by $\sum D$ the row-sum vector of a matrix D. Let $\underline{c}_1, \ldots, \underline{c}_k$ be the distinct columns of C (each appearing three times). Since M is a search matrix, we must have

$$0 = \sum(A \mid C) = \sum B_L + 2(\underline{c}_1 + \ldots + \underline{c}_k) = 2(\underline{c}_1 + \ldots + \underline{c}_k).$$

We conclude that the columns $\underline{c}_1, \ldots, \underline{c}_k$ make up an $(L \times k)$-matrix C' with all row-sums equal to 0. But the converse is also true: If we can find k vectors of length L which make up a matrix with all row-sums equal to 0, then by tripling each one of them, bordering each of them by $1, -1, 0$, and adding the other $3^L - k$ columns of length L, we clearly obtain a search-matrix M with $w(n) = nL + 3k$. So, our problem reduces to finding k such vectors of length L. This latter problem is, however, immediately settled by just invoking the previous theorem. If $3^{s-1} < k \leq 3^s$, $s \leq L$, we take a full $(s \times k)$-search matrix and add $L - s$ 0-rows at the bottom.

Case 2. n even, $n = 3^L + 2k + 1$, $0 \leq k < 3^L$; then $a = 3^L - k - 1 = n - 3k - 2$, $b = 3k + 2$, $w(n) = nL + 3k + 2$. Decompose M as in case 1):

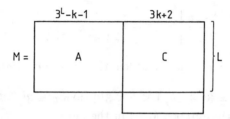

Figure 2.4

By the same reasoning as before it follows that C contains $k + 1$ distinct columns (all distinct from A), k of which appear three times whereas one column appears twice. Let these columns be $c_1, \ldots, c_k$ and c. Each column c_i must be bordered by $1, -1, 0$ whereas c must be bordered by $1, -1$ to ensure that the sum of the last row is 0. Taking the same approach as in case 1) we conclude

$$0 = \sum(A \mid C) = \sum B_L + 2(c_1 + \ldots + c_k) + c = 2(c_1 + \ldots + c_k) + c.$$

Since any entry in $2(c_1 + \ldots + c_k)$ is $\equiv 0 \pmod 2$ and c is a $1, -1, 0$-vector we see that c is, in fact, the 0-vector. Hence $c_i \neq 0$ for all i, and the c_i's make up an $(L \times k)$-matrix with all row-sums equal to 0. Since the reverse construction holds as well, we have reduced our problem to finding a full $(L \times k)$-search matrix with non-zero columns where we may assume $k \geq 1$, since otherwise there is nothing to do. Now we use the stonger assertion spelled out in the previous theorem. If $3^{L-1} < k < 3^L$, $k \neq 3^L - 2$, then we can find such a matrix by the construction in Theorem 2.1, whereas for $k = 3^L - 2$ this is not possible. If $3^{s-1} < k \leq 3^s$ with $1 \leq s < L$, then we take any $(s \times k)$-search matrix S, add $1, -1$ if there is a 0-column in S, and fill up with 0's (see figure 2.5):

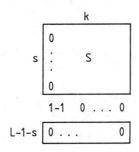

Figure 2.5

The only remaining case is $k = 1$, and here a proper construction is plainly not possible. So, our approach works for all n, except when $n = 3^L + 3$ or $n = 3^{L+1} - 3$. These two cases need precisely one more non-blank entry as seen by the following figure:

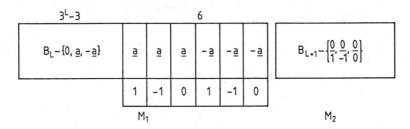

Figure 2.6

Theorem 2.2. *For* $|S| = n \geq 2$,

i) $\overline{L}\left(S, W; \frac{1}{n}, \ldots \frac{1}{n}\right) = \overline{L}\left(n, 3; \frac{1}{n}, \ldots, \frac{1}{n}\right)$

$$= \lceil \log_3 n \rceil - \frac{1}{n} \lfloor \frac{3^{\lceil \log_3 n \rceil} - n}{2} \rfloor$$

except for $n = 6$ *for which* $\overline{L}(S, W; \frac{1}{6}, \ldots, \frac{1}{6}) = 2$.

ii)

$$\overline{L}_{pre}(S, W; \frac{1}{n}, \ldots, \frac{1}{n}) = \lceil \log_3 n \rceil - \frac{1}{n} \lfloor \frac{3^{\lceil \log_3 n \rceil} - n}{2} \rfloor + \begin{cases} \frac{1}{n} & n = 3^L + 3 \text{ or} \\ & 3^{L+1} - 3, L \geq 1 \\ 0 & \text{otherwise.} \end{cases}$$

Proof. In view of $\overline{L}(S,W) \leq \overline{L}_{pre}(S,W)$ and our previous discussion, it remains to verify that

$$\overline{L}(S,W; \frac{1}{n}, \ldots, \frac{1}{n}) = h(n) \text{ for } n = 3^L + 3 \text{ and } n = 3^{L+1} - 3, L \geq 2.$$

Case 1. $n = 3^L + 3$, $L \geq 2$. We want to prove that there exists a tree T compatible with W with external length $e(T) = Ln + 5$. We proceed by induction on L. For $L = 2$, we have $n = 12$. Let $S = \{1, 2, \ldots, 12\}$. In the first test we weigh $\{1, 2, 3\}$ against $\{4, 5, 6\}$. If the defective coin is in either $\{1, 2, 3\}$ or $\{4, 5, 6\}$, then it can be determined with one more weighing whence $e(T_1) = e(T_3) = 3$ for these subtrees. If $x^* \in \{7, \ldots, 12\}$, then we weigh $\{7, 8, 9\}$ against $\{10, 11, 1\}$ where 1 is already known to be good. If $x^* \in \{7, 8, 9\}$, then we need one more weighing. If $x^* \in \{10, 11, 1\}$, then we weigh 10 against 11, and are done. In the remaining case $x^* = 12$. Hence for the subtree T_2 we have $e(T_2) = 3.2 + 2.2 + 1 = 11$, and thus

$$e(T) = 12 + \sum_{i=1}^{3} e(T_i) = 29 = 2.12 + 5 \text{ as required (see figure 2.7).}$$

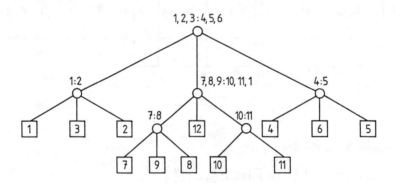

Figure 2.7

Now for $L \geq 3$, we weigh 3^{L-1} coins against 3^{L-1} other coins in the first test. For the subtrees T_1, T_2, T_3 we have $e(T_1) = e(T_3) = (L-1)3^{L-1}$, by induction $e(T_2) = (L-1)(3^{L-1} + 3) + 5$, and thus $e(T) = n + 2(L-1)3^{L-1} + (L-1)(3^{L-1} + 3) + 5 = n + (L-1)(3^L + 3) + 5 = Ln + 5$.

Case 2. $n = 3^{L+1} - 3, L \geq 2$. The proof is entirely analogous. For $L = 2$, i.e. $n = 24$, we first weigh 9 elements against 9 other elements. If we have balance, then x^* is one of the remaining 6 coins, and we proceed as before, using induction. $\square$

Remark. The proof of the sequential case apparently hinges on the fact that we have a coin available that is known to be good. Hence if we have a good coin available at the beginning then we can lower the bound for $\overline{L}$, even for $n = 6$.

A small variant of our problem immediately comes to mind. Suppose in a set of n coins there may be exactly one heavier coin or all coins may be good. The search domain consists now of $n + 1$ elements whence $\lceil \log_3(n + 1) \rceil$ is a lower bound, where we have to assume that there are at least two coins, since otherwise the problem is plainly unsolvable. A moment's reflection should convince the reader that for a sequential algorithm $\lceil \log_3(n+1) \rceil$ tests are all that is needed. For predetermined algorithms there is one exception when $n = 3^L - 2$, where one more weighing is needed. (See exercise 2.1.2.)

Let us turn to a more interesting version of our problem. We assume that there is precisely one defective coin x^*, but we do not know whether x^* is lighter or heavier than the good ones. If the coins are numbered $1, \ldots, n$, then the search domain is $S = \{1_L, 1_H, 2_L, 2_H, \ldots, n_L, n_H\}$. Hence the information-theoretic lower bound gives $\lceil \log_3 2n \rceil$. Again, we can almost achieve this bound both in the worst and the average case, even for predetermined algorithms. We just treat the worst-case problem, for the average case, see the exercises.

Theorem 2.3. *Let S be a set of $n \geq 2$ coins, one of which is lighter or heavier. Let L and L_{pre} denote the worst-case cost for sequential and predetermined algorithms, respectively. Then*

$$L = L_{pre} = \lceil \log_3(2n + 2) \rceil.$$

Proof. We first show $L \geq \lceil \log_3(2n + 2) \rceil$. Suppose $2n + 2 \geq 3^L + 1$. If $2n \geq 3^L + 1$, then the information-theoretic bound tells us that we need at least $L + 1$ weighings. The only other possibility is $2n = 3^L - 1, L \geq 2$. Suppose in the first test we use two sets of size ℓ. If the right arm goes down, one coin on the left-hand side may be lighter or a coin on the right-hand side may be heavier. Hence there are 2ℓ possible outcomes in this case. Similarly, there are 2ℓ possible outcomes if the left side goes down. We infer that in case of balance there are $2n - 2\ell - 2\ell = 2m$ possible outcomes. From $2n = 2\ell + 2\ell + 2m = 3^L - 1$ we conclude

$$\max(2\ell, 2m) \geq \frac{3^L - 1}{3} = 3^{L-1} - \frac{1}{3},$$

and thus

$$\max(2\ell, 2m) \geq 3^{L-1} + 1,$$

since $2\ell, 2m$ are even. Hence on at least one subtree we need L weighings, which means that we need at least $L + 1$ weighings overall.

Let $2n = 3^L + 2k + 1, -1 \leq k \leq 3^L - 2$. It remains to prove that for this n we can find a proper search matrix M. The assumptions on this weighing problem are apparently reflected by the fact that M not only has distinct columns but that no column is the negative of any other column which, in particular, implies that all columns of M must be non-zero. Hence we have to construct an $(L + 1) \times n$-matrix M with the stated property and with row-sums all equal to 0. Let us again call such matrices *admissible*.
Let A_1 be the 1×1-matrix consisting of 1. We declare A_L inductively by

$$
A_L = \begin{array}{|c|c|c|}
\hline
A_{L-1} & A_{L-1} & -A_{L-1} \\
\hline
1 \ \cdots \ 1 & -1 \ \cdots \ -1 & 0 \ \cdots \ 0 \\
\end{array}
\begin{array}{c}
0 \\
\vdots \\
0 \\
1
\end{array}
$$

By induction, A_L is an $\left(L \times \frac{3^L - 1}{2}\right)$-matrix with the following properties

   i) All columns are distinct and no column is the negative of another
      column.

   ii) $\sum A_L = \begin{pmatrix} 1 \\ \vdots \\ 1 \end{pmatrix}$

   iii) $\begin{pmatrix} 1 \\ \vdots \\ 1 \end{pmatrix} \in A_L$

   iv) $\begin{pmatrix} -1 \\ \vdots \\ -1 \end{pmatrix} \notin A_L$

v) $\begin{pmatrix} 0 \\ \vdots \\ 0 \end{pmatrix} \notin A_L.$

vi) By ii), the matrix $A'_L = A_L - \begin{pmatrix} 1 \\ \vdots \\ 1 \end{pmatrix}$ satisfies $\sum A'_L = 0.$

Case 1. $2n = 3^L - 1, L \geq 2$. The following matrix M_{-1} will do the job.

Case 2. $2n = 3^L + 2k + 1, k \geq 1$ odd. Let us first consider the case $k = 1$, i.e. $2n = 3^L + 3$. Considering iii), iv) and vi), the matrix M_1 below will be an admissible search matrix for this case.

Now suppose $k = 2\ell + 1 \geq 3$, and hence $1 \leq \ell = \frac{k-1}{2} \leq \frac{3^L-3}{2} = $ number of columns in A'_L. Take any ℓ columns $\underline{a}_1, \ldots, \underline{a}_\ell$ in A'_L and replace each one of them by three columns of length $L + 1$ in the following manner:

$$\underline{a}_i \longrightarrow \begin{array}{ccc} a_i & a_i & -a_i \\ 1 & -1 & 0 \end{array}.$$

The matrix $M_{2\ell+1}$ constructed below will be an admissible search matrix:

$$
\begin{array}{|c|ccccccc|ccc}
\multicolumn{1}{c}{\overset{\tfrac{3^L-k}{2}-1}{}} & \multicolumn{7}{c}{\overset{\tfrac{3(k-1)}{2}}{}} \\
\hline
 & & & & & & & & 1 & -1 & 0 \\
A'_L-\{\underline{a}_1,\dots,\underline{a}_l\} & \underline{a}_1 & \underline{a}_1 & -\underline{a}_1 & \cdots & \underline{a}_l & \underline{a}_l & -\underline{a}_l & \vdots & \vdots & \vdots \\
 & & & & & & & & 1 & -1 & 0 \\
\hline
\end{array}
$$

$$
0 \quad \dots\dots\dots \quad 0 \quad 1 \;\; -1 \quad 0 \qquad 1 \;\; -1 \quad 0 \qquad 0 \;\; -1 \;\; 1
$$

Case 3. $2n = 3^L + 2k + 1, k \geq 0$ even. For $k = 0$ we have the following admissible matrix:

$$
M_0 = \quad
\begin{array}{|c|cc}
\multicolumn{1}{c}{\overset{\tfrac{3^L-3}{2}}{}} & \\
\hline
 & 1 & -1 \\
A'_L & \vdots & \vdots \\
 & 1 & -1 \\
\hline
\end{array}
$$

$$
0 \;\; 0 \;\dots\; 0 \;\; 1 \;\; 0 \;\; -1
$$

For $k = 2\ell, 1 \leq \ell = \frac{k}{2} \leq \frac{3^L-3}{2}$, we take any ℓ columns $\underline{a}_1,\dots,\underline{a}_\ell$ from A'_L and replace each one of $\underline{a}_1,\dots,\underline{a}_{\ell-1}$ by three columns as in case 2, and the last column $\underline{a}_\ell$ by

$$
\underline{a}_\ell \longrightarrow \begin{array}{ccc} \underline{a}_\ell & \underline{a}_\ell & -\underline{a}_\ell \\ 1 & 0 & 1 \end{array}.
$$

Considering properties i) to vi) we see again that the matrix $M_{2\ell}$ below is admissible, thus finishing the proof. $\square$

$$
\begin{array}{|c|cccccccccc|cc}
\multicolumn{1}{c}{\overset{\tfrac{3^L-3-k}{2}}{}} & \multicolumn{10}{c}{\overset{\tfrac{3k}{2}}{}} \\
\hline
 & & & & & & & & & & & 1 & -1 \\
A'_L-\{\underline{a}_1,\dots,\underline{a}_l\} & \underline{a}_1 & \underline{a}_1 & -\underline{a}_1 & \cdots & \underline{a}_{l-1} & \underline{a}_{l-1} & -\underline{a}_{l-1} & \underline{a}_l & \underline{a}_l & -\underline{a}_l & \vdots & \vdots \\
 & & & & & & & & & & & 1 & -1 \\
\hline
\end{array}
$$

$$
0 \quad \dots\dots \quad 0 \;\; 1 \;\; -1 \quad 0 \qquad 1 \;\; -1 \quad 0 \qquad 1 \;\; 0 \;\; 1 \;\; -1 \;\; -1
$$

The following result settles the average case when uniform distribution is given. The details are very similar to the preceding proof.

Theorem 2.4. *Let S be a set of $n \geq 3$ coins where any coin is assumed to be lighter or heavier with probability $\frac{1}{2n}$. Let $\overline{L}$ and $\overline{L}_{pre}$ denote the average-case cost for sequential and predetermined algorithms, respectively. Suppose*

$2n = 3^L + 2k + 1, 0 \leq k < 3^L$. *Then*

$$\overline{L} = \overline{L}_{pre} = \overline{L}\left(2n, 3; \frac{1}{2n}, \ldots, \frac{1}{2n}\right) + \begin{cases} \frac{1}{2n} & \text{if } k \text{ odd} \\ \frac{1}{n} & \text{if } k \text{ even} \end{cases}$$

$$= \lceil \log_3 2n \rceil - \frac{1}{2n} \lfloor \frac{3^{\lceil \log_2 2n \rceil}}{2} \rfloor + \frac{1}{2} + \begin{cases} \frac{1}{2n} & \text{if } k \text{ odd} \\ \frac{1}{n} & \text{if } k \text{ even.} \end{cases}$$

Remark. It is easily seen that the assumption that one of the n coins is defective (lighter or heavier) or all of them are good leads to the same results as in Theorems 2.3 and 2.4.

Exercises 2.1.

1. Complete the proof of **2.2**, case 2.

2*. Suppose we know that at most one coin is heavier, $|S| = n$. Prove $L(S, \mathcal{W}) = \lceil \log_3(n+1) \rceil$, $L_{pre}(S, \mathcal{W}) = \lceil \log_3(n+1) \rceil$, except for $n = 3^L - 2$ when $L_{pre}(S, \mathcal{W}) = \lceil \log_3(n+1) \rceil + 1$.

3. Discuss the case analogous to the previous exercise, when we know that at most one coin is defective, but have no knowledge of whether the coin is heavier or lighter.

4. Prove Theorem 2.4.

5*. Suppose we are only allowed weighings $A : B$ with $|A| = |B| \leq k$. Denote by $L_{\leq k}(S, \mathcal{W})$ the worst case cost, $|S| = n \geq k$. Show $L_{\leq k}(S, \mathcal{W}) = t + \lceil \log_3(n - 2tk) \rceil$ with $t = \lceil \frac{n-3k}{2k} \rceil$. In particular, $L_{\leq 1}(S, \mathcal{W}) = \lfloor \frac{n}{2} \rfloor$.

6*. Treat the situation analogous to the previous exercise, when the defective coin is heavier or lighter. In particular, prove that for $k = 1$, $\lceil \frac{n+1}{2} \rceil$ is the worst-case cost.

7. Consider the situation as in exercise 5. Show by the method used in the proof of **1.27** that $L_{pre, \leq k}(S, \mathcal{W}) \geq \frac{n}{2k} \frac{\log_2 n}{\log_2 (en/k)}$.

8*. Suppose that at every stage of the algorithm we are only allowed to use elements that are still in doubt. Discuss the worst-case and average cost when the defective coin is known to be heavier.

9. Same situation as in the previous exercise, but the defective coin may be lighter or heavier.

10. Verify the remark at the end of the section.

11*. Generalize our weighing problem to an r-arms balance. That is, in every test we take r sets A_i of equal size, and receive as answer whether $x^* \in A_1, \ldots, x^* \in A_r$ or $x^* \in S - \bigcup_{i=1}^{r} A_i$. Show $L(n) = \lceil \log_{r+1} n \rceil$, $n \geq r$, and $L_{pre}(n) = \lceil \log_{r+1} n \rceil$ except when $n = (r+1)^L - i$, $2 \leq i \leq r-1$. In the latter case $L_{pre}(n) = \lceil \log_{r+1} n \rceil + 1$.

2.2 More Coins are Defective

A natural generalization of our counterfeit coin problem immediately comes to mind. Suppose in a set of n coins there are d defective (say, heavier) coins and $n - d$ good ones. The weight of the good coins is the same as is the weight of all defective coins. Determine the defective coins by using an equal arms balance. Note that by interchanging the roles of "good" and "defective", we may assume $d \leq \frac{n}{2}$. Let g be the weight of a good coin and h the weight of a defective coin. If $dh < (d+1)g$, i.e. $h < \frac{d+1}{d}g$, then it is easily seen that the larger of two numerically unequal sets will always be the heavier. Hence if we assume $h < \frac{d+1}{d}g$, as we shall do from now on, then information can only be gained when we weigh equal-sized sets against each other.

This general defective-coin problem is unsettled. Even for $d = 2$, the precise answer for all n is not known. Let us see where the additional difficulty arises. In the single-coin problem we know after a weighing $A : B$ in which of the three sets $A, B, S - (A \cup B)$ the defective coin lies. Now suppose $d \geq 2$ and the scale balances when weighing A against B. Then we only know that A and B contain the *same number of defective coins* but, in general, not how many they contain. Similarly, if $A < B$ then we can only be sure that B contains more defectives than A.

Still, as the following results mainly due to Tošić suggest, the worst-case cost will probably be very close to the information-theoretic bound for all n and d.

Proposition 2.5. *Let $L^{(2)}(n)$ denote the worst-case cost of our weighing problem when exactly two of $n \geq 2$ coins are known to be defective. Then*

$$\lceil \log_3 \binom{n}{2} \rceil \leq L^{(2)}(n) \leq \lceil \log_3 \binom{n}{2} \rceil + 1,$$

and equality is attained on the left-hand side for infinitely many n's.

Proof. Our search domain S consists of all possible pairs $\{i, j\} \subseteq \{1, \ldots, n\}$, hence $| S | = \binom{n}{2}$. It is easy to check that $n > 3^L$ implies $\binom{n}{2} > 3^{2L-1}$ and $n > 2.3^L$ implies $\binom{n}{2} > 3^{2L}$. The information-theoretic bound then yields for $L \geq 0$:

i) $L^{(2)}(n) \geq 2L$ for $n > 3^L$

ii) $L^{(2)}(n) \geq 2L + 1$ for $n > 2.3^L$.

Now we show, conversely, that for $L \geq 0$,

i') $L^{(2)}(n) \leq 2L + 1$ for $n \leq 2.3^L$

ii') $L^{(2)}(n) \leq 2L + 2$ for $n \leq 3^{L+1}$.

We prove i') and ii') simultaneously by induction. For $L = 0$ the assertions are trivial, so assume $L \geq 1$. To verify i') we weigh in our first test two sets A, B of cardinality $\lfloor \frac{n}{2} \rfloor$. If there is balance, in symbols $A = B$, then A and B must each contain a defective coin (since $| S - (A \cup B) | \leq 1$) which can then be determined individually with $2\lceil \log_3 \lfloor \frac{n}{2} \rfloor \rceil \leq 2L$ more weighings by Theorem 2.1. If, on the other hand, one of the sets is heavier, say A, in symbols $A > B$, then the two defectives are contained in $S - B$. Since $| S - B | = \lceil \frac{n}{2} \rceil \leq 3^L$, we conclude by induction on ii') that again $2L$ more weighings will do.

To verify ii') we split S into three sets A, B, C of cardinality $\lfloor \frac{n}{3} \rfloor$ each. Then $| S - (A \cup B \cup C) | \leq 2$. If $S - (A \cup B \cup C)$ contains two coins u, v, then we set $\overline{B} = B \cup \{u\}, \overline{C} = C \cup \{v\}$, otherwise we set $\overline{B} = B, \overline{C} = C$. Note that all sets $A, B, C, \overline{B}, \overline{C}$ have size $\leq 3^L$, and also that $| S - (A \cup \overline{B}) | = | S - (A \cup \overline{C}) | \leq 3^L$. In our first test we weigh A against B, and in the second test we weigh $\overline{B}$ against $\overline{C}$.

Case 1. $A = B$. If $\overline{B} = \overline{C}$, then $\overline{B} \supsetneq B$ and u must be one of the defectives, the other one being in $\overline{C}$ which can be determined with L more tests. If $\overline{B} > \overline{C}$, then each of A and B contains a heavier coin, so we are done with $2L$ more weighings. If $\overline{B} < \overline{C}$, then both defectives are in $S - (A \cup \overline{B})$. Since $| S - (A \cup \overline{B}) | \leq 3^L$, we may apply induction.

Case 2. $A > B$. If $\overline{B} = \overline{C}$, then both defectives are in A and we are done by induction. If $\overline{B} > \overline{C}$, then $\overline{B} \supsetneq B$, u must be one heavier coin, whereas the other one is in A which can be determined with L more weighings. If $\overline{B} < \overline{C}$, then each of A and $\overline{C}$ contains precisely one defective coin and we may find them by $2L$ more weighings.

Case 3. $A < B$. If $\overline{B} = \overline{C}$, then each of $\overline{B}$ and $\overline{C}$ contains a defective coin, now apply **2.1**. If $\overline{B} > \overline{C}$, then the defectives are in $S - (A \cup \overline{C})$, and we are again through by induction. The case where $\overline{B} < \overline{C}$ can clearly not arise.

To prove our final assertion, we sharpen the implications i) and ii). Solving for n we see that

i") $\binom{n}{2} > 3^{2L}$ for $n > \sqrt{\frac{1}{4} + 2.3^{2L}} + \frac{1}{2}$ and hence

$\qquad\qquad$ for $n \geq \lceil 3^L \sqrt{2} \rceil + 1$

and similarly

ii") $\binom{n}{2} > 3^{2L+1}$ for $n > \sqrt{\frac{1}{4} + 2.3^{2L+1}} + \frac{1}{2}$ and hence

$\qquad\qquad$ for $n \geq \lceil 3^L \cdot \sqrt{6} \rceil + 1$.

From i'), i") and ii'), ii"), respectively, we infer that the information-theoretic bound is attained by $L^{(2)}(n)$ for all n lying in intervals of the form $[\lceil 3^L \sqrt{2} \rceil + 1, 2.3^L]$ and $[\lceil 3^L \sqrt{6} \rceil + 1, 3^{L+1}]$, $L \geq 1$. $\square$

Remark. By a considerably more detailed analysis of the algorithm it can be shown that, in fact,

$$L^{(2)}(n) \leq 2L + 1 \quad \text{for} \quad n \leq 2.3^L + 3^{L-1}$$
$$L^{(2)}(n) \leq 2L + 2 \quad \text{for} \quad n \leq 3^{L+1} + 3^L$$

holds for all $L \geq 0$. This e.g. yields $L^{(2)}(n) = \lceil \log_3 \binom{n}{2} \rceil$ for all $n \leq 21$ except $n = 13$. The ad hoc algorithm below shows that again $L^{(2)}(13) = 4 = \lceil \log_3 \binom{13}{2} \rceil$, and it is plausible to surmise that indeed $L^{(2)}(n) = \lceil \log_3 \binom{n}{2} \rceil$ for all n.

Example 2.2. Let $S = \{1, 2, \ldots, 13\}$. In our first test we weigh $A = \{1, 2, 3, 4\}$ against $B = \{5, 6, 7, 8\}$. If we do not have balance, then w.l.o.g. we may assume $A > B$. In our second test we weigh $\{1, 9, 10\}$ against $\{2, 11, 12\}$. In the figure below we draw a line between elements i, j iff $\{i, j\}$ is a candidate for the defective pair after these weighings (check this!).

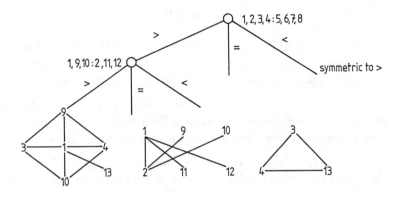

Figure 2.8

If we receive the answer $>$ in the 2nd test, then by weighing 3 against 4 in the third test we split the lines of figure 2.8 into three "stars":

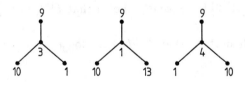

Figure 2.9

By our definition of the lines, the center of a star must be defective whence the other defective coin can be determined with one more test. The answer $<$ in the 2nd test is symmetric to this case, so let us assume we receive as answer $=$. In this case, we test 1 against 3 in the 3rd test, whence our point-line figure 2.8 splits into the three configurations of figure 2.10.

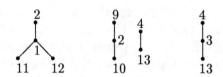

Figure 2.10

Clearly, all three possibilities can again be dealt with using one more test. The analysis of the case where we have equality $A = B$ in our first weighing can easily be supplied by the reader using the same approach.

The introduction of lines to designate the candidate pairs which has proved so useful in this example will be more fully exploited in the next chapter where we generalize the weighing problem to arbitrary graphs.

Tošić has considered the d-defective coin problem for $d \leq 5$. His results show that the optimum $L^{(d)}(n)$ differs again only slightly from the information-theoretic bound $\lceil \log_3 (\begin{smallmatrix} n \\ d \end{smallmatrix}) \rceil$, at least for certain series of n. It is clear that part of the difficulties lies in the number-theoretic problem of identifying the correct exponent L for which $3^{L-1} < (\begin{smallmatrix} n \\ d \end{smallmatrix}) \leq 3^L$. In addition, it is not even clear whether $L^{(d)}(n)$ is necessarily an increasing function of n, as for $d = 1$ or $d = 2$. Pyber [1986] has recently shown that $L^{(d)}(n) \leq \lceil \log_3 (\begin{smallmatrix} n \\ d \end{smallmatrix}) \rceil + 15d$, and it might well be true that $L^{(d)}(n) = \lceil \log_3 (\begin{smallmatrix} n \\ d \end{smallmatrix}) \rceil$ for most or all pairs (n, d).

Let us briefly look at the corresponding problem for $d = 2$ when only predetermined algorithms are permitted. Suppose M is a search matrix. Then as before M is an n-columned matrix over $\{1, -1, 0\}$ with all row-sums equal to 0. What is the condition on the columns that M must satisfy? Suppose the columns $\underline{a}$ and $\underline{b}$ correspond to the defective pair. If the outcome of the i-th test is 1 meaning that the left-hand side is heavier, then at least one of a_i and b_i must be 1 and neither one can be -1, i.e. $a_i + b_i \geq 1$ must hold. Similarly, if the outcome is -1, then $a_i + b_i \leq -1$. If the outcome is 0, then either $a_i = 1$, $b_i = -1$ or $a_i = -1$, $b_i = 1$ or $a_i = b_i = 0$, thus $a_i + b_i = 0$ must hold in this case.

Hence, if we define

$$sign(a_i + b_i) = \begin{cases} 1 & \text{if} \quad a_i + b_i \geq 1 \\ -1 & \text{if} \quad a_i + b_i \leq -1 \\ 0 & \text{if} \quad a_i + b_i = 0 \end{cases}$$

then the *signum-vector* $sign(\underline{a} + \underline{b}) = \begin{pmatrix} sign(a_1 + b_1) \\ \vdots \\ sign(a_L + b_L) \end{pmatrix}$

reflects precisely the outcome vector. We conclude that M is a search matrix iff all row-sums are equal to 0 and if the vectors $sign(\underline{a} + \underline{b})$ are distinct for all pairs of columns $\underline{a}, \underline{b}$ of M.

To estimate the minimal number L of rows of such a search matrix M is an intriguing and probably very difficult problem. The generalization to arbitrary d is straightforward. Nothing much is known even for $d = 2$.

Example 2.3. The reader may check that the following matrix is an admissible search matrix for $n = 7$, $d = 2$, thus proving $L_{pre}^{(2)}(7) = 3$.

$$M = \begin{array}{|ccccccc|} \hline 1 & 1 & 1 & -1 & -1 & -1 & 0 \\ 1 & -1 & 0 & 1 & -1 & 0 & 0 \\ 1 & 0 & -1 & -1 & 0 & 1 & 0 \\ \hline \end{array}$$

Since not even the worst-case problem is near solution it is not surprising that even less is known about the average cost when there are more than one defective coin present.

Exercises 2.2.

1*. Complete example 2.2.

2. Show that $L^{(2)}(n) = \lceil \log_2 \binom{n}{2} \rceil$ for $n \leq 36$. (Hint: There is only one doubtful case.)

3*. Prove $L^{(3)}(n) = \lceil \log_3 \binom{n}{3} \rceil$ for $n = 3^L$, and $L^{(3)}(n) \leq \lceil \log_3 \binom{n}{3} \rceil + 1$ for $n = 3^L + 3^{L-1}$ and $n = 2.3^L$. (Tošić).

4. Show $L^{(4)}(n) \leq \lceil \log_3(\begin{smallmatrix} n \\ 4 \end{smallmatrix}) \rceil + 1$, $L^{(5)}(n) \leq \lceil \log(\begin{smallmatrix} n \\ 5 \end{smallmatrix}) \rceil + 1$ for $n = 3^L$. (Tošić)

5*. Suppose at the outset we are given an arbitrary number of good coins, in addition to S. Denote by $L_g^{(d)}(n)$ the worst-case cost in this situation. Prove $L_g^{(3)}(n) \leq \lceil \log_3(\begin{smallmatrix} n \\ 3 \end{smallmatrix}) \rceil + 2$ for all n. (Tošić)

6. Suppose we are given two heavier coins, each of weight $h \geq \frac{3}{2}g$, where g is the weight of the good coins. What can you say about the worst-case cost in this situation?

7*. By iterating example 2.3 show that $L_{pre}^{(2)}(2^k - 1) \leq 2^{k-1} - 1$.

8. Derive a non-trivial lower bound for $L_{pre}^{(2)}(n)$.

2.3   Weighings With a Spring Scale

Let us now consider our second model concerning weighing problems. Suppose we are given a set S of n coins, d of which are heavier. We know the weight g of the good coins in advance and also the weight $h > g$ of the defective coins. If we weigh a subset $A \subseteq S$ with a spring scale, then the outcome will tell us precisely the number of defectives contained in S. Minimize the number $M^{(d)}(n)$ of weighings necessary to identify the set of defective coins! For fixed d, we have $d + 1$ possible outcomes of every test, as a test-set A may contain $0, 1, \ldots,$ or d defective coins. Hence our information-theoretic bound tells us that $\lceil \log_{d+1}(\begin{smallmatrix} n \\ d \end{smallmatrix}) \rceil$ is a lower bound for $M^{(d)}(n)$.

When $d = 1$, this bound can obviously be achieved, even for predetermined algorithms, since this case clearly reduces to a binary search process with no restriction on the test functions, treated in section 1.9.

Proposition 2.6. *For $n \geq 1$,*

$$M^{(1)}(n) = M_{pre}^{(1)}(n) = \lceil \log_2 n \rceil.$$

Already for $d = 2$, however, the problem becomes quite difficult. Suppose $A \subseteq S$ is the first test-set. According to the answer 2,1 or 0, A may contain both defectives, one defective, or none. In the first and third case, the problem is thus reduced to $M^{(2)}(\mid A \mid)$ and $M^{(2)}(\mid S - A \mid)$, where we may hope to apply induction. The second possibility where A and $S - A$ contain one defective each is new. So, let us turn our attention first to this case. Let $M^{(2)}(m, n)$ denote the worst-case cost when we know that one defective is in an m-set S while the other is in an n-set T which is disjoint to S. The best known algorithm for $M^{(2)}(m, n)$ due to Christen [1980] and Aigner [1986] involves the Fibonacci numbers F_n.

Definition. The numbers $F_0, F_1, F_2, \ldots$ with $F_0 = F_1 = 1$ and $F_n = F_{n-2} + F_{n-1}$ for $n \geq 2$ are called the *Fibonacci numbers*.

The Fibonacci numbers appear in virtually every field of combinatorics, and not only there. From the definition we have $F_0 = F_1 = 1$, $F_2 = 2$, $F_3 = 3$, $F_4 = 5$, $F_5 = 8$, $F_6 = 13$, and so on. What we are mainly interested in is how fast the numbers F_n grow. A a matter of fact, there is a closed formula for all F_n. Many proofs exist, but the following due to Polya must both be the simplest and most beautiful of all.

Lemma 2.7.

i) $F_n = \frac{1}{\sqrt{5}} \left[\left(\frac{1+\sqrt{5}}{2} \right)^{n+1} - \left(\frac{1-\sqrt{5}}{2} \right)^{n+1} \right] \quad (n \geq 0)$

ii) $\left(\frac{1+\sqrt{5}}{2} \right)^{n-1} \leq F_n \leq \left(\frac{1+\sqrt{5}}{2} \right)^{n} \quad (n \geq 1)$

iii) $\lim\limits_{n \to \infty} \frac{F_n}{F_{n-1}} = \frac{1+\sqrt{5}}{2} \sim 1.61803.$

Proof. Consider the equation $x^2 = x + 1$ and denote by y and z the roots, $y = \frac{1+\sqrt{5}}{2}$, $z = \frac{1-\sqrt{5}}{2}$. Let x be either one of the roots, then we claim that

$$x^n = F_{n-1}x + F_{n-2} \text{ for } n \geq 2.$$

For $n = 2$ this is clear. We proceed by induction. We have

$$
\begin{aligned}
x^{n+1} = x^n . x &= (F_{n-1}x + F_{n-2})x = F_{n-1}x^2 + F_{n-2}x \\
&= F_{n-1}(x+1) + F_{n-2}x = (F_{n-1} + F_{n-2})x + F_{n-1} \\
&= F_n x + F_{n-1},
\end{aligned}
$$

by the definition of the Fibonacci sequence. From $y^{n+1} = F_n y + F_{n-1}$, $z^{n+1} = F_n z + F_{n-1}$ we conclude $y^{n+1} - z^{n+1} = F_n(y - z)$, and thus by $y - z = \sqrt{5}$

$$F_n = \frac{y^{n+1} - z^{n+1}}{y - z} = \frac{1}{\sqrt{5}}\left[\left(\frac{1 + \sqrt{5}}{2}\right)^{n+1} - \left(\frac{1 - \sqrt{5}}{2}\right)^{n+1}\right]$$

which is precisely i). Assertion ii) follows easily by induction, whereas iii) is proved by writing $\frac{F_n}{F_{n-1}} = \frac{y^{n+1} - z^{n+1}}{y^n - z^n} = \frac{y - z(\frac{z}{y})^n}{1 - (\frac{z}{y})^n}$ and noticing that $|\frac{z}{y}| < 1$. $\square$

The positive root of $x^2 - x - 1$, often denoted by τ, is one of the fundamental numbers of all of mathematics. The Greeks called τ the "golden ratio" for the following reason. Take a rectangle of lengths a and b, $a \le b$. The rectangle is considered as particularly attractive from an aesthetic point of view (this has been verified empirically!), if the ratio of b to a is the same as that of a to $b - a$ (see figure 2.11). If $\tau = \frac{b}{a}$ is the wanted ratio, then $\tau = \frac{b}{a} = \frac{a}{b-a} = \frac{1}{\frac{b}{a}-1} = \frac{1}{\tau-1}$, and thus $\tau^2 - \tau - 1 = 0$, i.e. $\tau \sim 1.61803$.

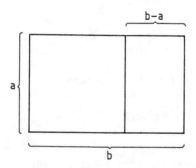

Figure 2.11

From our Lemma we see that the sequence F_n grows approximately as τ^n. Let us get back to our problem.

Proposition 2.8. Let $M^{(2)}(m, n)$ denote the worst-case cost when precisely one defective coin is in each of two disjoint sets S and T with $|S| = m$, $|T| = n$. Then

(2.1) $M^{(2)}(F_{n-1}, F_n) \le n - 1 \quad (n \ge 1)$.

Proof. In order to apply induction we actually have to prove a little more. Suppose we have four disjoint sets S_1, T_1, S_2, T_2 with sizes m_1, n_1, m_2, n_2, repectively, and suppose we know that the defective pair is either in $S_1 \cup T_1$ (one in S_1, one in T_1) or in $S_2 \cup T_2$ (one in S_2, one in T_2). Let $M^{(2)}(m_1, n_1; m_2, n_2)$ denote the worst-case cost for this situation. Then we claim in addition to (2.1):

$$(2.2) \qquad M^{(2)}(F_{n-1}, F_{n-1}; F_{n-2}, F_n) \leq n - 1 \quad (n \geq 2).$$

We prove both assertions by simultaneous induction. (2.1) is obvious for $n = 1$ and 2, as is (2.2) for $n = 2$. Let $n \geq 3$. For (2.1) we use as our first test-set A with $|A \cap S| = F_{n-2}$, $|A \cap T| = F_{n-1}$, whereas for (2.2) we use B with $|B \cap S_1| = F_{n-2}$, $|B \cap T_1| = F_{n-1}$, $|B \cap S_2| = 0$, $|B \cap T_2| = F_{n-2}$. The following figure reflects the outcomes in an obvious interpretation, and thus completes the proof by induction. □

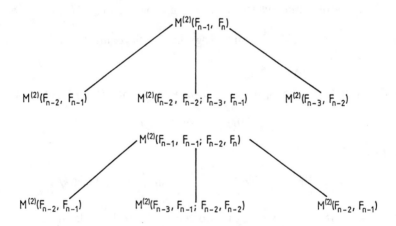

Figure 2.12

Theorem 2.9. *If F_n denotes the n-th Fibonacci number, then*

$$M^{(2)}(F_n) \leq n - 1 \quad (n \geq 1).$$

Proof. The assertion is trivial for $n = 1$. We proceed by induction on n. Choose a set of size F_{n-2} for the first test. Considering the three possible outcomes we have

$$M^{(2)}(F_n) \le 1 + \max(M^{(2)}(F_{n-2}), M^{(2)}(F_{n-2}, F_{n-1}), M^{(2)}(F_{n-1})).$$

By induction and Proposition 2.8 each of the terms on the righthand side is $\le n - 1$. $\square$

Individual values of $M^{(2)}(n)$ are, in general, very hard to determine, so let us just study the asymptotic growth of $M^{(2)}(n)$. Since $M^{(2)}(n)$ is obviously an increasing function of n, it is best to consider the "jump points" as in section 1.9 or, as we shall call it from now on, the *threshold function* $m^{(2)}(k)$ defined by

$$M^{(2)}(n) \le k \iff n \le m^{(2)}(k).$$

That is, $m^{(2)}(k)$ is the *largest* n with $M^{(2)}(n) \le k$.

From the preceding proposition we infer $m^{(2)}(k) \ge F_{k+1}$. Setting $n = m^{(2)}(k)$ in the information-theoretic bound $\log_3\binom{n}{2} \le M^{(2)}(n)$ one easily obtains $m^{(2)}(k) \le \sqrt{3}^{k+1}$ which together with Lemma 2.7(ii) yields the following result.

Corollary 2.10. *The threshold function $m^{(2)}(k)$ of $M^{(2)}(n)$ satisfies*

$$\tau^k \le m^{(2)}(k) \le \sqrt{3}^{k+1} \qquad (k \ge 1),$$

and thus

$$\tau \le \lim_{k \to \infty} \inf[m^{(2)}(k)]^{\frac{1}{k}} \le \lim_{k \to \infty} \sup[m^{(2)}(k)]^{\frac{1}{k}} \le \sqrt{3}.$$

Since $\tau \sim 1.618$ and $\sqrt{3} \sim 1.713$ we see that the bounds are not very far apart. The lower bound can be slightly improved by properly refining the Fibonacci algorithm. Very recently, Hao [1988] has shown that $\lim[m^{(2)}(k)]^{\frac{1}{k}}$ exists with $\tau < \lim[m^{(2)}(k)]^{\frac{1}{k}} \le \sqrt{3}$. Whether this limit actually equals $\sqrt{3}$ is an open question. The following table shows the threshold function for some small values. The reader may work on $m^{(2)}(6) = 22$ or $m^{(2)}(7) = 37$ to see that these values are not easy to come by.

k	2	3	4	5	6	7
$m^{(2)}(k)$	3	5	8	13	22	37

Figure 2.13

Let us take a look at the predetermined case for $d = 2$ defectives. A moment's reflection shows that we have to construct 0,1-matrices M with as few rows as possible such that all $\binom{n}{2}$ column sums $\underline{c}_i + \underline{c}_j$ are distinct.

Let us again consider the threshold function $m_{pre}^{(2)}(k)$ for the worst-case cost $M_{pre}^{(2)}(n)$. Then the problem reads: Consider all k-rowed matrices over $\{0,1\}$. What is the largest number $m_{pre}^{(2)}(k)$ of columns which a search matrix with k rows can have?

Let us take such a matrix M and number the rows $0, 1, \ldots, k-1$. To each column $\underline{c} = \begin{pmatrix} c_0 \\ \vdots \\ c_{k-1} \end{pmatrix}$ of M we associate the natural number $\bar{c}$ whose binary expansion is just $\underline{c}$, i.e. $\bar{c} = \sum_{i=0}^{k-1} c_i 2^i < 2^k$. Now it is clear that $\underline{c}_i + \underline{c}_j = \underline{c}_r + \underline{c}_s$ would imply $\bar{c}_i + \bar{c}_j = \bar{c}_r + \bar{c}_s$ (but not conversely, as the reader may easily convince himself). At any rate, if we can find n natural numbers $a_1, \ldots, a_n < 2^k$ all of whose sums $a_i + a_j$ are distinct, then by writing the a_i's in their binary expansions as columns, we will have constructed a $(k \times n)$-search matrix.

So we have reduced our problem to a very interesting question in additive number theory. What is the maximum $t(2^k)$ of numbers $a_1, \ldots, a_t$, $0 \leq a_i \leq 2^k - 1$, such that all sums $a_i + a_j$, $i \neq j$ are distinct. Let us call any such set of numbers *admissible*. An obvious choice of an admissible set is $\{0, 1, 2, 2^2, \ldots, 2^{k-1}\}$, thus $t(2^k) \geq k + 1$. Another method is suggested by a "greedy" construction. We set $a_1 = 0$, $a_2 = 1$ and inductively $a_i = a_{i-1} + a_{i-2} + 1$, yielding the set $\{0, 1, 2, 4, 7, 12, 20, 33, \ldots\}$. It should be clear that by this approach at most $2k - 1$ numbers are constructed, so this is not much of an improvement.

To do better, we employ a method first suggested by Singer [1938]. Let $GF(2^p)$ be the finite field with 2^p elements and $GF(2^{2p})$ its extension to a field containing 2^{2p} elements. We know from algebra that the multiplicative group of any finite field is cyclic. Let θ be a generating element of the multiplicative group of $GF(2^{2p})$. Thus the elements of $GF(2^{2p})$ are $\{0, \theta, \theta^2, \theta^3, \ldots, \theta^{2^{2p}-1}\}$. This is sometimes called the *multiplicative representation* of $GF(2^{2p})$. There is also an *additive representation*. Every element of $GF(2^{2p})$ can be uniquely written as $\alpha\theta + \beta$ where α and β run independently through the subfield $GF(2^p)$. Consider all 2^p elements

$\theta + \beta_i, \beta_i \in GF(2^p)$, and denote by $a_1, a_2, \ldots, a_{2^p}$ the integers defined by

$$\theta^{a_i} = \theta + \beta_i \quad (\beta_i \in GF(2^p)).$$

The a_i's satisfy $0 \leq a_i \leq 2^{2p} - 1$, and we claim that they form an admissible family. Suppose, on the contrary, that $a_i + a_j = a_r + a_s$. Then

$$\begin{aligned}
0 = \theta^{a_i + a_j} - \theta^{a_r + a_s} &= (\theta + \beta_i)(\theta + \beta_j) - (\theta + \beta_r)(\theta + \beta_s) \\
&= (\beta_i + \beta_j)\theta + \beta_i\beta_j - (\beta_r + \beta_s)\theta - \beta_r\beta_s \\
&= (\beta_i + \beta_j - \beta_r - \beta_s)\theta + \beta_i\beta_j - \beta_r\beta_s.
\end{aligned}$$

Since 0 has the unique additive representation $0 = 0.\theta + 0$, we conclude that

$$\beta_i + \beta_j = \beta_r + \beta_s, \beta_i\beta_j = \beta_r\beta_s.$$

Hence $\{\beta_i.\beta_j\}$ and $\{\beta_r, \beta_s\}$ are both solutions of the quadratic equation

$$x^2 - (\beta_i + \beta_j)x + \beta_i\beta_j = 0,$$

implying $\{\beta_i, \beta_j\} = \{\beta_r, \beta_s\}$, and thus $\{a_i, a_j\} = \{a_r, a_s\}$.
In terms of our function $t(2^k)$, this means $t(2^{2p}) \geq 2^p$. Relating this result to our original problem we obtain the following upper estimate for $M_{pre}^{(2)}(n)$.

Proposition 2.11. $M_{pre}^{(2)}(n) \leq 2\lceil \log_2 n \rceil$ *for $n \geq 2$.*

For the threshold function $m_{pre}^{(2)}(k)$ this means $m_{pre}^{(2)}(k) \geq \sqrt{2}^{k-1}$. Compare this to $m^{(2)}(k) \geq \tau^k$ obtained in Corollary 2.10.
We can express 2.11 in the form

$$\lim_{n \to \infty} \sup \frac{M_{pre}^{(2)}(n)}{\log_2 n} \leq 2.$$

What about lower bounds? Let M be an $(m \times n)$-search matrix with a minimal number of rows and columns $\underline{a}_1, \ldots, \underline{a}_n$. The following is the principal idea (due to Lindström [1972]) in estimating m from below. Let k be any integer between 1 and $m - 1$. We split each column $\underline{a}_i$ into its top part $\underline{b}_i$ and its bottom part $\underline{c}_i$ where $\underline{b}_i$ is of length k and $\underline{c}_i$ is of length $\ell = m - k$. Now suppose $\underline{u} \in \{0, 1\}^k$ is arbitrary, then we denote by $C(\underline{u}) \subseteq \{0, 1\}^\ell$ the set of all bottom vectors $\underline{v}$ such that $\binom{\underline{u}}{\underline{v}} = \underline{a}_i$ for some i. Hence $C(\underline{u}) \neq \emptyset$ iff $\underline{u} = \underline{b}_i$ for some i. Note that all vectors in $C(\underline{u})$ are distinct since all sums of two columns in M must be different. Let us number the vectors $\underline{u}$ from 1 to 2^k setting $\mid C(\underline{u}_i) \mid = s_i$, $i = 1, \ldots, 2^k$. Then

(2.3) $$n = s_1 + s_2 + \ldots + s_{2^k}.$$

Now we employ the fact that M is a search matrix. Consider the multiset $D(\underline{u}_i)$ of all s_i^2 ordered differences $\underline{v} - \underline{w}$ with $\underline{v}, \underline{w} \in C(\underline{u}_i)$. The vectors in $D(\underline{u}_i)$ have components equal to $1, -1$ or 0, where the 0-vector obviously appears s_i times. On the other hand, if $\underline{z} \in \{1, -1, 0\}^\ell$, $\underline{z} \neq 0$, then $\underline{z}$ appears *at most once* in $\bigcup\limits_{i=1}^{2^k} D(\underline{u}_i)$. Suppose otherwise, $\underline{z} = \underline{v} - \underline{w} \in D(\underline{u}_i)$, $\underline{z} = \underline{v}' - \underline{w}' \in D(\underline{u}_j)$ where $i = j$ is permitted. Then we clearly have

$$\binom{u_i}{v} + \binom{u_j}{w'} = \binom{u_i}{w} + \binom{u_j}{v'},$$

in contradiction to the definition of M.

Let us number the vectors $\underline{z} \in \{1, -1, 0\}^\ell$ from 1 to 3^ℓ with $\underline{z}_1 = \underline{0}$. If we denote by x_j the number of times $\underline{z}_j$ appears in $\bigcup\limits_{i=1}^{2^k} D(\underline{u}_i)$, then our remarks show that

(2.4) $$\sum_{j=1}^{3^\ell} x_j = \sum_{i=1}^{2^k} s_i^2 \text{ with } x_1 = n \text{ and } 0 \leq x_j \leq 1 \text{ for all } j \geq 2.$$

We know from Linear Algebra that for any two vectors $\underline{a}, \underline{b}$ the inequality $(\sum a_i b_i)^2 \leq (\sum a_i^2)(\sum b_i^2)$ holds (Cauchy's inequality). Setting $a_i = s_i$, $b_i = 1$ for all i this implies by (2.3)

$$n^2 \leq \left(\sum_{i=1}^{2^k} s_i^2 \right) \cdot 2^k,$$

and thus by (2.4)

(2.5) $$n^2 2^{-k} \leq \sum_{j=1}^{3^\ell} x_j.$$

It remains to bound $\sum x_j$ from above. Denote by W_h the set of all $\underline{z} \in \{1, -1, 0\}^\ell$ which have 0 in the h-th coordinate. We claim that

$$\sum_{\underline{z}_j \in W_h} x_j \geq \frac{1}{2} \sum_{j=1}^{3^\ell} x_j \quad (h = 1, \ldots, \ell).$$

To see this we are going to show that at least half the vectors $\underline{z} \in D(\underline{u}_i)$ have 0 in the h-th coordinate, for all i. Consider the s_i h-th coordinates of $C(\underline{u}_i)$, and suppose there are e 0's and f 1's. Then among the differences there are precisely $e^2 + f^2$ 0's from which

$$e^2 + f^2 \geq \frac{(e+f)^2}{2} = \frac{s_i^2}{2}$$

results. By setting $w_{jh} = 1$ if the h-th coordinate of $\underline{z}_j$ is 0 and -1 otherwise we can rewrite our inequality in the form

$$\sum_{j=1}^{3^\ell} w_{jh} x_j \geq 0 \quad (h = 1, \ldots, \ell).$$

Set, finally, $y_j = \max\left(0, 1 + \sum_{h=1}^{\ell} w_{jh}\right)$. Then

$$0 \leq \sum_{h=1}^{\ell} \sum_{j=1}^{3^\ell} w_{jh} x_j \leq \sum_{j=1}^{3^\ell}(y_j - 1) x_j,$$

and thus by (2.4)

(2.6) $$\sum_{j=1}^{3^\ell} x_j \leq \sum_{j=1}^{3^\ell} x_j y_j \leq n y_1 + \sum_{j=2}^{3^\ell} y_j.$$

So we have to bound $\sum y_j$. For $j = 1$ we have $\underline{z}_1 = \underline{0}$ and hence $y_1 = \ell + 1$. If $\underline{z}_j$ has r_j coordinates equal to 0, then $y_j = \max(0, 2r_j - \ell + 1)$, whence $y_j = 0$ whenever $r_j \leq \frac{\ell-1}{2}$. Fixing a set of r 0's among the ℓ coordinates, we have precisely $2^{\ell-r}$ possibilities to fill the other coordinates with 1's and -1's. Hence we infer

$$\sum_{j=1}^{3^\ell} y_j \leq \sum_{r > \frac{\ell-1}{2}} \binom{\ell}{r} 2^{\ell-r}(2r - \ell + 1) = 2^\ell \sum_{r > \frac{\ell-1}{2}} \binom{\ell}{r} 2^{-r}(2r - \ell + 1).$$

If ℓ is odd, then it is easily seen that $2^{-r}(2r - \ell + 1) \leq 2^{-\frac{\ell-1}{2}}$ for $r \geq \frac{\ell+1}{2}$ whence the right-hand side is bounded by $2^\ell \sum_{r > \frac{\ell-1}{2}} \binom{\ell}{r} 2^{-\frac{\ell-1}{2}} = 2^{\frac{3\ell-1}{2}}$. If ℓ is even, then we have $2^{-r}(2r - \ell + 1) \leq 3.2^{-\frac{\ell}{2}-1}$ for $r \geq \frac{\ell}{2} + 1$ and

$2^{-\frac{\ell}{2}}(2\frac{\ell}{2} - \ell + 1) = 2^{-\frac{\ell}{2}}$. Hence in this case the right-hand side is bounded by

$$2^{\ell}\left[\sum_{r \geq \frac{\ell}{2}+1} \binom{\ell}{r} 3.2^{-\frac{\ell}{2}-1} + \binom{\ell}{\ell/2} 2^{-\frac{\ell}{2}}\right] =$$

$$= 2^{\ell} \cdot 3.2^{-\frac{\ell}{2}-1} \cdot 2^{\ell-1} + 2^{\ell}\binom{\ell}{\ell/2} 2^{-\frac{\ell}{2}-2} = 3.2^{\frac{3\ell}{2}-2} + \binom{\ell}{\ell/2} 2^{\frac{\ell}{2}-2} \leq 2^{\frac{3\ell}{2}}$$

since $\binom{\ell}{\ell/2} \leq 2^{\ell}$. Taking (2.5) and (2.6) together we have thus proved

$$n^2 \leq 2^k(n(\ell + 1) + 2^{\frac{3\ell}{2}}).$$

It remains to properly choose k and ℓ. From the last inequality it is suggested that $k \sim \frac{3\ell}{2}$ will be the best choice. Suppose $m = 5q + r$, $0 \leq r < 5$. Then we choose $k = 3q$, $\ell = 2q + r$. Our inequality reads

$$n^2 - n2^{3q}(2q + r + 1) - 2^{6q+\frac{3}{2}r} \leq 0.$$

Viewing the expression on the left-hand side as a function in n, we infer that n must be smaller than the positive root of this quadratic, whence

$$
\begin{aligned}
n &\leq 2^{3q}(q + \frac{r+1}{2}) + \sqrt{2^{6q}[(q + \frac{r+1}{2})^2 + 2^{\frac{3}{2}r}]} \\
&\leq 2^{3q}(q + \frac{r+1}{2}) + Cq2^{3q} \quad \text{for some constant } C \\
&\leq C_1 2^{3q}q \quad \text{for some constant } C_1.
\end{aligned}
$$

With $q = \frac{m-r}{5}$ this, finally, becomes

$$n \leq C_1 2^{\frac{3m}{5} - \frac{3r}{5}} \frac{m-r}{5} \leq C_2 2^{\frac{3m}{5}} m \quad \text{for some constant } C_2,$$

and thus

$$\log_2 n \leq \log_2 C_2 + \frac{3m}{5} + \log_2 m.$$

Dividing this last inequality by $\log_2 n$ and recalling that $m \leq 2\lceil \log_2 n \rceil$ the following lower bound is established.

Proposition 2.12. *We have*

$$\liminf_{n \to \infty} \frac{M_{pre}^{(2)}(n)}{\log_2 n} \geq \frac{5}{3}.$$

In terms of the threshold function $m_{pre}^{(2)}(k)$, **2.11** and **2.12** yield the following inequalities.

Corollary 2.13. *Let $m_{pre}^{(2)}(k)$ be the threshold function for the cost $M_{pre}^{(2)}(n)$. Then*

$$\sqrt{2} \leq \lim_{k \to \infty} \inf[m_{pre}^{(2)}(k)]^{1/k} \leq \lim_{k \to \infty} \sup[m_{pre}^{(2)}(k)]^{1/k} \leq 2^{3/5}.$$

Comparing this to **2.10** we see from $2^{3/5} \sim 1.514 < \tau = 1.618$ that for this particular search problem, predetermined algorithms can never be as good as the best sequential procedures.

Exercises 2.3.

1. Verify the values in figure 2.13.

2*. Show: If $M^{(2)}(F_{n+1} + a) \leq n$, then $M^{(2)}(F_{k+1} + a) \leq k$ for all $k > n$.

3. Suppose we are only allowed test-sets A with $|A| \leq k$. Compute upper and lower bound for $M_{\leq k}^{(2)}(n)$.

4. For arbitrary n, let $t(n)$ be the largest number of integers m, $0 \leq m < n$, such that the sums of any two are distinct. Compute $t(n)$ for $n \leq 10$, and determine the first n for which the greedy series $(0, 1, 2, 4, 7, 12, 20, \ldots)$ is not optimal.

5. Generalize the idea of using Galois fields to arbitrary d.

6. Compute some small values of $M_{pre}^{(2)}(n)$.

7*. Suppose $S = T \dot\cup U$ with $|T| = m$, $|U| = n$. Denote by $M^{(2)}(m, n)$ the worst-case cost where we know that one defective is in T and the other is in U. Show that $\lceil \log_3 mn \rceil \leq M^{(2)}(m, n) \leq M_{pre}^{(2)}(m, n) \leq \lceil \log_2 mn \rceil + 1$.

8*. Prove $M_{pre}^{(2)}(2, n) = \lceil \log_2(n + 1) \rceil$. As we shall see in the next chapter, we also have $M^{(2)}(2, n) = \lceil \log_2(n + 1) \rceil$.

2.4 Spring Scale: Arbitrary Case

A very interesting situation arises when we have no advance knowledge what-soever as to what the set of defective elements is. Some of the coins may be defective, all of them or it may even happen that all coins are good. Our search domain consists therefore of the power set 2^S which with $q = n + 1$ yields the information theoretic bound

$$M_{pre}(n) \geq M(n) \geq \lceil \log_{n+1} 2^n \rceil = \lceil \frac{1}{\log_2(n+1)} n \rceil,$$

where $M(n)$ and $M_{pre}(n)$ denote the respective costs for this problem. We shall see that this bound is almost optimal, even for the predetermined case. In fact, we shall prove that

(2.7) $$\lim_{n \to \infty} \frac{M_{pre}(n) \log_2 n}{n} = 2.$$

We concentrate exclusively on predetermined algorithms, whether (2.7) can be improved for sequential algorithms is not known.

Let M be an $(m \times n)$-search matrix for this problem. As usual the rows are the $(0,1)$-incidence vectors for the test-sets $A_1, \ldots, A_m$. Suppose X^* is the set of defectives with incidence vector $\underline{x} = (x_1, \ldots, x_n)$, $x_j = 1$ iff the j-th coin is in X^*. The set of outcomes $e_1, \ldots, e_m$ is then given by $| A_1 \cap X^* |, \ldots, | A_m \cap X^* |$, i.e. by the matrix product

$$M \begin{pmatrix} x_1 \\ \vdots \\ x_n \end{pmatrix} = \begin{pmatrix} e_1 \\ \vdots \\ e_m \end{pmatrix}.$$

We conclude that M is a search matrix iff the vectors $M\underline{x}$ are pairwise distinct when $\underline{x}$ runs through all $0,1$-vectors of length n.

Example 2.4. Suppose we have $n = 4$ coins. It is clear that two tests cannot suffice since already for the 2-problem treated in the previous section we need 3 tests (cf. Figure 2.13). But the following matrix M shows three tests will do:

$$M = \begin{pmatrix} 1 & 0 & 1 & 1 \\ 0 & 1 & 1 & 0 \\ 1 & 1 & 0 & 0 \end{pmatrix}.$$

Suppose $\underline{e} = (e_1, e_2, e_3)$ is an outcome vector. M will be a search matrix if $M\underline{x} = \underline{e}$ allows us to uniquely recover the vector $\underline{x}$. The equations $M\underline{x} = \underline{e}$ are

$$
\begin{array}{ccccccc}
x_1 & & & + & x_3 & + & x_4 & = & e_1 \\
& & x_2 & + & x_3 & & & = & e_2 \\
x_1 & + & x_2 & & & & & = & e_3 \,.
\end{array}
$$

It follows that

$$2x_3 + x_4 = e_1 + e_2 - e_3.$$

Since x_3, x_4 are $= 0$ or 1 we see that the value of $e_1 + e_2 - e_3$ uniquely determines x_3, x_4. Considering the first two equations it is clear that, once x_3, x_4 are known, x_1 and x_2 are also uniquely determined. The reader can easily convince himself that for five coins three tests will not suffice.

In the above example we have determined the variables x_3 and and x_4 simultaneously, then x_2 and finally x_1. This grouping together of variables which are then simultaneously evaluated is the key to the following construction of a search matrix (due to Lindström [1965]) .
First we need a definition that will prove useful in many places later on.

Definition. Let T be a finite set and $\mathcal{F} \subseteq 2^T$ a collection of subsets. $\mathcal{F}$ is called a (simplicial) *complex* if $A \in \mathcal{F}$ and $B \subseteq A$ imply $B \in \mathcal{F}$.

Lemma 2.14. $\mathcal{F} \subseteq 2^T$ *be a complex, and suppose the function* $g : \mathcal{F} \longrightarrow \{0,1\}$ *has the property that for some fixed set* $F \in \mathcal{F}$

$$g(A \cap F) = g(A) \qquad \text{for all } A \in \mathcal{F}.$$

Then the following holds: If $C \in \mathcal{F}$ *and* $C \nsubseteq F$, *then*

$$
\sum_{\substack{A \subseteq C \\ |A|=odd}} g(A) \;=\; \sum_{\substack{B \subseteq C \\ |B|=even}} g(B).
$$

Proof. Since $C \nsubseteq F$ there exists $a \in C - F$. Half of the subsets A of C do not contain the element a. The map $A \longmapsto A \cup \{a\}$ is a bijection of these subsets onto the other half (those containing a), and it is clear that precisely one of A or $A \cup \{a\}$ has odd size. Now since $a \notin F$, we infer $A \cap F = (A \cup \{a\}) \cap F$ and thus

$$g(A) = g(A \cap F) = g((A \cup \{a\}) \cap F) = g(A \cup \{a\})$$

by our assumption. It follows that the terms in our two sums are pairwise equal, and hence so are the sums. $\square$

We proceed to the construction of the matrix. We take a complex $\mathcal{F} \subseteq 2^T$ and label the *non-empty* sets $F_1, \ldots, F_m$ in such a way that $F_i \subseteq F_j$ implies $i \leq j$. This is, of course, easily accomplished by, e.g., taking the 1-element sets first, then the 2-element sets, and so on.

We are now going to construct an $m \times n$-search matrix M with $n = \sum_{i=1}^{m} |F_i|$.

To do this we associate the rows of M with the sets $F_1, \ldots, F_m$, and group the columns according to $\mathcal{F}$. The first $|F_1|$ columns correspond to F_1, the next $|F_2|$ columns to F_2, and so on. Consider the group of columns associated with $F = F_k$. Let $a_1, \ldots, a_{|F|}$ be defined by $a_j = 2^{|F|-j}$. As noted before, any two sums of the a_j's are distinct. Now we define the j-th column of the F-group as follows. First we put 1's into a_j rows corresponding to odd-sized subsets of F, which is possible since $a_j \leq 2^{|F|-1}$. Next we place 0's into all rows corresponding to the remaining subsets of F. It remains to fill the positions corresponding to subsets $C \nsubseteq F$. This we do in a way suggested by the Lemma. The element in row C shall be the same as the one in row $C \cap F$, and 0 if $C \cap F$ is empty. Note that the vector c_j thus constructed is precisely the image of a function $g_j : \mathcal{F} \longrightarrow \{0, 1\}$ satisfying the assumption of the Lemma, where we set $g_j(\emptyset) = 0$.

Before proving that M is indeed a search matrix, let us pause to consider an example.

Example 2.5. Suppose $\mathcal{F}$ is the complex of all subsets of $\{1, 2, 3\}$. We arrange the 7 non-empty sets as required and obtain the following matrix. Note that we have some freedom in assigning the a_j 1's in the various columns.

	$\{1\}$	$\{2\}$	$\{3\}$	$\{1,2\}$	$\{1,3\}$	$\{2,3\}$	$\{1,2,3\}$
$\{1\}$	1	0	0	1 1	1 1	0 0	1 1 1
$\{2\}$	0	1	0	1 0	0 0	1 1	1 1 0
$\{3\}$	0	0	1	0 0	1 0	1 0	1 0 0
$\{1,2\}$	1	1	0	0 0	1 1	1 1	0 0 0
$\{1,3\}$	1	0	1	1 1	0 0	1 0	0 0 0
$\{2,3\}$	0	1	1	1 0	1 0	0 0	0 0 0
$\{1,2,3\}$	1	1	1	0 0	0 0	0 0	1 0 0

Consider, e.g., the group associated with $\{2,3\}$. In the column corresponding to 2 we place a 1 in the rows labeled $\{2\}$ and $\{3\}$ and 0 in the row $\{2,3\}$.

The remaining entries are determined by their intersections with $\{2,3\}$. E.g. $\{1,2\} \cap \{2,3\} = \{2\}$ hence there is a 1 in row $\{1,2\}$. Similarly in the column corresponding to 3 we place a 1 in row $\{2\}$ or in row $\{3\}$; in the example it is row $\{2\}$. Then we put 0's in the rows $\{3\}$ and $\{2,3\}$ and determine the remaining entries as before.

Let us now verify that the matrix M constructed in this fashion is indeed a search matrix. Let $e = (e_A : A \in \mathcal{F})$ be any outcome vector. As in example 2.4 we determine the variables from right to left. Set $| F_k | = f_k$ for $k = 1, \ldots, m$ and denote the variables belonging to the group F_k by $x_{k1}, x_{k2}, \ldots, x_{kf_k}$. Consider the group F_m. By adding all rows r_A belonging to odd-sized subsets A of F_m and subtracting from it the sum of all r_B corresponding to even-sized subsets B, we obtain

$$(2.8) \quad \Big(\sum_{\substack{A \subseteq F_m \\ |A| = odd}} r_A - \sum_{\substack{B \subseteq F_m \\ |B| = even}} r_B \Big)\underline{x} \;=\; \sum_{\substack{A \subseteq F_m \\ |A| = odd}} e_A - \sum_{\substack{B \subseteq F_m \\ |B| = even}} e_B.$$

Consider any group F_k, $k < m$ and column j in this group. We apply the lemma to the function g_j corresponding to this column and $F = F_k$. Since $F_m \not\subseteq F_k$ we have

$$\sum_{\substack{A \subseteq F_m \\ |A| = odd}} g_j(A) = \sum_{\substack{B \subseteq F_m \\ |B| = even}} g_j(B).$$

But this means precisely that $\sum r_A - \sum r_B$ has a 0 in the position corresponding to column j of group F_k. Applying this reasoning to all columns of all groups F_k, $k < m$, we infer that $\sum r_A - \sum r_B$ has non-zero entries only in the columns belonging to F_m. The entries there are, however, easily determined. In column 1 of group F_m there are $2^{|F_m|-1}$ 1's in the positions of the odd subsets and $2^{|F_m|-1}$ 0's in the position of the even subsets of F_m whence the coefficient in this column is $2^{|F_m|-1}$, and so on. We conclude that (2.8) reduces to the equation.

$$\sum_{j=1}^{|F_m|} 2^{|F_m|-j} x_{mj} \;=\; \sum e_A - \sum e_B,$$

and it is now obvious that the x_{mj}'s are indeed uniquely determined.

The rest is easy. Suppose we have already determined all variables belonging to the groups $F_{k+1}, \ldots, F_m$. We now consider the difference

$$
\left(\sum_{\substack{A \subseteq F_k \\ |A|=odd}} r_A - \sum_{\substack{B \subseteq F_k \\ |B|=even}} r_B \right) \underline{x} = \sum_{\substack{A \subseteq F_k \\ |A|=odd}} e_A - \sum_{\substack{B \subseteq F_k \\ |B|=even}} e_B.
$$

If j is a column of a group F_h with $h < k$, then by the same argument as before the coefficient in $\sum r_A - \sum r_B$ is 0. The coefficients in group F_k are $2^{|F_k|-1}, 2^{|F_k|-2}, \ldots, 1$. Thus by moving all variables $x_{\ell j}$ with $\ell > k$ to the right-hand side we uniquely recover the x_{kj}'s by our previous argument.

We can summarize our discussion in the following statement. Note that we exclude the empty set from $\mathcal{F}$.

Proposition 2.15. *Let $\mathcal{F}$ be a complex with $n = \sum_{A \in \mathcal{F}} |A|$, then $M_{pre}(n) \leq |\mathcal{F}| - 1$.*

According to **2.15** we are led to the construction of complexes $\mathcal{F}_m$ with $|\mathcal{F}_m| = m$ and $\sum_{A \in \mathcal{F}_m} |A|$ large. Write the numbers $0, 1, 2, 3, 4, 5, \ldots$ in their binary representation $0, 1, 10, 11, 100, 101, \ldots$. We associate to $m = \sum_{i=1}^{t} 2^{k_i}$ the subset $F_m = \{k_1, k_2, \ldots, k_t\} \subseteq \mathbb{N}_0$, with $F_0 = \emptyset$, and it is obvious that the first m subsets $F_0, F_1, \ldots, F_{m-1}$ form a complex $\mathcal{F}_m$ for every $m \geq 1$. As an example, $\mathcal{F}_7$ consists of the sets $\emptyset, \{0\}, \{1\}, \{0, 1\}, \{2\}, \{0, 2\}, \{1, 2\}$. Let $N(m) = \sum_{A \in \mathcal{F}_m} |A|$. Then we infer from **2.15** that there exists a search matrix M with $m - 1$ rows and $N(m)$ columns, i.e. $M_{pre}(N(m)) \leq m - 1$. To get an upper bound for $M_{pre}(n)$ we need therefore an estimate of $N(m)$.

Lemma 2.16. *For $m \geq 2$,*

$$
\frac{m}{2} \log_2 m - m < N(m) < m \log_2 m.
$$

Proof. Consider first $m = 2^\ell$. $\mathcal{F}_m$ consists then of all 2^ℓ subsets of an ℓ-set whence

$$
(2.9) \quad N(2^\ell) = \sum_{k=0}^{\ell} k \binom{\ell}{k} = \sum_{k=1}^{\ell} \ell \binom{\ell-1}{k-1} = \ell \sum_{k=0}^{\ell-1} \binom{\ell-1}{k} = \ell 2^{\ell-1}.
$$

Now suppose $m = 2^\ell + r$, $0 \le r < 2^\ell$. By the set-up of $\mathcal{F}_m$, we find that $\mathcal{F}_m = \mathcal{F}_{2^\ell} \cup \bigcup_{A \in \mathcal{F}_r} (A \cup \{\ell\})$. Hence

$$(2.10) \qquad\qquad N(m) = N(2^\ell) + r + N(r).$$

Now we proceed by induction on ℓ. For $\ell = 1$, we have $N(2) = 1, N(3) = 2$, so both inequalities are true. Now let $\ell \ge 2$. To prove the right-hand side we find, by (2.9), (2.10) and $\ell \le \log_2 m, \log_2 r < \ell$,

$$
\begin{aligned}
N(m) &= \ell 2^{\ell-1} + r + N(r) \le \ell 2^{\ell-1} + r + r \log_2 r \\
&< \ell 2^{\ell-1} + r + r\ell = \ell(2^\ell + r) - \ell 2^{\ell-1} + r \\
&\le \ell m - 2^\ell + r < \ell m \le m \log_2 m.
\end{aligned}
$$

To prove the left-hand side we use the fact that $x \log_2 x$ is a convex function for $x > 0$. This means that for any $a, b \in \mathbb{R}$ with $0 < a, b < 1$, $a + b = 1$ and $x, y > 0$

$$(x + y) \log_2 (x + y) \le x \log_2 \frac{x}{a} + y \log_2 \frac{y}{b}.$$

With $x = 2^\ell$, $y = r$ this becomes

$$m \log_2 m \le 2^\ell (\ell - \log_2 a) + r(\log_2 r - \log_2 b),$$

and thus by induction and (2.10)

$$
\begin{aligned}
\frac{m}{2} \log_2 m &\le \ell 2^{\ell-1} + \frac{r}{2} \log_2 r - 2^{\ell-1} \log_2 a - \frac{r}{2} \log_2 b \\
&< \ell 2^{\ell-1} + r + N(r) - 2^{\ell-1} \log_2 a - \frac{r}{2} \log_2 b \\
&= N(m) - 2^{\ell-1} \log_2 a - \frac{r}{2} \log_2 b.
\end{aligned}
$$

Now by choosing $a = b = \frac{1}{2}$ we obtain from the last inequality

$$\frac{m}{2} \log_2 m < N(m) + 2^{\ell-1} + \frac{r}{2} < N(m) + m. \qquad \square$$

As exercise 2.4.3 shows, the bounds in Lemma 2.16 can be strengthened. E.g., for the right-hand side we have, in fact, $N(m) \le \frac{m}{2} \log_2 m$ and this bound is sharp as seen by $m = 2^\ell$.

We proceed to the proof of $\limsup\limits_{n\to\infty} \frac{M_{pre}(n)\log_2 n}{n} \leq 2$. Choose m such that $N(m) \leq n < N(m+1)$. Then we know $M_{pre}(n) \leq m$, and if n goes to infinity, then so does m. From our Lemma we conclude

$$\frac{M_{pre}(n)\log_2 n}{n} \leq \frac{m\log_2 n}{n} < \frac{m\log_2(N(m+1))}{N(m)} = \frac{\log_2(N(m+1))}{N(m)/m}$$

$$< 2\frac{\log_2(m+1) + \log_2\log_2(m+1)}{\log_2 m - 2}$$

$$= 2\left[\frac{\log_2(m+1)}{\log_2 m - 2} + \frac{\log_2\log_2(m+1)}{\log_2 m - 2}\right].$$

On the right-hand side, the first summand goes to 2 with $m \longrightarrow \infty$, while the second summand goes to 0, and our proof is complete.

For a proof of the other half of assertion (2.7) we employ some very useful inequalities from probability theory.

Recall from section 1.8 that a random variable is a function $X : \Omega \longrightarrow T$ from some probability space Ω into the positive reals, where $p(x) = p(X = x) = \sum\limits_{X(\omega)=x} Pr(\omega)$ is the probability that X attains the value $x \in T$.

Definition. The *expectation* $E(X)$ of X is defined by $E(X) = \sum\limits_{x\in T} xp(x)$, and the *variance* $\mathrm{Var}(X)$ by $\mathrm{Var}(X) = E((X - E(X))^2)$.

Note that $E(X) = \sum\limits_{\omega\in\Omega} X(\omega)Pr(\omega)$. Very often $E(X)$ is denoted by μ (for mean) or $\overline{X}$. It follows directly from the definition that E is a multilinear function, i.e.

$$E(a_1 X_1 + \ldots + a_m X_m) = \sum_{i=1}^{m} a_i E(X_i), \quad a_1,\ldots,a_m \in \mathbb{R},$$

and in particular $E(a) = a$ for any $a \in \mathbb{R}$.

The interpretations of $E(X)$ and $\mathrm{Var}(X)$ are obvious. $E(X)$ gives the average value of X to be expected, while $\mathrm{Var}(X)$ measures how close the values of X are centered around μ. For the variance $\mathrm{Var}(X)$ we see $\mathrm{Var}(X) = E(X^2 - 2\mu X + \mu^2) = E(X^2) - 2\mu E(X) + \mu^2 = E(X^2) - \mu^2$, i.e.

$$\mathrm{Var}(X) = E(X^2) - E(X)^2.$$

Proposition 2.17. $X : \Omega \longrightarrow T$ *be a random variable. Then for any $a \geq 0$,*

i) $p(X \geq a) \leq \frac{E(X)}{a}$ whenever $X \geq 0$ (Markov's inequality)

ii) $p(|X - E(X)| \geq a) \leq \frac{\mathrm{Var}(X)}{a^2}$ (Chebysheff's inequality).

Proof. To prove i), we have

$$E(X) = \sum_{\omega} X(\omega)Pr(\omega) = \sum_{\omega : X(\omega) \geq a} X(\omega)Pr(\omega) + \sum_{\omega : X(\omega) < a} X(\omega)Pr(\omega)$$

$$\geq a \sum_{X(\omega) \geq a} Pr(\omega) = a \cdot p(X \geq a).$$

Note that $\sum\limits_{X(\omega) < a} X(\omega)Pr(\omega) \geq 0$ because of $X(\omega) \geq 0$ for all $\omega \in \Omega$. Now
let X be arbitrary, and define the variable Y by $Y = (X - E(X))^2$. Then
$Y \geq 0$ and $E(Y) = \mathrm{Var}(X)$, and thus by i)

$$p(|X - E(X)| \geq a) = p((X - E(X))^2 \geq a^2) = p(Y \geq a^2)$$

$$\leq \frac{E(Y)}{a^2} = \frac{\mathrm{Var}(X)}{a^2}. \qquad \square$$

Now suppose M is an optimal $(m \times n)$-search matrix for our problem. Let
$S = \{x_1, \ldots, x_n\}$ be the set of coins. We take as our probability space
$\Omega = 2^S$ and assume uniform distribution, that is every set $B \in \Omega$ is with
probability $Pr(B) = \frac{1}{2^n}$ the set of defective coins. Let $A_1, \ldots, A_m \subseteq S$ be
the sets corresponding to the rows of M. We define the random variables
$X_i : \Omega \longrightarrow \mathbb{R}^+$, by

$$X_i(B) = |A_i \cap B|, \quad B \in \Omega.$$

Let us compute $E(X_i)$ and $\mathrm{Var}(X_i)$. Set $\ell = |A_i|$, then

$$E(X_i) = \frac{1}{2^n} \sum_{B \subseteq S} |A_i \cap B| = \frac{1}{2^n} \sum_{k=0}^{\ell} k \binom{\ell}{k} 2^{n-\ell} =$$

$$= \frac{1}{2^\ell} \ell 2^{\ell-1} = \frac{\ell}{2} = \frac{|A_i|}{2} \quad (i = 1, \ldots, m),$$

$$\mathrm{Var}(X_i) = E(X_i^2) - E(X_i)^2 = \frac{1}{2^n} \sum_{k=0}^{\ell} k^2 \binom{\ell}{k} 2^{n-\ell} - \frac{\ell^2}{4}$$

$$= \frac{1}{2^\ell} \sum_{k=1}^\ell k\ell \binom{\ell-1}{k-1} - \frac{\ell^2}{4} = \frac{\ell}{2^\ell} \sum_{k=0}^{\ell-1} \left[k\binom{\ell-1}{k} + \binom{\ell-1}{k} \right] - \frac{\ell^2}{4}$$

$$= \frac{\ell(\ell-1)}{4} + \frac{\ell}{2} - \frac{\ell^2}{4} = \frac{\ell}{4} = \frac{|A_i|}{4} \quad (i = 1, \ldots, m).$$

From this we infer

$$E(\sum_{i=1}^m (X_i - \overline{X}_i)^2) = \sum_{i=1}^m \frac{|A_i|}{4} =: T \le \frac{mn}{4}.$$

Applying Markov's inequality to $Y = \sum_{i=1}^m (X_i - \overline{X}_i)^2$ we conclude

$$p(\sum_{i=1}^m (X_i - \overline{X}_i)^2 < 2T) = 1 - p(\sum_{i=1}^m (X_i - \overline{X}_i)^2 \ge 2T)$$

$$\ge 1 - \frac{1}{2} = \frac{1}{2}.$$

Thus there are at least 2^{n-1} sets $B \subseteq S$ for which $\sum_{i=1}^m (|A_i \cap B| - \frac{|A_i|}{2})^2 < 2T$,

i.e. $\sum_{i=1}^m (2|A_i \cap B| - |A_i|)^2 < 8T \le 2mn$.

Since M is a search matrix we note that the vectors $(|A_1 \cap B|, \ldots, |A_m \cap B|)$ are pairwise distinct, so this is also true for the vectors $(2|A_1 \cap B| - |A_1|, \ldots, 2|A_m \cap B| - |A_m|)$. Thus we conclude that the inequality

$$\sum_{i=1}^m t_i^2 < 2mn$$

has at least 2^{n-1} integral solutions $(t_1, \ldots, t_m)$. Invoking Cauchy's inequality we infer

$$\sum_{i=1}^m |t_i| \le \sqrt{\sum_{i=1}^m t_i^2} \cdot \sqrt{m} < \sqrt{2n}m$$

and thus

$$\sum_{i=1}^m |t_i| \le h,$$

where $h = \lfloor \sqrt{2nm} \rfloor$.

It is an easy exercise to show that the number of non-negative integral solutions to $\sum_{i=1}^{m} a_i \leq h$ is precisely $\binom{m+h}{m}$. Taking all our inequalities together and recalling $e^m > \frac{m^m}{m!}$ for any $m \geq 1$, we thus find

$$2^{n-1} \leq 2^m \binom{m+h}{m} < 2^m \frac{(m+h)^m}{m!} < (2e)^m (1 + \frac{h}{m})^m$$
$$\leq (2e)^m (1 + \sqrt{2n})^m,$$

and hence

$$2^n < C^m n^{m/2} \text{ for some constant } C.$$

From our previous result $\lim_{n \to \infty} \sup \frac{m \log_2 n}{n} \leq 2$ we know that $\lim_{n \to \infty} \frac{m}{n} = 0$. Taking logarithms in our last inequality we infer

$$n < m \log_2 C + \frac{m}{2} \log_2 n$$

or

$$2 < 2\frac{m}{n} \log_2 C + \frac{m \log_2 n}{n},$$

which finally yields

$$2 \leq \lim_{n \to \infty} \inf \frac{m \log_2 n}{n}.$$

Theorem 2.18. *We have*

$$\lim_{n \to \infty} \frac{M_{pre}(n) \log_2 n}{n} = 2.$$

Now that we have proved the asymptotic result as announced, we would like to get some precise values for $M_{pre}(n)$. This, however, seems to be a very difficult problem. It is tempting to conjecture that our construction is optimal for $n = \ell 2^{\ell-1}$, i.e. $M_{pre}(\ell 2^{\ell-1}) = 2^\ell - 1$, but this has not been shown.

Exercises 2.4.

1. Show that $M_{pre}(N(m)) = m - 1$ for $m \leq 8$.

2. Find some other good complexes $\mathcal{F}$.

3*. Sharpen **2.16** to $\frac{m}{2} \log_2 m - m + \frac{\log_2 3}{2} m < N(m) \leq \frac{m}{2} \log_2 m$. Note that the right-hand bound is sharp for $m = 2^\ell$. (Clements-Lindström).

4. Prove that $x \log_2 x$ is convex for $x > 0$.

5*. Show that the number of non-negative integral solutions of $\sum\limits_{i=1}^{m} a_i \leq h$

is $\binom{m+h}{m}$.

6. Estimate the constant C in $2^n < C^m n^{m/2}$.

7*. Suppose there are d defective sets A_i with 2^ℓ elements each. Denote by $M_{pre}(2^\ell, d)$ the (predetermined) worst-case cost of detecting the defective elements when each of A_i contains one defective. Show $\lim\limits_{d \to \infty} M_{pre}(2^\ell, d) \frac{\log_2 d}{d} \leq 2\ell$.

Problems

1. Consider an r-arms balance scale as in exercise 2.1.11. Determine $\overline{L}$ when uniform distribution is given. (2.1)

2. Estimate $\overline{L}(S, \mathcal{W}; \underline{p})$ for a given distribution $\underline{p}$. Is it true that $\overline{L}(S, \mathcal{W}; \underline{p}) \leq \overline{L}(S, \mathcal{W}; \frac{1}{n}, \ldots, \frac{1}{n})$? (2.1)

3. Prove or disprove $L^{(2)}(n) = \lceil \log_3 \binom{n}{2} \rceil$ for all n. (2.2)

4. What can be said about $L^{(2)}(n)$ when the weight h of the defective coin satisfies $h \geq \frac{3}{2} g$? In general, estimate $L^{(d)}(n)$ when $h \geq \frac{d+1}{d} g$? (2.2)

5. Estimate $\overline{L}^{(2)}(\mathcal{W}; \binom{n}{2}^{-1}, \ldots, \binom{n}{2}^{-1})$. (2.2)

6. Find a good upper bound for $L^{(d)}(n)$. Is it true that $L^{(d)}(n) \leq \lceil \log_3 \binom{n}{d} \rceil + C_d$? (2.2)

7. Suppose we only know that $d \leq \frac{n}{2}$ coins are defective, but have no prior knowledge of d. Estimate L. (2.2)

8. Discuss $L_{pre}^{(2)}(n)$ (see exercises 2.2.7, 2.2.8). (2.2)

9. Suppose we are given at the outset an arbitrary number of good coins (see exercise 2.2.5). Prove or disprove $L_g^{(d)}(n) \leq \lceil \log_3 \binom{n}{d} \rceil + C$. (2.2)

10. Prove or disprove $\lim_{k\to\infty} [m(k)]^{1/k} = \sqrt{3}$ (see **2.10**). (2.3)

11. Improve the upper bound in **2.13**. (2.3)

12. Is it true that $M_{pre}(\ell 2^{\ell-1}) = 2^{\ell} - 1$? (2.4)

13. Is $M(n)$ asymptotically better than $M_{pre}(n)$? (2.4)

Notes and References

Weighing questions are probably the oldest search problems ever studied. They appear in many variants in almost any collection of mathematical puzzles. The first problem studied in depth was the arbitrary spring scale case of section 4. It was posed by Söderberg-Shapiro [1963] and solved by Lindström [1964]. Lindström [1975] is a good account for the predetermined case, Hwang [1987] presents interesting variations for the two-coin problem. For weighing problems with partial information, the reader may refer to Christen-Hwang [1984].

Aigner M. [1986], Search problems on graphs. Discrete Appl. Math. 14, 215-230.

Bellman R., Glass B. [1961], On various versions of the defective coin problem. Inform. Control 4, 118-151.

Bose R., Chowla S. [1962], Theorems in the additive theory of numbers. Comm. Math. Helvet. 37, 141-147.

Cairns S.S. [1963], Balance scale sorting, Amer. Math. Monthly 70, 136-148.

Cantor D.G., Mills W.H. [1966], Determination of a subset from certain combinatorial properties. Can. J. Math. 18, 42-48.

Christen C. [1980], A Fibonaccian algorithm for the detection of two elements. Publ. 341, Dépt. d'IRO, Univ. Montreal.

Christen C. [1983], Optimal detection of two complementary coins. SIAM J. Alg. Disc. Methods. 4, 101 110.

Christen C., Hwang F.K. [1984], Detection of a defective coin with partial weight information. Amer. Math. Monthly 91, 173-179.

Clements G.H., Lindström B. [1965], A sequence of (±1)-determinants with large values. Proc. Amer. Math. Soc. 16, 548-550.

Conway J., Guy R. [1968], Sets of natural numbers with distinct sums. Notices Amer. Math. Soc. 15, 345.

Erdös P., Renyi A. [1963], On two problems of information theory. Publ. Math. Inst. Hung. Acad. Sci. 8, 241-254.

Erdös P., Turán P. [1941], On a problem of Sidon in additive number theory, and on some related problems. J. London Math. Soc. 16, 212-215.

Hao F.H. [1988], The optimal procedures for quantitive group testing. Discrete Math., to appear.

Hwang F.K. [1987], A tale of two coins. Amer. Math. Monthly 94, 121-129.

Linial N., Tarsi M. [1982], The counterfeit coin problem revisited. SIAM J. Computing 11, 409-415.

Lindström B. [1964], On a combinatory detection problem I. Publ. Math. Inst. Hung. Acad. Sci. 9, 195-207.

Lindström B. [1965], On a combinatorial problem in number theory. Can. Math. Bull. 8, 477-490.

Lindström B. [1969], Determination of two vectors from the sum. J. Combinatorial Theory 6, 402-407.

Lindström B. [1972], On B_2-sequences of vectors. J. Number Theory 4, 261-265.

Lindström B. [1975], Determining subsets by unramified experiments. In A Survey of Statistical Design and Linear Models, North Holland, 407-418.

Mead D.G. [1979], The average number of weighings to locate a counterfeit coin. IEEE Trans. Information Theory 25, 616-617.

Pyber L. [1986], How to find many counterfeit coins. Graphs and Combinatorics 2, 173-177.

Singer J. [1938], A theorem in finite projective geometry and some applications to number theory. Trans. Amer. Math. Soc. 43, 377-385.

Smith C.A.B. [1947], The counterfeit coin problem. Math. Gazette 31, 31-39.

Söderberg S., Shapiro H.S. [1963], A combinatory detection problem. Amer. Math. Monthly 70, 1066-1070.

Tošić R. [1983a], Two counterfeit coins. Discrete Math. 46, 295-298.

Tošić R. [1983b], A counterfeit coins problem. Review of Research Fac. Sci. Univ. Novi Sad 13, 361-365.

Tošić R. [1984], Four counterfeit coins. Review of Research Fac. Sci. Univ. Novi Sad 14, 99-108.

Winkelmann K. [1982], An improved strategy for a counterfeit coin problem. IEEE Trans. Information Theory 28, 120-122.

Chapter 3

Graph Problems

The problem of two defective coins treated in the previous chapter can be thought of as a special search problem on graphs as we will see in a moment. The notion of a graph is fundamental to a large part of combinatorics and related fields, and we shall find that, apart from a generalization of the weighing problem, there are some very interesting search problems of a purely graph-theoretical nature. We begin by collecting some important definitions and results.

3.1 Graph Notions

Let us recall the definition of a graph.

Definition. A *graph* G consists of a set of *vertices* V and a set of *edges* $E \subseteq \binom{V}{2}$. To emphasize these sets when necessary we write $G = G(V, E)$ and $V = V(G)$, $E = E(G)$. V and thus E are always supposed to be finite, and we mostly denote their cardinalities by $\mid V \mid = n$, $\mid E \mid = m$.

An edge $e \in E$ is therefore a pair of vertices $u, v \in V$, called the *end-vertices* of e. We often use the shorthand notation $e = uv$ and say, e *joins* u with v. To visualize graphs it is best to draw vertices as points and edges as curves or straight lines in the plane as in figure 3.1.

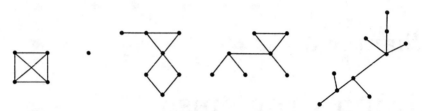

Figure 3.1

Two vertices are called *neighbors* or *adjacent* if they are joined by an edge, and we say vertex u is *incident* with edge e if u is an end-vertex of e. The *degree* $d(u)$ of a vertex u is the number of neighbors of u (equal to the number of incident edges). A vertex of degree 0 is called *isolated*. The following isomorphism concept for graphs is self-understood. $G(V, E)$ and $G'(V', E')$ are *isomorphic*, in symbols $G \cong G'$, iff there is a bijection $\varphi : V \longrightarrow V'$ such that $uv \in E$ iff $\varphi(u)\varphi(v) \in E'$.

A simple but very important fact is spelled out in our first result.

Proposition 3.1. *Let $G(V, E)$ be a graph. Then*

$$\sum_{u \in V} d(u) = 2 \mid E \mid .$$

Proof. We count the number of incident pairs (u, e), $u \in V$, $e \in E$ in two ways. Summing over V this gives $\sum_{u \in V} d(u)$, whereas summing over E we obtain $2 \mid E \mid$, since every edge has precisely two end-vertices.   □

Example 3.1. Let us single out two especially important classes of graphs. Suppose a graph G on n vertices has edges between any two vertices, i.e.
$E = (\begin{smallmatrix} V \\ 2 \end{smallmatrix})$, then we say G is a *complete graph* with the notation $G = K_n$.
Assume next that the vertex-set of G consists of two disjoint sets T and U, $\mid T \mid = m$, $\mid U \mid = n$, and that E comprises precisely all edges between T and U. Then G is said to be a *complete bipartite graph* $K_{m,n}$. Hence $K_{m,n}$ has $m + n$ vertices and mn edges.

It is clear what we mean by a subgraph. $H(V', E')$ is a *subgraph* of $G(V, E)$ if $V' \subseteq V$, $E' \subseteq E$, in symbols $H \subseteq G$. Hence any graph can be viewed as a subgraph of the complete graph on the same number of vertices. A subgraph of a complete bipartite graph is called *bipartite*.

The following specification of a subgraph is important. Suppose $A \subseteq V$, then G_A denotes the subgraph on A which contains all edges within A which are present in G, i.e. $V(G_A) = A$, $E(G_A) = E(G) \cap \binom{A}{2}$. G_A is called the subgraph *induced* by A. $G_{A,V-A}$ denotes the bipartite graph induced by A and $V - A$, i.e. $E(G_{A,V-A}) = E \cap \{uv : u \in A, v \in V - A\}$. We often tacitly identify a subgraph G_A with its underlying vertex-set A.

It should be clear what we mean by a *union* $G \cup H$ or *intersection* $G \cap H$ of the graphs G, H. If $V(G) \cap V(H) = \emptyset$, then we usually write $G + H$ for its union.

For the moment, we need just a few more definitions. Let $G(V, E)$ be a graph, and $u, v \in V$. A *trail* $T = (u = u_0, u_1, u_2, \ldots, u_t = v)$ is a sequence of vertices from u to v such that $u_i u_{i+1} \in E$ for all i. The *length* of a trail is the number of its edges. If all vertices u_i are distinct, then T is called a *path from u to v*. Finally, if in T all vertices are distinct except that $u = v$ then T is called a *cycle*.

Consider the graph in figure 3.2. The sequence (a, c, f, d, c, a) is a trail of length 5, (c, d, f, a, c) is a cycle of length 4.

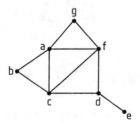

Figure 3.2

It is almost immediate that the relation $u \sim v$ iff there is a path from u to v is an equivalence relation on V (where we admit the trivial path (u) of length 0). The subgraphs induced by the equivalence classes are called the *connected components* of G, the number of which is denoted by $k(G)$. If $k(G) = 1$, then G is called *connected*.

Example 3.2. Two other important classes of graphs arise from these definitions. A *tree* is a connected graph without cyles. More generally, a *forest* is a graph all of whose components are trees. The tree with just one single vertex $(= K_1)$ is called *trivial*.

Consider the graph of figure 3.1. It consists of 5 components. The first component is K_4, the second K_1. The last component is a tree.

Proposition 3.2.

i) *Let $G(V, E)$ be a tree. Then $| E | = | V | - 1$.*

ii) *For a forest $G(V, E)$ we have $| E | = | V | - k(G)$.*

Proof. It obviously suffices to prove i). We use induction on $n = | V |$. For $n = 1$ or 2 there is nothing to prove. Suppose $n > 2$. Take any edge e. Since G has no cycles, we see that upon deleting e, G decomposes into two trees $G_1(V_1, E_1), G_2(V_2, E_2)$ with $| V_1 |, | V_2 | < n$. By induction, we have $| E | = | E_1 | + | E_2 | + 1 = (| V_1 | - 1) + (| V_2 | - 1) + 1 = | V | - 1$. □

Proposition 3.2 yields together with **3.1** an important property of trees. Suppose G is a tree and d_i is the number of vertices of degree i. We can then rewrite **3.1** as

$$\sum_{i=1}^{n-1} i d_i = 2 | E | = 2n - 2 = 2 \sum_{i=1}^{n-1} d_i - 2$$

or

$$d_1 = 2 + \sum_{i=2}^{n-1} (i - 2) d_i.$$

Hence any non-trivial tree G contains at least two vertices of degree 1, called *end-vertices* of G, and precisely two end-vertices u, v iff G has no vertices of degree ≥ 3, i.e. iff G is a path from u to v.

Note that any connected graph $G(V, E)$ contains a tree T on V (induction on $| V |$). We call any such tree a *spanning tree* of G.

The generalization of our spring scale weighing problems to arbitrary graphs should now be clear. We are given a graph $G(V, E)$ and an unknown edge e^*. As our test-sets we use sets of vertices $A \subseteq V$ and from the answers to these sets we are required to determine e^*. In chapter 2 any edge between two vertices was possible, so this was the special case where $G = K_n$, the complete graph.

Two models are suggested. First, we may receive as answer whether e^* is incident with *at least* one vertex of A or none; we call this the *binary variant*. Secondly, our answer may be threefold, whether e^* has both end-vertices in A, one end-vertex, or none. This is then called the *ternary variant*. Note that the latter case is precisely the generalization of the spring scale situation $M^{(2)}$ from K_n to arbitrary graphs.

Let us denote by $L(G)$ and $M(G)$ the respective worst-case costs. Since we receive more information in the ternary variant, we have

(3.1) $$M(G) \leq L(G)$$

for all G.
In the following two sections we discuss these two variants, concentrating on the graphs K_n, $K_{m,n}$ and the forests.

Exercises 3.1.

1. Draw all non-isomorphic trees up to 6 vertices.

2*. Let $G(V, E)$ be a graph with $E \neq \emptyset$ which has at most one vertex of degree 1. Show that G contains a cycle.

3. Prove that every connected graph contains a spanning tree. Develop a good algorithm for finding this tree.

4*. Prove the equivalence of the following statements: a. $G(V, E)$ is a tree, b. G is connected with $|E| = |V| - 1$, c. any two vertices are joined by exactly one path.

5. Show that any graph with at least two vertices contains at least two vertices of the same degree.

6*. Let $G(V, E)$ be a graph with n vertices and m edges. Prove: If $m > \binom{n-1}{2}$, then G is connected. Is the inequality best possible?

3.2   Searching For an Edge: Binary Variant

We begin with a simple but useful result that requires no further proof.

Lemma 3.3. *If $H \subseteq G$, then $L(H) \leq L(G)$.*

Let us make a first observation on this problem. Suppose in the course of our algorithm we have arrived at a graph $G(V, E)$ in which the unknown edge e^* lies. The next test $A \subseteq V$ splits G into two parts G_1, G_0. If the answer is "yes", then e^* lies in G_A or in $G_{A,V-A}$ whereas if the answer is "no", e^* lies in G_{V-A}. Thus $G_1 = G_A \cup G_{A,V-A}$, $G_0 = G_{V-A}$, and G_0 is an *induced* subgraph of G.

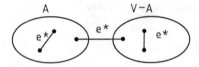

Figure 3.3

We conclude that any test corresponds to a partition of G into an induced subgraph and the remainder. It is convenient to interchange the roles of "yes" and "no" which obviously has no influence on $L(G)$. That is, after any test $A \subseteq V$ we receive as answer $e^* \in G_1 = G_A$ or $e^* \in G_0 = G_{A,V-A} \cup G_{V-A}$. From now on, we will always consider this latter version of our problem.

Our information-theoretic bound on $L(G)$ is

$$(3.2) \qquad\qquad L(G) \geq \lceil \log_2 |E| \rceil.$$

Let us first discuss the complete graphs K_n where for simplicity we write $L(n) = L(K_n)$. (3.2) reads in this case

$$(3.3) \qquad\qquad L(n) \geq \lceil \log_2 \binom{n}{2} \rceil.$$

Furthermore, Lemma 3.3 says that $L(n)$ is a non-decreasing function of n.

Example 3.3. The reader may easily check that for $n \leq 5$ the information-theoretic bound can indeed be achieved. But for $n = 6$ this is no longer true.

Consider K_6. The lower bound is $L(6) \geq \lceil \log_2 15 \rceil = 4$. Let us look at the first test. In order to achieve the information-theoretic bound we must be able to split K_6 into graphs G_1, G_0 with $\mid E(G_1) \mid, \mid E(G_0) \mid \leq 8$. Since any induced subgraph of a complete subgraph is itself complete we find from our observation above that $G_1 = K_i$ for some $i \leq 6$. From $\mid E(K_i) \mid = \binom{i}{2} \leq 8$ we infer $i \leq 4$, and thus $\mid E(G_1) \mid \leq 6$ implying $\mid E(G_0) \mid \geq 9$, so this is not possible. One more test is needed, i.e. $L(K_6) = 5$, as can be easily verified.

The fact that K_6 does not achieve the information-theoretic bound is no exception as the following result illustrates. First we need two lemmas.

Lemma 3.4. *We have*

$$\binom{n}{2} < 2^k \iff n < 2^{\frac{k+1}{2}} + \frac{1}{2} \quad (k \geq 1).$$

Proof. Note first that on neither side can we have equality. If $n < 2^{\frac{k+1}{2}} + \frac{1}{2}$ then $\binom{n}{2} < \frac{1}{2}((2^{\frac{k+1}{2}} + \frac{1}{2})(2^{\frac{k+1}{2}} - \frac{1}{2})) = 2^k - \frac{1}{8} < 2^k$. On the other hand, if $n > 2^{\frac{k+1}{2}} + \frac{1}{2}$, then $\binom{n}{2} > 2^k - \frac{1}{8}$ and thus $\binom{n}{2} > 2^k$ by our remark above. $\square$

Lemma 3.5. *If* $\binom{n+1}{2} > 2^k$ *and* $\binom{i+1}{2} < 2^{k-1}$, *then* $\binom{n}{2} - \binom{i}{2} > 2^{k-1}$ $(k \geq 2)$.

Proof. If $\binom{n}{2} > 2^k$, then there is nothing to prove, so we assume $\binom{n}{2} < 2^k$. Then $n < 2^{\frac{k+1}{2}} + \frac{1}{2} < n+1$ by the previous Lemma, i.e. $n = \lfloor 2^{\frac{k+1}{2}} + \frac{1}{2} \rfloor$. Again by the Lemma, $i \leq j = \lfloor 2^{\frac{k}{2}} - \frac{1}{2} \rfloor$.

Case 1. k odd. Then $n = 2^{\frac{k+1}{2}}$, $j \geq 2^{\frac{k-1}{2}}$, and thus by **3.4** applied to j

$$\binom{n}{2} - \binom{i}{2} \geq \binom{n}{2} - \binom{j}{2} = \frac{1}{2} \left[2^{\frac{k+1}{2}} (2^{\frac{k+1}{2}} - 1) - j(j-1) \right]$$

$$= (2^k - \binom{j+1}{2})) + (j - 2^{\frac{k-1}{2}}) > 2^k - 2^{k-1} = 2^{k-1}.$$

Case 2. k even. Then $j = 2^{\frac{k}{2}} - 1$, and therefore

$$\binom{n}{2} - \binom{i}{2} \geq \binom{n}{2} - \binom{j}{2} = \frac{1}{2}\left[n(n-1) - (2^{\frac{k}{2}} - 1)(2^{\frac{k}{2}} - 2)\right]$$

$$= \left[\binom{n+1}{2} - 2^{k-1}\right] + \left[3 \cdot 2^{\frac{k}{2}-1} - (n+1)\right].$$

It is easily seen that for $k \geq 6$, $\left(\dfrac{3 \cdot 2^{\frac{k}{2}-1}}{2}\right) > 2^k$ and thus $3 \cdot 2^{\frac{k}{2}-1} \geq n+1$

by the assumption on n. Together with $\binom{n+1}{2} > 2^k$ this yields $\binom{n}{2} - $

$\binom{i}{2} > 2^{k-1}$ for $k \geq 6$, whereas the cases $k = 2$ and 4 can be checked directly.   □

Proposition 3.6. *Let* $k \geq 4$ *and suppose* $\binom{n+1}{2} > 2^k$. *Then* $L(n) \geq k + 1$.

Proof. For $k = 4$, the only interesting case is $n = 6$ where $L(6) = 5$ was shown in example 3.3. We proceed by induction on k. Suppose A is the first test set with $|A| = a$. The resulting graphs are $G_1 = K_a$, $G_0 = K_{a,n-a} \cup K_{n-a}$. If $\binom{a+1}{2} > 2^{k-1}$, then $L(G_1) = L(a) \geq k$ by induction, and thus $L(n) \geq k + 1$. If, on the other hand, $\binom{a+1}{2} < 2^{k-1}$, then by the previous Lemma, $|E(G_0)| = \binom{n}{2} - \binom{a}{2} > 2^{k-1}$ whence $L(G_0) \geq k$, and thus again $L(n) \geq k + 1$.   □

Example 3.4. The preceding proposition shows that $L(n) > \lceil \log_2 \binom{n}{2} \rceil$ for all n with $\binom{n}{2} < 2^k < \binom{n+1}{2}$, $k \geq 4$. As an example, consider $n = 2^\ell$, $\ell \geq 3$. We have $\binom{n}{2} = 2^{\ell-1}(2^\ell - 1) = 2^{2\ell-1} - 2^{\ell-1} < 2^{2\ell-1}$, and

$$\binom{n+1}{2} = 2^{\ell-1}(2^\ell+1) = 2^{2\ell-1}+2^{\ell-1}, \text{ whence } \binom{2^\ell}{2} < 2^{2\ell-1} < \binom{2^\ell+1}{2},$$

$\ell \geq 3$. Our result implies therefore $L(2^\ell) \geq 2\ell = \lceil \log\binom{2^\ell}{2} \rceil + 1$.

On the other hand, let us show $L(2^\ell) \leq 2\ell$ for all $\ell \geq 1$. For $\ell = 1$ this is obvious. Now we use induction on ℓ. We split the vertex-set of K_{2^ℓ} into two equal-sized parts A, B with $|A| = |B| = 2^{\ell-1}$. As first test-set we take A and as second set we take B. After these two tests we know that the unknown edge e^* lies in $G_A = K_{2^{\ell-1}}$ or in $G_B = K_{2^{\ell-1}}$ or in $G_{A,B} = K_{2^{\ell-1},2^{\ell-1}}$. For the first two possibilities we have by induction $L(G_A) \leq 2\ell - 2$, $L(G_B) \leq 2\ell - 2$, and thus $L(2^\ell) \leq 2\ell$. If e^* is in $G_{A,B}$, then we know that one end-vertex u is in A while the other end-vertex v is in B. By the usual halving method, we can identify u with $\ell - 1$ tests on A, and similarly for v. Thus we again obtain $L(G_{A,B}) \leq 2\ell - 2$, i.e. $L(2^\ell) \leq 2\ell$. We have thus proved

$$L(2^\ell) = 2\ell \quad (\ell \geq 3).$$

Let us now tackle $L(n)$ in general. Since $L(n)$ is a non-decreasing function in n, we consider as usual the threshold function $m(k)$ with

$$L(n) \leq k \iff n \leq m(k).$$

From **3.6** and **3.4**, we know $m(k) \leq \lfloor 2^{\frac{k+1}{2}} - \frac{1}{2} \rfloor$ for $k \geq 4$, and in particular, $m(k) \leq 2^{\frac{k+1}{2}} - 1$ for $k \geq 5$, k odd. The following table gives the first values of $m(k)$ which the reader may check himself, showing that $m(k) = \lfloor 2^{\frac{k+1}{2}} - \frac{1}{2} \rfloor$ for $4 \leq k \leq 8$.

k	1	2	3	4	5	6	7	8
$m(k)$	2	3	4	5	7	10	15	22

Figure 3.4

In fact, it is known that $m(k) = \lfloor 2^{\frac{k+1}{2}} - \frac{1}{2} \rfloor$ up to $k = 11$, whereas $m(12) = 89 < \lfloor 2^{\frac{13}{2}} - \frac{1}{2} \rfloor = 90$. As for lower bounds of $m(k)$ we have the following result.

Proposition 3.7. *For $k \leq 4$, the values of $m(k)$ are $m(1) = 2$, $m(2) = 3$, $m(3) = 4$, $m(4) = 5$. For $k \geq 5$ we have*

$$m(k) \geq \begin{cases} 2^{\frac{k}{2}} + 2^{\frac{k}{2}-3} & k \text{ even} \\ 2^{\frac{k-1}{2}} + 2^{\frac{k-3}{2}} & k \text{ odd.} \end{cases}$$

Proof. For $k = 5$ and 6, the bounds are true by table 3.4. We proceed by induction on k.

Case 1. k even. We consider $G = K_n$ with $n = 2^{\frac{k}{2}} + 2^{\frac{k}{2}-3}$ and split the vertex-set into four parts A, B, C, D of cardinalities $|A| = 2^{\frac{k}{2}-1}$, $|B| = |C| = 2^{\frac{k}{2}-2}$, $|D| = 2^{\frac{k}{2}-3}$. As first test-set we take $A \cup B$. If the answer is "yes", then G_1 is the complete graph on $2^{\frac{k-2}{2}} + 2^{\frac{k-4}{2}}$ vertices whence we are done by induction. If the answer is "no", we test $A \cup C$. If the answer is "yes", then e^* has at least one end-vertex in C which we can find by testing half of C together with A etc. with $\frac{k}{2} - 2$ tests, while the other vertex is in $A \cup C$ which we can then find with $\frac{k}{2}$ tests. So altogether we need $2 + (\frac{k}{2} - 2) + \frac{k}{2} = k$ tests. Now, if the answer to the second test is "no" then we test $A \cup D$. If the answer to this test is "yes", then one end-vertex of e^* lies in D while the other is in $A \cup D$. Using the halving procedures as above we need $3 + (\frac{k}{2} - 3) + \frac{k}{2} = k$ tests. Finally, if the answer is "no", then we take as our fourth test-set $B \cup C$. If this time, we receive "yes", then one end-vertex of e^* is in B while the other is in C, whence we need altogether $4 + (\frac{k}{2} - 2) + (\frac{k}{2} - 2) = k$ tests again. On the other hand, if we receive "no", then e^* has one end-vertex in D and the other in $B \cup C$, implying that we need $4 + (\frac{k}{2} - 3) + (\frac{k}{2} - 1) = k$ tests again.

Case 2. k odd. We consider K_n with $n = 2^{\frac{k-1}{2}} + 2^{\frac{k-3}{2}}$, split the vertex-set into four parts A, B, C, D of sizes $|A| = 2^{\frac{k-1}{2}}$, $|B| = |D| = 2^{\frac{k-1}{2}-3}$, $|C| = 2^{\frac{k-1}{2}-2}$, and proceed as in case 1.   □

By a more detailed analysis, Chang, Hwang and Lin [1982] have strengthened **3.7** to

$$m(k) \geq \begin{cases} 43.2^{\frac{k}{2}-5} - 1 & k \text{ even} \\ 32.2^{\frac{k-1}{2}-4} - 1 & k \text{ odd.} \end{cases}$$

Further improvements were made by Chang, Hwang and Weng [1987]. But **3.7** together with **3.4** are at any rate good enough to determine $L(n)$ within an error of 1.

Theorem 3.8. *We have for all* n,

$$\lceil \log_2 \binom{n}{2} \rceil \leq L(n) \leq \lceil \log_2 \binom{n}{2} \rceil + 1,$$

and both sides of this inequality are attained for infinitely many n's, *respectively.*

Proof. We have already dealt with the cases $n \leq 6$, so assume $n \geq 7$. Suppose $\lceil \log_2 \binom{n}{2} \rceil = k$, i.e. $2^{k-1} < \binom{n}{2} < 2^k$. Then by **3.4**, $n \leq \lfloor 2^{\frac{k+1}{2}} + \frac{1}{2} \rfloor$. It is easily checked that

$$\lfloor 2^{\frac{k+1}{2}} + \frac{1}{2} \rfloor \leq \begin{cases} 2^{\frac{k+1}{2}} + 2^{\frac{k+1}{2}-3} & k \text{ odd} \\ 2^{\frac{k}{2}} + 2^{\frac{k-2}{2}} & k \text{ even} \end{cases}$$

which by **3.7** implies $L(n) \leq k + 1$.

The information-theoretic bound is attained for all n of the form

$$\lceil 2^{\frac{k}{2}} + \frac{1}{2} \rceil \leq n \leq \begin{cases} 2^{\frac{k}{2}} + 2^{\frac{k}{2}-3} & k \text{ even} \\ 2^{\frac{k-1}{2}} + 2^{\frac{k-3}{2}} & k \text{ odd} \end{cases} \quad (k \geq 5),$$

while the right-hand side is attained by all n of the form

$$n = \lfloor 2^{\frac{k+1}{2}} + \frac{1}{2} \rfloor \quad (k \geq 4)$$

as proved in **3.6** and **3.4**. $\square$

Corollary 3.9. *We have*

$$\lim_{k \to \infty} [m(k)]^{\frac{1}{k}} = \sqrt{2}.$$

Before proceeding to other classes of graphs let us briefly discuss the situation when only predetermined algorithms are permitted. Let M be a $k \times n$-search matrix. Suppose the defective pair corresponds to the columns $\underline{a}, \underline{b}$. If $\underline{e} = (e_1, \ldots, e_k)$ is the outcome vector, then clearly $e_1 = 1$ implies $a_i = b_i = 1$ whereas $e_i = 0$ implies $a_i = 0$ or $b_i = 0$. Hence $\underline{e}$ is precisely the Boolean product $\underline{e} = \underline{a} \wedge \underline{b}$, and we conclude that M is a search matrix if and only if any two Boolean products of columns of M are distinct.

This leads to a very interesting problem in extremal set theory. Let us identify the rows of M with a set T of k elements and the columns as subsets of T via the characteristic vector. Then our problem takes the following form in terms of the threshold function $m_{pre}(k)$: Given a set T of k elements. What is the maximal number $m_{pre}(k)$ of subsets of T such that the intersections of any two subsets are pairwise distinct?

Since $m_{pre}(k) \le m(k)$ we have as upper bound $m_{pre}(k) \le \lfloor 2^{\frac{k+1}{2}} - \frac{1}{2} \rfloor$, $k \ge 4$. To establish the following lower bound due to Frankl and Füredi [1984] we use the finite fields $GF(2^k)$ as in section 2.3.

Proposition 3.10. For $k \ge 1$,

$$m_{pre}(k) \ge 2^{\lfloor \frac{k}{4} \rfloor}.$$

Proof. It suffices to show $m_{pre}(4k) \ge 2^k$. We choose 4 disjoint sets A, B, C, D each of size k. The elements $x \in GF(2^k)$ can be identified with all 0,1-vectors of length k (with respect to a fixed basis). We number the elements of the four sets each from 1 to k, and denote by $\alpha, \beta, \gamma, \delta$ the natural embeddings of $GF(2^k)$ into A, B, C and D, respectively. E.g.,

$$\alpha(x) = \{a_i : x_i = 1\} \subseteq A.$$

Let us set $\underline{1} = (1, \dots, 1) \in GF(2^k)$. Then $\alpha(\underline{1} - x) = \alpha(x)^c$ where F^c denotes the set complement of F. Now we construct the $4k \times 2^k$-matrix M as follows. The rows correspond to the sets A, B, C and D in that order, and the columns to the elements $x \in GF(2^k)$ where column x corresponds to the set

$$X = \alpha(x) \cup \beta(\underline{1} - x) \cup \gamma(x^3) \cup \delta(\underline{1} - x^3) \quad (x \in GF(2^k)).$$

Suppose for columns x, y, u, v we have $X \cap Y = U \cap V$. Then $\alpha(x) \cap \alpha(y) = \alpha(u) \cap \alpha(v)$, $\beta(\underline{1} - x) \cap \beta(\underline{1} - y) = \beta(\underline{1} - u) \cap \beta(\underline{1} - v)$, i.e. $\beta(x) \cup \beta(y) = \beta(u) \cup \beta(v)$ by our remark above, and thus $x + y = u + v$. Hence if $x = y$, then $u = v$, and vice versa. So let us assume $x \ne y$, $u \ne v$. From $\gamma(x^3) \cap \gamma(y^3) = \gamma(u^3) \cap \gamma(v^3)$ and $\delta(\underline{1} - x^3) \cap \delta(\underline{1} - y^3) = \delta(\underline{1} - u^3) \cap \delta(\underline{1} - v^3)$, we conclude similarly $x^3 + y^3 = u^3 + v^3$. Since the field $GF(2^k)$ has characteristic 2 we infer $(x + y)^2 = x^2 + y^2$ and thus

$$\begin{aligned}
x^3 + y^3 &= (x+y)(x^2 - xy + y^2) = (x+y)((x+y)^2 + xy) \\
u^3 + v^3 &= (u+v)((u+v)^2 + uv).
\end{aligned}$$

Since $x \neq y$, $u \neq v$ we have $x + y = u + v \neq 0$ whence $x^3 + y^3 = u^3 + v^3$, $x + y = u + v$ imply $xy = uv$. But this means that $\{x, y\}$ and $\{u, v\}$ are both the sets of roots of the equation $z^2 + (x + y)z + xy = 0$, and we conclude that indeed $\{x, y\} = \{u, v\}$. $\quad\square$

Corollary 3.11. *For the threshold function* $m_{pre}(k)$ *of* $L_{pre}(n)$, *we have*

$$\sqrt[4]{2} \leq \lim_{k \to \infty} \inf[m_{pre}(k)]^{\frac{1}{k}} \leq \lim_{k \to \infty} \sup[m_{pre}(k)]^{\frac{1}{k}} \leq \sqrt{2}.$$

It is not known whether $\lim[m_{pre}(k)]^{\frac{1}{k}}$ exists.

Let us turn to the second interesting class, the bipartite graphs $K_{m,n}$ whose worst-case cost we denote by $L(m, n)$. The usual lower bound reads $L(m, n) \geq \lceil \log_2 mn \rceil$. By identifying the defective elements individually in each of the defining vertex-sets T and U, $|T| = m$, $|U| = n$ by the halving method we find $L(m, n) \leq \lceil \log_2 m \rceil + \lceil \log_2 n \rceil$. It is easily seen that $\lceil \log_2 m \rceil + \lceil \log_2 n \rceil \leq \lceil \log_2 mn \rceil + 1$ whence

$$\lceil \log_2 mn \rceil \leq L(m, n) \leq \lceil \log_2 mn \rceil + 1.$$

We now present a beautiful result of Chang and Hwang [1981] showing that, in fact, the information-theoretic bound is sharp for all m and n. First we need two lemmas. Let us call a graph $K_{1,n}$ a *star* with the single vertex the *center* of the star. More generally, we call a sum $K_{1,n_1} + \ldots + K_{1,n_t}$ a *star forest*.

Lemma 3.12. *Let* $G = \sum_{i=1}^{t} K_{1,n_i}$ *be a star forest, with* $|E(G)| = \sum_{i=1}^{t} n_i = 2^k + r$, $0 \leq r < 2^k$. *Then there is is an induced subgraph* G' *with* $|E(G')| = 2^k$ *if* $r > 0$, *resp.* $|E(G')| = 2^{k-1}$ *if* $r = 0$. *In particular* $L(G) = \lceil \log |E(G)| \rceil$.

Proof. Just collect 2^k edges if $r > 0$, and 2^{k-1} edges if $r = 0$, and notice that every subgraph of a star forest is again a star forest. $\quad\square$

Lemma 3.13. *Suppose* G *is a graph of the form depicted in figure 3.5, where* S *contains* $h2^r$ *isolated vertices, and each* U_i *contains* $2^r - 1$ *vertices. The figure means that vertex* v *is joined to all of* S, *the graphs on* $T_i \cup U_i$ *are disjoint complete bipartite graphs, and* v *is joined to all vertices in* $\bigcup_{i=1}^{t} T_i$ *(but to none of the* U_i's). *If* $|E(G)| = 2^\ell$, *then* $L(G) = \ell$.

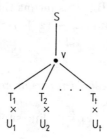

Figure 3.5

Proof. Set $j_s = |T_s|$, $s = 1, \ldots, t$, $q = \sum_{s=1}^{t} j_s$, and number the vertices of $\bigcup_{s=1}^{t} T_s$ by $t_1, \ldots, t_q$. Then $2^\ell = |E(G)| = h2^r + q + q(2^r - 1) = (h + q)2^r$, and thus $h + q = 2^{\ell - r}$. Let us divide S into h sets S_i of size 2^r each. By choosing $a \le h$, $b \le q$ with $a + b = \frac{h+q}{2}$ and the test-set $A = \{v\} \cup \bigcup_{i=1}^{a} S_i \cup \{t_1, \ldots, t_b\} \cup \bigcup_{i=1}^{t} U_i$, it is clear that $G_1 = G_A$ has $2^{\ell - 1}$ edges, as has G_0. Since both graphs G_1 and G_0 are of the same form as G, we arrive after $\ell - r$ tests at the star $K_{1,2^r}$, and the result follows by the previous lemma. $\square$

In order to apply induction in the following theorem we need to specify the optimal algorithms more precisely. Recall from section 1 that a subgraph of a complete bipartite graph is called *bipartite*. Suppose $G(T \cup U, E)$ is a bipartite graph on the defining vertex-sets T and U with $|E| = 2^r + 2^{r-1} + \ldots + 2^{r-p} + q$, where $0 \le q < 2^{r-p-1}$. We say that G is U-*optimal* if $L(G) = \lceil \log |E| \rceil$, and if for $|E| \ne 2^r$ the following holds: There is an optimal algorithm (of length $r + 1$) such that the graphs $G_{0,i}$ ($i = 0, \ldots, p$) corresponding to the all "no"-sequence ($G_{0,0} = G$) each contains an induced subgraph $G_{1,i+1}$ with $|E(G_{1,i+1})| = 2^{r-i}$, and such that further $G_{0,p+1}$ with $|E(G_{0,p+1})| = q$ is a star forest $G_{0,p+1} = \sum K_{j_s,1}$. That is, we must be able to split off induced subgraphs of sizes $2^r, 2^{r-1}, \ldots, 2^{r-p}$ in the "no"-sequence until we finally arrive at a star forest with all centers in U. Note that for $|E| = 2^r$ we just assume $L(G) = r$.

Theorem 3.14. *For all m and n,*

$$L(m, n) = \lceil \log_2 mn \rceil.$$

Proof. We fix m throughout. Let n_k be the largest n such that $mn \leq 2^k$. By **3.3**, it suffices to show that $L(m, n_k) \leq k$. Clearly, $n_k = 1$ for some k. Let T and U be the defining vertex-sets with $\mid T \mid = m$, $\mid U \mid = n_k$. We assume the following inductive hypothesis: If $n_h < n_k$, then $L(m, n_h) \leq h$ and further if n_h is odd, then K_{m,n_h} is U-optimal. For $n_h = 1$, this is satisfied by **3.12**. Now suppose $n_k > 1$. Note that $mn_k > 2^{k-1}$, since $mn_k \leq 2^{k-1}$ would imply $2^k < m(n_k + 1) \leq 2^{k-1} + m \leq 2^k$, which is absurd. Hence we have

$$2^{k-2} < mn_{k-1} \leq 2^{k-1} < m(n_{k-1} + 1),$$

and thus

$$2^{k-1} < m(2n_{k-1}) \leq 2^k < m(2n_{k-1} + 2),$$

which means that $n_k = 2n_{k-1}$ or $n_k = 2n_{k-1} + 1$. If $n_k = 2n_{k-1}$, then by testing $T \cup U'$ with $\mid U' \mid = n_{k-1}$, we obtain $G_1 = G_0 = K_{m,n_{k-1}}$, and are finished by induction. So we may assume $n_k = 2n_{k-1} + 1$. Let r be the largest integer such that

$$(3.4) \qquad\qquad n_k = 2^r n_{k-r} + 1.$$

Then $r \geq 1$ and n_{k-r} is odd. Setting

$$(3.5) \qquad mn_{k-r} = 2^{k-r-1} + 2^{k-r-2} + \ldots + 2^{k-r-p} + q$$

with $0 \leq q < 2^{k-r-p-1}$, we have

$$mn_k = m(2^r n_{k-r} + 1) = 2^{k-1} + 2^{k-2} + \ldots + 2^{k-p} + 2^r q + m.$$

By the induction hypothesis there exists a U-optimal algorithm $\mathcal{A}$ for $K_{m,n_{k-r}}$ with defining sets T and V, $\mid V \mid = n_{k-r}$. Let H be the graph on the all "no"-sequence in $\mathcal{A}$ corresponding to q edges, i.e. $H = \sum_{s=1}^{t} K_{j_s,1}$ with $\sum_{s=1}^{t} j_s = q$. From $\mathcal{A}$ we construct a U-optimal algorithm $\mathcal{A}'$ for K_{m,n_k}. For brevity, let us set $n = n_{k-r}$ and $n' = n_k$. We partition the $n' = 2^r n + 1$ vertices of U into n groups V_i each of size 2^r, and a single vertex v. $\mathcal{A}'$ is designed in two steps: First we replace every vertex $v_i \in V$ by the group V_i and split off induced subgraphs of size $2^r \cdot 2^{k-r-1} = 2^{k-1}, 2^{k-2}, \ldots, 2^{k-p}$ according to $\mathcal{A}$. Any end-node in $\mathcal{A}$ (except on the all "no"-sequence) corresponds then to a star $K_{1,2^r}$ which can then be searched in r more tests by **3.12**. Now consider the graph H' obtained by the replacement $v_i \longrightarrow V_i$ in the all "no"-sequence after p tests. It remains to verify that H' is U-optimal.

From the set-up of H in $\mathcal{A}$ we see that

$$H' = \left(\sum_{s=1}^{t} K_{j_s,2^r} \right) \cup K_{m,1}$$

with $\mid E(H') \mid = 2^r q + m$. Note that

$$2^r q < 2^r 2^{k-r-p-1} = 2^{k-p-1}.$$

Furthermore, since by (3.4) and (3.5)

$$2^{k-1} < m(n_{k-1}+1) \;=\; m(2^{r-1}n_{k-r}+1)$$
$$= \; 2^{k-2} + 2^{k-3} + \ldots + 2^{k-p-1} + 2^{r-1}q + m,$$

we have

$$2^{r-1}q + m > 2^{k-p-1},$$

and thus altogether

$$(3.6) \quad 0 < 2^{k-p-1} - 2^r q < 2^{r-1}q + m - 2^r q = m - 2^{r-1}q \le m - q.$$

Denote by T_s and V_s the defining vertex-sets of $K_{j_s,2^r}$ in H' ($s = 1,\ldots,t$). Pick a vertex $w_s \in V_s$ for every s and set $U_s = V_s - \{w_s\}$; thus $|U_s| = 2^r - 1$. As our first test-set for the graph H' we choose $A = \bigcup_{s=1}^{t} (T_s \cup U_s) \cup S \cup \{v\}$ where $S \subseteq T - \bigcup_{s=1}^{t} T_s$ has size $\mid S \mid = 2^{k-p-1} - 2^r q$. Note that the choice of S is possible by (3.6). The induced subgraph $H_1' = H_A'$ has $\mid E(H_1') \mid = q(2^r - 1) + q + 2^{k-p-1} - 2^r q = 2^{k-p-1}$ and thus fulfills the requirement on U-optimality of H_1'. Furthermore, we see that H_1' satisfies all the assumptions of Lemma 3.13, whence $L(H_1') = k - p - 1$. On the other hand, the "no"-graph H_0' is clearly a star forest with all centers in U. By **3.12**, our proof is complete.   □

Before going on to arbitrary graphs, let us take a brief look at predetermined algorithms for $K_{m,n}$. By the same argument as for the sequential case we infer

$$(3.7) \qquad \lceil \log_2 mn \rceil \le L_{pre}(m,n) \le \lceil \log_2 mn \rceil + 1.$$

The lower bound is sharp for infinitely many pairs (m, n), e.g. when m or n is a power of 2. But now, in contrast to our previous result, the information-theoretic bound also fails to hold for infinitely many pairs (m, n) as the following example shows.

Example 3.5. $L_{pre}(3, n) = 2 + \lceil \log_2 n \rceil$ for all n. So, e.g., when $n = 2^k + 2^{k-2}$, $k \geq 2$, then $L_{pre}(3, 2^k + 2^{k-2}) = k + 3 > \lceil \log_2 3(2^k + 2^{k-2}) \rceil$. To prove this, it obviously suffices to show $L_{pre}(3, 2^k + 1) \geq k + 3$ for $k \geq 0$. For $k = 0$ and 1 the inequality is true by (3.7), so we assume $k \geq 2$. Suppose, on the contrary, that a $(k + 2) \times (3 + 2^k + 1)$-search matrix M exists. In terms of sets this means, given the set $S = \{s_1, s_2, \ldots, s_{k+2}\}$, then there exist subsets A_1, A_2, A_3 and $B_1, B_2, \ldots, B_{2^k + 1}$ of S such that all intersections $A_i \cap B_j$ are distinct.

Suppose one of the sets A_i, say A_1, contains at most k elements. W.l.o.g., assume $s_1, s_2 \notin A_1$. Since $A_1 \cap (B_j \cup \{s_1, s_2\}) = A_1 \cap B_j$, we conclude that all $2^k + 1$ sets $B_j \cup \{s_1, s_2\}$ must be distinct, which is plainly impossible. If, on the other hand, $|A_i| \geq k + 1$ for all i, then $|\bigcap_{i=1}^{3} A_i| \geq k - 1 > 0$ because of $k \geq 2$. So there is an element, say s_{k+2}, contained in $\bigcap_{i=1}^{3} A_i$. Of the sets B_j, there are $2^{k-1} + 1$ sets, say $B_1, \ldots, B_{2^{k-1}+1}$, such that all of them contain s_{k+2} or none of them does. It follows that the sets $A_i' = A_i \cap \{s_1, \ldots, s_{k+1}\}$, $B_j' = B_j \cap \{s_1, \ldots, s_{k+1}\}$ $(i = 1, 2, 3; j = 1, \ldots, 2^{k-1} + 1)$ all must have distinct intersections, contradicting the induction hypothesis.

Theorem 3.15. *We have*

$$\lceil \log_2 mn \rceil \leq L_{pre}(m, n) \leq \lceil \log_2 mn \rceil + 1,$$

and both bounds are attained for infinitely many pairs (m, n), respectively.

Now we turn to general graphs. Let us call a graph $G(V, E)$ *optimal* if $L(G) = \lceil \log_2 |E(G)| \rceil$ and *near-optimal* if $L(G) \leq \lceil \log |E(G)| \rceil + 1$. Thus all graphs $K_{m,n}$ are optimal and all complete graphs K_n are near-optimal. Note that we may assume that G is connected, since joining two components A, B by identifying a pair of vertices $u \in A$ and $v \in B$ clearly does not lower $L(G)$. (See figure 3.6.)

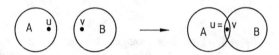

Figure 3.6

Exercise 3.2.1 states that K_6 is the unique smallest non-optimal graph. Hence all graphs G will $\mid E(G) \mid \leq 14$ are optimal. The following results have been obtained by Andreae [1988a]. Let us denote by $\Delta(G)$ and $\delta(G)$ the *maximal* and *minimal degree* of the vertices in G, respectively. A graph G is called k-*degenerate* if $\delta(H) \leq k$ for all subgraphs H of G. The reader can easily convince himself that the following alternate description is valid: A graph G is k-degenerate iff there exists a numbering of the vertices $v_1, \ldots, v_n$ such that every v_i is adjacent to at most k of its predecessors $v_1, \ldots, v_{i-1}$. We call $v_1, \ldots, v_n$ a *proper numbering* of the k-degenerate graph G. Note that any subgraph of a k-degenerate graph is again k-degenerate.

Obviously, a k-degenerate graph is also ℓ-degenerate for $\ell > k$. Furthermore, it should be clear, that the 1-degenerate graphs are precisely the forests. Just recall that any forest has a vertex of degree 1 and that subgraphs of forests are again forests.

Proposition 3.16. *Any forest is optimal.*

Proof. Let $G(V, E)$ be a forest, and let $v_1, \ldots, v_n$ be a proper numbering. Denote by H_i the induced subgraph on $\{v_1, \ldots, v_i\}$, $i = 1, \ldots, n$. Suppose G has m edges. Since by moving from H_i to H_{i+1} we add at most one edge, there must be a H_i with $\mid E(H_i) \mid = \lceil \frac{m}{2} \rceil$, and our claim follows by induction. $\square$

Before proving the next result, note that a k-degenerate graph G with m edges always contains an induced subgraph H with

$$(3.8) \qquad\qquad \max(\mid (E(H) \mid, m - \mid E(H) \mid) \leq \frac{m + k}{2}.$$

Indeed, choose a proper numbering $v_1, \ldots, v_n$ of the vertices, and denote by H_i the induced subgraph on $\{v_i, \ldots, v_i\}$. Since $\mid E(H_{i+1}) \mid \leq \mid E(H_i) \mid + k$, we deduce that there exists some i such that for $H = H_i$

$$\lfloor \frac{m}{2} \rfloor - \lceil \frac{k}{2} \rceil < | E(H) | \leq \lfloor \frac{m}{2} \rfloor + \lfloor \frac{k}{2} \rfloor \leq \frac{m+k}{2},$$

and further

$$m - | E(H) | \leq m - \lfloor \frac{m}{2} \rfloor + \lceil \frac{k}{2} \rceil - 1 = \lceil \frac{m}{2} \rceil + \lceil \frac{k}{2} \rceil - 1 \leq \frac{m+k}{2}.$$

Lemma 3.17. *For any graph G, we have $L(G) \leq \lceil 2\log_2 | E(G) | \rceil$.*

Proof. By our remark above we may assume that G is connected, and furthermore by **3.16** that G is not a tree. Suppose G has n vertices and m edges. Then $m \geq n$ by **3.2**(i). Making use of **3.3** and **3.8** we conclude

$$L(G) \leq L(K_n) \leq \lceil \log_2 \binom{n}{2} \rceil + 1 \leq \lceil \log_2 \binom{m}{2} \rceil + 1 \leq \lceil 2\log_2 m \rceil. \qquad \square$$

Theorem 3.18. *Let G be a k-degenerate graph, $k \geq 2$. Then $L(G) \leq \lceil \log_2 |E(G)| \rceil + \lceil \log_2(k-1) \rceil + 3$. For $k \leq 7$, this can be sharpened to $L(G) \leq \lceil \log_2 | E(G) | \rceil + 1$.*

Proof. Let us set $m = |E(G)|$. Note first that we may assume $m = 2^t$. Just add the right number of isolated edges (i.e. a sum of K_2's) to G and use **3.3**. If we choose the induced subgraph $H = H_i$ according to (3.8), then by picking $\{v_1, \ldots, v_i\}$ as first test-set we obtain a graph which in either case has at most $m_1 = \frac{m+k}{2}$ edges. Repeating this procedure i times we obtain a graph G_i (containing the unknown edge) with at most $m_i = \frac{m}{2^i} + \sum_{j=1}^{i} \frac{k}{2^j} = 2^{t-i} + \frac{2^i-1}{2^i} k$ edges. Thus $m_i \leq 2^{t-i} + (k-1)$. Let us set $i = \lceil \log_2 \frac{2^t}{k-1} \rceil$. Then $2^i \geq \frac{2^t}{k-1}$ implies $2(k-1) \geq (k-1) + 2^{t-i} \geq m_i$. Hence, after i tests, we have obtained a graph G_i with at most $2(k-1)$ edges. Making use of the previous lemma we infer

$$
\begin{aligned}
L(G) &\leq i + L(G_i) \leq \lceil \log_2 \frac{2^t}{k-1} \rceil + \lceil 2\log_2(2(k-1)) \rceil \\
&= t - \lfloor \log_2(k-1) \rfloor + \lceil 2\log_2(k-1) \rceil + 2 \leq t + \lceil \log_2(k-1) \rceil + 3 \\
&= \log_2 | E(G) | + \lceil \log_2(k-1) \rceil + 3.
\end{aligned}
$$

For the proof of the second claim it suffices to consider the case $k = 7$ (see the remark preceding **3.16**). Choose $i = t - 3$. Then by the same analysis as above, after i tests we arrive at a graph G_i with at most 14 edges. Thus G_i is optimal, and we conclude $L(G) \leq (t - 3) + \lceil \log_2 14 \rceil = t + 1 = \log_2 | E(G) | +1.$ □

Note that each graph G is $\Delta(G)$-degenerate. Hence we obtain the following strengthening of Lemma 3.17.

Corollary 3.19. *For each graph G with $\Delta(G) \geq 2$, we have*

$$L(G) \leq \lceil \log_2 | E(G) | \rceil + \lceil \log_2(\Delta(G) - 1) \rceil + 3,$$

and for $\Delta(G) \leq 7$, this can be sharpened to $L(G) \leq \lceil \log | E(G) | \rceil + 1$. That is, any graph G with $\Delta(G) \leq 7$ is near-optimal.

Example 3.6. A graph G is called *planar* if there exists a realization in the plane with the vertices as points of the plane and the edges as curves between their end-points such that the curves never cross inbetween. Figure 3.7 shows a planar realization of the graph K_5 minus an edge.

Figure 3.7

Planar graphs form an important class of graphs whose investigation goes back to the last century, mainly in connection with one of the most famous problems in all of mathematics, the *4-color problem*. It states that any planar graph can be 4-colored. That is, there is coloring of the vertices with 4 colors such that any two adjacent vertices receive different colors. The 4-color conjecture remained open for over 100 years until it was finally settled in 1976 by Appel and Haken with the massive help of computers. The interested reader may consult the book by Aigner [1987]. There he finds the easily proven fact that any planar graph has a vertex of degree

≤ 5. Since any subgraph of a planar graph is obviously planar, we conclude that planar graphs are 5-degenerate. Hence by **3.18**, we can assert that any planar graph is near-optimal. Whether optimality always holds is an open question, at any rate, no counterexample is known.

So far, no graph G is known with $L(G) > \lceil \log_2 \mid E(G) \mid \rceil + 1$. Two extremal cases can be imagined: Maybe *all* graphs are near-optimal, or maybe for every integer r there is a graph G such that $L(G) > \lceil \log_2 \mid E(G) \mid \rceil + r$. The following observation due to Triesch suggests that, answering this question, we may confine ourselves to *bipartite graphs*.

Proposition 3.20. *If $L(G) \leq \lceil \log_2 \mid E(G) \mid \rceil + r$ holds for all bipartite graphs G and some integer r, then $L(G) \leq \lceil \log_2 \mid E(G) \mid \rceil + r + 2$ holds for all graphs.*

Proof. Take any graph G. Let H be a bipartite subgraph of G with a maximal number of edges, and suppose A, B with $V = A \cup B$ are the defining vertex-sets of H. For $u \in A$ denote by $d_A(u)$ the degree of u in the subgraph G_A, and by $d_H(u)$ the degree in H. Then $d_A(u) \leq d_H(u)$ since otherwise the bipartite graph on $(A - u) \cup (B \cup u)$ would contain more edges than H. Similarly, we have $d_B(v) \leq d_H(v)$ for all $v \in B$. Hence we conclude by **3.1**

$$\mid E(G_A) \mid = \frac{1}{2} \sum_{u \in A} d_A(u) \leq \frac{1}{2} \sum_{u \in A} d_H(u) = \frac{1}{2} \mid E(H) \mid,$$

similarly $\mid E(G_B) \mid \leq \frac{1}{2} \mid E(H) \mid$, and thus $\mid E(G_A) \mid + \mid E(G_B) \mid \leq \mid E(H) \mid$. Suppose w.l.o.g. $\mid E(G_A) \mid \leq \mid E(G_B) \mid$, then $\mid E(G_A) \mid \leq \frac{1}{4} \mid E(G) \mid$, $\mid E(G_B) \mid \leq \frac{1}{2} \mid E(G) \mid$. We proceed by induction on $\mid E(G) \mid$, the small cases being clear by our previous results. Choose B as first test-set. If the answer is "yes", then $L(G) \leq L(G_B) + 1$, and hence by induction $L(G) \leq \lceil \log_2 \mid E(G_B) \mid \rceil + r + 3 \leq \lceil \log_2 \mid E(G) \mid \rceil + r + 2$. If, on the other hand, the answer is "no", then choose A as second test-set. If "yes", then $e^* \in E(G_A)$ and thus by induction $L(G) \leq L(G_A) + 2 \leq \lceil \log_2 \mid E(G) \mid \rceil + r + 2$. Finally, if the answer is "no", then $e^* \in E(H)$ which again implies by our hypothesis $L(G) \leq L(H) + 2 \leq \lceil \log_2 \mid E(H) \mid \rceil + r + 2 \leq \lceil \log_2 \mid E(G) \mid \rceil + r + 2$. □

Thus the main problem left concerns bipartite graphs. It was conjectured by several people that *all* bipartite graphs are optimal, which by our result would imply $L(G) \leq \lceil \log_2 \mid E(G) \mid \rceil + 2$. This has not been proved, but all available evidence (see the exercises) points to the fact that, at any rate, there may be a constant r such that $L(G) \le \lceil \log_2 |E(G)| \rceil + r$ holds for all bipartite graphs, and therefore with $r + 2$ for all graphs.

Exercises 3.2.

1. Show that K_6 is the unique smallest graph which is not optimal.

2. Verify the values of $m(k)$ in figure 3.4 and show further that $m(k) = \lfloor 2^{\frac{k+1}{2}} - \frac{1}{2} \rfloor$ up to $k = 11$, but $m(12) = 89 < \lfloor 2^{\frac{13}{2}} - \frac{1}{2} \rfloor = 90$. (Chang-Hwang)

3*. Use **3.14** to give a short proof of $L(n) \le \lceil \log_2 \binom{n}{2} \rceil + 1$.

4. Consider a set T of k elements and a family $\mathfrak{A} \subseteq 2^T$ such that no three sets A, B, C of $\mathfrak{A}$ satisfy $A \cap B = A \cap C$. Estimate how large $|\mathfrak{A}|$ can be.

5. Show $L_{pre}(5,5) = 6$.

6. Verify the alternate description of k-degenerate graphs.

7*. Show that every graph $G \neq K_3$ contains an induced subgraph H with $\frac{2}{5}|E(G)| \le |E(H)| \le \frac{3}{5}|E(G)|$. Note that the bounds are attained for $G = K_5$ or K_6.

8. Prove that any 2-degenerate graph is optimal.

9*. Consider the following search process on a graph $G(V, E)$. After testing $A \subseteq V$ we receive the answer "yes" if the unknown edge e^* has one end-vertex in A and the other in $V - A$, and "no" otherwise. This is called the "parity check model" since in the predetermined case we receive 1 if there is a 1 and a 0, i.e. $1=1+0=0+1$, and 0 if there are two 1's or two 0's, i.e. $0=1+1=0+0$. Let $P(n)$ be the cost for K_n in this model. Prove $\lceil \log_2 \binom{n}{2} \rceil \le P(n) \le \lceil \log_2 \binom{n}{2} \rceil + 1$, and show that equality may hold on the right-hand side. (Hwang)

10*. Show that $P_{pre}(n) \le 2\lceil \log_2 n \rceil \le \lceil \log_2 \binom{n}{2} \rceil + 2$.

3.3 Searching For an Edge: Ternary Variant

We turn to the second model, described in section 1. After every test A we receive as answer whether the unknown edge e^* has both end-vertices in A, one end-vertex, or none. Let us denote the worst-case cost by $M(G)$. As mentioned in section 1, $M(n) = M(K_n)$ is precisely the cost $M^{(2)}(n)$ studied in section 2.3. Recapitulating the results **2.10** and **2.13** for the threshold function $m(k)$ of $M(n)$ we have:

Proposition 3.21. *Let $m(k)$ and $m_{pre}(k)$ be the threshold function for $M(n)$ and $M_{pre}(n)$, respectively. Then*

$$\tau \;<\; \lim_{k\to\infty}[m(k)]^{\frac{1}{k}} \leq \sqrt{3},$$

$$\sqrt{2} \;\leq\; \lim_{k\to\infty}\inf[m_{pre}(k)]^{\frac{1}{k}} \leq \lim_{k\to\infty}\sup[m_{pre}(k)]^{\frac{1}{k}} \leq 2^{\frac{3}{5}}.$$

Let us now consider bipartite graphs $K_{m,n}$. We already know one result **2.8**: $M(K_{F_{n-1},F_n}) \leq n-1$ where the F_n's are the Fibonacci numbers. Arguing as there we arrive at the analogous asymptotic result for the threshold function $m(k)$ associated with the sequence $M(K_n, K_n)$.

Proposition 3.22. *Let $m(k)$ be the threshold function of $M(K_n, K_n)$, then*

$$\tau \leq \lim_{k\to\infty}\inf[m(k)]^{\frac{1}{k}} \leq \lim_{k\to\infty}\sup[m(k)]^{\frac{1}{k}} \leq \sqrt{3}.$$

What about exact results? First of all, we clearly have

$$(3.9) \qquad\qquad M(K_{1,n}) = \lceil \log_2 n \rceil,$$

since in this case there is no difference between the binary and ternary variant. Assume $m, n > 1$. As in the previous section we note the obvious implication:

$$(3.10) \qquad\qquad H \subseteq G \Longrightarrow M(H) \leq M(G).$$

Suppose as usual that the defining vertex-sets of $K_{m,n}$ are T and U, $|T| = m$, $|U| = n$. If we perform a test A on $K_{m,n}$, then we say the test is of *type* (i,j) if $|A \cap T| = i$, $|A \cap U| = j$. The resulting graphs of such a test are then

$$(3.11) \qquad G_2 = K_{i,j}, \;\; G_1 = K_{i,n-j} + K_{m-i,j}, \;\; G_0 = K_{m-i,n-j},$$

where $K_{a,b}$ is the empty graph if $a = 0$ or $b = 0$. Let us call G_2 and G_0 the *outer graphs* and G_1 the *mixed graph*. Since (3.11) is symmetric in i, j we may assume that $i \geq \frac{m}{2}$ always holds. Splitting G_1 further we are led to consider sums $K_{m_1,n_1} + \ldots + K_{m_t,n_t}$, with defining sets T_h, U_h, $h = 1, \ldots, t$. We then call A a test of *type* $(i_1, j_1) + \ldots + (i_t, j_t)$ if $|A \cap T_h| = i_h$, $|A \cap U_h| = j_h$ for all h.

Let us first study upper bounds, i.e. algorithms on $K_{m,n}$. The following results are due to Aigner [1986]. Since we want to apply induction it is desirable to concentrate on only one of the resulting graphs after each test. The following observation allows us to do this.

Consider $K_{m,n}$. If m is even, we choose a test of type $(\frac{m}{2}, j)$. Then

$$G_2 = K_{\frac{m}{2},j}, \quad G_1 = K_{\frac{m}{2},n-j} + K_{\frac{m}{2},j}, \quad G_0 = K_{\frac{m}{2},n-j}.$$

Since $G_0 \subseteq G_1$, $G_2 \subseteq G_1$ we may disregard the outer graphs in our further analysis by (3.10). For odd m, we choose a test of type $(\lceil \frac{m}{2} \rceil, j)$ with $j \leq \frac{n}{2}$. Since $j \leq n - j$ we have again $G_0 \subseteq G_1$, $G_2 \subseteq G_1$ by (3.11), and may thus concentrate on G_1. Now we apply analogous tests to each component of G_1, and so on.

Using this halving procedure, we arrive after $\lceil \log_2 m \rceil$ tests at a sum $K_{1,j_1} + K_{1,j_2} + \ldots + K_{1,j_t}$ with $\sum_{h=1}^{t} j_h = n$. As in the last section we call these graphs *star forests*.

Let us study star forests. Since $\sum K_{1,j_h}$ only depends on the numbers j_h we use the short notation $J = (j_1, \ldots, j_t)$ for $\sum K_{1,j_h}$. Our usual lower bound reads

$$M(J) \geq \lceil \log_3 \sum_{h=1}^{t} j_h \rceil.$$

Example 3.7. In contrast to the binary version the graphs J (which are forests) need not achieve the information-theoretic bound. The smallest examples are the stars $K_{1,3}$ and $K_{1,5}$ with $M(K_{1,3}) = 2$, $M(K_{1,5}) = 3$.

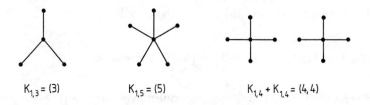

$K_{1,3} = (3)$ $K_{1,5} = (5)$ $K_{1,4} + K_{1,4} = (4,4)$

Figure 3.8

The reader can easily convince himself (or refer to **3.25**) that the same holds for the third graph of figure 3.8, $M(K_{1,4} + K_{1,4}) = 3 > \lceil \log_3 8 \rceil$.

We now discuss an important class of star forests with 3^k edges which do indeed achieve the lower bound.
Denote by $N(k)$ the sequence $(n_1, n_2, \ldots, n_{2^k})$ with

$$n_1 = 2^k, n_2 = \binom{k}{0} + \ldots + \binom{k}{k-1},$$

(3.12) $$n_3 = n_4 = \binom{k}{0} + \ldots + \ldots + \binom{k}{k-2}, \ldots,$$

$$n_{2^{i-1}+1} = \ldots = n_{2^i} = \binom{k}{0} + \ldots + \binom{k}{k-i}, \ldots,$$

$$n_{2^{k-1}+1} = \ldots = n_{2^k} = 1.$$

So, e.g., $N(0) = (1)$, $N(1) = (2,1)$, $N(2) = (4,3,1,1)$, $N(3) = (8,7,4,4,1,1,1,1)$.
The following relations are useful.

Lemma 3.23. *Set* $N(k) = (n_1(k), \ldots, n_{2^k}(k))$. *Then*

i) $\displaystyle\sum_{i=1}^{2^k} n_i(k) = 3^k \quad (k \geq 0)$

ii) $n_t(k-1) + n_{2t}(k-1) = n_{2t}(k),$

iii) $n_t(k-1) + n_{2t-1}(k-1) = n_{2t-1}(k).$

Proof. We have $\displaystyle\sum_{i=1}^{2^k} n_i(k) = 2^k + \sum_{\ell=0}^{k-1} 2^{k-1-\ell} [\binom{k}{0} + \ldots + \binom{k}{\ell}] = 2^k + \sum_{\ell=0}^{k-1} (2^0 + 2^1 + \ldots + 2^{k-1-\ell}) \binom{k}{\ell} = 2^k + \sum_{\ell=0}^{k-1} (2^{k-\ell} - 1) \binom{k}{\ell} = 2^k + (3^k - 1) - (2^k - 1) = 3^k$. ii) and iii) follow immediately from the definition. $\qquad \Box$

It is convenient to interpret $N(k)$ as infinite sequences by adding 0's at the end. The recursions ii) and iii) are then still valid.

Proposition 3.24. *We have* $M(N(k)) = k$ *for all* k.

Proof. Since $\sum_{i=1}^{2^k} n_i(k) = 3^k$ we certainly have $M(N(k)) \geq k$. To prove the converse we use induction on k. For $k = 0$ there is nothing to prove. Consider $N(k) = \sum_{i=1}^{2^k} K_{1,n_i(k)}$. For the first test we choose a set of the following type. Suppose $K_{1,n_i(k)}$ is a component, then we choose

$$(1, n_t(k-1)) \quad \text{if} \quad i = 2t - 1 \quad \text{is odd}$$
$$(0, n_{2t}(k-1)) \quad \text{if} \quad i = 2t \quad \text{is even}$$
$$(1 \leq t \leq 2^{k-1}).$$

The graph G_2 is then obviously $G_2 = \sum_{t=1}^{2^{k-1}} K_{1,n_t(k-1)} = N(k-1)$. Using **3.23**(ii) we obtain $n_t(k-1) = n_{2t}(k) - n_{2t}(k-1)$ and thus again $G_0 = N(k-1)$. Considering (3.11) and **3.23**(iii), we finally see for the mixed graph, $G_1 = \sum_{t=1}^{2^{k-1}} K_{1,n_{2t-1}(k-1)} + \sum_{t=1}^{2^{k-1}} K_{1,n_{2t}(k-1)}$ and thus again $G_1 = N(k-1)$. The result follows by induction. $\square$

Example 3.8. Consider $N(4) = (16, 15, 11, 11, 5, 5, 5, 5, 1, \ldots, 1)$. In the first test we use type $(1,8) + (0,7) + (1,7) + (0,4) + (1,4) + (0,1) + (1,4) + (0,1) + (1,1) + (0,0) + \ldots + (1,1) + (0,0)$. The resulting graphs are $(8, 7, 4, 4, 1, 1, 1, 1)$. Now we use type $(1,4) + (0,3) + (1,3) + (0,1) + (1,1) + (0,0) + (1,1) + (0,0)$ and obtain the graphs $(4, 3, 1, 1)$. We continue with type $(1,2) + (0,1) + (1,1) + (0,0)$ and obtain the graphs $(2,1)$. As final test we use type $(1,1) + (0,0)$ and obtain $(1,1)$ each time, i.e. three single edges.

The star forests $N(k)$ are quite useful for obtaining lower bounds. To do this we introduce an interesting ordering on sequences of natural numbers which has proved important in many fields, such as combinatorics, inequalities, or information theory.

Let $\underline{a} = (a_1, a_2, a_3, \ldots)$ be a sequence of integer ≥ 0 ordered according to magnitude, i.e. $a_1 \geq a_2 \geq \ldots$ We assume $\sum a_i < \infty$, or in other words that $a_\ell = 0$ for $\ell \geq \ell_0$. The *dominance order* on the set $\mathcal{S}$ of these sequences is declared by:

$$\underline{a} \preceq \underline{b} :\Longleftrightarrow \sum_{i=1}^{t} a_i \le \sum_{i=1}^{t} b_i \quad \text{for all} \quad t \ge 1.$$

The relation $\preceq$ is clearly transitive, in fact, S endowed with $\preceq$ forms a complete lattice with minimal element $(0, 0, 0, \dots)$.

Proposition 3.25. *Let* $A = (a_1, a_2, \dots) \in S$ *with* $a_1 \ge a_2 \ge a_3 \ge \dots$. *Then*

$$M(A) \le k \Longrightarrow A \preceq N(k).$$

Proof. Assume that A has m non-zero entries. We are going to show that $\sum_{i=1}^{t} a_{\sigma(i)} \le \sum_{i=1}^{t} n_i(k)$ for all t and all m-permutations σ. For $k = 0$ we have $A = (1) = N(0)$ so there is nothing to prove. We proceed by induction. Consider an optimal algorithm. We relabel the elements of A such that the first test has type $(1, q_i)$ on the first s graphs K_{1, a_i} and type $(0, a_i - q_i)$ on the remaining graphs, $0 \le s \le m$.
The resulting graphs are thus

$$G_2 = (q_1, \dots, q_s), \quad G_1 = (r_1, \dots, r_m), \quad G_0 = (q_{s+1}, \dots q_m)$$

with $q_i + r_i = a_i$ for all i. Since $M(G_i) \le k - 1$, $i = 0, 1, 2$, we have by induction

$$\sum_{i=1}^{t} r_{\sigma(i)} \le \sum_{i=1}^{t} n_i(k-1) \quad \text{for all } t \text{ and } \sigma.$$

Suppose of the t numbers $\sigma(i)$, τ belong to $\{1, \dots, s\}$ and $t - \tau$ to $\{s + 1, \dots, m\}$. Then again by induction

$$\sum_{i=1}^{t} q_{\sigma(i)} = \sum_{\sigma(i) \le s} q_{\sigma(i)} + \sum_{\sigma(i) > s} q_{\sigma(i)} \le \sum_{i=1}^{\tau} n_i(k-1) + \sum_{i=1}^{t-\tau} n_i(k-1),$$

$$\text{for all } t \text{ and } \sigma.$$

It is easily verified that $\sum_{i=1}^{\tau} n_i(k-1) + \sum_{i=1}^{t-\tau} n_i(k-1)$ is maximal for $\tau = \lfloor \frac{t}{2} \rfloor$. With $a_i = q_i + r_i$ we thus obtain by **3.23**

$$\sum_{i=1}^{t} a_{\sigma(i)} \le \sum_{i=1}^{t} n_i(k-1) + \sum_{i=1}^{\lfloor \frac{t}{2} \rfloor} n_i(k-1) + \sum_{i=1}^{\lceil \frac{t}{2} \rceil} n_i(k-1)$$

$$= \sum_{i=1}^{\lfloor \frac{t}{2} \rfloor} n_{2i}(k-1) + \sum_{i=1}^{\lceil \frac{t}{2} \rceil} n_{2i-1}(k-1) + \sum_{i=1}^{\lfloor \frac{t}{2} \rfloor} n_i(k-1) + \sum_{i=1}^{\lceil \frac{t}{2} \rceil} n_i(k-1)$$

$$= \sum_{i=1}^{\lfloor \frac{t}{2} \rfloor} (n_{2i}(k-1) + n_i(k-1)) + \sum_{i=1}^{\lceil \frac{t}{2} \rceil} (n_{2i-1}(k-1) + n_i(k-1))$$

$$= \sum_{i=1}^{\lfloor \frac{t}{2} \rfloor} n_{2i}(k) + \sum_{i=1}^{\lceil \frac{t}{2} \rceil} n_{2i-1}(k) = \sum_{i=1}^{t} n_i(k),$$

which is what we wanted to prove. $\square$

It is tempting to conjecture that the converse to **3.25** also holds: $A \preceq N(k) \implies M(A) \le k$. If true, this would provide a beautiful characterization of star forests with cost k, but so far only partial results are known.

As an illustration to **3.25** we can give the precise result for the complete bipartite graphs $K_{2,n}$. Some further results are contained in the exercises.

Corollary 3.26. *We have for all* $n \ge 1$,

$$M(K_{2,n}) = \lceil \log_2(n+1) \rceil.$$

Proof. Since $M(K_{2,n})$ is an increasing function in n, it suffices to show

(3.13) $M(K_{2,2^k-1}) \le k$

(3.14) $M(K_{2,2^k}) \ge k+1.$

(3.13) is easy. The result is obvious for $k = 1$. Let $k > 1$. For the first test we choose a set of type $(1, 2^{k-1})$ and split $K_{2,2^k-1}$ into the graphs $G_2 = K_{1,2^{k-1}}, G_1 = K_{1,2^{k-1}} + K_{1,2^{k-1}-1}, G_0 = K_{1,2^{k-1}-1}$. We see $M(G_2) \le k-1$, $M(G_0) \le k-1$ from (3.9), whereas $M(G_1) \le k-1$ follows from **3.24** and the fact that $G_1 \subseteq N(k-1)$.

The inequality (3.14) is trivial for $k = 0$. We proceed by induction. Suppose an optimal algorithm uses A as first set. By symmetry we have two cases: A may be of type $(2, j)$ or of type $(1, j)$. If we have type $(2, j)$, then $\max(j, 2^k - j) \ge 2^{k-1}$ implies $G_2 \supseteq K_{2,2^{k-1}}$ or $G_1 \supseteq K_{2,2^{k-1}}$ whence by induction $\max(M(G_2), M(G_1)) \ge k$ and thus $M(K_{2,2^k}) \ge k+1$. If A has type $(1, j)$ then we may assume $0 < j < 2^k$ since otherwise one of the outer graphs would be $K_{1,2^k}$ with $M(K_{1,2^k}) = k$. For $0 < j < 2^k$ we finally obtain

$G_1 = K_{1,j} + K_{1,2^k-j}$. Since $j + (2^k - j) > n_1(k-1) + n_2(k-1) = 2^k - 1$ we infer $M(G_1) \geq k$ from **3.25**, and thus again $M(G) \geq k + 1$. $\qquad\square$

Let us briefly discuss optimal graphs. For the binary model we have seen that infinitely many K_n's are optimal and all complete bipartite graphs $K_{m,n}$. In the ternary model the situation is completely different. Let us call a graph G 3-*optimal* if $M(G) = \lceil \log_3 | E(G) | \rceil$. It follows from the table in figure 2.13 that among the first K_n's ($n \geq 3$) only K_5 and K_8 are 3-optimal. We first look at complete bipartite graphs.

Lemma 3.27. *Suppose $K_{m,n}$ is split by a test into three non-empty graphs G_2, G_1, G_0. Set $t_i = \frac{|E(G_i)|}{mn}$ ($i = 0, 1, 2$). Then $t_1 \geq 2(\sqrt{t_2} - t_2)$.*

Proof. Suppose the test is of type (i,j). Then $G_2 = K_{i,j}, G_1 = K_{i,n-j} + K_{m-i,j}, G_0 = K_{m-i,n-j}$. We have $0 < t_1, t_2, t_3 < 1$ (since each G_i is non-empty) and $t_0 + t_1 + t_2 = 1$. Now

$$t_2 = \frac{ij}{mn}, t_1 = \frac{i(n-j) + (m-i)j}{mn} = \frac{i}{m} + \frac{j}{n} - 2t_2,$$

and thus $i = t_2 \frac{mn}{j}$ and

$$t_1 = t_2 \frac{n}{j} + \frac{j}{n} - 2t_2.$$

The function $f(j) = t_2 \frac{n}{j} + \frac{j}{n} - 2t_2$ has its minimum at $j = n\sqrt{t_2}$, whence $t_1 \geq \sqrt{t_2} + \sqrt{t_2} - 2t_2 = 2(\sqrt{t_2} - t_2)$. $\qquad\square$

Consider the function $g(t_2) = 2(\sqrt{t_2} - t_2)$ between 0 and 1. It is increasing from 0 to its maximum at $\frac{1}{4}$ when $g(\frac{1}{4}) = \frac{1}{2}$ and falls from then on. Furthermore we note for $t_2' = \frac{4-2\sqrt{3}}{3} < \frac{1}{4} < \frac{1}{3} = t_2''$ that $g(t_2') = g(t_2'') = \frac{2\sqrt{3}-2}{3}$, and thus

$$(3.15) \qquad g(t_2) \geq \frac{2\sqrt{3} - 2}{3} \quad \text{for} \quad \frac{4 - 2\sqrt{3}}{3} \leq t_2 \leq \frac{1}{3}.$$

Proposition 3.28. $M(K_{m,n}) \geq k + 1$ *for $mn > \lambda.3^{k-1}$ where $\lambda = \frac{3}{2\sqrt{3}-2}$. (Note that $2.049 < \lambda < 2.05$.) Hence a complete bipartite graph $K_{m,n}$ with $\lambda.3^{k-1} < mn \leq 3^k$ is not 3-optimal.*

Proof. For $k = 1$ we have $mn \geq 3$. $K_{m,n}$ contains therefore at least 4 edges or is the star $K_{1,3}$. In either case $M(K_{m,n}) \geq 2$ by our previous results. We proceed by induction. Suppose, on the contrary, that $M(K_{m,n}) \leq k$ and let G_2, G_1 and and G_0 be the graphs resulting after the first test. Let t_2, t_1, t_0 be defined as in the lemma. By induction $\mid E(G_2) \mid, \mid E(G_0) \mid \leq \lambda.3^{k-2}$ and thus $t_2, t_0 < \frac{1}{3}$ because of $mn > \lambda.3^{k-1}$. If $t_1 \geq \frac{1}{\lambda}$, then $\mid E(G_1) \mid \geq \frac{1}{\lambda} mn > 3^{k-1}$, in contradiction to $M(G_1) \leq k - 1$; hence $t_1 < \frac{1}{\lambda}$. It follows from $\frac{1}{3} > t_0 = 1 - t_1 - t_2 > 1 - \frac{1}{\lambda} - t_2$ that $t_2 > \frac{2}{3} - \frac{1}{\lambda} = \frac{4-2\sqrt{3}}{3}$, and thus $\frac{4-2\sqrt{3}}{3} < t_2 < \frac{1}{3}$. Applying (3.15) we conclude $t_1 \geq \frac{2\sqrt{3}-2}{3} = \frac{1}{\lambda}$, in contradiction $t_1 < \frac{1}{\lambda}$ as shown above. $\square$

The minimal value of λ which ensures $mn > \lambda.3^{k-1} \implies M(K_{m,n}) \geq k + 1$ is certainly ≥ 2 as the graph $K_{2,3}$ with $M(K_{2,3}) = 2$ shows (see **3.26**). **3.28** has an immediate corollary for complete graphs.

Corollary 3.29. $M(K_n) \geq k + 1$ whenever $\binom{n}{2} > \lambda.3^{k-1}$ with $\lambda = \frac{3}{2\sqrt{3}-2}$.

Hence a complete graph K_n with $\lambda.3^{k-1} < \binom{n}{2} \leq 3^k$ is not 3-optimal.

Proof. For $k = 1$ we have $\binom{n}{2} \geq 3$, i.e. $n \geq 3$ and we know from table 2.13 that $M(K_3) = 2$. Suppose, on the contrary, $M(K_n) \leq k$. If the first test-set A has size i, then $G_2 = K_i$, $G_1 = K_{i,n-i}$, $G_0 = K_{n-i}$. Hence by induction and **3.28** we must have $\binom{i}{2}, \binom{n-i}{2} \leq \lambda.3^{k-2}$, $i(n-i) \leq \lambda.3^{k-2}$, and thus $\binom{n}{2} = \binom{i}{2} + \binom{n-i}{2} + i(n-i) \leq \lambda.3^{k-1}$, contradicting the assumption. $\square$

The available data suggest that for fixed m, only finitely many $K_{m,n}$ are 3-optimal, while for the complete graphs it is quite possible that K_5 and K_8 are the only 3-optimal graphs.

Let us take a brief look at search matrices M for $K_{m,n}$. M is a 0,1-matrix of the form $M = A \mid B$ where A has m columns and B has n columns. The condition on M is that the mn sums $\underline{a} + \underline{b}$, $\underline{a} \in A$, $\underline{b} \in B$ are distinct.

Example 3.9. The following matrix shows $M_{pre}(K_{2,3}) = 2$.

$$\begin{pmatrix} 1 & 0 & 1 & 0 & 0 \\ 1 & 0 & 0 & 1 & 0 \end{pmatrix}.$$

The following inductive construction was proposed by Lindström [1975].

Lemma 3.30. *If $M = (A \mid B)$ is a k-rowed search matrix for $K_{m,n}$, then*

$$M' = \begin{pmatrix} A & B \\ \times & \times \\ B & A \end{pmatrix} \text{ is a 2k-rowed search matrix for } K_{mn,mn}, \text{ where } \begin{matrix} A \\ \times \\ B \end{matrix} \text{ is}$$

the matrix obtained from A and B by writing any column of A above any column of B; similarly for $\begin{matrix} B \\ \times \\ A \end{matrix}$.

Proof. Suppose $\frac{a_1}{b_1} + \frac{b_1'}{a_1'} = \frac{a_2}{b_2} + \frac{b_2'}{a_2'}$ in M'. Then $a_1 + b_1' = a_2 + b_2'$, $a_1' + b_1 = a_2' + b_2$ and thus $a_1 = a_2$, $a_1' = a_2'$, $b_1 = b_2$, $b_1' = b_2'$. □

Using our example $M_{pre}(K_{2,3}) = 2$, we find $M_{pre}(K_{6,6}) = 4$ and by induction $M_{pre}(K_{6^{2^k}, 6^{2^k}}) \leq 2^{k+2}$. From this and the usual probability arguments the following result can easily be derived. In fact, we can assert in this situation that $\lim_{k \to \infty} m_{pre}(k)$ exists (see the exercises).

Proposition 3.31. *Let $m_{pre}(k)$ be the threshold function for $M_{pre}(K_n, K_n)$. Then $\lim_{k \to \infty} [m_{pre}(k)]^{\frac{1}{k}}$ exists with*

$$6^{\frac{1}{4}} \leq \lim_{k \to \infty} [m_{pre}(k)]^{\frac{1}{k}} \leq 2^{\frac{3}{4}}.$$

We now turn to forests. For the binary variant we have seen in the last section that all forests are optimal. Again, this is no longer true in the ternary model.

Example 3.10. The star $K_{1,3}$ is not 3-optimal as remarked before. In general, we infer from (3.9) and (3.10) that a tree cannot be 3-optimal if it contains a vertex v of degree $d(v) > 2^{\lceil \log_3 m \rceil}$ where m is the number of edges. This condition is, however, not sufficient as the following two examples show.

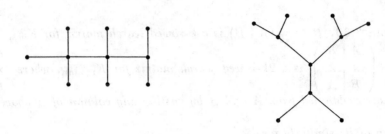

Figure 3.9

Both trees have 9 edges and the maximal degree is $\leq 4 = 2^{\lceil \log_3 9 \rceil}$, but it is easily verified that either of them needs 3 tests.

Let us denote by $\Delta(G)$ the maximal degree of the vertices in the graph G and by $\mathcal{F}_r$ the class of forests with $\Delta \leq r$. Andreae [1988b] has determined the precise difference of $M(G)$ for $G \in \mathcal{F}_r$ from the information-theoretic lower bound. We just state the result (see exercise 3.3.7).

Proposition 3.32. *Let* $F \in \mathcal{F}_r$ *with* m *edges. Then*

$$\lceil \log_3 m \rceil \leq M(F) \leq \lceil \log_3 m \rceil + f(r),$$

where $f(r) = 0$ *and* $f(r) = t - \lceil \log_3(2^{t-1} + 1) \rceil$, $2^{t-1} < r \leq 2^t$ *for* $r \geq 2$. *In addition, both bounds are sharp.*

In particular, it follows that any forest with $\Delta \leq 2$ is 3-optimal, but for $\Delta \geq 3$ this is no longer true, as seen by the examples in figure 3.9.

Exercises 3.3.

1*. Prove $M(K_{3,n}) \leq k \Longleftrightarrow n \leq 2^k - k$ $(k \geq 2)$.

2. Prove $M(K_{4,n}) \leq k \Longleftrightarrow n \leq 2^k - k + 2$ $(k \geq 2)$.

3. Show $M(K_{5,9}) = 4$ and $M(K_{9,14}) = 5$.

4*. Let G_2, G_1, G_0 be a decomposition of $K_{m,n}$ as in **3.27**, and t_i (i=0,1,2) as defined there. Prove $\max_i t_i \geq \frac{4}{9}$, and show further that $\frac{4}{9}$ cannot be improved.

5*. Show that K_n is not 3-optimal for infinitely many n's.

6. Verify that both of the trees in figure 3.9 are not 3-optimal.

7*. Show by example that both bounds in **3.32** are attained. (Andreae)

8. Show that a cycle is 3-optimal iff the length of the cycle is not a power of 3.

9*. Prove proposition **3.31**.

3.4 Searching For an Edge With Restricted Test Sets

So far, we have allowed any test-set A when searching for the unknown edge. A natural restriction on the tests would be to allow only sets $A \subseteq V(G)$ with $|A| \leq k$. Let us consider the extremal case when $k = 1$, i.e. the tests consist in asking questions of the form: Is v end-vertex of the unknown edge e^*? Clearly, the binary and ternary variants are the same in this situation. Let us denote by $L_1(G)$ the worst-case cost.

Since isolated vertices are clearly irrelevant, we assume that G does not contain any. Recall that $k(G)$ is the number of connected components of G.

Proposition 3.33. *Let $G(V, E)$ be a graph with $L_1(G) = L$. Then*

i) $| E | \leq (\begin{array}{c} L + 1 \\ 2 \end{array}) + 1$

ii) $| V | \leq (\begin{array}{c} L + 1 \\ 2 \end{array}) + 1 + k(G) \leq (\begin{array}{c} L + 2 \\ 2 \end{array}) + 1.$

Proof. We prove i) by induction on L. For $L = 1$, the information-theoretic bound says $| E | \leq 2 = (\begin{array}{c} L + 1 \\ 2 \end{array}) + 1$. Suppose v is the first test-vertex in an optimal algorithm for G. If $d(v) > L$ and the answer is "yes", then the second end-vertex w of e^* is among the $d(v)$ neighbors of v. It is clear that any algorithm will need at least $d(v) - 1 \geq L$ further tests to determine w in the worst case whence $L_1(G) \geq L + 1$, contrary to the assumption. We conclude that the first vertex v must satisfy $d(v) \leq L$. There is an edge not incident with v, since otherwise $G = K_{1,d(v)}$ and the choice of v would clearly not be optimal. Now, if the answer is "no", then the problem is reduced to the subgraph $G' = G - v$ with $L_1(G') \leq L - 1$. We conclude by induction $|E(G')| \leq \binom{L}{2} + 1$, and thus $|E(G)| = d(v) + |E(G')| \leq \binom{L+1}{2} + 1$.

The first inequality in ii) follows immediately from the observation $|V(G)| \leq |E(G)| + k(G)$ (see **3.2**(ii)). For the second, observe that the number of components of G is bounded by $L + 1$ since G has no isolated vertices. □

Example 3.11. To see that the bounds in **3.33** are sharp consider the graph G of Figure 3.10.

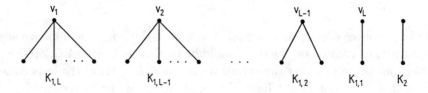

Figure 3.10

G consists of the sum $\sum_{i=1}^{L} K_{1,i}$ together with one further edge. Clearly, $L_1(G) = L$ (just ask $v_1, v_2, \ldots, v_L$ in this order), and we have $|E(G)| = \binom{L+1}{2} + 1$, $|V(G)| = \binom{L+2}{2} + 1$. Quite obviously, G is the only graph satisfying both inequalities. By successively identifying suitable vertices of G we obtain further examples of graphs G with $|E(G)| = \binom{L+1}{2} + 1$ and $|V(G)| = \binom{L+1}{2} + 1 + k(G)$.

No good characterization of the graphs with equality in **3.33**(i) is known, but there is a simple description of all graphs G with $|E(G)| = \binom{L_1+1}{2} + 1$ when only predetermined algorithms are permitted. The easy proof may be supplied by the reader.

Proposition 3.34. *Let $G(V,E)$ be a graph and L a natural number. The following conditions are equivalent.*

i) $L_{1,pre}(G) = L$ *and* $\mid E \mid = \binom{L+1}{2} + 1.$

ii) *There exists* $W \subseteq V$ *with* $\mid W \mid = L$ *such that* G_W *is complete, each vertex in* W *has degree* L, *and there is precisely one edge not incident with* W.

Example 3.12. Figure 3.11 gives an example of a graph G with $L_{1,pre}(G) = 4$ and $\mid E(G) \mid = 11$.

Figure 3.11

Solving the inequalities in **3.33** we obtain the following lower bounds for $L_1(G)$.

Corollary 3.35. *Let G be a graph with n vertices and m edges. Then*

i) $L_1(G) \geq \lceil \sqrt{2m - \frac{7}{4}} - \frac{1}{2} \rceil$

ii) $L_1(G) \geq \lceil \sqrt{2n - \frac{7}{4}} - \frac{3}{2} \rceil,$

and both bounds are sharp.

Let us turn to upper bounds. Since it is clearly not necessary to test all the vertices we have $L_1(G) \leq \mid V(G) \mid -1$ for all graphs G. The next result characterizes the extreme case. First we need a definition. Let $G(V, E)$ be a graph. The *complement* $\overline{G}$ of G has vertex-set V and edge-set $\binom{V}{2} - E$.

That is, the edge $e \in \binom{V}{2}$ is present in $E(\overline{G})$ precisely when it is not present in G.

For the proof we need one further observation. Suppose T is a tree on n vertices. We claim that the vertices of T can be labeled $v_1, \ldots, v_n$ in such a way that each $v_j (j \geq 2)$ is adjacent to at least one of its predecessors v_i, $i < j$. To see this, choose any vertex v_1. Suppose we have already picked vertices $v_1, \ldots, v_k$ satisfying the condition. If $k < n$ then it follows from the connectedness of T that there is a vertex v in $V - \{v_1, \ldots, v_k\}$ which is adjacent to at least one of $v_1, \ldots, v_k$. We set $v = v_{k+1}$, and the claim follows by induction.

Since any connected graph $G(V, E)$ contains a spanning tree, we can generalize our observation to arbitrary connected graphs. Let us call a labeling of $V = \{v_1, \ldots, v_n\}$ a *proper labeling* if the above condition is satisfied.

Proposition 3.36.   *Let $G(V, E)$ be a graph. Then $L_1(G) = |V| - 1$ iff $k(\overline{G}) \geq 3$.*

Proof.   Let us assume first that $k(\overline{G}) \leq 2$. In each of the connected components of $\overline{G}$ we choose a proper labeling $v_1, \ldots, v_r$ and $w_1, \ldots, w_s$ where the second set is empty if $k(\overline{G}) = 1$. Consider the sequence $S = (v_r, v_{r-1}, \ldots, v_2, w_s, w_{s-1}, \ldots, w_1, v_1)$. In G, no vertex of this sequence is adjacent to all of its successors except possibly w_1. We construct an algorithm $\mathcal{A}$ as follows: As long as the answer is "no", the vertices are asked according to S. When the answers are always "no", then the edge e^* is clearly determined after probing w_2. If, on the other hand, there is a "yes" before w_1, then we test the remaining neighbors of that vertex. By the way the sequence is set up we again need at most $|V| - 2$ tests.

Now suppose, conversely, that $\overline{G}$ has at least three components. If $v_1, \ldots, v_n$ is any permutation of the vertices, then among $\{v_1, \ldots, v_{n-2}\}$ there must be a vertex v_i not belonging to either the $\overline{G}$-component of v_{n-1} or v_n. Let v_k be such a vertex with largest index k, $k \leq n - 2$. It follows from the definition of k that v_k is adjacent in G to all successors v_j, $j > k$. This means that in any possible algorithm $v_1, v_2, \ldots$ there is a vertex v_k, $k \leq n - 2$, which is adjacent to all vertices not yet asked. Hence if the answer is "no" up to v_{k-1} and "yes" for v_k, then the algorithm will have length at least $n - 1$. $\square$

Using the same argument one can easily establish the following result.

Corollary 3.37. *Let $G(V, E)$ be a graph with $k(\overline{G}) = 2$. Then $L_1(G) = |V| - 2$.*

Example 3.13. The preceding result settles the complete graphs K_n and the complete bipartite graphs $K_{m,n}$. Looking at the complement we find $L_1(K_n) = n - 1$ and $L_1(K_{m,n}) = m + n - 2$. For forests, L_1 can attain any value between the lower bound **3.35** (see example 3.11) and $|V| - 2$ (for the stars).

For readers who are familiar with the complexity of algorithms (see e.g. the book by Garey-Johnson [1979]) we add that the determination of $L_1(G)$ is not so simple a problem as it may seem at first sight. In fact, determination of $L_1(G)$ for arbitrary graphs G is an NP-complete problem. Thus, although the test families in this situation are trivial to describe there is no hope to obtain fast search algorithms for arbitrary graphs.

Exercises 3.4.

1. Prove Proposition **3.34**.

2*. Prove Corollary **3.37**.

3. Discuss $L_{\leq 2}(G)$ when all test-sets of up to two vertices are allowed, and in general, $L_{\leq k}(G)$.

4*. Consider the following related recognition problem. Given the graph G. We are asked whether the unknown edge e^* belongs to G or to the complement $\overline{G}$. Let $L^r(G)$ be the worst-case cost. Obviously, $L^r(G) = L^r(\overline{G})$. Prove: $\min\{n - \alpha(G), n - \omega(G)\} \leq L^r(G) \leq \min\{n - \frac{\alpha(G)}{2}, n - \frac{\omega(G)}{2}\}$, where $\alpha(G)$ is the number of vertices in a largest subgraph without edges and $\omega(G)$ is the number of vertices in a largest complete subgraph.

5*. Denote by $\overline{L}_1(G)$ the average cost of determining e^* when all edges of G are equally likely. Show $\overline{L}_1(G) \leq \frac{2}{3}(n + 1)$.

6. Determine $\overline{L}_1(K_{m,n})$.

7*. Suppose the strategist player B employs the following "greedy" strategy. B says "no" as long as there is at least one possible edge left. Describe the length of this strategy S in terms of the graph.

8. Compute $L_1(P_n)$ and $L_1(C_n)$ where P_n and C_n are the path of length $n-1$ and cycle of length n, respectively. (Hint: Use the previous exercise.)

3.5   Searching For Subgraphs

In the last section our task consisted in identifying an unknown edge e^* by testing vertices. Now we go, so to speak, one dimension higher. Suppose we are given a class $\mathcal{G}$ of graphs on a fixed set V of n vertices. The unknown object G^* is a graph in $\mathcal{G}$ which we are required to determine by asking questions of the form: Is the edge e in G^*? Usually, we think of $\mathcal{G}$ as the set of all graphs enjoying a certain property. E.g., the property may be "without cycles", i.e. $\mathcal{G}$ is the set of all forests, or it may be "regular" meaning that all vertices have the same degree.

Let us denote by $L(\mathcal{G})$ the worst-case cost. Since there are $\binom{n}{2}$ possible edges to be asked we have

$$\lceil \log_2 |\,\mathcal{G}\,| \rceil \leq L(\mathcal{G}) \leq \binom{n}{2}.$$

It is convenient to think of the search process in question as a game between player A (Algy) and B (Strategist) as outlined in section 1.10. A wants to determine G^* with as few queries as possible and B tries to force A to ask as many questions as possible. We have seen in section 1.10 that $L(\mathcal{G})$ is the length of the game if both players play optimally. From our discussion there we know that the length $L(\mathcal{A})$ of any algorithm $\mathcal{A}$ is an upper bound for $L(\mathcal{G})$ whereas the length $L(\mathcal{S})$ of any strategy is a lower bound.

Consider the following strategy $\mathcal{S}_0$, called the *greedy strategy*. Player B says "no" as long as there is at least one member of $\mathcal{G}$ compatible with his answers. Suppose G is the graph consisting of the "yes"-edges at the end of the game, and H is the graph consisting of the unasked edges. Since the unknown graph $G^* \in \mathcal{G}$ is uniquely determined we infer that $G \cup H$ contains a unique subgraph in $\mathcal{G}$. Denote by $m(\mathcal{G})$ the maximal number of edges in a graph which has a unique subgraph in $\mathcal{G}$. Then

$$|\,E(H)\,| \leq |\,E(G \cup H)\,| \leq m(\mathcal{G}),$$

and thus

$$L(\mathcal{S}_0) = \binom{n}{2} - |E(H)| \geq \binom{n}{2} - m(\mathcal{G}).$$

Since $\mathcal{A}$ may choose the $\binom{n}{2} - m(\mathcal{G})$ edges first, we have in fact, $L(\mathcal{S}_0) = \binom{n}{2} - m(\mathcal{G})$, and thus the following general lower bound for $L(\mathcal{G})$, called the *greedy bound*.

Proposition 3.38. *Let $\mathcal{G}$ be a class of graphs on a fixed set V of n vertices, and let $m(\mathcal{G})$ be the maximal number of edges in a graph on V with a unique subgraph in $\mathcal{G}$. Then*

$$L(\mathcal{G}) \geq \binom{n}{2} - m(\mathcal{G}).$$

The greedy bound leads therefore to an extremal problem in graph theory. Before discussing the question of how good this bound is, let us look at an example.

Example 3.14. Suppose $\mathcal{G}$ is the class St of stars $K_{1,n-1}, n \geq 3$. Any star is determined by its center vertex. Hence there are n possible graphs in St leading to the information-theoretic lower bound $L(St) \geq \lceil \log_2 n \rceil$. Let us compute $m(St)$. Suppose a graph G on n vertices has a unique vertex v_0 with degree $d(v_0) = n - 1$. All other vertices must then satisfy $d(v) \leq n - 2$ from which we infer by **3.1**

$$|E(G)| \leq \frac{1}{2}(n - 1 + (n - 1)(n - 2)) = \frac{(n-1)^2}{2},$$

and thus $m(St) \leq \lfloor \frac{(n-1)^2}{2} \rfloor$, i.e. $L(St) \geq \binom{n}{2} - \lfloor \frac{(n-1)^2}{2} \rfloor = \lceil \frac{n-1}{2} \rceil$. The reader can easily convince himself that, in fact, $m(St) = \lfloor \frac{(n-1)^2}{2} \rfloor$ and further that $L(St) = \lceil \frac{n}{2} \rceil$. Hence the greedy bound is exact for n even and off by 1 if n is odd. Compare this with the information-theoretic bound $\lceil \log_2 n \rceil$.

Let us now discuss two more complicated classes of graphs where in the first case the greedy bound is exact, while in the second it is off by a linear term. First a definition: Let G be a graph with an even number n of vertices. A *matching* M in G is a set of $\frac{n}{2}$ edges which touch every vertex once and only once. Let us say that two edges are *independent* if they have no common end-vertex. A matching in G is then a set of $\frac{n}{2}$ pairwise independent edges.

Example 3.15. The bold edges in the graph of figure 3.12 form a matching.

Figure 3.12

The existence of matchings (particularly in bipartite graphs) is one of the fundamental problems in graph theory with applications in many other fields. The interested reader may consult the books by Mirsky [1971] or Bondy-Murty [1976].

Proposition 3.39. *Let $\mathcal{M}$ be the class of matchings on n vertices, $n \geq 2$ even. Then $L(\mathcal{M}) = \frac{n(n-2)}{4}$.*

Proof. We prove the upper bound first. For $n = 2$ there is nothing to show. We proceed by induction on n. For $u \in V$, let us call the unique vertex v such that uv is in the matching, the *mate* of u. Suppose $n \geq 4$. We pick any vertex $u \in V$ and test the edges ux, $x \in V$. To determine the mate v we clearly need at most $n - 2$ questions. The problem is now reduced to the remaining $n - 2$ vertices whence by induction

$$L(\mathcal{M}) \leq (n - 2) + \frac{(n - 2)(n - 4)}{4} = \frac{n(n - 2)}{4}.$$

To verify equality, we need to show by **3.38** that a graph G with a unique matching can have at most $\binom{n}{2} - \frac{n(n-2)}{4} = \frac{n^2}{4}$ edges, or in other words, that $m(\mathcal{M}) = \frac{n^2}{4}$. Suppose $v_1 w_1, \ldots, v_{n/2} w_{n/2}$ is the unique matching. Consider the first pair v_1, w_1. There are at most two edges leading from $\{v_1, w_1\}$ into any other pair $\{v_i, w_i\}$ since otherwise G would w.l.o.g. contain the edges $v_1 v_i, v_1 w_i, w_1 v_i$ whence we could replace $v_1 w_1, v_i w_i$ by $v_1 w_i, w_1 v_i$, thus obtaining a further matching of G. We conclude that $d(v_1) + d(w_1) \leq 2 + 2(\frac{n}{2} - 1) = n$. Applying the same reasoning to all pairs v_i, w_i we infer from **3.1**

$$\mid E(G) \mid = \frac{1}{2} \sum_{i=1}^{\frac{n}{2}} (d(v_i) + d(w_i)) \leq \frac{1}{2} \cdot \frac{n}{2} \cdot n = \frac{n^2}{4}. \qquad \square$$

The reader may show for himself that for any even n there is a unique graph G_n with a single matching achieving the maximum $\frac{n^2}{4}$. (Figure 3.13)

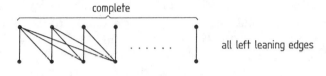

complete

all left leaning edges

Figure 3.13

As second example we consider the class T of trees on n vertices. We know that any such tree has precisely $n - 1$ edges. Now if a connected graph has at least n edges then it contains a cycle of length ≥ 3 and thus at least three spanning trees (just delete a different edge of the cycle each time). Hence $m(T) = n - 1$, leading to the greedy bound $L(T) \geq \binom{n}{2} - (n - 1)$. Invoking again the fact that any tree has the same number $n - 1$ of edges we certainly nedd not test all edges, i.e. $L(T) \leq \binom{n}{2} - 1$. The following result shows that the upper bound provides the correct answer.

Proposition 3.40. *Let T be the class of trees on n vertices. Then $L(T) = \binom{n}{2} - 1$.*

Proof. By our remarks above, we have to find a strategy S for player B with length $L(S) = \binom{n}{2} - 1$. Suppose A is an optimal algorithm of length ℓ. We define S step by step. Let G_0 be the graph without edges and let G_i be the graph induced by the "yes"-edges after i tests. Let us call an edge $uv \notin E(G_i)$ *feasible* if $G_i \cup \{uv\}$ is still without cycles. H_i shall denote the subgraph induced by the feasible edges. A cycle $C \subseteq G_i \cup H_i$ is termed *critical* if $| E(C) \cap E(H_i) | \geq 2$.

Suppose, player A uses the edge uv for the $(i + 1)$-st test. Of course, $uv \in E(H_i)$ since otherwise A would not be optimal. Player B now answers

$$
\begin{array}{ll}
\text{"no"} & \text{if } uv \text{ is in a critical cycle} \\
\text{"yes"} & \text{otherwise.}
\end{array}
$$

First, we have to verify that S is a valid strategy, i.e. $G_i \cup H_i$ is connected
and G_i contains no cycle for all i. This is obviously true for $i = 0$, and
from the definition of strategy S it is clear that G_i has no cycles. Finally,
if $G_i \cup H_i$ is connected while $G_{i+1} \cup H_{i+1}$ is not, then uv would disconnect
$G_i \cup H_i$ and hence could not be in any cycle at all. By the set-up of the
strategy S, the answer to the $(i+1)$-st test would be "yes", i.e. $G_{i+1} \cup H_{i+1}$
would still be connected.

Let T be the uniquely determined tree after ℓ tests, and suppose $e_1, \ldots, e_t$
are the unasked edges. We show that the assumption $t \geq 2$ leads to a
contradiction.

Case 1. $T = G_\ell$. Let $e_1 = uv$. Since T is connected there is a path W from
u to v in $T = G_\ell$ (figure 3.14).

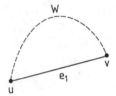

Figure 3.14

If xy is the edge in W that was tested last, say in the i-th test, then it is clear
that $e_1 \in H_{i-1}$. It follows that $W \cup \{e_1\}$ was a critical cycle at this point
whence $xy \in T$? would have received the answer "no", in contradiction to
$xy \in G_\ell = T$.

Case 2. $T = G_\ell \cup \{e_j\}$ for some j. G_ℓ must then consist of two components
joined by e_j (figure 3.15).

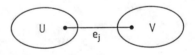

Figure 3.15

Any other edge e_k must also join U and V (same argument as in case 1). But this means that $G_\ell \cup \{e_k\}$ is also a tree in $G_\ell \cup H_\ell$, contradicting the uniqueness of T.

Case 3. $T = G_\ell \cup \{e_{j_1}, \ldots, e_{j_k}\}$, $k \geq 2$. G_ℓ contains at least three components U, V, W. Suppose w.l.o.g. that e_{j_1} joins U and V while e_{j_2} joins V and W (figure 3.16).

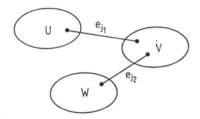

Figure 3.16

We infer that the last edge asked between U and W would have received the answer "yes" since it could not have been in a critical cycle. Since this edge is not present in G_ℓ, it must be in $\{e_1, \ldots, e_t\}$, say e. But then $(T \cup \{e\}) - \{e_{j_1}\}$ would be another tree in $G_\ell \cup H_\ell$, again contradicting the uniqueness of T. □

Denote by $\mathcal{B}$ the class of connected bipartite graphs on n vertices. Since $\mathcal{T} \subseteq \mathcal{B}$, we certainly have $L(\mathcal{B}) \geq \binom{n}{2} - 1$. The reader may verify that again not all edges need be tested thus establishing the following result.

Corollary 3.41. *Let $\mathcal{B}$ be the class of connected bipartite graphs on n vertices. Then $L(\mathcal{B}) = \binom{n}{2} - 1$.*

The exercises contain further results on other classes of graphs.

Remark. Why is the greedy bound good (in fact, exact) for matchings $\mathcal{M}$ while it is off by a linear term for $\mathcal{T}$? Observe that all matchings $\mathcal{M}$ are isomorphic to one another whereas there are many non-isomorphic trees. So it is tempting to conjecture that $L(\mathcal{G}) \sim \binom{n}{2} - m(\mathcal{G})$ if $\mathcal{G}$ contains only one or, at any rate, few isomorphism types. More generally, we know from Proposition **3.38** that $L(\mathcal{G})+m(\mathcal{G}) \geq \binom{n}{2}$. Perhaps it is true $L(\mathcal{G})+m(\mathcal{G}) \leq$

$\binom{n}{2} + f(n)$ where $f(n)$ grows slower than n^2, i.e. $\lim \frac{f(n)}{n^2} = 0$. Neither conjecture has been proved. A good condidate to test these claims is the class $\mathcal{C}$ of all cycles of length n. Clearly $\mathcal{C}$ has only one isomorphism type, but so far the best known algorithm differs from the greedy bound by a quadratic term in n (see exercises 3.5.5, 3.5.6).

Exercises 3.5.

1. Prove $L(St_n) = \lceil \frac{n}{2} \rceil, \ \ n \geq 3$.

2. Verify the uniqueness of the graph in figure 3.13.

3*. Show $L(\mathcal{B}) = \binom{n}{2} - 1$.

4*. Let $\mathcal{P}_n$ be the class of paths of length $n-1$ (called Hamiltonian paths). Show $m(\mathcal{P}_n) = \lfloor (\frac{n-1}{2})^2 \rfloor + 1$.

5. Let $\mathcal{H}_n$ be the class of cycles of length n (called Hamiltonian cycles). Show $m(\mathcal{H}_n) = \lfloor \frac{n^2}{4} \rfloor + 1$.

6*. Show $L(\mathcal{H}_n) \leq (n-1) + L(\mathcal{P}_{n-3})$.

7. Prove $L(\mathcal{P}_n) \leq \binom{n}{2} - (2n-9)$, and show a corresponding inequality for $L(\mathcal{H}_n)$.

8*. Let $\mathcal{K}_\ell$ be the class of complete graphs on $\ell \leq n$ vertices. Show $m(\mathcal{K}_\ell) = \binom{\ell}{2} + (\ell-2)(n-\ell) + \binom{\ell-1}{2}k^2 + \binom{r}{2} + rk(\ell-2)$ where $n - \ell = k(\ell-1) + r, 0 \leq r < \ell - 1$.

9. Prove $L(\mathcal{K}_\ell) = \binom{n}{2} - m(\mathcal{K}_\ell)$ for $n \geq (\ell-1)(\ell-2) + (r+1)$ where $n - \ell = k(\ell-1) + r, 0 < r < \ell - 1$, and $n \geq (\ell-1)^2 + 1$ when $r = 0$.

10. Generalize the class $\mathcal{M}$ of matchings to $\mathcal{M}_k$, the class consisting of k independent edges, $k \leq \frac{n}{2}$. Prove $m(\mathcal{M}_k) = k^2$ and show that the greedy bound is exact.

3.6 Recognizing Subgraphs

Some very interesting and entirely novel questions arise when we consider the recognition problem for graphs. We use again the terminology of section 1.10. Suppose a class G of graphs on a set V of n vertices is given. Player A wants to determine whether the unknown graph G^* lies in G or not, by asking questions: Is the edge e in G^*? Again we mostly think of G as a *graph property*. Player A is thus faced with the task of determining whether or not the unknown graph has the given property.

Let us look at this problem in full generality. We are given a set T of t elements $e_1, \ldots, e_t$, a family of subsets $\mathfrak{E} \subseteq 2^T$, and an unknown set $X \subseteq T$. Player A wants to decide whether or not $X \in \mathfrak{E}$ by asking questions: Is $x \in X$? for elements $x \in T$. The length of the game, provided both players perform optimally, is called the *recognition complexity* $C(\mathfrak{E})$ of $\mathfrak{E}$. If $\mathfrak{E} = \emptyset$ or $\mathfrak{E} = 2^T$, then obviously $C(\mathfrak{E}) = 0$ whence we call these two families *trivial*. For the sequel we tacitly assume that $\mathfrak{E}$ is always non-trivial.

Example 3.16. Suppose $\mathfrak{E}_k = \binom{T}{k}$ consists of all subsets of T of cardinality k. Player B uses the following simple strategy. He answers "yes" to the first k questions and "no" from then on. Now it is clear that A has to keep on asking till the end since if there is at least one element left, X could still contain $k + 1$ elements and hence not be in $\mathfrak{E}_k$. Thus $C(\mathfrak{E}_k) = t$.

Testing some small examples the reader will find that most of the families $\mathfrak{E}$ will enjoy the same property $C(\mathfrak{E}) = t$. Let us give them a name. We call a family $\mathfrak{E} \subseteq 2^T$ *elusive* if $C(\mathfrak{E}) = t$.

Let us note two facts. The recognition problem for $\mathfrak{E} \subseteq 2^T$ is clearly equivalent to that for $\mathfrak{E}^c = 2^T - \mathfrak{E}$, thus $C(\mathfrak{E}) = C(\mathfrak{E}^c)$. Now define $\mathfrak{E}^* = \{A \subseteq T : A^c = T - A \in \mathfrak{E}\}$. Then again $C(\mathfrak{E}) = C(\mathfrak{E}^*)$. To see this, one just has to note that an optimal strategy for $\mathfrak{E}$ induces an optimal strategy (of the same length) for $\mathfrak{E}^*$ by replacing every "yes" by a "no", and conversely. Let us call this fact the *duality principle*. It will prove quite useful in many instances.

The following simple strategy, called again the *greedy strategy* S_0, is probably the first that any player B will try. B says "yes" as long as there is at least one member of $\mathfrak{E}$ possible, and otherwise "no". Observe that this was precisely the strategy used in example 3.16.

The following result characterizes the families $\mathfrak{C}$ for which this strategy has length t, proving in particular that all these families are elusive.

Proposition 3.42. *Let $\mathfrak{C} \subseteq 2^T$ be given. The greedy strategy has length $L(S_0) = t$ precisely when the following exchange axiom on $\mathfrak{C}$ holds:*

(3.16)   *For all $U \in \mathfrak{C}$ and all $x \in U$ with $U - x \in \mathfrak{C}$ there*
            exist $y \in U^c$ and $V \in \mathfrak{C}$ such that $U - x \cup y \subseteq V$.

Proof. Suppose (3.16) is satisfied, and assume contrary to our claim that $L(S_0) < t$. Denote by Y the set of "yes"-elements or, as we say, the *accepted* elements, and by N the set of "no"-elements (the *refused* elements). Since not all elements were tested we must have $Y \cup N \neq T$, i.e. $N^c - Y \neq \emptyset$. By the definition of S_0 we infer that $W \in \mathfrak{C}$ for all W with $Y \subseteq W \subseteq N^c$. Setting $U = N^c$ and choosing any $x \in U - Y$ we conclude $U \in \mathfrak{C}, U - x \in \mathfrak{C}$. Condition (3.16) guaranties therefore the existence of $y \in N$ and $V \in \mathfrak{C}$ with $U - x \cup y \subseteq V$. This, however, implies $Y \subseteq U - x \cup y \subseteq V \in \mathfrak{C}$. Hence Player B would by his strategy have answered "yes" to the question $y \in X?$, in contradiction to $y \in N$.

We now assume that condition (3.16) is violated. Hence there exist $U \in \mathfrak{C}$ and $x \in U$ with $U - x \in \mathfrak{C}$ such that for all $y \in U^c$ the set $U - x \cup y$ is never contained in an $\mathfrak{C}$-set. Player A tests first the elements of $U - x$ and then those of U^c. Using S_0 player B answers "yes" to the first part of queries, and "no" from then on. After these $t - 1$ tests the unknown set X can only be $U - x$ or U, and since both of these sets are in $\mathfrak{C}$, A does indeed know the answer after $t - 1$ tests.   □

Remark. Looking at (3.16) one might be tempted to think that perhaps the condition $U - x \in \mathfrak{C}$ is superfluous. But this is not so. Since this altered condition is stronger than (3.16) it certainly implies $L(S_0) = t$. The converse, however, is not true. Just take $\mathfrak{C}$ to consist of a single set U, $\mathfrak{C} = \{U\}$, with $\emptyset \subsetneq U \subsetneq T$. The stronger condition is then certainly not satisfied, but it is obvious that $L(S_0) = t$ still holds.

Using the duality principle we can establish the following companion result to **3.42**. Denote by S_0^* the following strategy of B. B says "no" as long as there is at least one member of $\mathfrak{C}$ possible, and otherwise "yes".

Corollary 3.43. *Let $\mathfrak{C} \subseteq 2^T$ be given. The strategy $\mathcal{S}_0^*$ has length $L(\mathcal{S}_0^*) = t$ if and only if the following condition on $\mathfrak{C}$ holds:*

(3.17)   *For all $U \in \mathfrak{C}$ and all $y \in U^c$ with $U \cup y \in \mathfrak{C}$ there*
         exist $x \in U$ and $V \in \mathfrak{C}$ such that $U \cup y - x \supseteq V$.

Example 3.17. Quite a number of families $\mathfrak{C}$ satisfy (3.16) or (3.17) and are thus elusive. E.g., when $\mathfrak{C} \subseteq \binom{T}{k}$, i.e. all sets in $\mathfrak{C}$ have the same size, then (3.16) is trivially satisfied. In particular, if $\mid \mathfrak{C} \mid = 1$ then $\mathfrak{C}$ is elusive. Suppose $\mathfrak{C} = \{C, D\}$. If $|C| = |D|$, then $\mathfrak{C}$ is elusive as just remarked. So suppose $\mid C \mid < \mid D \mid$. For condition (3.16) to fail we must have $D = C \cup x$ for some x, so in this case neither the greedy strategy $\mathcal{S}_0$ nor its counterpart $\mathcal{S}_0^*$ works. By employing the same algorithm as in the second part of the proof of **3.42** it is clear that A can indeed determine X with less than t probes. For example, if $T = \{x_1, \ldots, x_t\}$ and $C = \{x_1, \ldots, x_k\}$, $D = C \cup \{x_{k+1}\}$, then A probes $x_1, \ldots, x_k$ first. If there is a "no", then the game is over since $X \notin \mathfrak{C}$. Otherwise, A proceeds to probe $\{x_{k+2}, \ldots, x_t\}$. If there is a "yes", then again the game is finished with $X \notin \mathfrak{C}$. But if B always answers "no", then A knows after $t - 1$ questions that X is in $\mathfrak{C}$. Incidentally, it is clear that $L(\mathfrak{C}) = t - 1$ in this situation. Another family that trivially satisfies (3.16) is $\mathfrak{C} = \bigcup_{i=0}^{k} \binom{T}{i}$ for all $k \leq n - 1$.

The families considered in example 3.17 are not really very interesting. E.g., for the graph properties to be considered later on, the families $\mathfrak{C}$ are much larger. In addition, they divide into certain isomorphism classes as remarked in the previous section. To generalize this isomorphism idea to arbitrary families $\mathfrak{C}$, the following concept is suggested. Consider the group Σ_T of all permutations of T. A subgroup $\Gamma \leq \Sigma_T$ is called *transitive* if to any $u, v \in T$ there is a permutation $\sigma \in \Gamma$ with $\sigma(u) = v$. Applying σ to a set $A \subseteq T$ we obtain the set A^σ. A^Γ denotes the family of all distinct sets A^σ, $\sigma \in \Gamma$, and $\mathfrak{C}^\Gamma = \bigcup\{A^\Gamma : A \in \mathfrak{C}\}$. Since $A^{id} = A$ we have, of course, $\mathfrak{C}^\Gamma \supseteq \mathfrak{C}$. We call $\mathfrak{C}$ *invariant under* Γ if $\mathfrak{C}^\Gamma = \mathfrak{C}$.

Proposition 3.44. *Let $\mathfrak{C} \subseteq 2^T$ be invariant under a transitive permutation group $\Gamma \leq \Sigma_T$. If $\mathfrak{C}$ satisfies:*

(3.18)   *there is no triple of $\mathfrak{C}$-sets $U \subseteq V \subseteq W$ with*

$$| W | = | V | + 1 = | U | + 2,$$

then $\mathfrak{C}$ *is elusive.*

Proof. If the strategy $\mathcal{S}_0^*$ has length $L(\mathcal{S}_0^*) = t$, then we are done. Hence we may assume $L(\mathcal{S}_0^*) < t$. By (3.17) this implies the existence of $U \in \mathfrak{C}$, $y \in U^c$ with $U \cup y \in \mathfrak{C}$ such that for all $x \in U$, $U \cup y - x$ never contains an $\mathfrak{C}$-set. Since $\mathfrak{C}$ is invariant under a transitive permutation group, we may clearly assume w.l.o.g. that player A probes first the element y. Player B uses now the following strategy $\mathcal{S}_1$. He says "yes" to y and thereafter "yes" to an element z iff $z \in U$. Let us look at the state of the game after $s < t$ questions with Y the set of accepted elements and N the set of refused elements. By the set-up of $\mathcal{S}_1$ we have

$$y \in Y \subseteq U \cup y \subseteq N^c.$$

If $Y = U \cup y$, then $U, Y = U \cup y \in \mathfrak{C}$ whence it follows from condition (3.18) that $Y \cup w \notin \mathfrak{C}$ for all $t - s$ elements w that have not yet been tested. It follows that player A cannot be sure whether or not the unknown set X is in $\mathfrak{C}$. If, on the other hand, $Y \subsetneq U \cup y$, then $Y \subseteq U \cup y - x$ for all $x \in U - Y$ (these x have not been probed), and thus $Y \notin \mathfrak{C}$ by the choice of U. Again, A cannot be certain about the outcome, and the proof is complete. $\square$

Before going further let us apply our results to graphs. We consider a fixed underlying set V of n vertices. The set T used in the preceding discussion is the set of all possible edges, i.e. $T = \binom{V}{2}$. Any graph $G(V, E)$ is then identified with $E \subseteq T$. In this way a family $\mathfrak{C} \subseteq 2^T$ corresponds to a family $\mathcal{G}$ of graphs on V precisely as in the last section. We again call $\mathcal{G}$ *elusive* if $C(\mathcal{G}) = \binom{n}{2}$, meaning that A has to probe all edges before he can be sure about the answer.

According to example 3.17, any family $\mathcal{G}$ is elusive all of whose members of $\mathcal{G}$ contain the same number of edges. In particular, this is the case for the family $\mathcal{T}$ of trees, for matchings $\mathcal{M}$ (for even n) and for the stars St. What about forests $\mathcal{F}$? Of course, $\mathcal{F}$ contains $\mathcal{T}$, but in the present situation it is not true that $\mathcal{G} \subseteq \mathcal{H}$ implies $C(\mathcal{G}) \leq C(\mathcal{H})$, as can be seen from the trivial example when $\mathcal{H} = 2^T$ is the family of all graphs for which $C(\mathcal{H}) = 0$ holds. Condition (3.16) is, however, satisfied for forests as the following figure shows: Let $A_1, \ldots, A_k$ be the components of the forest F, with, say,

$x \in E(A_1)$. The edge x disconnect A_1 and there must be another edge $y \in E(A_1)$ or from A_1 to A_2 making $F - x \cup y$ into a forest again.

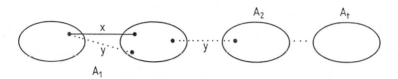

Figure 3.17

As remarked in several places before we will usually define a class $\mathcal{G}$ of graphs by a certain property, e.g. the class $\mathcal{F}$ of forests by the property of being without cycles or the class $\mathcal{C}$ by the property of being connected. This, in particular, means that $\mathcal{G}$ contains with G all graphs isomorphic to G. Let Σ_V be the symmetric group on V. Σ_V induces on $T = \binom{V}{2}$ the so-called *pair group* $\Sigma_T^{(2)}$. $\Sigma_T^{(2)}$ consists of all permutations $\sigma^{(2)}$ of T with $\sigma^{(2)}(uv) = (\sigma u, \sigma v)$, $uv \in E$, for $\sigma \in \Sigma_V$, and it is clear that two graphs $G(V, A)$ and $H(V, B)$ are isomorphic if and only if $B = \sigma^{(2)}(A)$ for some $\sigma^{(2)} \in \Sigma_T^{(2)}$.

The group $\Sigma^{(2)}$ is plainly transitive on T. Furthermore, if $\mathcal{G}$ consists of isomorphism classes of graphs, then $\mathcal{G}$ is invariant under $\Sigma^{(2)}$. Let us use the notation $\mathcal{P}$ (for property) instead of $\mathcal{G}$ to indicate the fact that $\mathcal{P}$ consists of isomorphism classes of graph. The *order* $o(\mathcal{P})$ is the number of different isomorphism classes in $\mathcal{P}$. Note the obvious fact that isomorphic graphs contain the same number of edges.

As a consequence of **3.44** we note a result first proved by Bollobás and Eldridge:

Corollary 3.45. *Any graph property $\mathcal{P}$ with $o(\mathcal{P}) \leq 2$ is elusive.*

The reader may show that any non-trivial graph property with $n \leq 5$ is elusive. But for $n = 6$ this is not so anymore. Figure 3.18 displays three non-isomorphic graphs on 6 vertices whose induced property $\mathcal{P}$ is non-elusive. In fact, there are non-elusive properties of order 3 for any $n \geq 6$ (see exercise 3.6.3).

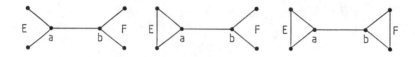

Figure 3.18

To verify $C(\mathcal{P}) \leq 14 < \binom{6}{2}$ for property $\mathcal{P}$ of figure 3.18 we proceed, in the role of player A, as follows. Note first that $d(a) = d(b) = 3$ and $d(u) \leq 2$ for $u \neq a, b$ in all three graphs. We pick any vertex v_1 and test all its 5 incident edges. If we always receive "no", then $X \notin \mathcal{P}$ and we are done. Otherwise we select a vertex v_2 adjacent to v_1 (in X) and test all 4 incident edges (other than v_1v_2). Now we pick a vertex v_3 adjacent in X to v_1 or v_2 and test all its edges. Either we know $X \notin \mathcal{P}$ after these tests or at least one of the center vertices a, b must have been among $\{v_1, v_2, v_3\}$. If exactly one of the v_i's has degree 3, say a, then v_1, v_2, v_3 are the vertices in $E \cup a$; in the other case we may assume that the vertex v_i of degree ≤ 2 is in E, say c (see figure 3.19 where the dashed lines may or may not be in the graph).

Figure 3.19

In the first case we test all edges incident with b, and in the second all edges incident with d. Either an edge arises not present in the graphs of figure 3.18 implying $X \notin \mathcal{P}$, or this is not so implying $X \in \mathcal{P}$. In either case, the edge in F need not be tested. The reader may easily construct a strategy of length 14, thus proving $C(\mathcal{P}) = 14$.

So far, all graph properties considered have been elusive or at any rate very close to it, needing cn^2 probes. The following ingenious example due to Best, van Emde Boas and Lenstra [1974] shows that there are, however, properties $\mathcal{P}$ whose complexity $C(\mathcal{P})$ is linear in n.

Call a graph a *scorpion graph* on n vertices if it contains a vertex b of degree $n-2$ (the *body*), a vertex t of degree 1 (the *tail*), and a vertex u of degree 2,

the *link*, which is joined to b and t. The remaining $n-3$ vertices are allowed
to form any graph whatsoever (figure 3.20).

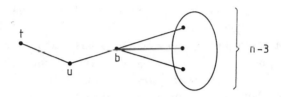

Figure 3.20

Proposition 3.46. *The property $\mathcal{P}$ of being a scorpion graph satisfies*
$C(\mathcal{P}) \le 6n - 10$.

Proof. We may assume $n \ge 5$. It is clear that player A is interested to pin
down the body b and the tail t. Suppose at some stage of the algorithm, G
is the graph induced by the accepted edges, and H the graph induced by
the refused edges. We call a vertex v a *candidate body* if at most one edge
incident with v has been refused till then, i.e. $d_H(v) \le 1$. The candidate
body has *weight* 2 or 1 according to whether $d_H(v) = 0$ or $d_H(v) = 1$. The
vertex v is a *candidate tail* if $d_G(v) \le 1$ with weight 2 or 1 if $d_G(v) = 0$ or
1, respectively.
Let $V = \{v_1, \ldots, v_n\}$. Player A uses the following algorithm. First, he tests
all edges around a cycle C, $v_1 v_2, v_2 v_3, \ldots, v_n v_1$. After these n tests, V splits
into three parts:

$$B = \{u : d_C(u) = 2\}, \quad M = \{u : d_C(u) = 1\}, \quad \text{and} \quad T = \{u : d_C(u) = 0\}.$$

Clearly, M contains an even number m of vertices. If $m = 0$, then one of the
sets B or T is empty, implying X is not a scorpion graph. If $m = 2$ and the
two vertices of M are neighbors in C, then we are in the situation $\beta = \tau = 2$
treated below, and A actually needs less than $5n$ tests. Otherwise there exist
$\frac{m}{2}$ edges, not yet asked, connecting the vertices of M in pairs. With these $\frac{m}{2}$
tests, M splits into $B_1 = \{u : d(u) = 2\}$ and $T_1 = \{u : d(u) = 1\}$. After these
$n + \frac{m}{2}$ probes we have the following situation: B and B_1 consist of candidate
bodies of weights 2 and 1, respectively, whereas T and T_1 consist of candidate

tails of weights 2 and 1, respectively. Note that the sum of the weights of all candidates is $2 \mid B \mid + \mid B_1 \mid +2 \mid T \mid + \mid T_1 \mid = 2(n - m) + m = 2n - m$.

In the next step, A asks only for edges between candidate bodies and candidate tails. With every question the sum of the weigths is reduced by 1. Hence after at most $2n - m - 2$ tests, all such edges have been probed, or else X is not a scorpion graph. So far A has asked at most $3n - \frac{m}{2} - 2$ questions. Suppose at this stage, B_0 is the set of candidate bodies, and T_0 the set of candidate tails with $\mid B_0 \mid = \beta$ and $\mid T_0 \mid = \tau$. The number of accepted edges between B_0 and T_0 is at most τ, and the number of refused edges is at most β. Since all edges between B_0 and T_0 have been probed, we conclude $\beta\tau \leq \beta + \tau$, i.e. $(\beta - 1)(\tau - 1) \leq 1$. Therefore either $\min(\beta, \tau) \leq 1$ or $\beta = \tau = 2$.

If $\min(\beta, \tau) = 0$, then X is not a scorpion graph. Suppose G is the graph composed of the accepted edges at this stage. If $\beta = 1$, then in order for G to be extendable to a scorpion graph, the unique candidate body b must be joined to all candidate tails in T_0 except one, t, which must be the unique tail. If $\tau = 1$, then the tail is uniquely determined. Now suppose $\beta = \tau = 2$, with $B_0 = \{a, b\}$, $T_0 = \{c, d\}$. If G is to be extendable to a scorpion graph, there must be precisely two disjoint edges in G joining B_0 and T_0, say ac, bd. Hence there are two possibilities: a is the body, d the tail and therefore b the link, or else b is the body, c the tail and a the link. Testing ax for any $x \notin B_0 \cup T_0$, we conclude a is the body (if the answer is "yes") or b is the body (if the answer is "no").

Now that player A has isolated the candidate body b or candidate tail t, it is clear from the set-up of the algorithm that he needs at most $3n - 7$ more questions, testing successively the edges incident with b, t and the link to determine the outcome where he may spare one question, already asked, if $\beta = \tau = 2$. Hence the total number of probes does not exceed $6n - \frac{m}{2} - 9 \leq 6n - 10$. $\quad\square$

The last proposition raises the question whether there is a general lower bound for non-trivial graph properties. The following observation, due to Milner and Welsh [1976], leads the way to establishing such a bound. Let $\mathcal{P}$ be a non-trivial property and suppose G is a graph, $G \notin \mathcal{P}$, all of whose proper subgraphs are in $\mathcal{P}$, $\mid E(G) \mid = e \geq 0$. Player B chooses a fixed copy of G and answers "yes" to the first $e - 1$ questions whenever an edge of G is probed, and otherwise "no". In this way, A is obviously forced to make at least e probes, whence $C(\mathcal{P}) \geq e$.

To complement this observation we give the following definition: Let G, H be two graphs on n vertices. We say that G and H can be *packed* if there are two edge-disjoint copies of G and H (in K_n). Figure 3.21 shows a packing of the graphs on the lefthand side.

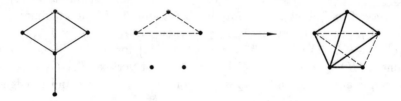

Figure 3.21

In other words, G and H can be packed if $G \subseteq \overline{H}$ or equivalently $H \subseteq \overline{G}$, where the subgraph inclusion refers to the isomorphism types. Suppose m is the largest integer, $m \leq (\begin{smallmatrix} n \\ 2 \end{smallmatrix})$, such that any graphs G and H with $\mid E(G) \mid + \mid E(H) \mid \leq m$ can be packed. Then we claim that m is a lower bound for the complexity $C(\mathcal{P})$ of any non-trivial property $\mathcal{P}$. Suppose $\emptyset \in \mathcal{P}$. Let e be the number of edges in a graph $G \notin \mathcal{P}$ all of whose proper subgraphs are in $\mathcal{P}$. If $e \geq m$, then $C(\mathcal{P}) \geq m$ by our remark above. If, on the other hand, $e < m$, then B answers "no" to the first $m - e$ questions. Let H be the graph composed of these edges. Since we know that G and H can be packed, B can now choose a suitable copy of $G \notin \mathcal{P}$ and answers "yes" to the next $e - 1$ questions if the edge is in G and "no" otherwise. Doing so he clearly forces A to ask at least e more questions whence again $C(\mathcal{P}) \geq m$. If, however, $\emptyset \notin \mathcal{P}$ then the reader may easily supply a similar reasoning by considering a graph $G \in \mathcal{P}$, all of whose proper subgraphs are not in $\mathcal{P}$.

The following result due to Sauer and Spencer [1978] determines the best possible m for a packing.

Proposition 3.47. *Let G and H be graphs on n vertices. If $\mid E(G) \mid + \mid E(H) \mid \leq \lfloor \frac{3}{2}(n-1) \rfloor$, then G and H can be packed, and this bound is best possible.*

Proof. That $\lfloor \frac{3}{2}(n - 1) \rfloor$ cannot be improved follows immediately from the example when $G = K_{1,n-1}$ and H is a set of $\lfloor \frac{n-1}{2} \rfloor + 1$ disjoint edges, which graphs can obviously not be packed.

By adding edges we may assume $|E(G)| + |E(H)| = \lfloor \frac{3}{2}(n-1) \rfloor$ and $|E(G)| \le |E(H)|$. The result is obvious for $n \le 4$, so let us assume $n \ge 5$. We proceed by induction on n. If one of the graphs has an isolated vertex u and the other graph has a vertex v of degree ≥ 2, then we can put u on top of v and proceed by induction. Denote by $\Delta(G)$ and $\Delta(H)$ the maximal degree of G and H, respectively. If $\Delta(H) \le 1$, then $| E(H) | \le \frac{n}{2}$ by **3.1**, and thus $| E(G) | + | E(H) | \le \frac{n}{2} + \frac{n}{2} = n < \lfloor \frac{3}{2}(n-1) \rfloor$ for $n \ge 5$. Hence we may assume $\Delta(H) \ge 2$ and that G has no isolated vertex. Let $G_1, \ldots, G_k$ be the components of G and suppose G_i contains n_i vertices and e_i edges. If $e_i \ge \frac{3}{4}n_i$ for all i, then $| E(G) | = \sum_{i=1}^{k} e_i \ge \frac{3}{4} \sum_{i=1}^{k} n_i = \frac{3}{4}n$, in contradiction to $| E(G) | \le \frac{1}{2}\lfloor \frac{3}{2}(n-1) \rfloor < \frac{3}{4}n$. Hence we conclude there exists a component G_1 of G with $\frac{e_1}{n_1} < \frac{3}{4}$. Since G_1 has no isolated vertex, G_1 must be either a single edge or a path of length 2.

Case 1. G_1 is an edge xy. From $| E(H) | \le \lfloor \frac{3}{2}(n-1) \rfloor - \frac{n}{2} < n - 1$ we know that H contains at least 2 components and further $\Delta(H) \le n - 2$. Let $u \in V(H)$ be a vertex of maximal degree, $d_H(u) \ge 2$, and v another vertex of H not adjacent to u. We put x on top of u, y on top of v, and can now complete the packing on the remaining $n - 2$ vertices by induction, since $\lfloor \frac{3}{2}(n-1) \rfloor - 3 = \lfloor \frac{3}{2}n - \frac{9}{2} \rfloor = \lfloor \frac{3}{2}(n-3) \rfloor$ (see figure 3.22 where the solid edges correspond to G and the dashed edges to H).

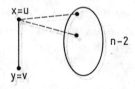

Figure 3.22

Case 2. G_1 is a path x, y, z. Since $d_G(y) = 2$ we infer that H has no isolated vertex. Let u be a vertex of maximal degree in H. If one of the H-components is a single edge, then we are back to case 1 with the roles of G and H interchanged. Otherwise choose a vertex v not in the H-component of u with at least two neighbors w, w'. Putting y on top of u, x on v, and

z on w we can complete the packing on the remaining $n - 3$ vertices by induction (figure 3.23). □

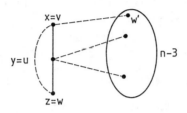

Figure 3.23

Corollary 3.48. *Any non-trivial graph property* $\mathcal{P}$ *satisfies* $C(\mathcal{P}) \geq \lfloor \frac{3}{2}(n - 1) \rfloor$.

By a careful analysis of the packing method, Bollobás and Eldridge [1978b] have shown that, in fact, $C(\mathcal{P}) \geq 2n - 4$ holds for any non-trivial property. So there is a gap for the precise lower bound between $2n$ and $6n$ which up to now remains unsettled.

In the remainder of this chapter we concentrate on elusive properties. First, we consider again the general situation when a non-trivial family $\mathfrak{E} \subseteq 2^T$ is given.

Definition. Let $\mathfrak{E} \subseteq 2^T$. The *counting polynomial* of $\mathfrak{E}$ in the indeterminate z is $p(\mathfrak{E}; z) = \sum\limits_{X \in \mathfrak{E}} z^{|X|} = \sum\limits_{i=0}^{t} a_i z^i$ where $a_i = |\,\{X \in \mathfrak{E} : |\,X\,| = i\}\,|$.

The following important result, obtained by several authors, shows how the counting polynomial is related to our recognition problem. As preparation we need a detailed description of families $\mathfrak{E}$ with $C(\mathfrak{E}) = k$. Let us call a family $\mathfrak{E} \subseteq 2^T$ $(t - k)$-*divisible* if $\mathfrak{E}$ is the disjoint union of intervals in the lattice 2^T, each of length $t - k$. That is, there exist families $I_j = [A_j, B_j] = \{X : A_j \subseteq X \subseteq B_j\}$ with $|\,B_j - A_j\,| = t - k$ for $j = 1, \ldots, s$, $I_j \cap I_{j'} = \emptyset$ for $j \neq j'$ and $\mathfrak{E} = \bigcup\limits_{j=1}^{s} I_j$. It is clear that for a disjoint union $\mathfrak{E} = \mathfrak{E}_1 \cup \mathfrak{E}_2$, one of the $\mathfrak{E}_i$'s is not $(t - k)$-divisible if $\mathfrak{E}$ is not $(t - k)$-divisible. Note further that $\emptyset$ is trivially $(t - k)$-divisible.

Proposition 3.49. *If $C(\mathfrak{E}) = k$, then $\mathfrak{E}$ is $(t-k)$-divisible.*

Proof. Let $\mathcal{A}$ be an optimal algorithm of length k and suppose $\mathfrak{E}$ is not $(t-k)$-divisible. We construct a strategy S for player B which forces A to ask more than k questions. As before we denote by Y_i the accepted elements at stage i and by N_i the refused elements.
In the beginning, $Y_0 = N_0 = \emptyset$. Suppose e_1 is the first element tested. We set

$$\mathfrak{E}_0 = \mathfrak{E}$$
$$\mathfrak{E}_{0,1} = \{X \in \mathfrak{E} : e_1 \in X\}$$
$$\mathfrak{E}_{0,2} = \{X \in \mathfrak{E} : e_1 \notin X\}.$$

Since $\mathfrak{E}_0 = \mathfrak{E}_{0,1} \mathbin{\dot\cup} \mathfrak{E}_{0,2}$ and $\mathfrak{E}_0$ is not $(t-k)$-divisible, we know one of $\mathfrak{E}_{0,1}$ or $\mathfrak{E}_{0,2}$ is not $(t-k)$-divisible, say $\mathfrak{E}_{0,j_1}$. Player B says "yes" precisely when $j_1 = 1$. Defining $\mathfrak{E}_1 = \mathfrak{E}_{0,j_1} = \{X \in \mathfrak{E} : Y_1 \subseteq X \subseteq N_1^c\}$ we conclude that $\mathfrak{E}_1$ is not $(t-k)$-divisible.
Let Y_i, N_i and $\mathfrak{E}_i = \{X \in \mathfrak{E} : Y_i \subseteq X \subseteq N_i^c\}$ for $1 \leq i < k$ already be determined, with $\mathfrak{E}_i$ not $(t-k)$-divisible. Suppose e_{i+1} is the next element to be probed. We set

$$\mathfrak{E}_{i,1} = \{X \in \mathfrak{E} : Y_i \cup e_{i+1} \subseteq X \subseteq N_i^c\}$$
$$\mathfrak{E}_{i,2} = \{X \in \mathfrak{E} : Y_i \subseteq X \subseteq (N_i \cup e_{i+1})^c\}.$$

Since $\mathfrak{E}_i$ is the disjoint union of $\mathfrak{E}_{i,1}$ and $\mathfrak{E}_{i,2}$ we infer again that one of $\mathfrak{E}_{i,1}$ or $\mathfrak{E}_{i,2}$ is not $(t-k)$-divisible, say $\mathfrak{E}_{i,j_{i+1}}$. Player B now answers "yes" if and only if $j_{i+1} = 1$. We now set $\mathfrak{E}_{i+1} = \mathfrak{E}_{i,j_{i+1}} = \{X \in \mathfrak{E}_i : Y_{i+1} \subseteq X \subseteq N_{i+1}^c\}$. In this way, the game ends after k tests with Y_k, N_k and $\mathfrak{E}_k = \{X \in \mathfrak{E} : Y_k \subseteq X \subseteq N_k^c\}$ where $\mathfrak{E}_k$ is not $(t-k)$-divisible. Since the outcome is now certain, $\mathfrak{E}_k$ must be either $\mathfrak{E}_k = \emptyset$ or $\mathfrak{E}_k = [Y_k, N_k^c]$. But $\mid N_k^c - Y_k \mid = t - \mid Y_k \cup N_k \mid = t - k$. So $\mathfrak{E}_k$ is in either case $(t-k)$-divisible, and this is our desired contradiction. $\square$

Very recently, Grieser has shown the following partial converse of **3.49**: Suppose $\mathfrak{E}$ is $(t-k)$-divisible, $\mathfrak{E} = \bigcup_{j=1}^{s} I_j$, then $C(\mathfrak{E}) \leq 2k \ln s$.

Theorem 3.50. *Let $\mathfrak{E} \subseteq 2^T$. If $C(\mathfrak{E}) = k$, then the counting polynomial $p(\mathfrak{E}; z)$ is divisible by $(1+z)^{t-k}$.*

Proof. By our previous proposition, $\mathfrak{C} = \bigcup_{j=1}^{s} I_j$ where the I_j's are pairwise disjoint intervals of length $t - k$. Clearly, $p(I_j; z) = z^{|A_j|}(1 + z)^{t-k}$ with $I_j = [A_j, B_j]$ for all j, and thus

$$p(\mathfrak{C}; z) = \sum_{X \in \mathfrak{C}} z^{|X|} = \sum_{j=1}^{s} \sum_{X \in I_j} z^{|X|} = (1 + z)^{t-k} \sum_{j=1}^{s} z^{|A_j|}. \qquad \square$$

To compute the counting polynomial for a family $\mathfrak{C}$ is, in general, quite difficult. Still, as we shall see in a moment, many interesting graph properties can be shown to be elusive by an application of **3.50**. Let us turn the statement around. If $(1 + z)^i | p(\mathfrak{C}; z)$, then $C(\mathfrak{C}) \geq t - i + 1$. In particular, $(1 + z) | p(\mathfrak{C}; z)$ or, in other words, $p(\mathfrak{C}; -1) \neq 0$ implies that $\mathfrak{C}$ is elusive. Since $p(\mathfrak{C}; -1) = | \{X \in \mathfrak{C} : |X| \text{ even}\} | - | \{X \in \mathfrak{C} : |X| \text{ odd}\} |$ we have the following result.

Corollary 3.51. *Let* $\mathfrak{C} \subseteq 2^T$.

i) *If the number of sets in $\mathfrak{C}$ with even cardinality is not equal to the number of sets in $\mathfrak{C}$ with odd cardinality, then $\mathfrak{C}$ is elusive.*

ii) *If $| \mathfrak{C} |$ is odd, then $\mathfrak{C}$ is elusive.*

Example 3.18. Let us compute the counting polynomial for the scorpion graphs $\mathcal{S}c_n$, $n \geq 5$. We can choose the three distinguished vertices in $n(n - 1)(n - 2)$ ways. Hence $p(\mathcal{S}c_n; z) = n(n - 1)(n - 2)z^{n-1}(1 + z)^{\binom{n-3}{2}}$ and thus $C(\mathcal{S}c_n) \geq \binom{n}{2} - \binom{n-3}{2} = 3n - 6$. Note that this bound is not exact since for $n = 5$ there are only two non-isomorphic scorpion graphs implying $C(\mathcal{S}c_5) = 10$ by **3.45**, whereas $3n - 6 = 9$ for $n = 5$. Grieser has recently improved the lower bound to $C(\mathcal{S}c_n) \geq (3 + \alpha)n - C_\alpha$ for every α with $0 < \alpha < 1.5$ and $n > N_\alpha$. Let us look at two more properties. Suppose St is the property that the graph is a star (of any degree). Since a star is uniquely determined by its center, if it contains at least two edges, we compute

$$p(St; -1) = 1 - \binom{n}{2} + n \sum_{i=2}^{n-1} \binom{n-1}{i}(-1)^i$$

$$= \binom{n-1}{2} \neq 0.$$

Hence St is elusive.

As our final example, we consider connected graphs $\mathcal{C}$. Let $g_n(z)$ be the counting polynomial of all graphs with n vertices, thus $g_1(z) = 1$ and $g_n(z) = (1+z)^{\binom{n}{2}}$ for $n \geq 2$. Let $c_n(z)$ be the counting polynomial of connected graphs. We fix one vertex u and classify the graphs according to the component H containing u. Suppose H contains k vertices. We can choose the $k-1$ vertices different from u in $\binom{n-1}{k-1}$ ways and obtain as counting polynomial of H precisely $c_k(z)$. The remaining $n-k$ vertices form any graph so their counting polynomial is $g_{n-k}(z)$. Combining these two polynomials we arrive at the recursion

$$g_n(z) = \sum_{k=1}^{n} \binom{n-1}{k-1} c_k(z) g_{n-k}(z),$$

with the convention $g_0(z) = 1$.

At $z = -1$ this yields $g_n(-1) = 0$ for $n \geq 2$, and thus

$$
\begin{aligned}
1 &= c_1(-1) \\
0 &= c_n(-1) + (n-1)c_{n-1}(-1) \quad \text{for } n \geq 2.
\end{aligned}
$$

We conclude $c_n(-1) = (-1)^{n-1}(n-1)! \neq 0$. Thus property $\mathcal{C}$ is elusive.

Our final results take us to the beginning of this topic. In 1973, Rosenberg conjectured that every non-trivial graph property $\mathcal{P}$ has a complexity $\geq cn^2$ for some positive constant c. As we have seen, the scorpion graphs are a counterexample to this conjecture. Together with Aanderaa, Rosenberg weakened his conjecture stating that every non-trivial *monotone* graph property $\mathcal{P}$ satisfies $C(\mathcal{P}) \geq cn^2$ for some constant c. This latter conjecture has been proved true by Rivest and Vuillemin [1976], and we conclude this chapter with a presentation of their elegant results.

Definition. A graph property $\mathcal{P}$ is called *monotone* if $G \in \mathcal{P}$ and $H \subseteq G$ implies $H \in \mathcal{P}$.

We might as well have defined monotone by the ascending condition $G \in \mathcal{P}$, $H \supseteq G \implies H \in \mathcal{P}$. But since the complementary family $\mathcal{P}^c$ of every monotone ascending property $\mathcal{P}$ is monotone in our sense, this would yield nothing new.

We begin again with arbitrary families $\mathfrak{C} \subseteq 2^T$. In analogy to our definition for graphs, we call $\mathfrak{C}$ *monotone*, if $\mathfrak{C}$ contains with U every subset of U.

Monotone families are called *complexes* in topology (see section 2.4), and we will use this latter term from now on. Let us denote by $\Gamma(\mathfrak{C}) \leq \Sigma_T$ the group of all permutations of T which leave $\mathfrak{C}$ invariant. Intuition leads to the guess that player B will have good strategies if the group $\Gamma(\mathfrak{C})$ is "large" enough. A natural condition for this seems to be that $\Gamma(\mathfrak{C})$ is transitive on T, which, as remarked before, trivially holds if $\mathfrak{C}$ is a graph property. The following very interesting conjecture was advanced by Rivest and and Vuillemin: If $\mathfrak{C}$ is a complex with transitive group $\Gamma(\mathfrak{C})$, then $\mathfrak{C}$ is elusive. The truth of this conjecture would thus imply the elusiveness of any monotone graph property.

Rivest and Vuillemin went even further to conjecture that any family $\mathfrak{C} \subseteq 2^T$ with $\emptyset \in \mathfrak{C}$, $T \notin \mathfrak{C}$ and transitive group $\Gamma(\mathfrak{C})$ is elusive. While this is false in general (see example 3.19 below), they succeeded in verifying the conjecture whenever the size of T is a prime power.

Let us first make a few observations on $\Gamma = \Gamma(\mathfrak{C})$. We write $C \sim D$ for two subsets $C, D \subseteq T$ if $D = C^\sigma$ for some $\sigma \in \Gamma$. The relation $\sim$ is obviously an equivalence relation on the power set 2^T (Γ is a group!). The equivalence classes of $\sim$ are called the *orbits* of 2^T under Γ. Thus the orbits are all of the form A^Γ for some $A \subseteq T$. Clearly, all sets of an orbit have the same size, and since $\Gamma(\mathfrak{C})$ leaves $\mathfrak{C}$ invariant, we note that $\mathfrak{C}$ is the disjoint union of orbits. Now we use the assumption that Γ is transitive on T. Consider any orbit $\theta = \{A_1, \ldots, A_m\}$ with $\mid A_i \mid = s$ for all i. Take any element $e \in T$ and suppose e is in h of the sets A_i, say $A_1, \ldots, A_h$. If e' is any other element, then by the transitivity of Γ, there exists $\sigma \in \Gamma$ which carries e into e'. Hence e' is in the distinct sets $A_1^\sigma, \ldots, A_h^\sigma \in \theta$. Reversing the role of e and e' we infer that e and e', and thus all elements are in precisely h of the sets in θ. From this we conclude

$$ms = ht, \quad s \leq t.$$

Now if $t = p^r$ is a prime power, then $ms = hp^r$, and thus $s = 0$ or p^r or else, $p \mid m = \mid \theta \mid$. In other words, there are exactly two orbits of size not divisible by p, namely $\theta = \{\emptyset\}$ and $\theta = \{T\}$.

Theorem 3.52. *Let* $\mid T \mid = p^r$ *be a prime power,* $\mathfrak{C} \subseteq 2^T$, $\emptyset \in \mathfrak{C}$, $T \notin \mathfrak{C}$, *and* $\Gamma(\mathfrak{C})$ *transitive on* T. *Then* $\mathfrak{C}$ *is elusive.*

Proof. We know from our discussion above that $\mathfrak{C}$ consists of orbits under Γ. Let $\mathfrak{C}_0 = \{X \in \mathfrak{C} : \mid X \mid \text{ even}\}$ and $\mathfrak{C}_1 = \{X \in \mathfrak{C} : \mid X \mid \text{ odd}\}$. The orbit $\{\emptyset\}$ is in $\mathfrak{C}_0$ while all other orbits have size divisible by p. Hence $p \mid \mid \mathfrak{C}_1 \mid$

while $p\!\!\!/\ \mid \mathfrak{C}_0 \mid$. We conclude $\mid \mathfrak{C}_0 \mid \neq \mid \mathfrak{C}_1 \mid$ and thus that $\mathfrak{C}$ is elusive by **3.51**(i).   □

Example 3.19. As mentioned above, the conclusion of the previous theorem may fail when t is not a prime power. The following counterexample with $t = 12$ is due to Illies. We set $T = \{1, 2, \dots, 12\}$, and denote by $\Sigma \leq \Sigma_T$ the group generated by the cyclic permutation $\begin{pmatrix} 1 & 2 & 3 & \cdots & 12 \\ 2 & 3 & 4 & \cdots & 1 \end{pmatrix}$. The family $\mathfrak{C}$ is defined as $\mathfrak{C} = \{\emptyset\} \cup \{1\}^\Sigma \cup \{1,4\}^\Sigma \cup \{1,5\}^\Sigma \cup \{1,4,7\}^\Sigma \cup \{1,5,9\}^\Sigma \cup \{1,4,7,10\}^\Sigma$. (Recall the notation A^Σ before **3.44**.). Thus e.g. $\{1,4\}^\Sigma = \{\{1,4\}, \{2,5\}, \{3,6\}, \dots \{12,3\}\}$. Obviously, $\emptyset \in \mathfrak{C}$, $T \notin \mathfrak{C}$, and $\Gamma(\mathfrak{C})$ is transitive since $\Gamma(\mathfrak{C})$ contains the transitive group Σ. Note that $\mid \mathfrak{C} \mid = 56$. We are now going to exhibit an algorithm of length 11. For brevity, we use the following short-hand notation. Suppose in our decision tree, we have arrived at the node v (after having tested $i_1, i_2, \dots, i_k$). The symbol $(j_1, j_1, \dots, j_\ell)$ with $j_r \neq i_s$ for all r and s stands for the following subtree:

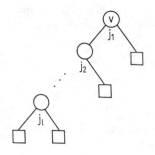

Figure 3.24

That is, we test $j_1, j_2, \dots, j_\ell$ in this order, and whenever an answer is "yes", then the outcome $X \notin \mathfrak{C}$ is determined, as is the outcome $X \in \mathfrak{C}$ when all answers are "no". The reader may now verify that the algorithm in figure 3.25 indeed solves the recognition problem. Vertical lines refer to "no" and horizontal lines to "yes". The $\mathfrak{C}$-sets determined at each stage are inside the boxes, where we omit the curly braces for brevity.

```
1 ——————— 4 ——————— (2,3,5,6,8,9,11,12)    ┌─────────────────────────┐
                                            │1,4;1,4,7;1,4,10;1,4,7,10│
│               │                           └─────────────────────────┘
│              10 ——————— (2,3,5,6,8,9,11,12)    ┌──────────┐
│                                                │1,10;1,7,10│
│            (2,3,6,7,8,11,12)                ┌─────────────┐
│                                            │1;1,5;1,9;1,5,9│
2 ——————— 5 ——————— (3,4,6,7,9,10,12)    ┌─────────────────────────┐
                                         │2,5;2,5,8;2,5,11;2,5,8,11│
│               │                        └─────────────────────────┘
│              11 ——————— (3,4,6,7,9,10,12)    ┌──────────┐
│                                              │2,11;2,8,11│
│            (3,4,7,8,9,12)                ┌────────────────┐
│                                         │2;2,6;2,10;2,6,10│
3 ——————— 6 ——————— (4,5,7,8,10,11)    ┌─────────────────────────┐
                                       │3,6;3,6,9;3,6,12;3,6,9,12│
│               │                      └─────────────────────────┘
│              12 ——————— (4,5,7,8,10,11)    ┌──────────┐
│                                           │3,12;3,9,12│
│            (4,5,8,9,10)                ┌────────────────┐
│                                        │3;3,7;3,11;3,7,11│
4 ——————— 7 ——————— (5,6,8,9,11,12)    ┌──────────┐
                                       │4,7;4,7,10│
│            (5,6,9,10,11)           ┌────────────────┐
│                                    │4;4,8;4,12;4,8,12│
12 ——————— 9 ——————— (5,7,8,10,11)    ┌──────────┐
                                      │9,12;6,9,12│
│            (5,6,7,10,11)           ┌──────┐
│                                    │12;8,12│
11 ——————— 8 ——————— (6,7,9,10)    ┌──────────┐
                                   │8,11;5,8,11│
│            (5,6,9,10)            ┌──────┐
│                                  │11;7,11│
7 ——————— (5,6,8,9)              ┌────┐
                                 │7;7,10│
│
10 ——————— (5,8,9)              ┌──────┐
                                │10;6,10│
│
6 ——————— (5,8)              ┌────┐
                             │6;6,9│
│
9 ——————— (8)              ┌────┐
                           │9;5,9│
│                         ┌────────┐
                          │∅;5;8;5,8│
                          └────────┘
```

Figure 3.25

We return to graphs. Although $\binom{n}{2}$ is not a prime power for $n \geq 4$, **3.52** provides nevertheless a proof of the Aanderaa-Rosenberg conjecture as we shall now demonstrate.

Proposition 3.53. *If P is a non-trivial monotone graph property on $n = 2^m$ vertices, then $C(P) \geq \frac{n^2}{4}$.*

Proof. For $i = 0,\dots,m$, let H_i be the sum of 2^{m-i} disjoint copies of the complete graph K_{2^i}. Thus H_0 is the empty graph, H_1 consists of 2^{m-1} disjoint edges, and so on. Obviously, $H_0 \subseteq H_1 \subseteq \dots \subseteq H_m = K_{2^m}$. Since P is non-trivial and monotone there is a largest index j, $j < m$, such that $H = H_j \in P$. Let J be the sum of 2^{m-j-1} copies of K_{2^j}, and let $K = J * J$, meaning that K is the union of two copies of J plus all edges between them (figure 3.26).

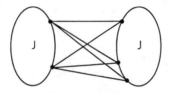

Figure 3.26

We have $H = J + J$ and $H_{j+1} \subseteq J * J = K$, since clearly $K_{2^j} * K_{2^j} = K_{2^{j+1}}$. Hence $K \notin P$ by the monotonicity of P. Player B pursues the following strategy. He gives away the information that the unknown graph contains H and is contained in K. In other words, we consider the family

$$\mathcal{F} = \{E(G) - E(H) : H \subseteq G \subseteq K, \ G \in P\}.$$

Obviously, $C(P) \geq C(\mathcal{F})$ and it thus remains to show that $C(\mathcal{F}) \geq \frac{n^2}{4}$. Since $|E(K)| - |E(H)| = 2|E(J)| + \frac{n^2}{4} - 2|E(J)| = \frac{n^2}{4}$, we have to show, in fact, that $\mathcal{F}$ is elusive. To deduce this we check that the conditions of Theorem 3.52 are satisfied. T is the edge-set between the two copies of J. Since $H \in P$ and $K \notin P$, we have $\emptyset \in \mathcal{F}$ and $T \notin \mathcal{F}$, and furthermore that $|T| = 2^{2m-2}$ is a prime power. Finally, if e and e' are any two edges connecting the two J's, then there obviously exists a permutation σ of the vertices which keeps the two copies invariant and maps e into e'. The corresponding permutation $\sigma^{(2)}$ on the edges maps therefore H and K into themselves and sends e into e'. Hence $\Gamma(\mathcal{F})$ is transitive on the edges, and the proof is complete. $\square$

Theorem 3.54. *If $\mathcal{P}$ is a non-trivial monotone graph property on n vertices, then $C(\mathcal{P}) > \frac{n^2}{16}$.*

Proof. Denote by $c(n)$ the minimum of all non-trivial monotone graph properties on n vertices. If $n = 2^m$, then the result follows from **3.53**. Suppose $2^m \leq n < 2^{m+1}$, $m \geq 1$. If we can show $c(n) \geq 2^{2m-2}$, we are through since $2^{2m-2} = 2^{2m+2-4} > \frac{n^2}{16}$. We prove $c(n) \geq 2^{2m-2}$ by induction on $n - 2^m$. For $n = 2^m$, Proposition **3.53** will do. If the star St_n is in $\mathcal{P}$, then player B gives away that a certain vertex u has degree $n - 1$ and concentrates on the set V' of neighbors of u. If G is a graph on V' we denote by $G * u$ the graph where every vertex of G is joined to u. The family $\mathcal{F} = \{G : G * u \in \mathcal{P}\}$ is a non-trivial monotone graph property on $n - 1$ vertices ($K_n \notin \mathcal{P}!$) whence $C(\mathcal{P}) \geq C(\mathcal{F}) \geq c(n - 1) \geq 2^{2m-2}$ where the last inequality is implied by induction. Similarly, if $K_1 + K_{n-1} \notin \mathcal{P}$, then B gives the information that a vertex u has degree 0 and concentrates on the set V' of vertices different from u. The family $\mathcal{F} = \{G : G + u \in \mathcal{P}\}$ is again a non-trivial monotone property on $n - 1$ vertices ($\emptyset \in \mathcal{P}!$) and we argue as before.

Let us, finally, assume $St_n \notin \mathcal{P}$ and $K_1 + K_{n-1} \in \mathcal{P}$. Set $r = 2^{m-1}$ and $s = n - 2r$. The monotonicity of $\mathcal{P}$ implies that $H = (K_r * K_s) + E_r \in \mathcal{P}$ where E_r is the empty graph on r vertices, since it is a subgraph of $K_1 + K_{n-1}$. Similarly, $K = K_r * (K_s + E_r) \notin \mathcal{P}$ since it contains St_n. Player B gives away that the unknown graph lies between H and K, i.e. he considers the property $\mathcal{F} = \{E(G) - E(H) : H \subseteq G \subseteq K, G \in \mathcal{P}\}$. Precisely as in the proof of the previous proposition it is shown that $\mathcal{F}$ is a family which satisfies all assumptions of **3.52**. Hence $\mathcal{F}$ is elusive and we conclude $C(\mathcal{P}) \geq C(\mathcal{F}) = | E(K) | - | E(H) | = r^2 = 2^{2m-2}$ (see figure 3.27) and the proof is complete. $\square$

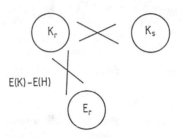

Figure 3.27

By an ingenious application of ideas from algebraic topology, Kahn, Saks and Sturtevant [1984] have sharpened **3.54** to $C(\mathcal{P}) \geq (\frac{1}{4} - \varepsilon)n^2$ for all $\varepsilon > 0$ and n large enough. Furthermore, they have shown that any non-trivial monotone graph property is elusive whenever n is a prime power, and it is plausible that the same may hold for any n, and indeed, in full generality, for any non-trivial complex.

Exercises 3.6.

1. Prove that families $\mathfrak{C} \subseteq 2^T$ satisfying one of the following conditions are elusive: a. $\emptyset \in \mathfrak{C}$, $\{x\} \notin \mathfrak{C}$ for all $x \in T$; b. $\emptyset \notin \mathfrak{C}$, $\{x\} \in \mathfrak{C}$ for all $x \in T$; c. $T \in \mathfrak{C}$, $\binom{T}{t-1} \cap \mathfrak{C} = \emptyset$; d. $T \notin \mathfrak{C}$, $\binom{T}{t-1} \subseteq \mathfrak{C}$.

2*. Show that any non-trivial graph property $\mathcal{P}$ on $n \leq 4$ vertices is elusive.

3. Find a non-elusive graph property $\mathcal{P}$ with $o(\mathcal{P}) = 3$ for all $n \geq 6$.

4* Generalize the example in figure 3.18 to $n \geq 6$, n even. Let $\mathcal{P}$ be the class of graphs   A⟨▷—◁⟩B   where A and B may be any graphs on $\frac{n}{2} - 1$ vertices. Prove: $C(\mathcal{P}) \leq \frac{3n^2}{8} + \frac{n}{4} - 1$. (Kleitman)

5. Consider the following property $\mathcal{P}$. There is a vertex of degree $n - 4$, and the vertices adjacent to it have degree 1. Prove that $\mathcal{P}$ is not elusive.

6. Apply **3.51** to conclude that the following properties $\mathcal{P}$ are elusive:
   a. all graphs with at most k isolated vertices; b. all graphs with 2 independent edges; c. bipartite graphs.

7*. Suppose $\mathfrak{E} \subseteq 2^T$ has transitive group $\Gamma(\mathfrak{E})$. Show that $\mathfrak{E}$ is elusive if $(1+z)^2 \nmid p(\mathfrak{E}; z)$. In particular this implies $\mathfrak{E}$ is elusive if $4 \nmid |\mathfrak{E}|$. (Best, van Emde Boas, Lenstra)

8. Show that G and H can be packed if $\Delta(G) = 1$ and $\Delta(H) \leq \frac{n-1}{2}$.

9*. Show that G and H can be packed if $\Delta(G)\Delta(H) < \frac{n}{2}$, and give an example that a packing need not exist if $(\Delta(G)+1)(\Delta(H)+1) \geq n+2$. (Sauer-Spencer)

10*. Let T_1, T_2 be two trees which are not stars. Show that they can be packed.

Problems

1. Compute $L(n)$ for all n. (3.2)

2. Estimate $\overline{L}(n)$ and $\overline{L}_{pre}(n)$. (3.2)

3. Are all 3-degenerate graphs optimal? (3.2)

4. Are all planar graphs optimal? (3.2)

5. Compute $L_{pre}(m, n)$. In particular, is it true that $L_{pre}(2^{t-1}+1, 2^{t-1}+1) = 2t$ for all t? (3.2)

6. Prove or disprove the existence of a constant r such that $L(G) \leq \lceil \log_2 |E(G)| \rceil + r$ for all graphs G. (3.2)

7. Prove or disprove: $M(A) \leq k \iff A \preceq N(k)$ (see **3.25**). (3.3)

8. Is K_n ($n \geq 3$) 3-optimal only for $n = 5$ and 8? (3.3)

9. Are there only finitely many 3-optimal graphs $K_{m,n}$ for fixed m? (3.3)

10. Characterize the 3-optimal trees or forests. (3.3)

11. Is the following true? For any r, there are only finitely many forests in $\mathcal{F}_r$ which are not 3-optimal. (3.3)

12. Find a non-trivial upper bound for $M(G)$ when G is an arbitrary graph. (3.3)

13. Estimate $L_{\leq k}(G)$. (3.4)

14. Extend the results of section 3.4 to k-uniform hypergraphs. (3.4)

15. Prove or disprove: $L(\mathcal{G}) + m(\mathcal{G}) \leq \binom{n}{2} + o(n^2)$. (3.5)

16. Is it true that $L(\mathcal{G}) + m(\mathcal{G}) \leq \binom{n}{2} + Cn$ when $\mathcal{G}$ consists of isomorphic graphs? (3.5)

17. Determine $L(\mathcal{P})$ and $L(\mathcal{H})$ (see exercises 3.5.4, 3.5.5). (3.5)

18. Is $L(\mathcal{K}_\ell) = \binom{n}{2} - m(\mathcal{K}_\ell)$ precisely when n satisfies the bounds in exercise 3.5.9? (3.5)

19. Close the gap between $2n$ and $6n$ as lower bound for non-trivial graph-properties. (3.6)

20. Prove or disprove: Any non-trivial monotone graph property is elusive. (3.6)

21. Find non-elusive families $\mathfrak{C} \subseteq 2^T$ with $\emptyset \in \mathfrak{C}$, $T \notin \mathfrak{C}$, $\Gamma(\mathfrak{C})$ transitive, for infinitely many t, $t = |T|$. (3.6)

22. Prove or disprove: If $(\Delta(G) + 1)(\Delta(H) + 1) \leq n + 1$, then G and H can be packed. (Bollobás-Eldridge) (3.6)

23. Prove that any family of trees T_i , where T_i is a tree on i vertices, $i = 1, \ldots, n$, can be packed on n vertices. (Gyarfás-Lehel) (3.6)

Notes and References

The material in this chapter has three origins: the group testing problem leading up to the binary variant in graph search; the scale weighing questions with its natural graph generalizations; finally the Aanderaa-Rosenberg conjecture focusing on recognition problems. Edge identification for arbitrary graphs was first formulated in Aigner [1986]. For packing and recognition problems, Bollobás [1978a] and Yap [1986] are good references. Best, van Emde Boas, Lenstra [1974], Rivest, Vuillemin [1976] and Kahn-Saks-Sturtevant [1984] contain some of the deepest results on these questions.

Aigner M. [1986], Search problems on graphs. Discrete Appl. Math. 14, 215-230.

Aigner M. * [1987], Graph Theory, A Development From the 4-Color Problem. BCS Associates, Moscow. (Translation from the German book: Graphentheorie, eine Entwicklung aus dem 4-Farben Problem. Teubner, Stuttgart, 1983).

Aigner M., Triesch E. [1988a], Searching for an edge in a graph. J. Graph Theory, to appear.

Aigner M., Triesch E. [1988b], Searching for subgraphs. Combinatorica, submitted.

Andreae T. [1988a], A search problem on graphs which generalizes some group testing problems with two defectives. Preprint.

Andreae T. [1988b], A ternary search problem on graphs. Discrete Appl. Math., to appear.

Best M.R., van Emde Boas P., Lenstra Jr. H.W. [1974], A sharpened version of the Aanderaa-Rosenberg conjecture. Math. Center Tracts, Amsterdam.

Bollobás B. * [1978a], Extremal Graph Theory. Academic Press, London-New York-San Francisco.

Bollobás B., Eldridge S.E. [1978b], Packings of graphs and applications to computational complexity. J. Combinatorial Theory B 25, 105-124.

Bondy J.A., Murty U.S.R. * [1976], Graph Theory with Applications. MacMillan Press, London.

Chang G.J., Hwang F.K. [1981], A group testing problem on two disjoint sets. SIAM J. Alg. Discrete Methods 2, 35-38.

Chang G.J., Hwang F.K., Lin S. [1982], Group testing with two defectives. Discrete App. Math. 4, 97-102.

Chang X.M., Hwang F.K., Weng J.F. [1988], Group testing with two or three defectives. To appear.

Christen C. [1983], Optimal detection of two complementary defectives. SIAM J. Alg. Discrete Methods 4, 101-110.

Frankl P., Füredi Z. [1984], Union-free hypergraphs and probability theory. Europ. J. Combinatorics 5, 127-131.

Garey M.R., Johnson D.S. * [1979], Computers and Intractability. Freeman & Co., San Francisco.

Gyarfás A., Lehel J. [1978], Packing trees of different order into K_n. Colloq. Math. Soc. J. Bolyai 18, 463-469.

Illies N. [1978], A counter-example to the generalized Aanderaa-Rosenberg conjecture. Information Proceeding Letters 7, 154-155.

Kahn J., Saks M., Sturtevant D. [1984], A topological approach to evasiveness. Combinatorica 4, 297-306.

Kleitman D.J., Kwiatkowski D.J. [1980], Further results on the Aanderaa-Rosenberg conjecture. J. Combinatorial Theory B 28, 85-95.

Milner E.C., Welsh D.J.A. [1976], On the computational complexity of graph theoretical properties. Proc. Fifth British Combinatorial Conference, 471-487.

Mirski L. * [1971], Transversal Theory. Academic Press, London- New York-San Francisco.

Rivest R.L., Vuillemin J. [1975], A generalization and proof of the Aanderaa-Rosenberg conjecture. Proc. 7th Annual ACM Symposium on Theory of Computing, 6-11.

Rivest R.L., Vuillemin J. [1976], On recognizing graph properties from adjacency matrices. Theoretical Comp. Sci. 3, 371-384.

Rosenberg A.L. [1973], On the time required to recognize properties of graphs: a problem. SIGACT News 5, 15-16.

Sauer N., Spencer J. [1978], Edge-disjoint placement of graphs. J. Combinatorial Theory B, 295-302.

Tošić R. [1980], An optimal search procedure. J. Stat. Planning and Inference 4, 169-171.

Triesch E. [1984], Über die Komplexität von Grapheneigenschaften. Diss. Univ. Aachen.

Yap H.P. * [1986], Some Topics in Graph Theory. Cambridge University Press, Cambridge.

Chapter 4

Sorting Problems

A standard question in theoretical computer science calls for sorting a previously unsorted or partially sorted list of keys. Apart from the weighing problems discussed in chapter 2, sorting questions were probably the first search problems treated in depth. There is a vast literature focusing on sorting algorithms and related topics - volume III of Knuth's celebrated series on the art of computer programming is exclusively devoted to this theme. Observing the general outline of this book, we will solely concentrate on questions of optimality, neglecting the feasibility or implementation of the various sorting methods to be discussed.

Let us get an overview of the subject. The standard situation is as follows. At the outset we are given a set $R = \{x_1, \ldots, x_n\}$ of n distinct elements, the set of *keys* or the *reservoir*. We know that R is ordered according to an unknown linear order which we are required to determine. The tests at our disposal are comparisons $x_i : x_j$ between any two keys. Since the outcome of any such test is $x_i < x_j$ or $x_i > x_j$, we see that a sorting algorithm corresponds to a binary tree with the leaves being associated to the $n!$ possible orderings. If $S(n)$ denotes the complexity of the sorting problem, then our information-theoretic bound yields

$$S(n) \geq \lceil \log_2 n! \rceil.$$

Example 4.1. For $n = 2, 3, 4$ we obtain $S(2) \geq 1$, $S(3) \geq 3$, $S(4) \geq 5$, and algorithms of this length are trivially obtained. But already for $n = 5$, it is not altogether obvious how to find an algorithm of length $\lceil \log_2 5! \rceil = 7$. First we compare two disjoint pairs and then the two maxima. After these three tests we arrive at a partially ordered set P of the form

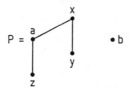

Figure 4.1

where we read the relations from top to bottom, i.e. $x > a$, $x > z$, $a > z$, $x > y$. Now compare $a : b$. The following figure shows the two possible outcomes.

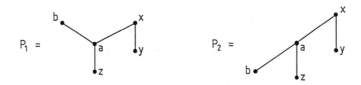

Figure 4.2

If P_1 arises, then we take as 5th test $b : x$ and are now faced with inserting y into the proper place of the chain $\{z < a < b\}$ (if $b < x$) or $\{z < a\}$ (if $b > x$). By testing $y : a$ first, this can clearly be done with two more comparisons. If, on the other hand, P_2 arose, then we take as 5th test $b : z$. The remaining task calls for inserting y into the chain $\{b < z < a\}$ or $\{z < b < a\}$ which can again be done with two more tests by comparing y to the middle element first.

Let us stress an important point. After the first three comparisons our decision tree is split into $2^3 = 8$ subtrees with $\frac{120}{8} = 15$ leaves each. Why can we say that? The leaves below an inner node corresponding to the poset P of figure 4.1 represent precisely the possible linear orderings compatible with P, or as we say from now on, the *linear extensions* $L(P)$ of P. We use the notation $e(P) =| L(P) |$, and it is easily seen that $e(P) = 15$. It is clear that the next comparison $x_i : x_j$ divides $L(P)$ into two disjoint sets $L(P; x_i < x_j)$ and $L(P; x_j < x_i)$, those extensions of P for which $x_i < x_j$ holds and those for which $x_j < x_i$ holds. In order to complete our sorting with 7 tests we must thus find a test which splits $L(P)$ into two sets of size 8 and 7, respectively. The reader can easily verify that our choice $a : b$ for the 4th test is the *only* comparison which accomplishes this partition. Following this line of reasoning it is readily seen that, apart from comparing the two minima in the 3rd test, any optimal algorithm for sorting 5 elements must perform the first four steps as in our example.

The lesson to be learned from this example is, that in order to design an optimal or at least near optimal algorithm we have to tackle the general sorting problem when an arbitrary poset P is given at the outset, with the central question how to find a comparison $x : y$ which partitions $L(P)$ into nearly equal parts. This will be the subject of the next chapter culminating in the famous theorem of Kahn and Saks that we can always sort a given poset P with $C.\log_2 | L(P) |$ comparisons for a fixed constant C, independent of P. But first let us get back to our original sorting problem.

4.1   Linear Sorting

Let us state once more the information-theoretic bound:

$$S(n) \geq \lceil \log_2 n! \rceil.$$

To get a closer picture of $\lceil \log_2 n! \rceil$ we use Stirling's approximation known from Analysis:

$$\sqrt{2\pi n}(\frac{n}{e})^n < n! < \sqrt{2\pi n}(\frac{n}{e})^n e^{\frac{1}{4n}}.$$

From this follows immediately that for some constant C,

$$(4.1) \qquad | \lceil \log_2 n! \rceil - n\log_2 n + n\log_2 e - \frac{1}{2}\log_2 n | \leq C,$$

so about $n\log_2 n$ comparisons are needed.

Let us see how close we can get to the lower bound $\lceil \log_2 n! \rceil$. Practically, all known algorithms are recursive and fall into two categories.

Algorithms of the first kind split the reservoir R in any fashion into two subsets R_1 and R_2, sort R_1, R_2 separately, and complete the sorting by *merging* R_1 and R_2 into its proper list. The cost of these algorithms is thus composed of the (recursive) sorting cost of R_1, R_2 plus the cost of merging the sorted lists R_1 and R_2 (the splitting being trivial).

Algorithms of the second kind work dually. First we partition R into its top part R_1 and its bottom part R_2, i.e. every element of R_2 is below every element of R_1, sort each R_i recursively, and after that glue them together. Here the cost arises in the (recursive) sorting of R_1, R_2 and the *splitting* process in the beginning. The following figure shows schematically the two approaches:

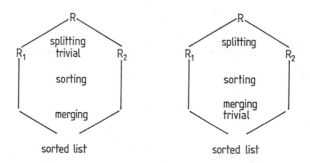

Figure 4.3

Let us consider the two extremal cases when one of R_1, R_2, say R_1, contains a single element x, or when the sizes of R_1 and R_2 differ by at most one.

Let us discuss the merging approach first. In the first case we split R into $\{x\}$ and $R - \{x\}$, sort $R - \{x\}$ and at the end insert x into its proper place. We call this algorithm *sorting by insertion*. If x is to be inserted into an ordered list $\{x_1 > x_2 \ldots > x_i\}$, then x may be greater than x_1, or between x_1 and x_2, and so on. The worst-case cost is thus at least $\lceil \log_2(i+1) \rceil$ (see example 1.5). Comparing x with a middle element each time, this bound can clearly be achieved. The recursive procedure of inserting one element after the other is usually called *binary insertion*. Steinhaus described this method in his famous book "Mathematical Snapshots" [1950] and suggested that it may be optimal for every n. We shall see in a moment that this is far from being true, in fact, binary insertion is optimal only for $n \leq 4$. The observation that $\lceil \log_2(i+1) \rceil$ tests are required to insert x into a list of i elements leads to the following result.

Proposition 4.1. *Let $B(n)$ be the worst-case cost of binary insertion. Then*

$$B(n) = \sum_{i=2}^{n} \lceil \log_2 i \rceil.$$

Using the formula $\sum_{i=1}^{k} i 2^{i-1} = (k-1)2^k + 1$ we compute

(4.2) $$B(n) = \lceil \log_2 n \rceil n - 2^{\lceil \log_2 n \rceil} + 1$$

and hence together with (4.1)

$$\lim_{n \to \infty} \frac{S(n)}{n \log_2 n} = 1.$$

Our sorting problem is thus asymptotically settled, but, of course, there is still ample room for improvements as far as exact results are concerned.

In the second extremal case we split R into two sets R_1, R_2 of size $\mid R_1 \mid = \lfloor \frac{n}{2} \rfloor$ and $\mid R_2 \mid = \lceil \frac{n}{2} \rceil$, respectively, sort R_1 and R_2, and merge the sorted lists. Let us denote by $M(i,j)$ the worst-case cost of merging two ordered lists S,T containing i and j elements, respectively. Suppose $S = \{a_1 < a_2 < \ldots < a_i\}$, $T = \{b_1 < b_2 < \ldots < b_j\}$. The following algorithm is called *linear merge*. We first compare $a_1 : b_1$. The smaller of the two must be the overall minimum which we now delete. In the two remaining lists we again compare the two bottom elements, and so on. Clearly, this algorithm stops after at most $i + j - 1$ test whence

$$M(i,j) \le i + j - 1.$$

When i is small as compared to j, this bound will obviously be no good since we already know $M(1,j) = \lceil \log_2(j+1) \rceil$ while linear merge needs j comparisons. In the next section, the problem of merging two or more chains will be treated in depth. For the moment, let us show that we can do no better than in linear merge when $\mid T - S \mid \le 1$.

Proposition 4.2. *Suppose* $\mid j - i \mid \le 1$, *then* $M(i,j) = i + j - 1$.

Proof. Consider first the case $i = j$, with $S = \{a_1 < a_2 < \ldots a_i\}$, $T = \{b_1 < b_2 < \ldots < b_i\}$. As in the previous chapters we view the sorting process as a game between two players A and B. Player B employs the following strategy. He answers $a_h < b_k$ if and only if $h \le k$. In other words, B aims for the final ordering $\{a_1 < b_1 < a_2 < b_2 < \ldots < a_i < b_i\}$. Since none of the $2i - 1$ relations $a_h < b_h$, $1 \le h \le i$, and $b_h < a_{h+1}$, $1 \le h \le i - 1$, can be implied transitively by any other test, player A must, in fact, test all of them to be sure of the outcome whence indeed $M(i,i) \ge 2i - 1$, and thus $M(i,i) = 2i - 1$ holds. For $j = i + 1$, player B answers $a_h < b_k$ iff $h < k$ yielding the ordering $\{b_1 < a_1 < b_2 < a_2 < \ldots < b_i < a_i < b_{i+1}\}$. Again, player A must test all $2i$ covering relations $a_h < b_{h+1}$, $b_h < a_h$, $1 \le h \le i$, whence $M(i,i+1) \ge 2i$, and thus $M(i,i+1) = 2i$. □

Denoting by $M(n)$ the recursive cost of this sorting method, called *sorting by merging*, we thus conclude

$$M(n) = M(\lfloor\frac{n}{2}\rfloor) + M(\lceil\frac{n}{2}\rceil) + (n-1).$$

It is an easy exercise to show that $M(n) = B(n)$ for all n, so these two algorithms covering the extremal cases have precisely the same length.

Let us turn to the second approach, sorting by splitting. The case when $\mid R_1 \mid = 1$, $\mid R_2 \mid = n-1$ calls for extracting the overall maximum of R, then of $R - \{x\}$, and so on. Algorithms of this kind are called *sorting by selection*. How many tests $W_1(n)$ do we need to determine the maximum of a set of n elements? Since anyone of the n elements may be the maximum, we note that $\lceil\log_2 n\rceil$ tests are certainly called for in the worst case. To see that the information-theoretic bound is no great help in this situation we employ the terminology of tennis tournaments. We shall make extensive use of this idea in section 3. Let us view the elements of R as n tennis players. Any comparison $x : y$ is a *game* between x and y, and we say x is the *winner* over y if $x > y$. Given the (admittedly unrealistic) assumption that the relative strength of the players induces a transitive relation on R, our sorting problem can be viewed as a tennis tournament determining the precise ranking of the players.

In our situation we are only interested in selecting the overall champion. In every game there is exactly one loser and since everyone of the $n-1$ players different from the champion must lose at least once, we infer $W_1(n) \geq n-1$. On the other hand, by always pairing players that have never been defeated before, the champion is certainly determined after $n-1$ games.

Proposition 4.3. *The cost of determining the maximum (minimum) of n elements is $W_1(n) = n - 1$.*

Selecting the maximum recursively yields a cost of $(n-1)+(n-2)+\ldots+1 = \binom{n}{2}$, so this algorithm needs in the worst case *all* comparisons and is thus far inferior to the methods discussed before.

There is a well-known method, called QUICKSORT, which partitions the reservoir R into its top-part R_1 and its bottom part R_2. Initially, we are given the sequence $a_1, a_2, \ldots, a_n$. We partition R into its top-part R_1 containing all elements $\geq a_1$, and its bottom-part R_2 with all elements $< a_1$

as follows. We keep two pointers i and j, meaning that all elements with index $\leq i$ belong to R_1, and those with index $\geq j$ belong to R_2. Initially, we set $i = 1$, $j = n + 1$ with the assumption $a_{n+1} < \min\{a_i : i = 1, \ldots, n\}$. In the first run we go to the smallest index $h > i$ with $a_h < a_1$ and to the heighest index $k < j$ with $a_k \geq a_1$. If $h < k$, then we exchange the positions of a_h and a_k and set $h = i$, $k = j$. Now we know that $a_s \geq a_1$ for all $s \leq i$ and $a_t < a_1$ for all $t \geq k$, and repeat the procedure for the new pointer positions. If, on the other hand, $k < h$, then we have arrived at the desired partition with the first k elements forming the top part and the remaining $n - k$ forming the bottom part.

Example 4.2. Consider the sequence 6 2 1 5 8 9 4 3 7. QUICKSORT performs then the following runs, where the elements to be exchanged are underlined.

$$
\begin{array}{ccccccccc}
\downarrow & & & & & & & & \downarrow \\
6 & \underline{2} & 1 & 5 & 8 & 9 & 4 & 3 & \underline{7} \\
 & \downarrow & & & & & & & \downarrow \\
6 & 7 & \underline{1} & 5 & 8 & \underline{9} & 4 & 3 & 2 \\
 & & \downarrow & & & \downarrow & & & \\
6 & 7 & 9 & \underline{5} & \underline{8} & 1 & 4 & 3 & 2 \\
 & & & \downarrow & \downarrow & & & & \\
6 & 7 & 9 & \underline{8} & \underline{5} & 1 & 4 & 3 & 2 \\
\end{array}
$$

The number of comparisons is $2 + 4 + 2 + 1 = 9$.

The reader will find that there are sequences which need Cn^2 comparisons in the worst-case, but on the average QUICKSORT will do its job with $Cn \log_2 n$ comparisons (see exercises 4.1.3, 4.1.4).

Many other sorting algorithms have been studied in depth (Heapsort, bubble-sort and others). The interested may consult Knuth [1973] or Mehlhorn [1984].

Let us get back to the main problem of estimating $S(n)$. So far, binary insertion or merge sort were the best, showing that $S(n) \leq \sum_{i=2}^{n} \lceil \log i \rceil$. A famous method due to Ford and Johnson [1959] allows us to lower the upper bound to $F(n) = \sum_{i=2}^{n} \lceil \log \frac{3i}{4} \rceil$.

Let us look at the example $n = 11$. First we compare $\lfloor \frac{n}{2} \rfloor = 5$ disjoint pairs, and sort the 5 maximal elements recursively (with 7 comparisons, see example 4.1). Let us call these elements $a_1, \ldots, a_5$ and their counterparts of the first round $b_1, \ldots, b_5$ with b_6 the remaining element. After these 12 comparisons we arrive at the following picture

$$
\begin{array}{ccccc}
a_1 & a_2 & a_3 & a_4 & a_5 \\
\cdot \longrightarrow & \cdot \longrightarrow & \cdot \longrightarrow & \cdot \longrightarrow & \cdot \\
\uparrow & \uparrow & \uparrow & \uparrow & \uparrow \\
\cdot & \cdot & \cdot & \cdot & \cdot \quad \cdot \\
b_1 & b_2 & b_3 & b_4 & b_5 \quad b_6
\end{array}
$$

We call $b_1 < a_1 < a_2 < a_3 < a_4 < a_5$ the *main chain*. Now we insert b_3 into the main chain using 2 comparisons, then b_2 using again 2 comparisons, thus arriving after 16 comparisons at

$$
\begin{array}{ccccc}
c_1 & c_2 & c_6 & c_7 = a_4 & c_8 = a_5 \\
\cdot \longrightarrow & \cdot \ldots \longrightarrow & \cdot \longrightarrow & \cdot \longrightarrow & \cdot \\
& & & \uparrow & \uparrow \\
& & & \cdot & \cdot \quad \cdot \\
& & & b_4 & b_5 \quad b_6
\end{array}
$$

Now we insert b_5 into the main chain $\{c_1 < \ldots < c_8\}$ using 3 comparisons and after that we insert b_4 using again 3 comparisons. So after 22 comparisons we have constructed a main chain $\{d_1 < \ldots < d_{10}\}$ and we can now insert b_6 using 4 more comparisons. Altogether, we have used 26 tests (as compared to 29 for binary insertion) which is optimal since $\lceil \log_2 11! \rceil > 25$.

The main idea in the Ford-Johnson algorithm is to insert in the k-th series of insertions that b_{t_k} first (and then $b_{t_k-1}, \ldots, b_{t_{k-1}+1}$), which needs at most k insertions ($k \geq 2$). The optimal choice for these insertions is thus

$$
b_3, b_2; b_5, b_4; b_{11}, b_{10}, \ldots, b_6; b_{21}, \ldots, b_{12}; \ldots.
$$

Let us determine the sequence $(t_1, t_2, t_3, \ldots)$ such that $b_{t_k}, \ldots, b_{t_{k-1}+1}$ can each be inserted with at most k comparisons. Before the k-th series we have the diagram

$$
\begin{array}{cccc}
c_1 & c_{2t_{k-1}} & a_{t_{k-1}+1} & a_{t_k-1} \\
\cdot \longrightarrow \ldots & \cdot \longrightarrow & \cdot \longrightarrow \ldots \longrightarrow & \cdot \quad \ldots \quad \cdot \\
& & \uparrow & \uparrow \\
& & \cdot & \cdot \qquad \vdots \\
& & b_{t_{k-1}+1} & b_{t_k-1} \quad b_{t_k}
\end{array}
$$

The number of elements in the main chain up to a_{t_k-1} is $2t_{k-1}+(t_k-t_{k-1}-1)$. To insert b_{t_k} with $\leq k$ comparisons, this number must be less than 2^k, so the best choice of t_k is $2t_{k-1} + (t_k - t_{k-1} - 1) = 2^k - 1$, or $t_{k-1} + t_k = 2^k$. Setting $t_0 = 1$, we find

$$\begin{aligned} t_k &= 2^k - t_{k-1} = 2^k - 2^{k-1} + t_{k-2} = \ldots = 2^k - 2^{k-1} + \ldots + (-1)^k \\ &= \frac{2^{k+1} + (-1)^k}{3}. \end{aligned}$$

Let us now compute the length $F(n)$ of our algorithm. We have

$$(4.3) \qquad F(n) = \lfloor \frac{n}{2} \rfloor + F(\lfloor \frac{n}{2} \rfloor) + G(\lceil \frac{n}{2} \rceil),$$

where G counts the number of comparisons involved in the sequence of insertions. The first values are $F(1) = 0$, $F(2) = 1$, $F(3) = 3$, $F(4) = 5$, $F(5) = 7$ which are all optimal. If $t_{k-1} \leq h \leq t_k$, then

$$\begin{aligned} G(h) &= \sum_{j=1}^{k-1} j(t_j - t_{j-1}) + k(h - t_{k-1}) \\ &= kh - \sum_{j=0}^{k-1} t_j. \end{aligned}$$

Let us set

$$(4.4) \qquad w_k = \sum_{j=0}^{k-1} t_j = \lfloor \frac{2^{k+1}}{3} \rfloor.$$

Notice that $w_{k-1} = \lfloor \frac{w_k}{2} \rfloor$ and $t_{k-1} = \lceil \frac{w_k}{2} \rceil$. We claim that

$$(4.5) \qquad F(n) - F(n - 1) = k \text{ iff } w_k < n \leq w_{k+1}.$$

For $k = 1$ or 2 this is certainly true. We proceed by induction on k. If n is even, then by (4.3)

$$F(n) - F(n - 1) = 1 + F(\frac{n}{2}) - F(\frac{n}{2} - 1).$$

Hence by induction, (4.5), and $w_{k-1} = \lfloor \frac{w_k}{2} \rfloor$,

$$\begin{aligned} F(n) - F(n - 1) = k \quad &\Longleftrightarrow \quad F(\frac{n}{2}) - F(\frac{n}{2} - 1) = k - 1 \\ &\Longleftrightarrow \quad w_{k-1} < \frac{n}{2} \leq w_k \\ &\Longleftrightarrow \quad w_k < n \leq w_{k+1}. \end{aligned}$$

For n odd we obtain

$$F(n) - F(n-1) = G(\lceil \tfrac{n}{2} \rceil) - G(\lfloor \tfrac{n}{2} \rfloor) = k$$

iff $t_{k-1} < \lceil \tfrac{n}{2} \rceil \le t_k$. Using $t_{k-1} = \lceil \tfrac{w_k}{2} \rceil$, this latter condition is again equivalent to $w_k < n \le w_{k+1}$.
By (4.4), we see that

$$w_k < n \le w_{k+1} \iff \frac{2^{k+1}}{3} < n \le \frac{2^{k+2}}{3} \iff k+1 < \log_2(3n) \le k+2.$$

This, in turn, implies

$$F(n) - F(n-1) = \lceil \log_2 \frac{3n}{4} \rceil,$$

and thus the following result, first obtained by Hadian.

Proposition 4.4. *The number of comparisons needed by the Ford- Johnson algorithm in the worst case is*

$$F(n) = \sum_{i=2}^{n} \lceil \log_2 \frac{3i}{4} \rceil.$$

The following table summarizes the information-theoretic lower bound and the cost of binary insertion and the Ford-Johnson algorithm for $n \le 16$.

n	2	3	4	5	6	7	8	9	10	11	12	13	14	15	16
$\lceil \log_2 n! \rceil$	1	3	5	7	10	13	16	19	22	26	29	33	37	41	45
$B(n)$	1	3	5	8	11	14	17	21	25	29	33	37	41	45	49
$F(n)$	1	3	5	7	10	13	16	19	22	26	30	34	38	42	46

$F(n)$ gives thus the exact value up to 11 and again for $n = 20, 21$ with $F(20) = 62$, $F(21) = 66$. It can be shown that $F(n) > \lceil \log n! \rceil$ for $n \ge 22$ (see exercise 4.1.8). For $n = 12$ a computer search showed $S(12) = F(12) = 30 > 29 = \lceil \log 12! \rceil$, and it was thought for a while that $F(n)$ might be optimal for all n. However, Manacher [1979b] improved the Ford-Johnson algorithm for infinitely many n by ingeniously merging small chains. Whether $F(n)$ is the true value for infinitely many n is an open question.

Still more difficult than determining $S(n)$ is the problem of estimating the average cost $\overline{S}(n)$ of sorting n elements. We have, of course, the lower bound established in Theorem 1.8:

$$\overline{S}(n) \geq \lceil \log_2 n! \rceil - \frac{1}{n!} 2^{\lceil \log_2 n! \rceil} + 1$$

The average cost $\overline{F}(n)$ of the Ford-Johnson algorithm achieves this lower bound for $n \leq 5$ but not for $n = 6$ (see exercise 4.1.9). There exist, however, procedures attaining the lower bound for $n = 6$ and also for $n = 9, 10$ while for $n = 7$ this is not possible. Beyond that, nothing much is known.

Exercises 4.1.

1.* Prove $M(n) = B(n)$ for all n.

2. Compute the average $\overline{W}_1(n)$ of determining the overall maximum.

3. Show that there are inputs which require all comparisons in QUICKSORT.

4. Investigate the average behavior of QUICKSORT, when all $n!$ orderings are equally likely.

5. Draw the comparison trees for sorting 4 elements when a. binary insertion, b. merging, c. selection, d. Ford-Johnson is used and compute $\overline{S}$ for each of these methods.

6.* Let $S'(n)$ be the worst-case cost when some of the keys are equal, and you are required to determine the chain and all equations. Prove $S'(n) = S(n)$.

7.* Suppose we know that all keys are equal to 0 or 1. What is the worst-case cost? What is the average cost? (Knuth)

8.* Show that $F(n) > \lceil \log_2(n)! \rceil$ for $n \geq 22$.

9.* Show that $\overline{F}(6) > \overline{S}(6)$.

10. Discuss $\overline{S}(n)$ up to $n = 10$.

4.2 Merging Chains

In our first approach to the sorting problem, the main task consisted in merging two chains. In this section we will study this problem in detail. As before, we denote by $M(m, n)$ the cost of merging two chains of size m and n, respectively.

In the last section we have discussed an algorithm, called *linear merge* which needs $m + n - 1$ comparisons in the worst case, whence

(4.6) $$M(m, n) \leq m + n - 1 \text{ for all } m, n \geq 1.$$

Since the possible linear extensions of two disjoint chains $\{a_1 < \ldots < a_m\}$ and $\{b_1 < \ldots < b_n\}$ correspond uniquely to the position of the elements $b_1, \ldots, b_n$ in the final chain of length $m + n$, we conclude that there are precisely $\binom{m+n}{n}$ such extensions. The information-theoretic bound thus reads

(4.7) $$M(m, n) \geq \lceil \log_2 \binom{m+n}{n} \rceil.$$

We have already seen that for $\mid n - m \mid \leq 1$, bound (4.6) gives the correct value whereas for $m = 1$, the lower bound (4.7) applies. So, it seems that the case when m and n are roughly equal is quite different from the situation when m is very small as compared to n. Note, however, that in both these extreme cases the true cost is (apart from a constant) equal to the information-theoretic lower bound (4.7). Our first result shows that this is indeed true for all m and n. The following is the key idea of the proof. At the outset we are given a poset P_0 consisting of two disjoint chains $S = \{a_1 < a_2 < \ldots < a_m\}$, $T = \{b_1 < b_2 < \ldots < b_n\}$. Let $L(P_0)$ be the set of $\binom{m+n}{n}$ linear extensions of P_0. In the course of an algorithm we add relations between the a_i's and b_j's. All posets P so arising have the property that they can be covered by the two chains S and T, or, equivalently, that there are no three pairwise unrelated elements. We say that these posets have *width* 2 (with the linear orders having width 1). In general, P is of width k if P can be decomposed into k chains, but not into fewer than k chains. Equivalently, P is of width k if the largest set of pairwise unrelated elements in P contains k elements (see exercise 4.2.1). Whenever P is such a poset obtained at some stage of the algorithm and $x : y$ is the next pair to be compared, then as noted at the beginning of this chapter

$$\mid L(P) \mid = \mid L(P; x < y) \mid + \mid L(P; y < x) \mid.$$

Now comes the crux of the argument. Suppose there is a *universal constant* δ, $0 < \delta \leq \frac{1}{2}$, such that for *every* poset P of width 2 there is a pair x, y satisfying

$$\delta \leq \frac{|\,L(P; x < y)\,|}{|\,L(P)\,|} \leq 1 - \delta.$$

Then the same is true for $\frac{|L(P; y < x)|}{|L(P)|}$ whence after the comparison $x : y$, the linear extensions left number at most $(1 - \delta)\,|\,L(P)\,|$. Let us call such a pair x, y a *δ-central pair* for P.

Now suppose we are given any poset P of width 2 (e.g. two disjoint chains), with $e(P) = |\,L(P)\,|$. The information-theoretic bound says that any sorting procedure with P at the outset will need at least $\lceil \log_2 e(P) \rceil$ queries. On the other hand, if $\mathcal{A}$ is an algorithm of length L which chooses a δ-central pair at each stage, then the number of possible linear extensions at the end is at most $(1 - \delta)^L e(P)$ whence

$$1 \leq (1 - \delta)^L e(P)$$

or

$$L \leq \left(-\frac{1}{\log_2(1 - \delta)} \right) \log_2 e(P),$$

where $-\frac{1}{\log_2(1-\delta)} = K(\delta)$ is a positive constant independent of P. The larger δ is, the smaller and therefore the better the constant $K(\delta)$ will be, with the extreme case $\delta = \frac{1}{2}$, $K(\frac{1}{2}) = 1$.

The following result due to Linial [1984] shows that in every poset of width 2 there is a $\frac{1}{3}$-central pair. In the next section we will discuss the great result of Kahn and Saks that indeed *every* poset has a δ-central pair with $\delta > \frac{3}{11}$.

Theorem 4.5. *Let P be a poset of width 2, and $S(P)$ its sorting complexity. Then there exists a $\frac{1}{3}$-central pair in P, and thus*

$$\lceil \log_2 e(P) \rceil \leq S(P) \leq \frac{1}{(\log_2 3) - 1} \log_2 e(P) \sim 1.7095.\log_2 e(P).$$

Proof. Suppose P is covered by the two chains $\{a_1 < a_2 < \ldots < a_m\}, \{b_1 < b_2 < \ldots < b_n\}$ with possibly further relations between the chains. For a_i, b_j we define $Pr(a_i < b_j)$ as the proportion of linear extensions which put b_j above a_i, i.e.

$$Pr(a_i < b_j) = \frac{|\,L(P; a_i < b_j)\,|}{e(P)}.$$

A similar definition applies to more than two arguments, e.g.,

$$Pr(a_i < b_j < a_k) = \frac{|\, L(P; a_i < b_j \wedge b_j < a_k)\,|}{e(P)}.$$

We may assume that a_1 and b_1 are unrelated, since otherwise we just ignore the smaller of the two. Suppose w.l.o.g. $Pr(a_1 < b_1) \leq \frac{1}{2}$. If $Pr(a_1 < b_1) = \frac{1}{2}$, then we have found our central pair, so assume $Pr(a_1 < b_1) < \frac{1}{2}$. Obviously, $Pr(a_1 < b_1) \leq Pr(a_1 < b_2) \leq \ldots \leq Pr(a_1 < b_n)$. Let j be the largest index such that $Pr(a_1 < b_j) < \frac{1}{2}$. Note that $j < n$, since $Pr(a_1 < b_n) < \frac{1}{2}$ would imply $Pr(a_1 > b_n) = \frac{1}{e(P)} > \frac{1}{2}$ and thus $e(P) = 1$, i.e. P would be a chain. Now if $Pr(a_1 < b_j) \geq \frac{1}{3}$, then we are finished, so assume $Pr(a_1 < b_j) < \frac{1}{3}$. From the choice of j we further have $\frac{1}{2} \leq Pr(a_1 < b_{j+1})$. Note, finally, $Pr(b_j < a_1 < b_{j+1}) \leq Pr(a_1 < b_1)$ since every linear extension with $b_j < a_1 < b_{j+1}$ corresponds uniquely to a linear extension with $a_1 < b_1$ by moving a_1 all the way down and keeping all other positions unchanged. We conclude

$$
\begin{aligned}
\frac{1}{2} \leq Pr(a_1 < b_{j+1}) &= Pr(a_1 < b_j) + Pr(b_j < a_1 < b_{j+1}) \\
&\leq Pr(a_1 < b_j) + Pr(a_1 < b_1) \\
&\leq 2Pr(a_1 < b_j) < \frac{2}{3},
\end{aligned}
$$

and thus $\frac{1}{3} \leq Pr(a_1 < b_{j+1}) < \frac{2}{3}$. The elements a_1 and b_{j+1} are therefore a $\frac{1}{3}$-central pair. $\square$

Remark. The value $\delta = \frac{1}{3}$ is best possible as the poset $Q = \begin{array}{c} b\, \bullet \\ | \quad \bullet\, c \\ a\, \bullet \end{array}$ demonstrates. Here $Pr(c < a) = \frac{1}{3}$, $Pr(c < b) = \frac{2}{3}$. It can be shown (Aigner [1985]) that this poset is essentially the only one with $\delta = \frac{1}{3}$, meaning that the only width 2-posets which have no central pair with $\delta > \frac{1}{3}$ arise by stacking copies of Q and chains on top of each other. By taking into account previously determined comparisons, the constant $\frac{1}{\log_2 3 - 1} \sim 1.71$ can be lowered to $\frac{1}{\log_2((1+\sqrt{5})/2)} \sim 1.44$, and this is the best possible general constant (Linial [1984]).

Corollary 4.6. *Let $M(m,n)$ be the cost of merging two chains of size m and n, respectively. Then*

$$\lceil \log_2 \binom{m+n}{n} \rceil \leq M(m,n) \leq 1.44 \log_2 \binom{m+n}{n}.$$

After these asymptotic considerations we discuss precise results. We look first at the case when m is small as compared to n, and determine then the range of m and n when the method of linear merge is known to be best possible.

Let us make a general remark before. In the course of an algorithm we encounter posets P which are to be sorted. We have denoted the sorting complexity of P by $S(P)$. Let us introduce an ordering on the set of all non-isomorphic posets on n elements. Set $P \preceq Q$ if there exists a one-to-one mapping φ from the elements of P to those of Q such that $a \underset{P}{<} b \Rightarrow \varphi a \underset{Q}{<} \varphi b$. In other words, P is isomorphic to a sub-poset of Q. The ordering $\prec$ has a unique minimal element, the poset consisting of n unrelated elements, called the *antichain* on n elements, and a unique maximal element, the *chain* on n elements. A moment's reflection shows that $P \preceq Q$ implies $S(P) \geq S(Q)$. Just think of P as a sub-poset of Q; any sorting algorithm for P will then also sort Q.

Example 4.3. Figure 4.4 shows posets P, Q, R with $P \prec Q \prec R$. The respective embeddings are given by the identity mapping.

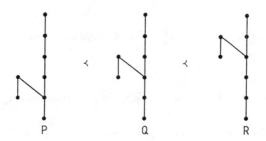

Figure 4.4

We have noted the obvious result $M(1, n) = \lceil \log_2(n + 1) \rceil$. But already for $m = 2$, to determine the precise cost $M(2, n)$ is far from easy. It was established by Hwang-Lin [1971] and Graham [1971].

Theorem 4.7. *We have*

$$M(2, n) = \lceil \log_2 \frac{7}{12}(n + 1) \rceil + \lceil \log_2 \frac{14}{17}(n + 1) \rceil.$$

Proof. Since $M(2,n)$ is obviously increasing in n, it is best to prove our claim in terms of the threshold function $m(t)$

$$M(2,n) \le t \Longleftrightarrow n \le m(t).$$

The reader can easily convince himself that the stated formula for $M(2,n)$ is equivalent to

(4.8) $$m(2k) = \lfloor \frac{17}{14}2^k \rfloor - 1.$$

(4.9) $$m(2k+1) = \lfloor \frac{12}{7}2^k \rfloor - 1.$$

We have $m(1) = 0$, $m(2) = 1$, $m(3) = 2$, $m(4) = 3$, so (4.8) and (4.9) hold for $t \le 4$. We proceed by induction on t.

Case 1. $t = 2k+1$, $k \ge 2$. Let the chains be $S = \{a_1 < a_2\}$ and $T = \{b_1 < b_2 < \ldots < b_n\}$. We show first that $m(2k+1) \ge \lfloor \frac{12}{7}2^k \rfloor - 1$, i.e. we set $n = \lfloor \frac{12}{7}2^k \rfloor - 1$ and prove that S and T can be merged with $2k+1$ comparisons.

Let the first comparison be $a_2 : b_{m(2k)+1}$. If $a_2 < b_{m(2k)+1}$, then S and $\{b_1 < \ldots < b_{m(2k)}\}$ can be merged with $2k$ tests by induction, hence we may assume $a_2 > b_{m(2k)+1}$ (Figure 4.5).

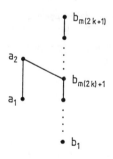

Figure 4.5

Since $m(2k+1) - m(2k) = \lfloor \frac{12}{7}2^k \rfloor - \lfloor \frac{17}{14}2^k \rfloor = \lfloor \frac{24}{7}2^{k-1} \rfloor - \lfloor \frac{17}{7}2^{k-1} \rfloor = 2^{k-1}$, a_2 can be inserted into its proper place with $k-1$ comparisons. After that we insert a_1 into T using at most $k+1$ tests since $m(2k+1)+1 = \lfloor \frac{12}{7}2^k \rfloor < 2^{k+1}$; so altogether we need $1 + (k-1) + (k+1) = 2k+1$ comparisons.
Now we exhibit a strategy $\mathcal{S}$ which forces player A to use more than $2k+1$ tests when $n = \lfloor \frac{12}{7}2^k \rfloor$, thus proving $m(2k+1) = \lfloor \frac{12}{7}2^k \rfloor - 1$.

We may assume w.l.o.g. that the first comparison involves a_2. Obviously, a_2 must be compared to some b_j with $j \le m(2k) + 1$. Strategy S answers $a_2 > b_j$ for every such j. Since player A gets the most information when $j = m(2k) + 1$ (see figure 4.4 for the case $t = 5$), we may assume that the first comparison is indeed $a_2 : b_{m(2k)+1}$. For the remainder of the game, S stipulates $a_1 < b_{m(2k)+2}$. In this way, player A is forced to insert a_2 into the chain $\{b_{m(2k)+2} < \ldots < b_n\}$ and a_1 into the chain $\{b_1 < \ldots < b_{m(2k)+1}\}$. Since $n - (m(2k) + 1) = \lfloor \frac{12}{7} 2^k \rfloor - \lfloor \frac{17}{14} 2^k \rfloor + 1 = 2^{k-1} + 1$ and $m(2k) + 2 = \lfloor \frac{17}{14} 2^k \rfloor + 1 > 2^k$, the two insertions take at least $k + (k + 1) = 2k + 1$ comparisons, whence player A needs at least $2k + 2$ tests overall.

Case 2. $t = 2k$, $k \ge 3$. Again, we exhibit first an algorithm of length $2k$ when $n = m(2k) = \lfloor \frac{17}{14} 2^k \rfloor - 1$.

Our first comparison is $a_2 : b_{m(2k-1)+1}$. If the answer is $<$, then we are through by induction. If the answer is $>$, then we compare $a_2 : b_{m(2k)+1-2^{k-3}}$. If the answer is $>$, then we need to insert a_2 into the chain $\{b_{m(2k)+2-2^{k-3}} < \ldots < b_{m(2k)}\}$ taking $k - 3$ tests, and a_1 into $\{b_1 < \ldots < b_{m(2k)}\}$ taking $k + 1$ tests (since $m(2k) + 1 = \lfloor \frac{17}{14} 2^k \rfloor < 2^{k+1}$) and thus $2k$ tests altogether. Suppose then $a_2 < b_{m(2k)+1-2^{k-3}}$. Since $m(2k) - 2^{k-3} - m(2k - 1) = \lfloor \frac{17}{7} 2^{k-1} \rfloor - 2^{k-3} - \lfloor \frac{12}{7} 2^{k-1} \rfloor \le 2^{k-2}$, we can certainly insert a_2 into its proper place with $k - 2$ comparisons, which together with the two previous comparisons give k tests. Hence if as 3rd test we take $a_1 : b_{2^{k-1}}$, after that $a_1 : b_{2^{k-1}+2^{k-2}}$, and finally $a_1 : b_{2^{k-1}+2^{k-2}+2^{k-3}}$, we can always assume that the answer is $>$. Note that $2^{k-1} + 2^{k-2} + 2^{k-3} > \lfloor \frac{12}{7} 2^{k-1} \rfloor$. Hence after these 5 tests we arrive at the following figure:

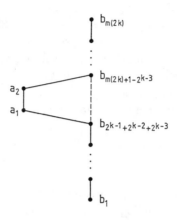

Figure 4.6

So it remains to merge $\{a_1 < a_2\}$ with the chain $\{b_{2^{k-1}+2^{k-2}+2^{k-3}+1} < \cdots < b_{m(2k)-2^{k-3}}\}$ and, since $m(2k) - 2^{k-3} - (2^{k-1} + 2^{k-2} + 2^{k-3}) = m(2k) - 2^k = \lfloor \frac{17}{14}2^k \rfloor - 1 - 2^k = \lfloor \frac{3}{14}2^k \rfloor - 1 = \lfloor \frac{12}{7}2^{k-3} \rfloor - 1 = m(2k-5)$, we may apply induction.

Now suppose $n = m(2k) + 1 = \lfloor \frac{17}{14}2^k \rfloor$. To construct a strategy S which forces player A to make $2k + 1$ tests is not quite as easy as in the previous case. Again, we may assume that the first test is $a_2 : b_{m(2k-1)+1}$ with answer $>$.

We declare the first steps of S as follows:

First three tests involving a_1:

      1st test: $a_1 > b_j$ iff $j \le 2^{k-1}$

      2nd test: $a_1 > b_j$ iff $j \le 2^{k-1} + 2^{k-2}$

      3rd test: $a_1 > b_j$ iff $j \le 2^{k-1} + 2^{k-2} + 2^{k-3}$.

Tests involving a_2:

      2nd test: $a_2 < b_j$ iff $j \ge n + 1 - 2^{k-3}$

      3rd test: $a_2 < b_j$ iff $j \ge n + 1 - 2^{k-3} - 2^{k-4}$

Case 2a. The 3rd test involving a_1 comes before the 3rd test involving a_2. Suppose after the overall first test $a_2 : b_{m(2k-1)+1}$, there come 3 tests involving a_1. Since $n - m(2k - 1) = \lfloor \frac{34}{7}2^{k-2} \rfloor + 1 - \lfloor \frac{24}{7}2^{k-2} \rfloor > 2^{k-2}$, it takes $k - 1$ further comparisons to insert a_2. Furthermore, $2^{k-1} + 2^{k-2} \le m(2k - 1) + 1 < 2^{k-1} + 2^{k-2} + 2^{k-3}$. Hence we may assume that a_1 is first compared to $b_{2^{k-1}}$ and then to $b_{2^{k-1}+2^{k-2}}$. If, in the next test, a_1 is compared to b_j with $j > 2^{k-1} + 2^{k-2} + 2^{k-3}$, (with answer $<$), then by stipulating

$a_2 > b_{2^{k-1}+2^{k-2}+2^{k-3}}$ and $a_1 < b_{2^{k-1}+2^{k-2}+2^{k-3}+1}$, it takes $k-2$ tests to insert a_1, and $k-1$ tests to insert a_2, since $n+1-(2^{k-1}+2^{k-2}+2^{k-3}) = \lfloor \frac{17}{14}2^k \rfloor + 1 - 7.2^{k-3} > 2^{k-2}$, and thus with the 4 previous tests $2k+1$ altogether. If, on the other hand, there is another test involving a_2, then by employing a similar reasoning it is readily seen that that the only potentially successful line for player A is to compare $a_2 : b_{n+1-2^{k-3}}$ and $a_1 : b_{2^{k-1}}$, $a_1 : b_{2^{k-1}+2^{k-2}}$, $a_1 : b_{2^{k-1}+2^{k-2}+2^{k-3}}$. But then the situation is as in figure 4.6. We now have to merge $\{a_1 < a_2\}$ with $\{b_{2^{k-1}+2^{k-2}+2^{k-3}+1} < \ldots < b_{n-2^{k-3}}\}$ and since $n - 2^{k-3} - (2^{k-1} + 2^{k-2} + 2^{k-3}) = m(2k - 5) + 1$, this takes $2k - 4$ more comparisons by induction.

Case 2b. The 3rd test involving a_2 comes before the 3rd test involving a_1. The argument is entirely analogous to the previous case and may be filled in by the reader.   □

Hwang [1980] has also computed the precise result for $m = 3$ whose proof is, as expected, enormously involved.

Theorem 4.8. *We have for $n \geq 8$,*

$$M(3,n) = \lceil \log_2 \frac{28}{43}(n + 2) \rceil + \lceil \log_2 \frac{56}{107}(n + 2) \rceil + \lceil \log_2 \frac{1}{17}(7n + 13) \rceil.$$

Now we turn to the other end and discuss the question when the method of linear merge cannot be further improved. We have seen

$$M(m,m) = 2m - 1 \quad \text{for } m \geq 1,$$
$$M(m,m + 1) = 2m \quad \text{for } m \geq 1,$$

and it is an easy matter to prove that

(4.10) $M(m,m + 2) = 2m + 1$ for $m \geq 2$

(4.11) $M(m,m + 3) = 2m + 2$ for $m \geq 4$.

We have already noted $M(1,3) = 2$, and from our results it follows further that $M(1,4) = 3$, $M(2,5) = 5$. Furthermore, it is easily seen that $M(3,6) = 7$. So, linear merge is not optimal outside the range given in (4.10) and (4.11).

The following result obtained by Stockmeyer and Yao [1980] generalizes (4.10) and (4.11) to

(4.12) $M(m, m + d) = 2m + d - 1$ for $m \geq 2d - 2$.

Thus we can say that linear merge is optimal whenever $m \leq n \leq \lfloor \frac{3m}{2} \rfloor + 1$. It is an open problem whether (4.12) gives the precise range of the optimality of linear merge for fixed d.

In order to prove (4.12) we must also consider two restricted merging problems. Suppose the chains to be merged are $S = \{a_1 < \ldots < a_m\}$ and $T = \{b_1 < \ldots < b_n\}$. We interpret the merging problem as usual as a game between two players. By $/M(m, n)$ we denote the worst-case cost of merging S and T when player B is only allowed to use strategies compatible with $a_1 > b_1$ (unknown to player A). $/M\backslash(m, n)$ denotes the cost when the strategies must be consistent with $a_1 > b_1$ and $a_m < b_n$ (again unknown to player A). Unknown to player A means that A does not know that B uses these restricted strategies, i.e. he must still determine the precise linear order. Sometimes we make use of the cost $M\backslash(m, n)$ when player B uses only strategies compatible with $a_m < b_n$. By symmetry, we, of course, have $/M(m, n) = M\backslash(m, n)$.

To see the difference between these notions consider, e.g., $m = 2$, $n = 4$. We know from (4.10) that $M(2, 4) = 5$. Let us prove, however, that $/M(2, 4) = 4$. We first compare $a_1 : b_2$. If $a_1 > b_2$, then we have reduced our problem to $M(2, 2) = 3$. On the other hand, if $a_1 < b_2$, then we compare $a_1 : b_1$ and with the answer $a_1 > b_1$ we have reduced our problem to $M(1, 3) = 2$. Thus $/M(2, 4) \leq 4$ and since clearly $/M(2, 4) \geq M(2, 3) = 4$ we deduce $/M(2, 4) = 4$.

In the following we make frequent use of two strategies. In the *simple strategy* player B chooses numbers h and k with $0 \leq h \leq m, 0 \leq k \leq n$ and stipulates $a_i < b_j$ for $i \leq h, j > k$ and $a_i > b_j$ for $i > h, j \leq k$ (see figure 4.7).

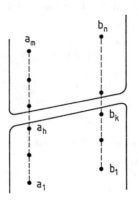

Figure 4.7

Thus

$$(4.13) \qquad M(m,n) \geq M(h,k) + M(m-h,n-k).$$

In the *complex strategy* player B chooses h and k and stipulates $a_i < b_j$ for $i \leq h$, $j \geq k$ and $a_i > b_j$ for $i > h$, $j \leq k$ (figure 4.8).

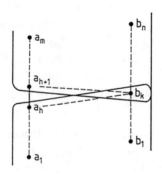

Figure 4.8

Thus

$$(4.14) \qquad M(m,n) \geq M\backslash(h,k) + /M(m-h,n-k+1).$$

To simplify our inductive argument we first prove the following easy lemma.

Lemma 4.9. *We have*

   i) $M(m,n) \geq /M(m,n) \geq /M\backslash(m,n)$

  ii) $/M(m+1, n+1) \geq /M(m,n) + 2$

 iii) $/M\backslash(m+1, n+1) \geq /M\backslash(m,n) + 2.$

Proof. i) is obvious. In part ii), player B stipulates for the $/M(m+1, n+1)$-problem $b_1 < a_1 < b_2 < a_2$. Player A must then solve the $/M(m,n)$-problem and must make in addition the comparisons $a_1 : b_1$ and $a_1 : b_2$. The proof of iii) is analogous. □

Theorem 4.10. *We have*

   i) $M(m, m+d) \geq 2m + d - 1$ *for* $m \geq 2d - 2$

  ii) $/M(m, m+d) \geq 2m + d - 1$ *for* $m \geq 2d - 1$

 iii) $/M\backslash(m, m+d+2) \geq 2m + d$ *for* $m \geq 2d - 1.$

Proof. Although we are mainly interested in part i) we must prove all three inequalities since in the inductive proof we make use of all inequalities. From the Lemma we know that ii) and iii) are true once we know that they hold for the smallest value $m = 2d - 1$. Again, since $M(m,n) \geq /M(m,n)$, we have to consider in i) just the value $m = 2d - 2$. So our task consists in showing

$$M(2d - 2, 3d - 2) \geq 5d - 5$$
(4.15) $$/M(2d - 1, 3d - 1) \geq 5d - 3$$
$$/M\backslash(2d - 1, 3d + 1) \geq 5d - 2,$$

for every $d \geq 1$. The inequalities are trivial for $d = 1$. We proceed by induction on d, and assume that (4.15) and hence the theorem is true for all $d' < d$.

Proof of i). Let the first comparison be $a_i : b_j$. Note that by reversing the order of both chains we may assume that i is odd, say $i = 2\ell - 1$ with $1 \leq \ell < d$, since $m = 2d - 2$ is even. If $j \leq 3\ell - 2$, then player B says $>$ and pursues the simple strategy with $h = 2\ell - 2$, $k = 3\ell - 2$. By (4.13) and induction we have

$$
\begin{aligned}
M(2d - 2, 3d - 2) &\geq 1 + M(2\ell - 2, 3\ell - 2) + M(2(d - \ell), 3(d - \ell)) \\
&\geq 1 + (5\ell - 5) + (5(d - \ell) - 1) \\
&= 5d - 5.
\end{aligned}
$$

If $j \geq 3\ell - 1$, then player B says $<$ and uses then the complex strategy with $h = 2\ell - 1$, $k = 3\ell - 2$. Hence by (4.14), Lemma 4.9(i) and induction we obtain

$$
\begin{aligned}
M(2d - 2, 3d - 2) \; &\geq \; 1 + M\backslash(2\ell - 1, 3\ell - 2) + /M(2(d - \ell) - 1, 3(d - \ell) + 1) \\
&\geq \; 1 + /M(2\ell - 1, 3\ell - 2) + /M\backslash(2(d - \ell) - 1, 3(d - \ell) + 1) \\
&\geq \; 1 + (5\ell - 4) + (5(d - \ell) - 2) \\
&= \; 5d - 5.
\end{aligned}
$$

Proof of ii). Suppose the first comparison is $a_i : b_j$ with $i = 2\ell - 1$, $j \leq 3\ell - 2$ for some $1 \leq \ell \leq d$. Player B says $>$ and pursues the complex strategy with $h = 2\ell - 2$, $k = 3\ell - 1$. As before we obtain

$$
\begin{aligned}
/M(2d - 1, 3d - 1) \; &\geq \; 1 + /M\backslash(2\ell - 2, 3\ell - 1) + /M(2(d - \ell) + 1, 3(d - \ell) + 1) \\
&\geq \; 1 + (5\ell - 5) + (5(d - \ell) + 1) \\
&= \; 5d - 3.
\end{aligned}
$$

If $i = 2\ell - 1$, $j \geq 3\ell - 1$, then player B proclaims $<$ and uses the simple strategy with $h = 2\ell - 1$, $k = 3\ell - 2$. Thus

$$
\begin{aligned}
/M(2d - 1, 3d - 1) \; &\geq \; 1 + /M(2\ell - 1, 3\ell - 2) + M(2(d - \ell), 3(d - \ell) + 1) \\
&\geq \; 1 + (5\ell - 4) + 5(d - \ell) \\
&= \; 5d - 3.
\end{aligned}
$$

Now suppose $i = 2\ell$, $j \leq 3\ell$ with $1 \leq \ell < d$. Player B pronounces $a_i > b_j$ and uses the complex strategy with $h = 2\ell - 1$, $k = 3\ell + 1$, leading to

$$
\begin{aligned}
/M(2d - 1, 3d - 1) \; &\geq \; 1 + /M\backslash(2\ell - 1, 3\ell + 1) + /M(2(d - \ell), 3(d - \ell) - 1) \\
&\geq \; 1 + (5\ell - 2) + (5(d - \ell) - 2) \\
&= \; 5d - 3.
\end{aligned}
$$

If, finally, $i = 2\ell$, $j \geq 3\ell + 1$, then player B says $<$ and pursues the simple strategy with $h = 2\ell$, $k = 3\ell$. Thus

$$
\begin{aligned}
/M(2d - 1, 3d - 1) \; &\geq \; 1 + /M(2\ell, 3\ell) + M(2(d - \ell) - 1, 3(d - \ell) - 1) \\
&\geq \; 1 + (5\ell - 1) + (5(d - \ell) - 3) \\
&= \; 5d - 3.
\end{aligned}
$$

Proof of iii). The argument is entirely analogous and may be supplied by the reader. $\square$

As mentioned before, no values $M(m,n)$ outside the range $m \le n \le \lfloor \frac{3m}{2} \rfloor + 1$ have been found where linear merge is optimal. The first open case is $m = 7$, $n = 12$ where $18 \ge M(7,12) \ge M(7,11) = 17$.

Now that we have analyzed the extreme cases $m \ll n$ and $m \sim n$, what about the range in between? Hwang and Lin[1972] advanced a common generalization of binary insertion and linear merging which we now briefly discuss.

The idea is simple enough. We assume $m \le n$ and compare first $a_1 : b_{i(m,n)}$ where $i(m,n)$ is a suitably chosen function. If $a_1 > b_{i(m,n)}$, then we have reduced our problem to $M(m, n - i(m,n))$. If $a_1 < b_{i(m,n)}$, then we insert a_1 into its proper place using $\lceil \log_2 i(m,n) \rceil$ comparisons and consider then the remaining problem $M(m - 1, n')$, where n' is the smallest index such that $a_1 < b_{n'}$. By choosing $i(m,n) = 2^{\lfloor \log \frac{n}{m} \rfloor} \sim \lceil \frac{n}{m+1} \rceil$ it can be shown that the cost of this algorithm is smaller than $\lceil \log_2 \binom{m+n}{n} \rceil + \min(m,n)$ (see exercise 4.2.10). Note that for $m = 1$ we obtain precisely binary insertion, whereas for $m = n$ linear merge results.

Our final topic concerns the merging of several chains. Suppose we have k chains $C_1, \ldots, C_k$ each of size n. The information-theoretic bound is

$$M(n, \ldots, n) \ge \lceil \log_2 \binom{kn}{n \ldots n} \rceil,$$

where on the right-hand side the argument of the logarithm is a k-fold multinomial coefficient. Assume $k = 2^\ell + r$, $0 \le r < 2^\ell$. Then by recursively merging the 2^ℓ chains (using linear merge) we arrive after at most $\ell.2^\ell n$ tests at a chain of length $2^\ell n$. Similarly, by merging the r remaining chains we need by induction at most $\lceil \log_2 r \rceil rn$ tests to produce a chain of length rn. Finally, using linear merge on the big chains we obtain the linear order after another $(2^\ell + r)n$ comparisons. Hence the total number of tests does not exceed

$$\ell 2^\ell n + \lceil \log_2 r \rceil rn + (2^\ell + r)n \le (2^\ell + r)n \, (\ell + 1) \le \lceil \log_2 k \rceil kn.$$

We have proved therefore

$$M(\underbrace{n, \ldots, n}_{k}) \le \lceil \log_2 k \rceil kn.$$

When the sizes of the chains are not equal, then the Hwang-Lin procedure is suggested. Suppose the chains have sizes $n_1, \ldots, n_k$, respectively. Merge the first two chains, and then merge in every one of the following chains, using the Hwang-Lin algorithm. The reader may easily verify that this method yields the following result.

$$\lceil \log_2 \left(\frac{n_1 + \cdots + n_k}{n_1 \ldots n_k} \right) \rceil \leq M(n_1, \ldots, n_k) \leq \lceil \log_2 \left(\frac{n_1 + \cdots + n_k}{n_1 \ldots n_k} \right) \rceil + \sum_{i=2}^{k} n_i.$$

Exercises 4.2.

1.* Show that P has width k iff the largest set of pairwise unrelated elements in P has size k. (Dilworth)

2. Verify the formulae (4.8) and (4.9).

3. Complete the remaining case in the proof of **4.7**.

4.* Consider the following posets P_n of width 2 on the chains $S = \{a_1 < a_2 < \ldots\}$, $T = \{b_1 < b_2 < \ldots\}$. If $n = 2m$, Let S and T contain m elements each with the additional relations $a_j > b_{j-1}$ $(j = 2, \ldots, m)$, $b_j > a_{j-2}$ $(j = 3, \ldots, m)$. If $n = 2m - 1$, let S contain m elements, and T $m - 1$ elements, with the additional relations $a_j > b_{j-2}$ $(j = 3, \ldots, m)$, $b_j > a_{j-1}$ $(j = 2, \ldots, m)$. Determine $| L(P_n) |$ and show that we need $n - 1$ tests to merge them.

5. Show $M(m + m', n) \leq M(m, n) + M(m', n)$.

6.* Prove $M(m, n) \leq M(m, \lfloor \frac{n}{2} \rfloor) + m$.

7.* Show: $M(m, n) \leq 1 + \max(M(m, n - k), M(m - 1, n) + \lceil \log_2 k \rceil)$, $m \geq 1$, $n \geq k$.

8. Complete the proof of Theorem 4.10.

9.* Show that Theorem 4.10 gives precisely the range of optimality for linear merge, when $n - m \leq 4$, $m \leq n$.

10.* Show that the method of Hwang-Lin yields $M(m, n) < \lceil \log_2 \left(\frac{m + n}{n} \right) \rceil + \min(m, n)$.

11. Verify $M(4, 1, 1) = 6$.

4.3 Selection Problems

Let us now consider questions arising from the second approach to sorting outlined in section 1. Our method consisted in isolating the maximal element, then the maximal element of the remaining set, i.e. the second largest element overall, and so on. More generally, we want to determine a certain part at the top (or by symmetry at the bottom) of the eventual linear order. Three possible top parts immediately come to mind, depicted in the following figure.

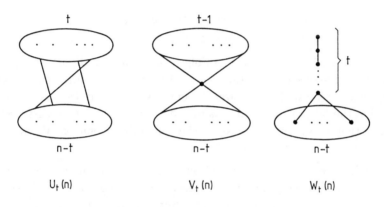

Figure 4.9

The left poset calls for determining the t largest elements (without regard to their respective ordering), the middle poset corresponds to selecting the t-th largest element whereas the poset on the right calls for finding the t largest elements in order. Note that once the t-th element v is determined, its relation to any other element must be known, i.e. there is no element $\neq v$ unrelated to v (see exercise 4.3.1). Hence the second poset of the figure corresponds indeed to $V_t(n)$.

Let us denote the respective worst-case costs by $U_t(n)$, $V_t(n)$, and $W_t(n)$ for $1 \leq t \leq n$. Since any algorithm of the $W_t(n)$- problem yields algorithms for $V_t(n)$ and $U_t(n)$, and similarly any algorithm for $V_t(n)$ obviously also solves the $U_t(n)$-problem, we note

$$U_t(n) \leq V_t(n) \leq W_t(n) \text{ for all } t \text{ and } n.$$

By symmetry, we further have

$$U_t(n) = U_{n-t}(n), \quad V_t(n) = V_{n+1-t}(n),$$

whence in a table for $U_t(n)$, $V_t(n)$ we may assume $t \leq \lfloor \frac{n}{2} \rfloor$ and $t \leq \lceil \frac{n}{2} \rceil$, respectively. Furthermore

$$W_{n-1}(n) = W_n(n) = S(n).$$

For $t = 1$, all three selection problems are the same, namely determination of the maximum which by **4.3** yields

$$U_1(n) = V_1(n) = W_1(n) = n - 1.$$

Already for $t = 2$, however, the precise answer requires some thought. Note first that

(4.16) $\qquad\quad U_2(n) \;\leq\; V_2(n) = W_2(n) \leq U_2(n) + 1.$
$\qquad\qquad\quad\;\; U_2(n) \;\leq\; V_2(n-1) + 1 = W_2(n-1) + 1.$

$V_2(n) = W_2(n)$ is clear from the definition, whereas $W_2(n) \leq U_2(n) + 1$ follows from the observation that we need at most one more comparison for $W_2(n)$ once we know the two largest elements. To verify the last inequality, determine the largest two elements in order out of $n - 1$ elements first, and compare then the second largest to the remaining element. Whatever the answer, the top two elements will then be known.

Let us look at $W_2(n)$ first. As in section 1 we view an algorithm as a sequence of tennis games played between n players. Our task consists then in selecting the best and second best competitors. Suppose first that $n = 2^k$. As in a knock-out tennis tournament we pair the players in 2^{k-1} pairs, determine the winner of each pair, pair the winners again, and so on. In this way we determine the overall winner with $2^{k-1} + 2^{k-2} + \ldots + 2 + 1 = 2^k - 1 = n - 1$ games. (See figure 4.10 for n=16.)

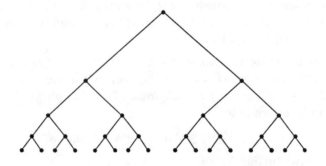

Figure 4.10

Note that every player except the overall winner w has lost precisely once. Hence we know at this point that the second best player s must be among the losers to w (since he can only lose to w). Since w has played in k games, there are k possible candidates for s. The best player among these (which must be s) can then be determined with $k - 1$ more games by **4.3**. Thus we conclude $W_2(n) \leq (n - 1) + (k - 1) = (n - 2) + \log_2 n$.

If $n = 2^k + r$, $0 < r < 2^k$, then by playing a preliminary round involving $2r$ players, we arrive at 2^k possible candidates for w and proceed as before. In the worst case the eventual winner w was involved in $k + 1 = \lceil \log_2 n \rceil$ games whence by the same reasoning as before we obtain

$$(4.17) \qquad V_2(n) = W_2(n) \leq (n - 2) + \lceil \log_2 n \rceil.$$

Using the last inequality in (4.16) we further have

$$(4.18) \qquad U_2(n) \leq (n - 2) + \lceil \log_2(n - 1) \rceil.$$

Steinhaus who discusses these algorithms in his book "Mathematical Snapshots" conjectured that they give the true values for all n. After some erroneous attempts it was Kislitsyn [1964] who first showed that (4.17) is indeed the correct value, while equality in (4.18) was established a little later. Before we turn to lower bounds and a proof of these results let us generalize the tournament method to arbitrary t.

Proposition 4.11. *Let $1 \leq t \leq n$. Then*

i) $W_t(n) \leq (n - t) + \sum\limits_{i=n-t+2}^{n} \lceil \log i \rceil$

ii) $V_t(n) \leq (n - t) + (t - 1)\lceil \log(n - t + 2) \rceil$

iii) $U_t(n) \leq (n - t) + (t - 1)\lceil \log(n - t + 1) \rceil.$

Proof. To prove i) we set up a knock-out tournament as before with a possible pre-round if n is not a power of 2. As before we determine the best player w using $n - 1$ games. Now we remove w from its initial position, move up its first opponent and replay the games along the path that w climbed up to the top. This takes at most $\lceil \log_2 n \rceil - 1$ games, and the second best player s is determined. Figure 4.11 shows this procedure for $n = 11$.

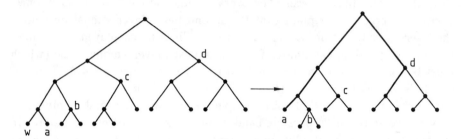

Figure 4.11

Note that the third best player must have lost to the second best (in the first or second round of games) by this set-up. Hence we delete now the second best from its initial position, move up its first opponent into his place and replay the games in the path that moved s up to the top. It is immediately seen that in the worst case we need no more than $\lceil \log_2(n-1) \rceil - 1$ games to move the third best player up to the top. Continuing in this way, we need another $\lceil \log_2(n-2) \rceil - 1$ to determine the 4th ranking player, and so on. Summing up all terms yields formula i). Observe that i) yields for $t = n$ or $t = n - 1$ precisely the formula $B(n)$ for binary insertion in **4.1**.

To verify ii) we use the tournament idea in a slightly different way suggested by Hadian and Sobel [1969]. First we set up a knock-out tournament for $n - t + 2$ players. This takes $n - t + 1$ games. The winner v_0 of this tournament is better than $n - t + 1$ others and hence can't be the t-th best. We discard v_0 as before and replace v_0 by one of the remaining $t - 2$ players. By replaying the games that moved v_0 to the top we obtain the new winner v_1 after at most $\lceil \log_2(n-t+2) \rceil$ games. Again, we see that v_1 is better than $n - t + 1$ others and hence cannot possibly be the t-th best. Repeating this procedure $t - 2$ times until we have used up all $t - 2$ remaining elements, we have discarded precisely the $t - 1$ players that are better than the t-th best. Now in the last series (after having discarded v_{t-2}) we can move up the first opponent of v_{t-2} one step (as in the proof if i)). Replaying the games in the chain that moved v_{t-2} to the top, we determine the best player w of the $n - t + 1$ players left with $\lceil \log_2(n-t+2) \rceil - 1$ games, and w is now precisely the t-th best. Summing up all terms yields ii).

The proof of iii) is entirely analogous to ii). Just start with a tournament on $n - t + 1$ players and proceed as before. $\square$

Now we turn to lower bounds. We will prove a general result in section 2 of the next chapter which will give good bounds on all these selection problems as well as some others. For the moment we confine ourselves to a proof of $W_2(n) \geq (n-2) + \lceil \log_2 n \rceil$ and $U_2(n) \geq (n-2) + \lceil \log_2(n-1) \rceil$.

Proposition 4.12. *We have for all* $n \geq 2$,

   i) $W_2(n) = V_2(n) = (n-2) + \lceil \log_2 n \rceil$

   ii) $U_2(n) = (n-2) + \lceil \log_2(n-1) \rceil$.

Proof. Consider an optimal algorithm $\mathcal{A}$ of, say, length ℓ determining the largest two elements in order. Denote by d_i the number of players who were defeated at least i times. Clearly, $\ell = \sum_{i \geq 1} d_i$ and $d_1 = n - 1$. Suppose the overall winner w has played p times, then $d_2 \geq p - 1$ since, as we remarked before, every player (except the second best) who has been defeated by w must lose at least one other time. It remains to show that $p \geq \log_2 n$ or equivalently $2^p \geq n$.

As usual we view the sorting process as a game between two players A and B. Let S be the set of elements. To each stage i (after i tests) we associate a function $f_i : S \longrightarrow \mathbb{N}_0$ $(i = 0, \ldots, \ell)$. At the outset we set $f_0(x) = 1$ for all $x \in S$. Now suppose $x : y$ is the $(i+1)$-st comparison. Player B says $x > y$ if $f_i(x) > f_i(y)$, $y > x$ if $f_i(y) > f_i(x)$, making an arbitrary choice if $f_i(x) = f_i(y)$. Suppose the outcome according to this rule is $x > y$. The new function $f_{i+1} : S \longrightarrow \mathbb{N}_0$ is then declared by

$$
\begin{aligned}
f_{i+1}(x) &= f_i(x) + f_i(y) \\
f_{i+1}(y) &= 0 \\
f_{i+1}(z) &= f_i(z) \quad \text{for } z \neq x, y.
\end{aligned}
$$

We observe two things:

   i) $\sum_{x \in S} f_i(n) = n$ for all $i = 0, \ldots, \ell$.

   ii) If $f_i(x) = 0$ then $f_j(x) = 0$ for all $j > i$.

In other words, once player x has lost, its value $f_i(x)$ drops to 0 and stays at 0 thereafter. In particular, at the end we must have $f_\ell(x) = 0$ for all $x \neq w$, and thus $f_\ell(w) = n$ by i).

The rest is easy. Denote by $v_i(x)$ the number of victories of x up to stage i. We claim that $2^{v_i(x)} \geq f_i(x)$ for all x and all i. This certainly holds for

$i = 0$, since $2^0 = 1 = f_0(x)$. We proceed by induction on i. If z is not involved in the $(i+1)$-st game, then $v_{i+1}(z) = v_i(z)$ and $f_{i+1}(z) = f_i(z)$, so that nothing has changed. If the outcome of game $i+1$ is $x > y$, then $2^{v_{i+1}(y)} \geq f_{i+1}(y) = 0$ holds trivially, while for x we have $2^{v_{i+1}(x)} = 2.2^{v_i(x)} \geq 2f_i(x) \geq f_i(x) + f_i(y) = f_{i+1}(x)$ by the set-up of the strategy. Now at the end, we have $v_\ell(w) = p$ and thus $2^p = 2^{v_\ell(w)} \geq f_\ell(w) = n$, and the proof is complete.

The reader can now easily adjust the strategy to prove the corresponding result for $U_2(n)$.   □

For general t, we have the following lower bounds which are corollaries of Theorem 5.6 of the next chapter.

Theorem 4.13. *For all t and n,*

i) $W_t(n) \geq (n - t) + \lceil \log_2 n(n-1)\ldots(n-t+2) \rceil$

ii) $V_t(n) \geq (n - t) + \lceil \log_2 (\begin{smallmatrix} n \\ t-1 \end{smallmatrix}) \rceil$

iii) $U_t(n) \geq (n - t) + \lceil \log_2 \frac{1}{t} (\begin{smallmatrix} n \\ t-1 \end{smallmatrix}) \rceil$.

A comparison of the bounds in **4.13** and **4.11** shows that for fixed t the bounds differ only in a function of t, i.e. a constant. For example, for $W_t(n)$, we have

$$\sum_{i=n-t+2}^{n} \lceil \log_2 i \rceil < \sum_{i=n-t+2}^{n} \log_2 i + (t-1)$$
$$= \log_2(n(n-1)\ldots(n-t+2)) + (t-1)$$
$$\leq \lceil \log_2 n(n-1)\ldots(n-t+2) \rceil + (t-1).$$

Hence the two bounds are at most $t - 2$ apart for $t \geq 2$. Furthermore, it is easily shown that for infinitely many n the bounds coincide, giving thus the precise value. Note also, that for $t = 2$ we again obtain $W_2(n) = V_2(n) \geq (n-2) + \lceil \log_2 n \rceil$.

For $t = 3$, the bounds for $W_3(t)$ are at most 1 apart. The precise result requires a considerably more refined argument. We just state the result (due to Aigner [1982a]).

Theorem 4.14. *Let $n \geq 6$, $n = 2^k + r$ with $0 \leq r < 2^k$. Then*

$$W_3(n) = \begin{cases} (n-3) + 2k & r = 0 \\ (n-3) + 2k + 1 & 1 \leq r \leq 2^{k-2} \\ (n-3) + 2k + 2 & otherwise. \end{cases}$$

The small values are $W_3(3) = 3$, $W_3(4) = 5$, $W_3(5) = 7$.

No general formula is known for any other t, the best bounds being due to Kirkpatrick [1974].

Let us now discuss one of the most intensively studied selection problems. Suppose n is odd. The unknown chain has then a unique middle element, called the *median*. Our task is to find the median. Let us denote the cost of this problem by $Med(n)$; thus $Med(n) = V_{\frac{n+1}{2}}(n)$. Our bounds **4.11** and **4.13** are quite far apart in this case, the lower bound being linear in n, while the upper bound is of the order $\frac{1}{2}n\log_2 n$, i.e. about half of the full sorting problem although we are asking for much less information. The following beautiful algorithm, first suggested by Blum et al [1973], shows that the median can indeed be found with cost linear in n. In fact, we show that $V_t(n)$ can be determined with linear cost in n for all t.

Proposition 4.15. *We have for all n,*

$$V_t(n) \leq 15n.$$

Proof. The assertion is trivial for $n \leq 2^{10}$ since $V_t(n) \leq S(n) \leq \sum_{i=2}^{n} \lceil \log i \rceil \leq 10n$. For $n \geq 2^{10}$ we are going to prove by induction that in fact $V_t(n) \leq 15n - 163$. For $n = 2^{10}$ we have $V_t(n) \leq S(n) \leq 10n \leq 15n - 163$. Now suppose $n > 2^{10}$. By adding at most 13 dummy minimal elements we may assume that $n = 7(2q + 1)$ with $q \geq 73$.

Step 1. We divide the n elements into $2q+1$ groups of 7 elements each and sort the groups. This takes at most $(2q + 1)S(7) = 13(2q + 1)$ comparisons.

Step 2. Now we determine the median of the $2q+1$ medians; call it x. This requires by induction at most $15(2q + 1) - 163 = 30q - 148$ tests.

Step 3. The $n - 1$ elements different from x are now partitioned into 4 parts A, B, C, D (see figure 4.12):

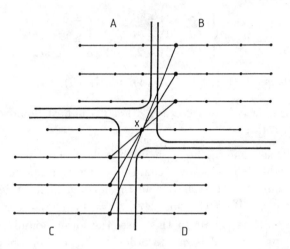

Figure 4.12

All $4q+3$ elements in B are known to be greater than x. All $4q+3$ elements in C are known to be smaller than x.

The $6q$ elements in $A \cup D$ are still undecided in relation to x. By inserting x into each 3-chain of A and D, we can tell with at most $4q$ comparisons which elements of $A \cup D$ are smaller or greater than x.

Step 4. We have now established the exact position of x. Suppose r elements are greater than x and $n-1-r$ elements are smaller. If $t = r+1$, then we are done. If $t < r + 1$, then we need to find the t-th largest of the r large elements. If $t > r+1$, then we have to find the $(t-1-r)$-largest of the $n-1-r$ small elements. Now $r \leq \mid A \cup B \cup D \mid \leq 10q + 3$, $n-1-r \leq \mid A \cup C \cup D \mid \leq 10q + 3$. Hence by induction this last step can be performed with at most $15(10q + 3) - 163$ comparisons. Taking all steps together we need at most

$$(26q + 13) + (30q - 148) + (4q) + (150q - 118) = 210q - 253$$
$$= 15(14q - 6) - 163 \leq 15n - 163$$

comparisons, and the proof is complete.   □

It is clear that this algorithm is not best possible since it ignores a lot of information in step 4. Blum et al [1973] have shown that we can improve the factor 15 to 5.43 for large n. For the median problem itself Schönhage et al [1976] have shown that $Med(n) \leq 3n$ for n large, whereas the best known lower bound for large n is $Med(n) \geq 2n$ (Bent-John [1985]).

There is a beautiful conjecture due to Backelin which relates our selection problem to the entropy function $H(x) = -x \log_2 x - (1 - x) \log_2(1 - x)$ discussed in previous chapters. Let $t = \lfloor xn \rfloor$, $0 < x < 1$. Then the conjecture says $\lim\limits_{n \to \infty} \frac{V_t(n)}{n} = 1 + H(x)$. If true, it would mean for the median $\lim\limits_{n \to \infty} \frac{Med(n)}{n} = 2$.

There is another class of selection problems that immediately comes to one's mind. In the simplest instance we want to determine the maximal and minimal element of the unknown chain. More generally, we aim to produce the s-th and t-the largest elements with $1 \leq s < t \leq n$. Let us denote the cost of this double selection problem by $V_{s,t}(n)$, with $W_{s,t}(n)$ denoting the cost when we want to determine the first s and the last $n - t + 1$ elements in order. Thus $V_{1,n}(n) = W_{1,n}(n)$ corresponds precisely to the problem of determining the maximal and minimal elements. Let us look at this problem first.

Proposition 4.16. *For any* $n \geq 2$,

$$W_{1,n}(n) = V_{1,n}(n) = U_{1,n}(n) = \lceil \frac{3n}{2} \rceil - 2.$$

Proof. An algorithm of this length is easily constructed. Suppose n is even. We first make $\frac{n}{2}$ disjoint comparisons. The overall winner can now be determined with $\frac{n}{2} - 1$ comparisons involving the winners of this first round, similarly for the overall loser. Hence $\frac{3n}{2} - 2$ comparisons suffice. For n odd, we determine the overall winner w and loser ℓ of $n - 1$ elements first, using $\frac{3(n-1)}{2} - 2$ tests and compare then the remaining element to w and ℓ. Thus, we are finished after $\frac{3(n-1)}{2} = \frac{3n+1}{2} - 2 = \lceil \frac{3n}{2} \rceil - 2$ comparisons.

To establish the lower bound, we use the following strategy. Let $Max(P)$ and $Min(P)$ be the sets of maximal elements and minimal elements of a poset P. Suppose that at stage i of the algorithm the poset P_i has been determined, and $x : y$ is the next test. We proclaim $x > y$ if $x \in Max(P_i)$, $y \notin Max(P_i)$ or $y \in Min(P_i)$, $x \notin Min(P_i)$, making an arbitrary choice in all other cases. It is clear that by this strategy the number $|Max(P)| + |Min(P)|$ is reduced by at most 1 each time, unless the two elements to be compared are both maximal and minimal at this stage, i.e. they have never been part of any comparison before. Then the number $\mid Max(P) \mid + \mid Min(P) \mid$ will be reduced by 2. Clearly, there are at most $\lfloor \frac{n}{2} \rfloor$ such tests. Suppose ℓ is the length of the algorithm. At the outset, every element is both maximal and minimal, hence $\mid Max(P_0) \mid + \mid Min(P_0) \mid = 2n$. At the end we have $\mid Max(P_\ell) \mid + \mid Min(P_\ell) \mid = 2$. By the set-up of our strategy we conclude

$$2 \geq 2n - \ell - \lfloor \frac{n}{2} \rfloor = \lceil \frac{3n}{2} \rceil - \ell$$

i.e. $\ell \geq \lceil \frac{3n}{2} \rceil - 2$.   □

In section 2 of the next chapter we will derive a general theorem producing a "top-part" and a "bottom-part". We just state the pertinent results for our selection problems.

Proposition 4.17. *Let $1 \leq s < t \leq n$, and denote by $W_{s,t}(n)$ the cost of selecting the first s and the last $n - t + 1$ elements in order; similarly for $V_{s,t}(n)$ and $U_{s,t}(n)$. Then*

i) $W_{s,t}(n) \geq \lceil \frac{3}{2}(t - s - 1) + 1 + \log_2 n(n-1) \ldots (t - s + 2) \rceil$,

ii) $V_{s,t}(n) \geq \lceil \frac{3}{2}(t - s - 1) + 1 + \log_2 \binom{n}{t} \binom{t}{s-1} \rceil$

iii) $U_{s,t}(n) \geq \lceil \frac{3}{2}(t - s - 1) + 1 + \log_2 \frac{1}{s(n-t+1)} \binom{n}{t} \binom{t}{s-1} \rceil$.

Notice that for $s = 1$, $t = n$, we again obtain our result **4.16**.
What about the average case? Here the problem becomes as usual much harder. Let us briefly look at the selection problem $\overline{V}_t(n)$ when all $n!$ orderings are equally likely. Clearly $\overline{V}_1(n) = n - 1$, since it always takes at least $n - 1$ comparisons to determine the top element. But already for $\overline{V}_2(n)$, the precise result is far from known.
Everybody's first try will be, to use the same tournament procedure as outlined in figure 4.10. An easy computation shows that for $n = 2^k + r$ the average-cost of this algorithm is $(n - 2) + \lfloor \log_2 n \rfloor + \frac{2r}{n}$. For $n \leq 4$ this actually yields the exact values $\overline{V}_2(2) = 1$, $\overline{V}_2(3) = 2\frac{2}{3}$, $\overline{V}_2(4) = 4$. However, already for $n = 5$ the value $5\frac{2}{5}$ obtained is not optimal as the following decision tree shows.

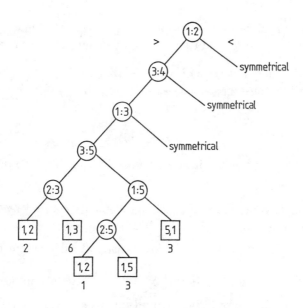

Figure 4.13

The end-nodes give the largest and second largest element with the number underneath denoting the number of orderings leading to this leaf. The cost for this procedure is therefore $\frac{1}{15}(11.5 + 4.6) = \frac{79}{15} = 5\frac{4}{15}$. It can be shown that this algorithm actually yields the optimal value $\overline{V}_2(5) = 5\frac{4}{15}$.

It would seem that for $n = 2^k$ the average value of $\overline{V}_2(n)$ cannot be improved upon $V_2(n) = (n-2) + k$, but this is not true (exercise 4.3.12). In fact, it is known that for fixed $t \geq 2$

$$ct\ln\ln n \leq \overline{V}_t(n) - n \leq c't\ln\ln n \quad (n \longrightarrow \infty)$$

for constants c and c'. (Matula [1973], Yao-Yao [1982]).

Let us, finally, look at the average cost $\overline{Med}(n)$ of determining the median. We have stated the best bounds known as $2n \leq Med(n) \leq 3n$ $(n \longrightarrow \infty)$. In the average-case the best bounds are

$$1.375n \leq \overline{Med}(n) \leq 1.5n \quad (n \longrightarrow \infty),$$

a result due to Floyd and Rivest [1975].

Exercises 4.3.

1.* Suppose an algorithm $\mathcal{A}$ selects the t-th largest element. Then this element must be related to any other element in any of the end-posets.

2. Verify the inequalities: a) $U_t(n) < U_t(n+1) \le U_t(n)+(t-1)$ $(t \ge 3)$, b) $V_t(n) < V_t(n+1) \le V_t(n)+(t-1)$ $(t \ge 3)$, c) $W_t(n) < W_t(n+1) \le W_t(n) + \lceil \log_2(t+1) \rceil$, d) $U_t(n+1) \le V_t(n)+1$.

3.* Show $U_2(n) \ge (n-2) + \lceil \log_2(n-1) \rceil$.

4. Show that the bounds in **4.11** and **4.13** coincide for infinitely many n.

5.* Suppose P_i consists of a_i unrelated elements covered by a single maximum, and suppose P is the disjoint union of s such P_i's. Then it takes $(s - 2) + \lceil \log_2 \sum_{i=1}^{s} 2^{a_i} \rceil$ comparisons to determine the first two in order, and $(s - 2) + \lceil \log_2 \left(\sum_{i=1}^{s} 2^{a_i} - 1 \right) \rceil$ to determine the first two without regard to ordering. Note that for $s = n$, $a_i = 0$ $(i = 1, \ldots, s)$ we obtain **4.12**. (Floyd)

6.* Give algorithms to verify the upper bound in **4.14**.

7. Show $W_3(5) = 7$, $V_3(5) = 6$ and $U_3(5) = 5$.

8. Determine $Med(n)$ for $n \le 11$.

9. Try to lower the constant 15 in **4.15**.

10. Determine $\overline{U}_2(n)$ and $\overline{V}_2(n)$ up to $n = 6$.

11.* Show that the knockout tournament method yields $\overline{V}_2(n) \le (n-2) + \lfloor \log_2 n \rfloor + \frac{2r}{n}$, where $n = 2^k + r$, $0 \le r < 2^k$.

12.* Prove $\overline{V}_2(2^k) < V_2(2^k)$ for $k \ge 3$.

4.4   Sorting Networks

So far, we have exclusively discussed sequential algorithms to solve various sorting problems. A very interesting predetermined analogue is provided by the following set-up.

Suppose we are given n slots numbered $S_1, S_2, \ldots, S_n$. The algorithm lays down once and for all a sequence of comparisons $S_i : S_j$. Suppose the current content of S_i is x and the content of S_j is y where $i < j$. After the comparison $S_i : S_j$ the larger of x and y is put in S_i whereas the smaller of the two is placed in S_j. At the end the largest element is to be in S_1, the second largest in S_2, and so on, no matter what the initial input was. Any such (successful) procedure is called a *sorting network*.

Let us look at $n = 4$. A network is pictured conveniently by drawing horizontal lines for each slot, marking the comparisons by vertical bars from left to right. Figure 4.14 gives a network that sorts 4 elements with 5 comparisons.

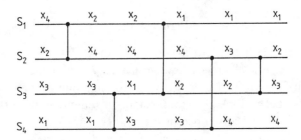

Figure 4.14

As an example, if $x_1 > x_2 > x_3 > x_4$ is the correct ordering and the input is x_4, x_2, x_3, x_1, then figure 4.14 shows the various stages in the network terminating in the proper ordering.

The reader may easily verify for himself that the network works indeed for every input sequence.

We denote by $\hat{S}(n)$ the network complexity of sorting n elements. Similarly, if we are interested to find the t largest elements (without regard to order), then after a sequence of network comparisons, the t largest elements are supposed to be in slots S_1 to S_t, no matter what the input was. Or, if the t-th largest element is to be selected, then it should be in slot S_t at the end. We use the symbols $\hat{U}_t(n)$ or $\hat{V}_t(n)$ or $\hat{M}(m, n)$ for the corresponding network problems. Obviously, the network cost is always at least as large as the corresponding sorting cost, so e.g.,

$$\hat{S}(n) \geq S(n), \quad \hat{V}_t(n) \geq V_t(n), \quad \hat{M}(m, n) \geq M(m, n).$$

Example 4.4. The following network obviously selects the largest element, thus proving $\hat{V}_1(n) = V_1(n) = n - 1$. In figure 4.15 and thereafter we denote the slots simply by $1, \dots, n$.

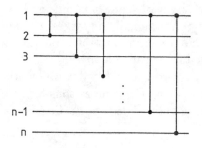

Figure 4.15

At first sight, it seems hard to decide whether a given network does what it is supposed to do. There is, however, a very useful method which gets around this difficulty. To this end, we generalize our problem by allowing equal elements. Let us look at the full sorting problem. A successful network is now supposed to sort any input into non-increasing order. In the simplest case the input consists of a sequence of 0's and 1's and at the end all 1's should be on top of all 0's. The following result shows that a network which properly sorts all 2^n sequences of 0's and 1's, in fact sorts any sequence whatsoever.

Proposition 4.18. *If a network on n lines sorts all 2^n sequences of 0's and 1's into non-increasing order, then it will sort any input into non-increasing order.*

Proof.   Suppose a given network transforms the input $(x_1, \dots, x_n)$ into the output $(y_1, \dots, y_n)$. If f is a monotone function from the x_i's into another set, i.e. $x_i \le x_j$ implies $f(x_i) \le f(x_j)$, then we claim that the network carries the input $(f(x_1), \dots, f(x_n))$ into $(f(y_1), \dots, f(y_n))$. To see this, suppose that at some stage, x and x' are to be compared where x is in slot i and x' is in slot j with $i < j$. We assume inductively that in the f-sequence, $f(x)$ is in slot i at this stage and $f(x')$ is in slot j. If $x \ge x'$ then $f(x) \ge f(x')$ by assumption and both contents remain unchanged. If, on the other hand, $x < x'$, then $f(x) \le f(x')$. In the first case x and x' interchanged. In the second case, $f(x)$ and $f(x')$ are also interchanged if $f(x) < f(x')$ while for $f(x) = f(x')$ the correspondence, slot $i : x' \longleftrightarrow f(x') = f(x)$, slot $j : x \longleftrightarrow f(x) = f(x')$ is trivially satisfied.

Now suppose that an arbitrary input sequence $(x_1, \ldots, x_n)$ is not properly sorted, where in the output $(y_1, \ldots, y_n)$ the relation $y_i < y_{i+1}$ holds. Consider the monotone function f which takes all numbers $\leq y_i$ into 0 and all numbers $> y_i$ into 1. This 0,1-sequence would be carried, by our remark above, into the sequence $(f(y_1), \ldots, f(y_n))$ which is 0 in slot i and 1 in slot $i + 1$, contrary to the assumption that all 0,1-sequences are properly sorted. □

Precisely the same argument shows that we may restrict our attention to 0,1-sequences when considering merging networks or selection networks. **4.18** is usually called the 0,1-*principle*. The usefulness of the 0,1-principle is best demonstrated by the following merging method due to Batcher [1968], called the *odd-even-merge*.

Suppose we have $m + n$ lines where the input in the first m lines is sorted as is the input in the last n lines. A *merging network* produces the proper ordering in the output lines, with the worst-case cost denoted by $\hat{M}(m, n)$. The algorithm of Batcher proceeds as follows. Let the sequences to be merged be $(x_1, \ldots, x_m)$ and $(y_1, \ldots, y_n)$. If $m = n = 1$, then we make the single comparison $x_1 : y_1$. If $mn > 1$, then we recursively merge the *odd* sequences $(x_1, x_3, \ldots, x_{2\lceil \frac{m}{2} \rceil - 1})$, $(y_1, y_3, \ldots, y_{2\lceil \frac{n}{2} \rceil - 1})$ first and then the *even* sequences $(x_2, x_4, \ldots, x_{2\lfloor \frac{m}{2} \rfloor})$, $(y_2, y_4, \ldots, y_{2\lfloor \frac{n}{2} \rfloor})$. Let the result of the first merge be $(v_1, v_2, \ldots, v_{\lceil \frac{m}{2} \rceil + \lceil \frac{n}{2} \rceil})$ and that of the second merge $(w_1, w_2, \ldots, w_{\lfloor \frac{m}{2} \rfloor + \lfloor \frac{n}{2} \rfloor})$. Now we make the comparisons $w_1 : v_2, w_2 : v_3, \ldots,$ $w_{\lfloor \frac{m}{2} \rfloor + \lfloor \frac{n}{2} \rfloor} : v_{\lfloor \frac{m}{2} \rfloor + \lfloor \frac{n}{2} \rfloor + 1}$, where the last comparisons is superfluous if both m and n are even. The result will be sorted.

To see that this method works we use the 0,1-principle. Suppose the x-input contains k 1's (in the top positions) and $m - k$ 0's, and the y-input contains ℓ 1's and $n - \ell$ 0's. After the odd merge the v-sequence will consist of $\lceil \frac{k}{2} \rceil + \lceil \frac{\ell}{2} \rceil$ 1's followed by 0's, and the w-sequence will consist of $\lfloor \frac{k}{2} \rfloor + \lfloor \frac{\ell}{2} \rfloor$ 1's followed by 0's. Observe that

$$(\lceil \frac{k}{2} \rceil + \lceil \frac{\ell}{2} \rceil) - (\lfloor \frac{k}{2} \rfloor + \lfloor \frac{\ell}{2} \rfloor) = 0, 1, \text{ or } 2.$$

If the difference is 0 or 1, then the sequence is already sorted. If the difference is 2, then we have the situation

v_1	w_1	v_2	w_2	$\ldots$	v_s	w_s	v_{s+1}	w_{s+1}	$\ldots$	
1	1	1	1		1	0	1	0	$\ldots$	0

where $s = \lfloor \frac{k}{2} \rfloor + \lfloor \frac{\ell}{2} \rfloor + 1$. Hence the comparison $w_s : v_{s+1}$ will yield the proper ordering.

Before further pursuing merging networks let us see what sorting cost we obtain by using the odd-even merge. Let $\hat{B}(n,n)$ be the cost of merging two chains of length n using Batchers's algorithm. We have $\hat{B}(0,0) = 0$, $\hat{B}(1,1) = 1$. By the set-up of the algorithm we infer

$$\hat{B}(n,n) = \hat{B}(\lceil\frac{n}{2}\rceil,\lceil\frac{n}{2}\rceil) + \hat{B}(\lfloor\frac{n}{2}\rfloor,\lfloor\frac{n}{2}\rfloor) + (n-1).$$

Hence

$$
\begin{aligned}
\hat{B}(n,n) - \hat{B}(n-1,n-1) &= \hat{B}(\lfloor\frac{n-1}{2}\rfloor + 1, \lfloor\frac{n-1}{2}\rfloor + 1) \\
&\quad -\hat{B}(\lfloor\frac{n-1}{2}\rfloor, \lfloor\frac{n-1}{2}\rfloor) + 1 \\
&= \vdots \\
&= \hat{B}(1,1) - \hat{B}(0,0) + \lceil\log_2 n\rceil \\
&= \lceil\log_2 n\rceil + 1.
\end{aligned}
$$

It follows that

$$\hat{B}(n,n) = \sum_{i=1}^{n}\lceil\log i\rceil + n,$$

and in particular $\hat{B}(2^k,2^k) = \sum_{i=1}^{k} i2^{i-1} + 2^k = (k-1)2^k + 1 + 2^k$, i.e

$$(4.19) \qquad\qquad \hat{B}(2^k,2^k) = k2^k + 1 = n\log_2 n + 1.$$

Hence we obtain as upper bound for the merging cost in a network

$$(4.20) \qquad\qquad \hat{M}(n,n) \le \sum_{i=1}^{n}\lceil\log i\rceil + n.$$

Let $b(n)$ denote the cost of a Batcher sorting network by recursively merging chains using odd-even merge each time. We have

$$(4.21) \qquad\qquad b(n) = b(\lceil\frac{n}{2}\rceil) + b(\lfloor\frac{n}{2}\rfloor) + \hat{B}(\lceil\frac{n}{2}\rceil,\lfloor\frac{n}{2}\rfloor).$$

Consider $n = 2^k$. With the initial condition $b(1) = 0$, we conclude from (4.19) and the recursion (4.21)

$$b(2^k) = 2b(2^{k-1}) + (k-1)2^{k-1} + 1$$

$$= 2^2 b(2^{k-2}) + (k-2)2^{k-1} + (k-1)2^{k-1} + 2 + 1$$

$$\vdots$$

$$= 2^{k-1} \sum_{i=1}^{k-1} i + \sum_{i=0}^{k-1} 2^i$$

$$= 2^{k-2}(k-1)k + 2^k - 1$$

$$= (k^2 - k + 4)2^{k-2} - 1.$$

It follows that $\hat{S}(n) \leq Cn(\log_2 n)^2$ for some constant C.

For a long time it was thought that this was the best possible asymptotic result until Ajtai, Komlós and Szémerédi [1983] constructed a network which uses only $C'n \log_2 n$ comparisons for a universal constant C'. This result, which is far beyond this book, rates without doubt among the greatest recent discoveries in this field.

As to the precise value of $\hat{S}(n)$, Batcher's method is known to be optimal up to $n = 8$. No further value of $\hat{S}(n)$ is known. The following table gives the cost $b(n)$ of Batcher's algorithm as compared to the best known value.

n	2	3	4	5	6	7	8	9	10	11	12
$b(n)$	1	3	5	9	12	16	19	26	31	37	41
$\hat{S}(n) \leq$	1	3	5	9	12	16	19	25	29	35	39

Figure 4.16 shows a Batcher network for sorting 7 elements.

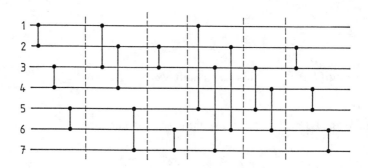

Figure 4.16

Back to merging networks. We have seen in **4.2** that $M(n, n) = 2n - 1$ holds for sequential algorithms, so there is a gap between n for the sequential case and $n \log_2 n$ for networks. Unlike for the full sorting problem this gap cannot be bridged in the case of merging. We claim

(4.22) $\hat{M}(2n, 2n) \geq 2\hat{M}(n, n) + n$ for all $n \geq 1$.

By interchanging lines we may assume that the first sorted list $x_1 > x_2 > \ldots > x_{2n}$ appears on lines $1, 3, 5, \ldots, 4n - 1$ and the second sorted list $y_1 > y_2 > \ldots > y_{2n}$ on lines $2, 4, 6, \ldots, 4n$. Any comparison $i : j, i < j$, falls into three disjoint classes:

    a) $i \leq 2n, j \leq 2n$
    b) $i > 2n, j > 2n$
    c) $i \leq 2n, j > 2n$.

Class (a) must contain at least $\hat{M}(n, n)$ comparisons, since the input values in the first $2n$ lines may all be above the values of the lower half. Similarly, class (b) must contain at least $\hat{M}(n, n)$ comparisons. Finally, if $y_{2n} > x_1$, then all n values $y_{n+1}, \ldots, y_{2n}$ mut be moved into the upper half whence there are at least n comparisons in class (c). By noting that no comparison in one of the classes furnishes any information about the other classes, we have proved (4.22).

Repeatedly using (4.22) we obtain

$$
\begin{aligned}
\hat{M}(2^k, 2^k) &\geq 2\hat{M}(2^{k-1}, 2^{k-1}) + 2^{k-1} \\
&\geq 2^2 \hat{M}(2^{k-2}, 2^{k-2}) + 2^{k-1} + 2^{k-1} \\
&\vdots \\
&\geq 2^k + k2^{k-1} \\
&= \frac{k+2}{2} 2^k.
\end{aligned}
$$

Summarizing (4.19) and this last result we obtain:

Proposition 4.19. *For the merging cost in a network, we have*

$$\frac{k+2}{2} 2^k \leq \hat{M}(2^k, 2^k) \leq k2^k + 1.$$

By the same argument as in the proof of (4.22) it is readily seen that

(4.23) $\hat{M}(m_1 + m_2, n_1 + n_2) \geq \hat{M}(m_1, n_1) + \hat{M}(m_2, n_2) + \min(m_2, n_1)$
        for $m_1, m_2, n_1, n_2 \geq 0$.

Let us turn to the other extreme when m is small as compared to n. First we make use of the 0,1-principle to reduce the merging problem to a more convenient form.

Let m and n be natural numbers, $m, n \geq 1$. The vectors $\underline{b}_i \in \mathbf{Z}^m$ and $\underline{a}_i \in \mathbf{Z}^{m+n}$ are defined as follows:

$$
\underline{b}_i = \begin{pmatrix} n+m-i \\ \vdots \\ n+2 \\ n+1 \\ 0 \\ -1 \\ \vdots \\ -(i-1) \end{pmatrix}, \quad
\underline{a}_i = \begin{pmatrix} \underline{b}_i \\ \hline n \\ n-1 \\ \vdots \\ 2 \\ 1 \end{pmatrix} \quad (i = 1, \ldots, m).
$$

Thus e.g.

$$
\underline{a}_1 = \begin{pmatrix} n+m-1 \\ \vdots \\ n+1 \\ 0 \\ \hline n \\ \vdots \\ 1 \end{pmatrix}, \quad
\underline{a}_m = \begin{pmatrix} 0 \\ -1 \\ \vdots \\ -(m-1) \\ \hline n \\ \vdots \\ 1 \end{pmatrix}.
$$

Lemma 4.20. *An (m,n)-merging network which sorts all inputs $\underline{a}_i$ ($i = 1, \ldots, m$), sorts all possible inputs.*

Proof. Let $\underline{c} = (\underline{d} \mid \underline{e})^T$ be any 0,1-input where $\underline{d} = (1, \ldots, 1, \underbrace{0, \ldots, 0}_{i})^T \in \{0,1\}^m$ and $\underline{e} = (1, \ldots, 1, 0, \ldots, 0)^T \in \{0,1\}^n$. The mapping f which carries $\underline{a}_i$ into $\underline{c}$ is monotone. Since our network sorts $\underline{a}_i$ it will carry $\underline{c}$ into the sorted sequence $(1, 1, \ldots, 1, 0, \ldots, 0)^T$. Now by the 0,1-principle, if all 0,1-sequences are sorted, then so are all possible inputs. $\square$

Let us describe the action of a given network π by $\pi\underline{a}$, i.e. the input $\underline{a}$ is carried into $\pi\underline{a}$. The following easily proved result shows that π is monotone.

Lemma 4.21. *Let π be an (m,n)-merging network. If $\underline{a},\underline{a}' \in \mathbf{Z}^{m+n}$ satisfy $\underline{a} \le \underline{a}'$ (i.e. $a_i \le a_i'$ for all i), then at stage k of π we have again $\underline{a}^{(k)} \le \underline{a}'^{(k)}$ for the respective contents. In particular, $\pi\underline{a} \le \pi\underline{a}'$ holds at the end.*

Note that $\underline{a}_1 \ge \underline{a}_2 \ge \ldots \ge \underline{a}_m$. Now we turn to some small cases.

Proposition 4.22. *We have for all n,*

$$\hat{M}(1,n) = n.$$

Proof. By 4.20, we just have to sort the input $\underline{a} = (0 \mid n, n-1, \ldots, 1)^T$. Clearly, this can be done with n comparisons by moving 0 down step by step. Let us analyze an arbitrary network sorting $\underline{a}$. We claim that the content $a_1, \ldots, a_{n+1}$ (read from top to bottom) at a certain stage can be described as follows. The lines are uniquely divided into groups $F_1 \mid F_2 \mid \ldots \mid F_r$ from top to bottom such that

  i) $i \in F_k, j \in F_\ell, k < \ell \Rightarrow a_i > a_j$,

 ii) if $F_k = \{f_k, f_k+1, \ldots, f_{k+1}-1\}$, then $a_{f_k+1} > a_{f_k+2} > \ldots > a_{f_{k+1}-1} > a_{f_k}$.

In other words, within each group the top element is the smallest in this group, with the others appearing in their natural order.

To see this, we note that at the start we have one group $F_1 = \{0, n, n-1, \ldots, 1\}$ satisfying ii). Now assume that we compare at a certain stage lines $i : j$.

If i and j are in different groups, then nothing happens by i). If i and j are in the same group F_k with $f_k < i < j \le f_{k+1} - 1$, then again no change occurs by ii). If, finally, i and j are in the same group F_k with $i = f_k$ and $f_k < j \le f_{k+1} - 1$, then the contents of lines i and j are interchanged, and F_k splits into two groups $F_k' = \{j, f_k + 1, \ldots, j - 1\}$ and $F_k" = \{i = f_k, j + 1, \ldots, f_{k+1} - 1\}$. With F_k' and $F_k"$ replacing F_k we see that i) and ii) are again satisfied.

We conclude that any comparison, which changes the current content at all, increases the number of groups by precisely 1. Since, at the end, we have $n + 1$ groups $\{n\}, \{n - 1\}, \ldots, \{1\}, \{0\}$, we infer that indeed n comparisons are required to sort $\underline{a}$. □

Note that any comparison which changes the content does raise the number of groups by 1. Hence in any sorting algorithm of $\underline{a}$, there are precisely n comparisons which change the content. Let us call them *essential* comparisons.

Note also that after a first essential comparison involving line j, j moves to the top of its group and stays at the top thereafter.

Proposition 4.23. *We have for all n,*

$$\hat{M}(2,n) = \lceil \frac{3n}{2} \rceil.$$

Proof. Batcher's odd-even merge uses $\hat{M}(\lceil \frac{n}{2} \rceil, 1) + \hat{M}(\lfloor \frac{n}{2} \rfloor, 1) + \lfloor \frac{n+1}{2} \rfloor = n + \lfloor \frac{n+1}{2} \rfloor = \lceil \frac{3n}{2} \rceil$ comparisons, hence $\hat{M}(2,n) \leq \lceil \frac{3n}{2} \rceil$. To prove the converse inequality we use again **4.20.** We have to sort the two vectors $\underline{a} = (n+1, 0 \mid n, \ldots, 1)^T$ and $\underline{b} = (0, -1 \mid n, \ldots, 1)^T$. Suppose an optimal network uses ℓ comparisons. Let $(a_1, \ldots, a_{n+2})$ and $(b_1, \ldots, b_{n+2})$ be the contents after the k-th comparison. We set $d_k = \mid \{i : a_i \neq b_i\} \mid$. Thus at the beginning $d_0 = 2$. At the end we arrive at the sequences $(n+1, n, \ldots, 1, 0)$ and $(n, n-1, \ldots, 0, -1)$ whence $d_\ell = n + 2$.

Since in $\underline{a}$ the first entry $n+1$ will never be moved, the action of the network on $\underline{a}$ will be that of the previous proposition (by disregarding $n+1$). We know that there are precisely n comparisons which change the content of $\underline{a}$; let us call them *inner* comparisons with the others called *outer* comparisons. Let $(a_1, \ldots, a_{n+2})$ and $(b_1, \ldots, b_{n+2})$ be the contents at stage k, and suppose $i : j$, $i < j$, is the next comparison.

We claim $d_{k+1} \leq d_k + 1$.

Case 1. If $a_i > a_j$, $b_i > b_j$ or $a_i < a_j$, $b_i < b_j$, then either everything remains unchanged or both a_i, a_j and b_i, b_j are interchanged. Hence in this case $d_{k+1} = d_k$.

Case 2. $a_i < a_j$, $b_i > b_j$. Since $\underline{a} \geq \underline{b}$ we have by Lemma 4.21, $b_j < b_i \leq a_i < a_j$. Since a_i and a_j are interchanged and b_i and b_j stay unchanged, we have $d_{k+1} = d_k$ unless $b_i = a_i$ in which case $d_{k+1} = d_k + 1$ results.

Case 3. $a_i > a_j$, $b_i < b_j$. By the monotonicity we have $b_i < b_j \leq a_j < a_i$, and conclude as before $d_{k+1} \leq d_k + 1$.

Consider the inner comparisons. If such a comparison raises d_k, then we call it *red*, otherwise *green*. Let r be the number of red comparisons and g be the number of green comparisons. Hence $r + g = n$. The red comparisons are precisely those of case ii) above, when $b_j < b_i = a_i < a_j$ where $j \geq 3$, since $j = 2$ would imply $i = 1$, which is not an essential comparison for $\underline{a}$. Since line j was not involved in an inner comparison until then (see the remark before **4.23**), we conclude from $a_j \neq b_j$ that line j must have been part of a previous outer comparison $s : j$.

We thus infer that the number of outer comparisons $\ell - n$ is at least r. Since $d_\ell - d_0 = n$ and $d_{k+1} \leq d_k + 1$ for all k, we have

$$\begin{aligned}
(\ell - n) + r &\geq n, \\
\ell - n &\geq r,
\end{aligned}$$

and thus

$$2(\ell - n) \geq n,$$

i.e., $\ell \geq \frac{3n}{2}$. $\square$

By the same method one can also establish the precise result for $\hat{M}(3, n)$. (Aigner-Schwarzkopf)

Proposition 4.24. *For all n,*

$$\hat{M}(3, n) = \lceil \frac{7n + 3}{4} \rceil.$$

Note that odd-even merge is by **4.23** and **4.24** again optimal for $m = 3$ and arbitrary n, and it is quite plausible that Batcher's algorithm is indeed optimal for all m and n.

Propositions 4.23 and 4.24 together with (4.23) yield the exact value $\hat{M}(n, n)$ for some small values of n, given in the following table:

n	1	2	3	4	5	7	8	9
$\hat{M}(n, n)$	1	3	6	9	13	21	25	30

The algorithms are all provided by odd-even merge. As for lower bounds, we can settle all numbers except $n = 6$ by using **4.23**, **4.24** and (4.23). Consider, e.g., $\hat{M}(9, 9)$. By (4.23) and **4.24** we have

$$\hat{M}(9, 9) \geq \hat{M}(3, 6) + \hat{M}(6, 3) + \min(6, 6) = 30.$$

For $n = 6$, Batcher's algorithm yields $\hat{M}(6,6) \leq 17$, but the best we can do by (4.23) is $\hat{M}(6,6) \geq 16$.

Before discussing selection problems let us make a few general remarks. Since at the start we have no prior information, the first comparison is of no significance, we may compare the contents of any two lines $i : j$. It will be sometimes convenient to assume that $1 : n$ is the first comparison.

A second remark. So far, we have assumed that any comparison $i : j$, $i < j$, puts the larger element into line i and the smaller into line j. It seems plausible at first sight that we might do better in general if we allow us the freedom of designating the line into which the larger element should go. In a comparison $i : j$, where $i > j$ is also allowed, let us assume that the larger element always goes into the line i (the first coordinate). Let us call such networks *non-standard*.

Example 4.5. Figure 4.17 shows a non-standard network which sorts 4 elements. The arrows point to the lines where the larger element should end up.

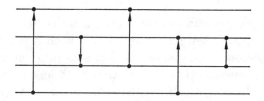

Figure 4.17

Let us denote any network π, standard or not, by the sequence $[i_1 : j_1][i_2 : j_2]$ $\dots [i_s : j_s]$ of comparisons. We transform π step by step into a standard network of the same length s. If for all k, $i_k < j_k$, then π is already a standard network. Otherwise, let m be the smallest index with $i_m > j_m$. We replace every i_m by j_m and every j_m by i_m and do that for all comparisons $i_k : j_k$, $k \geq m$. In this new network π' we look again for the smallest index m' with $i'_m > j'_m$ and proceed as before. After at most s such rounds of interchanges we obtain a standard network $\tilde{\pi}$. Since by these interchanges we permuted the lines by a certain fixed permutation σ we conclude that $\tilde{\pi}\underline{a} = \sigma(\pi\underline{a})$ for any input $\underline{a}$. Now if $\underline{a}$ is already ordered at the outset, $\underline{a} = a_1 > a_2 > \dots > a_n$, then both $\pi\underline{a}$ and $\tilde{\pi}\underline{a}$ leave $\underline{a}$ unchanged whence we conclude that σ is, in fact, the identity permutation. Thus, $\tilde{\pi}\underline{a} = \pi\underline{a}$, for all $\underline{a}$, which means that $\tilde{\pi}$ is indeed a proper sorting network of the same length.

In our example above, we have the interchanges

$$[1:4][3:2][1:3][2:4][2:3] \quad \longrightarrow$$
$$[1:4][2:3][1:2][3:4][3:2] \quad \longrightarrow$$
$$[1:4][2:3][1:2][3:4][2:3].$$

Now let us consider the selection problems $\hat{U}_t(n)$, $\hat{V}_t(n)$ and $\hat{W}_t(n)$. We have already seen

$$(4.24) \qquad\qquad \hat{U}_1(n) = \hat{V}_1(n) = \hat{W}_1(n) = n - 1.$$

The corresponding results for $t = 2$ are also easily established. Note first that for $n \geq t + 1$, $t \geq 2$,

$$(4.25) \qquad \begin{aligned} \hat{U}_t(n) &\geq \hat{U}_t(n-1) + 2, \quad \hat{V}_t(n) \geq \hat{V}_t(n-1) + 2, \\ \hat{W}_t(n) &\geq \hat{W}_t(n-1) + 2. \end{aligned}$$

To verify (4.25), let π be an optimal network which selects the top t elements. By our remark above we may assume w.l.o.g. that $[1:n]$ is the first comparison. Now if the element x that goes into line n after the first comparison is the smallest, then the remaining network must select the top t elements of $n - 1$ elements. If, on the other hand, x is among the top t, then there must be at least one more comparison involving line n. Clearly, the same argument works for $\hat{V}_t(n)$ and $\hat{W}_t(n)$ as well. The starting values $\hat{U}_2(2) = 0$, $\hat{V}_2(2) = \hat{W}_2(2) = 1$ yield therefore

$$\hat{U}_2(n) \geq 2n - 4, \quad \hat{V}_2(n) = \hat{W}_2(n) \geq 2n - 3.$$

A network for selecting the top two with $2n - 4$ comparisons is, on the other hand, immediately constructed. First we select the top element among the first $n - 1$ entries (taking $n - 2$ comparisons by (4.24)) and then the top element out of lines $2, \ldots, n$, using again $n - 2$ comparisons. Thus $\hat{U}_2(n) \leq 2n - 4$. By adding the comparison 1:2, we conclude further $\hat{V}_2(n) \leq 2n - 3$.

Proposition 4.25. *For $n \geq 2$,*

$$\hat{U}_2(n) = 2n - 4, \quad \hat{V}_2(n) = \hat{W}_2(n) = 2n - 3.$$

For $t = 3$, the precise results are not known, but we are going to determine the correct values within an error of 2. Let us look at upper bounds first. Consider $\hat{U}_t(n)$ for general t. We make the $\lfloor \frac{n}{2} \rfloor$ comparison $1 : n$, $2 : n - 1, \ldots, \lfloor \frac{n}{2} \rfloor : \lceil \frac{n}{2} \rceil + 1$ first. After this round of comparisons there can be at most $\lfloor \frac{t}{2} \rfloor$ of the top t elements in the lowest $\lfloor \frac{n}{2} \rfloor$ lines. Next we use networks of length $\hat{U}_{\lfloor \frac{t}{2} \rfloor}(\lfloor \frac{n}{2} \rfloor)$ on the bottom $\lfloor \frac{n}{2} \rfloor$ lines to move the $\lfloor \frac{t}{2} \rfloor$ largest elements to the top of this half. After this we know that the top t elements are contained in lines $1, 2, \ldots, \lceil \frac{n}{2} \rceil + \lfloor \frac{t}{2} \rfloor$. By applying a network of length $\hat{U}_t(\lceil \frac{n}{2} \rceil + \lfloor \frac{t}{2} \rfloor)$ we then move these elements into the top t lines (see figure 4.18).

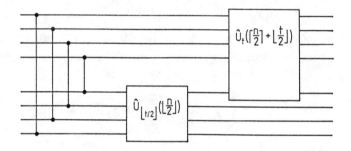

Figure 4.18

Clearly, the same approach works for $\hat{V}_t(n)$ and $\hat{W}(n)$ as well.

Proposition 4.26. *For all t and n,*

$$\hat{U}_t(n) \leq \left\lfloor \frac{n}{2} \right\rfloor + \hat{U}_{\lfloor \frac{t}{2} \rfloor}(\lfloor \frac{n}{2} \rfloor) + \hat{U}_t(\lceil \frac{n}{2} \rceil + \lfloor \frac{t}{2} \rfloor)$$

$$\hat{V}_t(n) \leq \left\lfloor \frac{n}{2} \right\rfloor + \hat{U}_{\lfloor \frac{t}{2} \rfloor}(\lfloor \frac{n}{2} \rfloor) + \hat{V}_t(\lceil \frac{n}{2} \rceil + \lfloor \frac{t}{2} \rfloor)$$

$$\hat{W}_t(n) \leq \left\lfloor \frac{n}{2} \right\rfloor + \hat{U}_{\lfloor \frac{t}{2} \rfloor}(\lfloor \frac{n}{2} \rfloor) + \hat{W}_t(\lceil \frac{n}{2} \rceil + \lfloor \frac{t}{2} \rfloor)$$

Let us consider $t = 3$. The inequality for $\hat{U}_3(n)$ reads in this case

$$(4.26) \quad \hat{U}_3(n) \leq \left\lfloor \frac{n}{2} \right\rfloor + \left\lfloor \frac{n}{2} \right\rfloor - 1 + \hat{U}_3(\lceil \frac{n}{2} \rceil + 1) = \hat{U}_3(\lceil \frac{n}{2} \rceil) + 1) + 2\left\lfloor \frac{n}{2} \right\rfloor - 1.$$

So, e.g. $\hat{U}_3(6) \leq \hat{U}_3(4) + 5 = 8$. Since, on the other hand, by (4.25), $\hat{U}_3(6) \geq \hat{U}_3(5) + 2 = \hat{U}_2(5) + 2 = 8$, we infer $\hat{U}_3(6) = 8$. To solve the recursion in (4.26), we start with $\hat{U}_3(5) = 6$, $\hat{U}_3(6) = 8$. By moving from n to $\lceil \frac{n}{2} \rceil + 1 = n'$, then to $\lceil \frac{n'}{2} \rceil + 1$, and so on, we see that the numbers $n = 2^k + 3, \ldots, 2^k + 2^{k-1} + 2$ move to $n' = 2^{k-1} + 3, \ldots, 2^{k-1} + 2^{k-2} + 2$, and thus in $k - 1$ iterations of (4.26) to $n" = 5$.

Similarly, the numbers $n = 2^k + 2^{k-1} + 3, \ldots, 2^{k+1} + 2$ move to $n' = 2^{k-1} + 2^{k-2} + 3, \ldots, 2^k + 2$, and thus with $k - 1$ iterations to $n" = 6$. Note that $k = \lfloor \log_2(n - 3) \rfloor$.

Let us rewrite (4.26) as

$$\hat{U}_3(n) - \hat{U}_3(\lceil \frac{n}{2} \rceil + 1) \leq 2\lfloor \frac{n}{2} \rfloor - 1.$$

With $d_1 = n - (\lceil \frac{n}{2} \rceil + 1) = \lfloor \frac{n}{2} \rfloor - 1$ the right-hand side is $2d_1 + 1$, similarly for the following iterations. By summing up all inequalities we thus arrive at

$$\hat{U}_3(n) - \begin{cases} \hat{U}_3(5) \\ \hat{U}_3(6) \end{cases} \leq 2\sum_{i=1}^{k-1} d_i + (k - 1),$$

where $n = \sum_{i=1}^{k-1} d_i + \begin{cases} 5 \\ 6 \end{cases}$.

Hence we conclude

$$\hat{U}_3(n) \leq \begin{cases} \hat{U}_3(5) \\ \hat{U}_3(6) \end{cases} + 2n - \begin{cases} 10 \\ 12 \end{cases} + (k - 1),$$

and thus

$$\hat{U}_3(n) \leq 2n - 5 + \lfloor \log_2(n - 3) \rfloor.$$

With the easily proved values $\hat{V}_3(5) = 7$, $\hat{V}_3(6) \leq 10$ and $\hat{W}_3(5) \leq 8$, $\hat{W}_3(6) \leq 10$ (from **4.26**), we can similarly solve the corresponding recursions for $\hat{V}_3(n)$ and $\hat{W}_3(n)$.

$$\hat{V}_3(n) \leq \hat{W}_3(n) \leq 2n - 3 + \lfloor \log_2(n - 3) \rfloor.$$

Now to lower bounds. The following approach is due to Yao [1980]. Let us consider $\hat{U}_3(n)$ first. The network in figure 4.19(a) selects the top three of 8 elements.

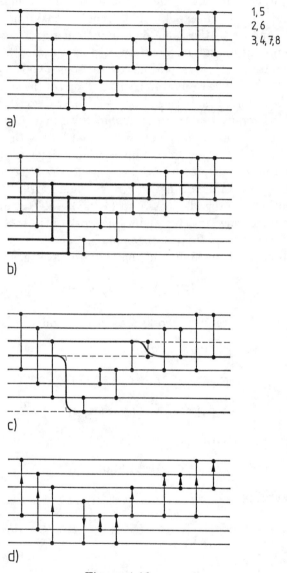

1, 5
2, 6
3, 4, 7, 8

a)

b)

c)

d)

Figure 4.19

Suppose the largest element occurs in line j at the start, then it must end up in one of the 3 top lines. The numbers to the right of our network show where the top element will finish if it is on line j in the beginning. Now there is the crucial idea. One of the 3 top lines ℓ must contain at least $\lceil \frac{n}{3} \rceil$ of thes j's. In our example it is line 3. Looking at the paths of these j's (all belonging to the same end-line) from right to left we notice that the collection of paths can be interpreted as a rooted binary tree with the starting positions as leaves and the comparisons involved as inner nodes (see figure 4.19(b)). Hence by our old result **1.2**, one of the starting positions, say j_0, must be involved in at least $\lceil \log_2 \lceil \frac{n}{3} \rceil \rceil$ comparisons. Now we delete this path and its comparisons (in our example, we take $j_0 = 8$). The resulting network on $n - 1$ lines may contain "twisted " lines (as indicated in figure 4.19(c)), by moving the elements involved in a deleted comparison down to the line formerly occupied by j_0. Straightening out the lines we thus arrive at a possibly non- standard network π (see figure 4.19(d)) which at any rate puts the other two top elements into $\{1, 2, 3\} - \ell$. By our previous remark, π can be transformed into a standard network of the same length and hence must perform at least $\hat{U}_2(n - 1)$ comparisons.

Taking all parts of the argument together we have thus proved

$$\hat{U}_3(n) \geq \hat{U}_2(n - 1) + \lceil \log_2 \lceil \frac{n}{3} \rceil \rceil.$$

Clearly, the same argument works for general t and also for $\hat{V}_t(n)$ and $\hat{W}_t(n)$.

Theorem 4.27. *For $t \geq 2$ and all n,*

$$\hat{U}_t(n) \geq \hat{U}_{t-1}(n - 1) + \lceil \log_2 \lceil \frac{n}{t} \rceil \rceil$$

$$\hat{V}_t(n) \geq \hat{V}_{t-1}(n - 1) + \lceil \log_2 \lceil \frac{n}{t - 1} \rceil \rceil$$

$$\hat{W}_t(n) \geq \hat{W}_{t-1}(n - 1) + \lceil \log_2 n \rceil.$$

Using our previous result **4.26** we obtain:

Corollary 4.28. *For all n,*

$$2n - 6 + \lceil \log_2 \lceil \frac{n}{3} \rceil \rceil \leq \hat{U}_3(n) \leq 2n - 5 + \lfloor \log_2(n - 3) \rfloor$$

$$2n - 5 + \lceil \log_2 \lceil \frac{n}{2} \rceil \rceil \leq \hat{V}_3(n) \leq 2n - 3 + \lfloor \log_2(n - 3) \rfloor$$

$$2n - 5 + \lceil \log_2 n \rceil \leq \hat{W}_3(n) \leq 2n - 3 + \lfloor \log_2(n - 3) \rfloor.$$

In particular, we see that the bounds differ by at most 2. Finally, we note that Propositions 4.26 and 4.27 can, of course, be used to determine asymptotic upper and lower bounds for general t.

Exercises 4.4.

1. Verify that the network in figure 4.14 sorts 4 elements.

2.* Show $\hat{S}(n) \geq \hat{S}(n-1) + \lceil \log_2 n \rceil$.

3. Verify the values for $\hat{S}(n)$ up to $n = 6$.

4. Find a sorting network for 9 elements with 25 comparisons (one better than Batcher's network).

5. Prove **4.21**.

6.* Prove $\hat{M}(m,n) \geq \hat{M}(m-1,n) + 1$ for $n \geq m$.

7. Verify the values of $\hat{M}(n,n)$ in the table after Proposition 4.24.

8.* Show $\hat{V}_3(5) = 7$.

9.* Let $x, y \in \{0,1\}^n$. We say x *covers* y, if $x_k = 1, y_k = 0$ for some k, and $x_i = y_i$ for all $i \neq k$. Suppose a sequence π of comparisons carries the permutation p (of $\{1,\ldots,n\}$) into πp. Show $(\pi p)_i = k$ iff there exist $x, y \in \{0,1\}^n$ with x covering y, such that $(\pi x)_i = 1$, $(\pi y)_i = 0$ and y has k 0's.

10.* Show: i) $\hat{U}_t(n) \geq (n-t)\lceil \log_2(t+1) \rceil$, ii) $\hat{V}_t(n) \geq (n-t)\lceil \log_2(t+1) \rceil + \lceil \log_2 t \rceil$, iii) $\hat{W}_t(n) \geq \sum_{i=2}^{t} \lceil \log_2 i \rceil + (n-t)\lceil \log_2(t+1) \rceil$. (Alekseyev)

11. Using the previous exercise and **4.26**, derive asymptotic expressions for $\hat{U}_t(n), \hat{V}_t(n), \hat{W}_t(n)$, t fixed.

12.* Suppose a network can only compare adjacent lines $i, i+1$. Prove: i) $\hat{S}(n) = \binom{n}{2}$ in this case, ii) what is $\hat{V}_1(n), \hat{V}_2(n), \hat{U}_2(n)$?

4.5 Parallel Sorting

Take a look at the network in figure 4.16 sorting 7 elements. You see that there are groups of consecutive comparisons which are disjoint and can thus be performed simultaneously. In figure 4.16 there are 6 such groups. We say that the network has *delay time* 6. The reader may verify that we can do no better than 6.

Of course, we may consider this situation in the sequential case as well. In any round of comparisons we are allowed to test up to $\lfloor \frac{n}{2} \rfloor$ disjoint pairs of elements. Denote by $S^{(p)}(n)$ the minimal delay time in any algorithm sorting n elements. $S^{(p)}(n)$ is also called the *parallel cost* of sorting n elements.

It is convenient to think of the n elements as tennis players (or football teams) and of $S^{(p)}(n)$ as the minimum number of rounds required to determine the correct ordering. Similarly, we may define $U_t^{(p)}(n)$ or $M^{(p)}(m,n)$ as the parallel cost of the corresponding problems. When dealing with networks we, of course, use the notation $\hat{U}_t^{(p)}(n)$ and $\hat{M}^{(p)}(m,n)$, where we have $S^{(p)}(n) \leq \hat{S}^{(p)}(n)$, $U_t^{(p)}(n) \leq \hat{U}_t^{(p)}(n)$, and so on.

Let us consider the merging problem first. What is the delay time $\hat{B}^{(p)}(m,n)$ of Batcher's odd-even merge? The last set of comparisons $w_1 : v_2, w_2 : v_3, \ldots$ may be performed in a single round. Similarly, the odd and even merge can be executed in parallel. Hence we have the recursion

$$\hat{B}^{(p)}(m,n) = \hat{B}^{(p)}(\lceil \frac{m}{2} \rceil, \lceil \frac{n}{2} \rceil) + 1.$$

The reader may easily solve this recursion obtaining

$$\hat{B}^{(p)}(m,n) = \max(\lceil \log_2 m \rceil, \lceil \log_2 n \rceil) + 1.$$

Hence

$$\lceil \log_2(m+n) \rceil \leq \hat{B}^{(p)}(m,n) \leq \lceil \log_2(m+n) \rceil + 1.$$

$\hat{B}^{(p)}(m,n)$ achieves the lower bound for some m and n, but whenever $2n > 2^k \geq m+n$, then the upper bound gives the correct value. A simple modification yields, however, a network C with delay time $\lceil \log_2(m+n) \rceil$. Instead of merging odd-odd and even-even as in Batcher's method, C merges odd-even and then even-odd, with the final round of comparisons $1 : 2, 3 : 4, 5 : 6, \ldots$. By the 0,1-principle, it is readily seen that C is indeed a merging network. Now in this case we have the recursion

$$\hat{C}^{(p)}(m,n) = \max(\hat{C}^{(p)}(\lceil \frac{m}{2} \rceil, \lfloor \frac{n}{2} \rfloor), \hat{C}^{(p)}(\lfloor \frac{m}{2} \rfloor, \lceil \frac{n}{2} \rceil)) + 1.$$

Assuming inductively $\hat{C}^{(p)}(k,\ell) = \lceil \log_2(k+\ell) \rceil$ for $k + \ell < m + n$, we immediately obtain

$$\hat{C}^{(p)}(m,n) = \lceil \log_2(m+n) \rceil \quad \text{for all } m \text{ and } n.$$

Example 4.6. Figure 4.20 shows Batcher's network $B(3,5)$ to the left and the network $C(3,5)$ to the right. We have $\hat{B}^{(p)}(3,5) = 4$ and $\hat{C}^{(p)}(3,5) = 3$, but note that the total number of comparisons in C is one more than in B.

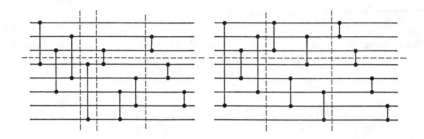

Figure 4.20

Proposition 4.29. *For all* $m, n \geq 1$,

$$M^{(p)}(m,n) = \hat{M}^{(p)}(m,n) = \lceil \log_2(m+n) \rceil.$$

Proof. Since $M^{(p)}(m,n) \leq \hat{M}^{(p)}(m,n)$ we just have to show $M^{(p)}(m,n) \geq \lceil \log_2(m+n) \rceil$. Let the chains to be merged be $\{a_1 < a_2 < \ldots < a_m\}$ and $\{b_1 < b_2 < \ldots < b_n\}$ and assume $m \leq n$. If $m = 1$, then every round contains only one essential comparison (involving a_1), hence $M^{(p)}(1,n) = \lceil \log_2(1+n) \rceil$. Furthermore, $M^{(p)}(m+1,n) \geq M^{(p)}(m,n)$, since we may declare the new element to be the smallest, and thus $M^{(p)}(m,n) \geq \lceil \log(1+n) \rceil$.

Suppose $n = 2^k + r$, $0 \leq r < 2^k$. If $m \leq 2^k - r$, then $k+1 = \lceil \log_2(1+n) \rceil \leq \lceil \log_2(m+n) \rceil = \lceil \log_2(m + 2^k + r) \rceil \leq k+1$. Hence $M^{(p)}(m,n) \geq \lceil \log_2(1+n) \rceil = \lceil \log_2(m+n) \rceil$. Now assume $m > 2^k - r$, then $\lceil \log_2(m+n) \rceil = k+2$. Suppose in the first round there is an element a_i which is compared to some b_j among the top r elements in the b-chain. If we declare as outcome $a_i < b_j$, $a_\ell < \{b_1, \ldots, b_n\}$ for $\ell < i$, $a_h > \{b_1, \ldots, b_n\}$ for $h > i$, then our algorithm needs to insert a_i among $\{b_1 < b_2 < \ldots < b_{j-1}\}$. Since $j \geq n+1-r$, this takes at least $\lceil \log_2 j \rceil \geq \lceil \log_2(n+1-r) \rceil = k+1$ further rounds, and thus $k+2 = \lceil \log_2(m+n) \rceil$ rounds altogether. The same argument applies when a_i is compared in the first round to some b_j among the bottom r elements in the b-chain. Hence, we may assume that in the first round all a_i's are compared to b_j's with $r+1 \leq j \leq n-r$. But there are only $n-2r = 2^k - r < m$ such b_j's implying that there is an element a_i which is not compared at all in the first round. Choosing the outcome $a_\ell < \{b_1, \ldots, b_n\}$ for $\ell < i$, $a_h > \{b_1, \ldots, b_n\}$ for $h > i$, we have to insert a_i among $\{b_1 < \ldots < b_n\}$, and this takes $\lceil \log(1 + n) \rceil = k + 1$ further rounds, whence again $k + 2 = \lceil \log_2(m + n) \rceil$ rounds are seen to be necessary. $\square$

4.29 shows, in particular, that $\hat{M}^{(p)}(2^{k-1}, 2^{k-1}) = k$ for every k. Hence, by repeatedly merging chains of length 2^i (doing all steps at the i-th iteration in parallel), we deduce

$$\hat{S}^{(p)}(2^k) \leq k + (k - 1) + \ldots + 1 = \binom{k + 1}{2},$$

and thus for arbitrary n

$$S^{(p)}(n) \leq \hat{S}^{(p)}(n) \leq \binom{\lceil \log n \rceil + 1}{2} \sim (\log_2 n)^2.$$

On the other hand, we trivially have $S^{(p)}(n) \geq \lceil \log_2 n \rceil$.

For a long time it was thought that $(\log_2 n)^2$ gives the correct growth of $S^{(p)}(n)$. But the remarkable construction of Ajtai, Komlós and Szémerédi [1983] uses, in fact, only $C' \log_2 n$ rounds for some (large) constant C', so it is now known that

$$C \log_2 n \leq S^{(p)}(n) \leq \hat{S}^{(p)}(n) \leq C' \log_2 n.$$

The following table gives the best known values for $S^{(p)}(n)$ up to $n = 10$. They are exact for $n \leq 8$, in fact, we always have $S^{(p)}(n) = \hat{S}^{(p)}(n)$.

n	3	4	5	6	7	8	9	10
$S^{(p)}(n)$	3	3	5	5	6	6	7	7

Let us briefly consider selection problems. $U_1^{(p)}(n)$ is easily determined. Since every round can reduce the number of maximal elements by at most a factor of 2 (in the worst case) we have $U_1^{(p)}(n) \geq \lceil \log_2 n \rceil$. The network in figure 4.21

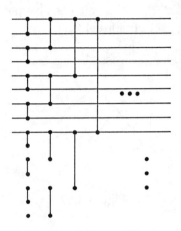

Figure 4.21

shows, on the other hand, $\hat{U}_1^{(p)}(n) \leq \lceil \log_2 n \rceil$; thus $U_1^{(p)}(n) = \hat{U}_1^{(p)}(n) = \lceil \log_2 n \rceil$. By the result on $\hat{S}^{(p)}(n)$ we note that all functions $U_t^{(p)}, \hat{U}_t^{(p)}(n), \ldots$ are of the order $\log_2 n$. But what about exact results? Let us just consider $W_t^{(p)}(n)$.

Proposition 4.30. *For all n and t,*

$$W_t^{(p)}(n) \leq \lceil \log_2 n \rceil + (t - 1).$$

Proof. Let $n = 2^k + r$, $0 \leq r < 2^k$. If $r > 0$, then we make a preliminary round of r comparisons to obtain the poset

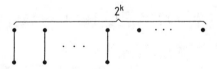

Suppose that after i more rounds after that we obtain a poset P_i which is the disjoint union $P_i = P_{i,1} \cup \ldots \cup P_{i,2^{k-i}}$ where each component $P_{i,j}$ is a binary tree (looked down from top to bottom). In the $(i + 1)$-st round we

match the 2^{k-i} maximal elements in pairs and compare two non-maximal elements if and only if they have a common predecessor. The resulting poset P_{i+1} is then a union of 2^{k-i-1} binary trees. By induction, we arrive after $\lceil \log_2 n \rceil$ rounds at the poset of figure 4.22,

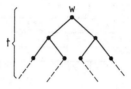

Figure 4.22

where we may discard all elements which are more than $t-1$ levels afar from w. Now we compare the elements immediately below w, observing the same rules as before. In this way we find the 2nd, 3rd,...,t-th largest element in at most $t-1$ more rounds.   □

As an example, we have $W_2^{(p)}(8) \leq 4$. The reader may prove (somewhat tediously) that $\hat{W}_2^{(p)}(8) = 5$, so $\hat{W}_t^{(p)}(n) = W_t^{(p)}(n)$ need not hold anymore for $t > 1$.

To derive a lower bound we notice that

$$W_t^{(p)}(n) \geq W_t^{(p)}(\lceil \tfrac{n}{2} \rceil) + 1 \ \ \text{for} \ \ 1 \leq t \leq \lceil \tfrac{n}{2} \rceil.$$

Indeed, if we declare the $\lceil \tfrac{n}{2} \rceil$ winners of the 1st round (including the non-compared element if n is odd) to be better than any of the losers, then our algorithm will select the t largest elements in order among $\lceil \tfrac{n}{2} \rceil$ elements after the 1st round. In particular, we obtain

$$W_2^{(p)}(n) \geq W_2^{(p)}(\lceil \tfrac{n}{2} \rceil) + 1 \ \ \text{for} \ \ n \geq 3,$$

and thus

$$W_2^{(p)}(n) \geq \lceil \log_2 n \rceil + 1 \ \ \text{for} \ \ n \geq 3$$

by induction. Hence we have proved

$$W_2^{(p)}(n) = \lceil \log_2 n \rceil + 1 \ \ (n \geq 3).$$

With the same argument, $W_t^{(p)}(n) \geq \lceil \log_2 n \rceil + (t-1)$ would be established for $n \geq 2^{t-1} + 1$, if we can prove

$$(4.27) \qquad W_t^{(p)}(2^{t-1} + 1) = 2t - 1 \quad (t \geq 1).$$

It is conjectured that (4.27) holds for all t, but this has been verified only for $t \leq 5$.

As our final topic we consider a parallel model suggested by Valiant [1975] where we are allowed to make *non-disjoint* comparisons in any round of the algorithm. Of course, if we were permitted to make all $\binom{n}{2}$ comparisons at once then we would be finished in one round. To keep an analogy to the disjoint comparison model considered thus far, we assume that in any round we are allowed to make up to n comparisons. Let us consider only the problem of selecting the top element. Related results are contained in the exercises.

Suppose $\mathcal{A}$ is a successful parallel algorithm of length ℓ making at most n comparisons in each round. Let us denote by C_i the set of possible candidates for the top element after round i, with $c_i = |C_i|$. Thus $c_0 = n$ and $c_0 \geq c_1 \geq c_2 \geq \ldots \geq c_\ell = 1$. Now in the $(i+1)$-st round it clearly makes no sense to compare two elements that are both non-candidates. Similarly, if a comparison pairs a candidate x with a non-candidate y, then the outcome might be $x > y$ and we would have gained no information on x. So, the $(i+1)$-st round will consist of comparisons just involving the candidates. It is most convenient to view this round as a graph G on the vertex-set C_i joining two vertices by an edge iff they are compared. After round $i+1$ the set C_{i+1} of candidates will then consist of vertices of G with no edge between any two of them. We call such a set of vertices a *stable* set of the graph. In the worst case the *largest* stable set might consist of the new candidates C_{i+1} (they might be above all the other elements). Hence our task consists in selecting such a graph where this maximum is as small as possible.

We have therefore reduced the design of an optimal algorithm to the following graph-theoretical question. Let the vertex-set V with $|V| = p$ $(= c_i)$ be given. For any graph G on V we set $\alpha(G) = \max\{|S| : S \subseteq V, S \text{ stable}\}$. The problem then reads: Given n, what is

$$\alpha(p, n) = \min_G \{\alpha(G) : G \text{ has at most } n \text{ edges}\}?$$

An optimal choice of comparisons in the $(i+1)$-st round will then correspond to a graph G with $\alpha(G) = \alpha(c_i, n)$ where $c_{i+1} = \alpha(c_i, n)$.

Let us turn the question around. Given α, *at least how many* edges must a graph G have with $\alpha(G) = \alpha$? Any graph G which consists of α disjoint complete subgraphs will have this property, and we will obtain a minimal number of edges among these graphs if we choose the complete subgraphs as equally sized as possible. A famous theorem of Turán in graph theory (see Bondy-Murty [1976], p.109) asserts that those are precisely the extremal graphs G with $\alpha(G) = \alpha$ and a minimal number of edges.

The extremal graph $G_{p,\alpha}$ looks therefore as follows. Let $q = \lceil \frac{p}{\alpha} \rceil$. $G_{p,\alpha}$ consists of α disjoint complete subgraphs where $p - \alpha(q - 1)$ of them have q vertices and $\alpha q - p$ of them have $q - 1$ vertices. The number of edges in $G_{p,\alpha}$ is easily computed as $\frac{1}{2}(q - 1)(2p - \alpha q)$. The following figure shows $G_{16,6}$ with $|E(G_{16,6})| = 14$.

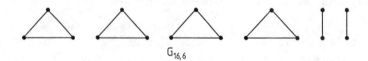

$G_{16,6}$

Figure 4.23

Turning back to our sorting problem, we infer from our analysis that

(4.28) $$c_{i+1} = \min\{\alpha : \frac{1}{2}(\lceil \frac{c_i}{\alpha} \rceil - 1)(2c_i - \alpha \lceil \frac{c_i}{\alpha} \rceil) \leq n\}.$$

Before estimating the length of an optimal algorithm let us consider the example $n = 16$. With disjoint comparisons we need $\lceil \log_2 16 \rceil = 4$ rounds. In the present situation we can do better. Choosing the comparisons in the first round according to the graphs $G_{16,\alpha}$ we see from (4.28) that $c_1 = 6$ where $G_{16,6}$ as in figure 4.23 is an optimal choice. After this round we are left with 6 candidates. Since $\binom{6}{2} = 15 < 16$ we can now perform *all* comparisons and are thus finished after only 2 rounds. Let us look at one more example $n = 2^8 = 256$. It is seen that $c_1 = 86$ and $c_2 = 13$. Since $\binom{13}{2} = 78 < 256$ we need just one more round, and thus 3 rounds altogether. Since $\log_2 \log_2 16 = 2$ and $\log_2 \log_2 256 = 3$, these two examples suggest that $\log_2 \log_2 n$ may be the correct growth of our selection problem, when n goes to infinity. We are now going to confirm this guess.

Consider (4.28). Let us set $\lceil \frac{c_i}{\alpha} \rceil = \frac{c_i}{\alpha} + r$ with $0 \le r < 1$. The inequality within the parentheses reads

$$(\frac{c_i}{\alpha} + r - 1)(2c_i - \alpha(\frac{c_i}{\alpha} + r)) \le 2n$$

or

$$(\frac{c_i}{\alpha} + r - 1)(c_i - \alpha r) \le 2n,$$

i.e.

$$\frac{c_i^2}{\alpha} - c_i + \alpha r(1 - r) \le 2n.$$

Since $r(1 - r) \le \frac{1}{4}$, the inequality is certainly satisfied if

$$\frac{c_i^2}{\alpha} - c_i + \frac{\alpha}{4} \le 2n,$$

or by $c_i \ge \alpha$ if

$$\frac{c_i^2}{\alpha} - \frac{3c_i}{4} \le 2n.$$

We conclude

$$c_{i+1} \le \lceil \frac{c_i^2}{2n + \frac{3}{4}c_i} \rceil.$$

On the other hand, the inequality is certainly not satisfied if

$$\frac{c_i^2}{\alpha} - c_i > 2n$$

whence we conclude

$$c_{i+1} \ge \lceil \frac{c_i^2}{2n + c_i} \rceil.$$

So we have to solve the recursive inequalities

$$\lceil \frac{c_i^2}{2n + c_i} \rceil \le c_{i+1} \le \lceil \frac{c_i^2}{2n + \frac{3}{4}c_i} \rceil$$

with $c_0 = n$.

Let us look at the upper bound first. The small values are trivially disposed of. We need one round for $n \le 3$ and at least 2 rounds for $n \ge 4$. Let us assume that the length ℓ of the algorithm is at least 2, i.e. $n \ge 4$. For c_1 we obtain $c_1 \le \lceil \frac{4n}{11} \rceil \le \frac{n}{2}$ for $n \ge 4$. Before the final ℓ-th round (making all

comparisons) we will have $\binom{c_i}{2} > n$, i.e. $c_i^2 > 2n$ for $i = 0, 1, \ldots, \ell - 2$.
Hence up to $i = \ell - 2$ we have

$$\lceil \frac{c_i^2}{2n + \frac{3}{4}c_i} \rceil \le \lceil \frac{c_i^2}{2n} \rceil \le \frac{c_i^2}{2n} + 1 \le \frac{c_i^2}{2n} + \frac{c_i^2}{2n} = \frac{c_i^2}{n}.$$

From the inequality $c_{i+1} \le \frac{c_i^2}{n}$ for $i = 1, \ldots, \ell - 2$ and $c_1 \le \frac{n}{2}$ we conclude
$c_i \le \frac{n}{2^{2^{i-1}}}$ $(i = 1, \ldots, \ell - 1)$. The algorithm will terminate after ℓ rounds if
$\binom{c_{\ell-1}}{2} \le n$. Substituting this into the inequality $c_{\ell-1} \le \frac{n}{2^{2^{\ell-2}}}$ we conclude
that the length of the algorithm will not exceed ℓ when

$$\frac{n^2}{2^{2^{\ell-1}}} - \frac{n}{2^{2^{\ell-2}}} \le 2n,$$

or

$$n \le 2^{2^{\ell-1}+1} + 2^{2^{\ell-2}} \le 2^{2^{\ell}} \text{ for } \ell \ge 2.$$

Thus we obtain the result that the worst-case cost of our problem is at most
$\lceil \log_2 \log_2 n \rceil$ whenever $\lceil \log_2 \log_2 n \rceil$ is at least 2, i.e. for $n > 4$.
The proof of the lower bound follows the same pattern. We have

$$c_{i+1} \ge \frac{c_i^2}{2n + c_i} \ge \frac{c_i^2}{4n},$$

and hence by induction and the starting value $c_1 \ge \frac{n}{4}$,

$$c_i \ge \frac{n}{2^{2^{i+1}-2}}.$$

Hence, the length ℓ of the algorithm will exceed i as long as

$$n > 2^{2^{i+1}}.$$

We conclude that we need at least $\lceil \log_2 \log_2 n \rceil - 1$ comparisons to solve our
sorting problem.

Let us summarize our discussion.

Proposition 4.31. *Let $Max(n)$ be the worst-case cost of maximal element
selection in the parallel model when in any round up to n arbitrary comparisons are permitted. Then*

$$\lceil \log_2 \log_2 n \rceil - 1 \le Max(n) \le \lceil \log_2 \log_2 n \rceil \quad (n > 4).$$

For $n = 4$ we obtain $Max(4) = 2$, so the upper bound is not satisfied. We remark that the lower bound may be attained. For example, we have $Max(21) = 2 < \lceil \log_2 \log_2 21 \rceil = 3$. Notice also that $Max(n)$ is not a monotone function in n since, e.g., $Max(19) = Max(20) = 3$ while $Max(21) = 2$.

Exercises 4.5.

1. Show that 6 is the minimal delay time for sorting 7 elements, even in the sequential case.

2. Verify that Batcher's odd-even merge has delay time $\max(\lceil \log_2 m \rceil, \lceil \log_2 n \rceil) + 1$.

3.* Prove that the network C before example 4.6 is a merging network.

4. Compare the total number of comparisons in Batcher's network and in C of the previous exercise. When does C use more comparisons than B?

5. Verify $\hat{W}_2^{(p)}(8) = 5$.

6. Prove $W_t^{(p)}(2^{t-1} + 1) = 2t - 1$ for $t \leq 5$.

7.* Prove $S^{(p)}(n) \geq \lceil \log_2 n \rceil + \lfloor \log_2 n \rfloor$ $(n \geq 5)$.

8. Determine $V_{1,n}^{(p)}(n)$.

9. Give bounds for $V_t^{(p)}(n)$, $U_t^{(p)}(n)$.

10.* Determine $Max(2^{2^\ell})$ for all ℓ. Is it ℓ?

11. Discuss $MaxMin(n)$, the parallel cost of determining the first and last elements, using at most n comparisons in each round.

12.* Suppose we want to complete the sorting in one round. Show that we need $\binom{n}{2}$ comparisons.

13.* Suppose we want to find the maximum in one round. How many comparisons do we need? In 2 rounds?

14.* Show that $Merge(n,n) \leq 2\log_2 \log_2 n + C$, where $Merge(n)$ is the cost of merging two n-chains with $\leq n$ comparisons in each round. (Valiant)

15. Apply the previous exercise to the full sorting problem $Sort(n)$ with $\leq n$ comparisons in each round.

Problems

1. Is $F(n) = S(n)$ for infinitely many n? (4.1)

2. Estimate $\overline{F}(n)$. (4.1)

3. Estimate $\overline{S}(n)$. (4.1)

4. Prove or disprove that Theorem 4.10i) gives the precise range when linear merge is optimal. (4.2)

5. Does $/M\backslash(m,n) \geq \lceil \log_2 \binom{m+n}{n} \rceil$ always hold? (4.2)

6. Prove or disprove the following inequalities (Knuth): a. $M(m,n+1) \leq M(m,n)+1 \leq M(m+1,n)$ for $m \leq n$, b. $M(m,n)+2 \leq M(m+1,n+1)$. (4.2)

7. Improve the bounds for $M(n,n,n)$ or for k chains. (4.2)

8. A sequence $a_1, \ldots, a_n$ is unimodal if $a_1 \leq a_2 \leq \ldots \leq a_k \geq a_{k+1} \geq \ldots \geq a_n$. Are $\{U_t(n) : t = 1, \ldots, n\}$ and $\{V_t(n) : t = 1, \ldots, n\}$ unimodal sequences for all n? (4.3)

9. Is it true that $(1-x) + H(x) \leq \frac{V_{\lfloor xn \rfloor}(n)}{n} \leq (1+x) + H(x), 0 < x < 1$, $H(x) =$entropy. More strongly, is $\lim\limits_{n \to \infty} \frac{V_{\lfloor xn \rfloor}}{n} = 1 + H(x)$? (4.3)

10. Determine $\overline{V}_2(n)$ for all n. (4.3)

11. Compute further values of $\hat{S}(n)$. (4.4)

12. Is Batcher's odd-even merge optimal for $m = 4$ and arbitrary n? Is it optimal for all m and n? (4.4)

13. Does $\hat{M}(m, n) \geq \hat{M}(m - 1, n) + 2$ hold for $n \geq m + 1$? (4.4)

14. Determine $\hat{U}_3(n)$, $\hat{V}_3(n)$ and $\hat{W}_3(n)$ for infinitely many n. (4.4)

15. Do there exist merging networks which are optimal both in the total number of comparisons and in the time delay $(= \lceil \log_2(m + n) \rceil)$? (4.5)

16. Prove or disprove: $W_t^{(p)}(2^{t-1} + 1) \geq 2t - 1$ for all t. (4.5)

17. Establish a non-trivial constant C with $S^{(p)}(n) \geq C \log_2 n$. (4.5)

Notes and References

The origin of today's sorting techniques takes us back to the 19th century. Knuth [1973] reports that Hollerith, an employee of the US Census Bureau, devised an ingeneous tabulating machine around 1880 to cope with statistics problems encountered in the census rolls. A comprehensive account of modern sorting methods can also be found in Knuth [1973]. As for optimality questions, Batcher [1968], Valiant [1975] and Ajtai-Komlós-Szémerédi [1983] are landmarks for sorting networks and parallel computations. Ford-Johnson's [1959] merge-insertion method stood for a long time as the best general sorting procedure until Manacher [1979b] bettered it. Apart from Knuth [1973] a wealth of information can also be found in Mehlhorn [1984].

Aigner M. [1981], Producing posets. Discrete Math. 35, 1-15.

Aigner M. [1982a], Selecting the top three elements. Discrete Appl. Math. 4, 247-267.

Aigner M. [1982b], Parallel complexity of sorting problems. J. Algorithms 3, 79-88.

Aigner M. [1985], A note on merging. Order 2, 257-264.

Ajtai M., Komlós J. Szémerédi E. [1983], Sorting in $c \log n$ parallel steps. Combinatorica 3(1), 1-19.

Alekseyev V.E. [1969], Certain algorithms for classification with minimal memory (Russian, English summary). Kibernetika 5, 99-103.

Batcher K.E. [1968], Sorting networks and their applications. Proc. AFIPS Spring Joint Computer Conf. 32, 307-314.

Bent S.W., John J.W. [1985], Finding the median requires $2n$ comparisons. In: Proc. 17th ACM Symposium Theory of Computing, 213-216.

Blum M., Floyd R.W., Pratt V., Rivest R.L., Tarjan R.E. [1973], Time bounds for selection. J. Computer System Sci. 7m, 448-461.

Bollobás B., Hell P. [1985], Sorting and graphs. In: Graphs and Order, Reidel, 169-184.

Bondy J.A., Murty U.S.R. * [1976], Graph Theory With Applications. The McMillan Press, London.

Bose R.C., Nelson R.J. [1962], A sorting problem. J. Ass. Comp. Mach. 9, 282-296.

Dilworth R.P. [1950], A decomposition theorem for partially ordered sets. Annals Math. 51, 161-166.

Floyd R.W., Knuth D. [1971], The Bose-Nelson sorting problem. In: A Survey of Combinatorial Theory, Proc. Intern. Symposium, Fort Collins, North Holland, 163-172.

Floyd R.W., Rivest R.L. [1975], Expected time bounds for selection. Comm. Ass. Comp. Mach. 18, 165-172.

Ford L.R., Johnson S.B. [1959], A tournament problem. Amer. Math. Monthly 66, 387-389.

Fussenegger F., Gabow H. [1979], A counting approach to lower bounds for selection problems. J. Ass. Comp. Mach. 26, 227-238.

Graham R.L. [1971], On sorting by comparisons. Proc. Second Atlas Conf., 263-269.

Green M.W. [1970], Some observations on sorting. Cellular Logic in Memory Arrays Final Report, Stanford Res. Inst., 49-71.

Hadian A. [1969], Thesis, Univ. Minnesota.

Hadian A., Sobel M. [1969], Selecting the t-largest using binary errorless comparisons. Coll. Math. Soc. János Bolyai, 585-599.

Häggkvist R., Hell P. [1981], Parallel sorting with constant time for comparisons. SIAM J. Comp. 10, 465-472.

Häggkvist R., Hell P. [1982], Sorting and merging in rounds. SIAM J. Alg. Discrete Methods 3, 465-473.

Hoare C.A.R. [1962], QUICKSORT. Computer J. 5, 10-15.

Hwang F.K. [1980], Optimal merging of 3 elements with n elements. SIAM J. Computing 9, 298-320.

Hwang F.K., Lin S. [1969], An analysis of Ford and Johnson's sorting algorithm. Proc. Third Annual Princeton Conf. on Information Sci. and Systems, 292-296.

Hwang F.K., Lin S. [1971], Optimal merging of two elements with n elements. Acta Informatica 1, 145-158.

Hwang F.K., Lin S. [1972], A simple algorithm for merging two disjoint linearly-ordered sets. SIAM J. Computing 1, 31-39.

Hyafil L. [1976], Bounds for selection. SIAM J. Computing 5, 109-114.

Kahn J., Saks M. [1984], Balancing poset extensions. Order 1, 113-126.

Kirkpatrick D.G. [1974], Topics in the complexity of combinatorial algorithms. Comp. Sci. Dept. Technical Report Tr74, Univ. Toronto.

Kislitsyn S.S. [1964], On the selection of the k-th element of an ordered set by pairwise comparisons. Sibirsk Math. Zk. 5, 557-564.

Knuth D. * [1973], The Art of Computer Programming, vol. 3, Sorting and Searching. Addison-Wesley, Reading.

Linial N. [1984], The information-theoretic bound is good for merging. SIAM J. Computing 13, 795-801.

Manacher G.K. [1979a], Significant improvements to the Hwang-Lin merging algorithm. J. Ass. Comp. Mach. 26, 434-440.

Manacher G.K. [1979b], The Ford-Johnson algorithm is not optimal. J. Ass. Comp. Mach. 26, 441-456.

Matula D.W. [1973], Selecting the t-th best in average $n + 0(\log\log n)$ comparisons. Techn. Report Tr 73-9, Washington Univ.

Mehlhorn K. * [1984], Data Structures and Algorithms 1: Sorting and Searching. Springer-Verlag, Berlin.

Picard C. *[1965], Théorie des questionnaires. Gauthiers-Villars, Paris.

Pohl I. [1972], A sorting problem and its complexity. Comm. Ass. Comp. Mach. 15, 462-464.

Pratt V., Yao F.F. [1973], On lower bounds for computing the i-th largest element. Proc. 14th IEEE Symposium on Switching and Automata Theory, 70-81.

Schönhage A., Paterson M., Pippenger N. [1976], Finding the median. J. Comput. System Sci. 13, 184-199.

Steinhaus H. * [1969], Mathematical Snapshots. Oxford Univ. Press, New York.

Stockmeyer P.K., Yao F.F. [1980], On the optimality of linear merge. SIAM J. Computing 9, 85-90.

Turán P. [1941], Eine Extremalaufgabe aus der Graphentheorie. Mat. Fiz. Lapok 48, 436-452.

Valiant L. [1975], Parallelism in comparison problems. SIAM J. Computing 4, 348-355.

Varecza A. [1982a], Finding two consecutive elements. Studia Sci. Math. Hung. 17, 291-302.

Varecza A. [1982b], Are two given elements neighboring? Discrete Math. 42, 107-117.

Yao A.C.C. [1980], Bounds on selection networks. SIAM J. Computing 9, 566-582.

Yao A.C.C., Yao F.F. [1976], Lower bounds on merging networks. J. Ass. Comp. Mach. 23, 566-571.

Yao A.C.C., Yao F.F. [1982], On the average-case complexity of selecting the k-th best. SIAM J. Computing 11, 428-447.

Chapter 5

Poset Problems

In many instances in the last chapter we were required to sort partially ordered lists. That is, we are given a set S of n elements and know that S is ordered according to an unknown linear order. At the outset we are further given a set of relations forming a poset P on S. Our task is again to determine the unknown linear order (which, of course, must be compatible with P) with as few comparisons as possible. In section 4.2 we discussed at length an example of such a situation, namely when P consisted of a pair of disjoint chains. General poset problems of this type provide some very new and interesting insights into sorting, culminating in some of the finest theorems obtained thus far.

5.1   The General Sorting Problem

We are given a poset P on n elements and are required to sort the underlying set with with as few comparisons as possible. Let us call this the *general sorting problem*, with $S(P)$ denoting the worst-case cost. Thus our original sorting problem corresponds to the case when P is an antichain.

The possible outcomes of our problem are in one-to-one correspondence with the set $L(P)$ of linear extensions of P, whose cardinality we again denote by $e(P) = |L(P)|$. The usual information-theoretic bound yields therefore

$$S(P) \geq \lceil \log_2 e(P) \rceil.$$

How close can we come to this bound? In particular, can we come to within a constant factor of the lower bound? For the full sorting problem ($P =$

antichain) and for the merging problem (P =disjoint union of chains) we have answered this question affirmatively.

Before proving the analogous fact for any poset P (with a constant ~ 2.2 independent of P) we discuss a somewhat simpler result due to Fredman [1976] which shows that the information-theoretic bound is nearly exact as long as $e(P)$ is large as compared to 2^n.

Proposition 5.1. *Let P be a poset on n elements. Then*

$$S(P) \leq \log_2 e(P) + 2(n - 1).$$

Proof. The idea of the algorithm is as follows. As in binary insertion we insert the elements one-by-one. Suppose we already know $x_1 < x_2 < \ldots < x_{k-1}$. Let $L_{k-1} \subseteq L(P)$ be the set of linear extensions compatible with this chain, thus $L_1 = L(P)$. Now we insert any one of the remaining elements, say x, into $\{x_1 < \ldots < x_{k-1}\}$. Suppose we can do this with s_k comparisons so that

(5.1) $$| L_k | \leq \frac{| L_{k-1} |}{2^{s_k - 2}} \quad (k \geq 2).$$

Since at the end, $| L_n |= 1$, we conclude

$$| L(P) |\geq \prod_{k=2}^{n} 2^{s_k - 2},$$

and thus

$$\log_2 e(P) \geq \sum_{k=2}^{n} s_k - 2(n - 1) \geq S(P) - 2(n - 1).$$

as required.

So it remains to verify (5.1).

Define two dummy elements x_0, x_k with $x_0 < x_1 < \ldots < x_{k-1} < x_k$, and set

$$p(i, j) = \frac{| L_{k-1}(x_i < x < x_j) |}{| L_{k-1} |},$$

i.e. $p(i, j)$ is the proportion of linear extensions in L_{k-1} for which $x_i < x < x_j$ holds.

We insert x into $\{x_1 < \ldots < x_{k-1}\}$ inductively. Suppose we have performed r comparisons involving x; let $i = i(r)$ be the largest index for which $x_i < x$ is known to hold at this stage, and let $j = j(r)$ be the smallest index with $x < x_j$ at this point. If $j(r) = i(r) + 1$, then we are finished. Otherwise, let h be the largest index such that

(5.2) $\qquad p(i, h) + p(i + 1, h - 1) < p(h - 1, j) + p(h, j - 1).$

Note that (5.2) is satisfied for $h = i + 1$, whereas (5.2) is violated for $h = j$. Hence h exists with $i < h < j$. The $(r + 1)$-st comparison is now $x : x_h$. We claim that for $i(r) + 1 < j(r)$

(5.3) $\qquad p(i(r), j(r)) + p(i(r) + 1, j(r) - 1) \leq \dfrac{1}{2^{r-1}}.$

This is certainly true for $r = 0$, since the right-hand side is then 2. We proceed by induction on r.
If the outcome of $x : x_h$ is $x < x_h$, then by (5.2)

(5.4)
$$
\begin{aligned}
p(i(r + 1), j(r + 1)) \quad &+ \quad p(i(r + 1) + 1), j(r + 1) - 1) \\
&\leq \quad p(i, h) + p(i + 1, h - 1) \\
&< \quad p(h - 1, j) + p(h, j - 1).
\end{aligned}
$$

If the outcome is $x > x_h$, then by the choice of h

(5.5)
$$
\begin{aligned}
p(i(r + 1), j(r + 1)) \quad &+ \quad p(i(r + 1) + 1), j(r + 1) - 1) \\
&\leq \quad p(h, j) + p(h + 1, j - 1) \\
&\leq \quad p(i, h + 1) + p(i + 1, h).
\end{aligned}
$$

Now both $(p(i, h) + p(i + 1, h - 1)) + (p(h - 1, j) + p(h, j - 1))$ and $(p(h, j) + p(h + 1, j - 1)) + (p(i, h + 1) + p(i + 1, h))$ sum to $p(i, j - 1) + p(i + 1, j) = p(i, j) + p(i + 1, j - 1) \leq \frac{1}{2^{r-1}}$ by induction, whence (5.4) and (5.5) establish (5.3).
Thus if x is inserted in s_k steps, then

$$
p(i(s_k), j(s_k)) \leq p(i(s_k - 1), j(s_k - 1)) \leq \dfrac{1}{2^{s_k - 2}},
$$

and hence

$$
\mid L_k \mid = \mid L_{k-1} \mid p(i(s_k), j(s_k)) \leq \dfrac{\mid L_{k-1} \mid}{2^{s_k - 2}},
$$

which is just (5.1). $\square$

Now we begin the discussion of the main theorem of this section. Recall the notion of a δ-*central pair* (x, y) in a poset P, meaning that

$$\delta \le \frac{|\, L(P; x < y)\,|}{|\, L(P)\,|} \le 1 - \delta.$$

We will outline a proof that any poset (which is not a chain) has a δ-central pair with $\delta > \frac{3}{11}$. By our previous discussion this will imply that the sorting complexity $S(P)$ of any poset is bounded by

$$S(P) \le \left(-\frac{1}{\log_2 \frac{8}{11}} \right) \log_2 e(P) \sim 2.1766 \log_2 e(P).$$

As in section 4.2 we will only prove that a pair x, y with

(5.6) $$\frac{3}{11} < \frac{|\, L(P; x < y)\,|}{|\, L(P)\,|} < \frac{8}{11}$$

exists, but give no indication of how to find this central pair. Which pair (x, y) might be a good candidate? Let us picture the linear extensions $\sigma \in L(P)$ as order-preserving injections from P into $\{1 < 2 < \ldots < n\}$. If $\sigma(x) = k$, then we say the element x has *height* $h(x; \sigma) = k$ in the extension σ. We are thus searching for a pair x, y such that in about half the extensions σ, $h(x; \sigma) < h(y; \sigma)$ while otherwise $h(y; \tau) < h(x; \tau)$. This observation suggests that we look for two elements x, y whose *expected heights* $h(x) := \frac{1}{|L(P)|} \sum_\sigma h(x; \sigma)$ and $h(y) := \frac{1}{|L(P)|} \sum_\sigma h(y; \sigma)$ are about the same.

Clearly, $1 \le h(x) \le n$ for every $x \in P$. We may assume that P contains neither a unique minimal nor a unique maximal element, whence $1 < h(x) < n$ for all $x \in P$. Therefore there exists a pair x, y with $|\, h(y) - h(x)\,| < 1$ and this pair is our candidate for proving (5.6). Note that x, y are necessarily incomparable in P since $x \underset{P}{<} y$ obviously implies $h(y; \sigma) \ge h(x; \sigma) + 1$ for all $\sigma \in L(P)$ and thus $h(y) - h(x) \ge 1$.

Let us use the short notation $p(x < y) = \frac{|L(P; x<y)|}{|L(P)|}$. The quantity $p(x < y)$ can be interpreted as the *probability* that $x < y$ occurs in the eventual liner extension. Our claim (5.6) is thus true if we can show that

(5.7) $$h(y) - h(x) < 1 \quad \text{implies} \quad p(x < y) < \frac{8}{11}.$$

The proof of (5.7) splits into an order-theoretic part and a lot of arithmetic involved.

Let us first connect the quantities $h(x), h(y)$ and $p(x < y)$. To this end, we define $E_k(x < y) = \{\sigma \in L(P) : \sigma(y) - \sigma(x) = k\}$, $e_k(x < y) = \mid E_k(x < y) \mid$ and $p_k(x < y) = \frac{e_k(x < y)}{e(P)}$ for every integer k. That is, $p_k(x < y)$ is the proportion of extensions σ for which $\sigma(y) - \sigma(x) = k$. Note that $p_k(x < y) = p_{-k}(y < x)$. Since

$$p(x < y) = \sum_{k \geq 1} p_k(x < y)$$

$$h(y) - h(x) = \sum_{k \in \mathbf{Z}} k p_k(x < y),$$

(5.7) becomes

(5.8) $$\sum_{k \in \mathbf{Z}} k p_k(x < y) < 1 \text{ implies } \sum_{k \geq 1} p_k(x < y) < \frac{8}{11}.$$

The two parts of the proof of (5.8) are now as follows:
First we derive a number of properties enjoyed by the sequence $p_k = p_k(x < y)$ $(k \in \mathbf{Z})$ - this is the order-theoretic part -, and show then that these properties imply the truth of (5.8).

Proposition 5.2. *Let P be a poset, $x, y \in P$ incomparable elements and $p_k = p_k(x < y)$, $k \in \mathbf{Z}$, as defined before. Then*

i) $\sum_{k \in \mathbf{Z}} p_k = 1$

ii) $p_0 = 0$, $p_1 = p_{-1}$

iii) $p_k = 0 \Rightarrow p_{k+1} = 0$ for $k \geq 1$

iv) $p_2 + p_{-2} \leq p_1 + p_{-1}$

v) $p_k \leq p_{k-1} + p_{k+1}$ for $\mid k \mid \geq 2$

vi) $p_k^2 \geq p_{k-1} p_{k+1}$ for $\mid k \mid \geq 2$.

Proof. i) and ii) are trivially true. To prove iii) it suffices to show that every extension σ with $\sigma(y) - \sigma(x) = k + 1$ can be turned into an extension τ with $\tau(y) - \tau(x) = k$. Since x, y are incomparable, denoted by $x \parallel y$, no z with $\sigma(x) < \sigma(z) < \sigma(y)$ can be comparable to both x and y. By symmetry, we may assume $x \parallel z$ and that z is the first element above x in the chain, which is incomparable to x. Then $z \parallel w$ for every w with $\sigma(x) < \sigma(w) < \sigma(z)$ since otherwise $z > w$, $w > x$ and thus $z > x$. Hence we may adjust σ by moving z below x, obtaining a required extension τ.

To prove iv) we exhibit an injective mapping f from $E_2(x < y) \cup E_2(y < x) \longrightarrow E_1(x < y) \cup E_1(y < x)$. Suppose z is between x and y in a linear extension where x and y are two apart. If $z \parallel x$ then f switches x and z. If z is comparable to x, then y is incomparable to both x and z, and f moves y to the other side of x. In the first case, x is incomparable to both its neighbors in the new extension $f(\sigma)$ and is in the same relative position to y as before, while in the second case x is comparable to one of its neighbors in $f(\sigma)$ and reverses its position relative to y. Hence the extensions $f(\sigma)$ so generated are all distinct.

The proof of v) is considerably more difficult. Since $p_k = p_{-k}$ we may assume $k \geq 2$, and are thus only concerned with extensions σ where $\sigma(y) > \sigma(x)$. Note that (since $x \parallel y$) $e_k(x < y; P) = e_k(x < y; Q)$, $k \geq 1$, where Q arises from P by adding the single relation $x < y$. We then say y *covers* x, denoted by $x < \cdot y$. The proof is by induction on $n = \mid P \mid$. Let n be the minimal number where the inequality v) fails to hold (clearly $n \geq 3$), and among all counterexamples let Q, $\mid Q \mid = n$, be a poset with a maximal number of relations, $x < \cdot y$.

Claim 1. If $v, w \in Q$, $v \parallel w$, then one of v, w must be $\geq x$ while the other must be $\leq y$. Let $Q' = Q \cup \{v < w\}$, i.e. Q' is the poset arising from Q by adding $v < w$ and all relations implied transitively therefrom; similarly let $Q" = Q \cup \{w < v\}$. Clearly, $e_i(x < y; Q) = e_i(x < y; Q') + e_i(x < y; Q")$ for all $i \geq 1$. Hence if $x < \cdot y$ still holds in Q' and $Q"$, then the inequality v) is true for both Q' and $Q"$ (since they contain more relations than Q) and thus also for Q, contrary to our assumption. Hence $x < \cdot y$ can no longer hold in one of Q' or $Q"$, which can only arise if $x \leq v$, $w \leq y$ or $x \leq w$, $v \leq y$.

Claim 2. In Q, x is a minimal element, and y is a maximal element. Let $w \leq x$, $w \neq x$ be a minimal element. Then by Claim 1, w is comparable to (and hence less than) every other element v, i.e. w is the unique minimum of P. But then $e_i(x < y; Q) = e_i(x < y; Q - w)$ for all $i \geq 1$, contradicting the minimality of $n = \mid Q \mid$. Thus $w = x$, and x is minimal. An analogous argument shows that y is maximal.

Claim 3. Q is covered by two disjoint chains $A = \{x < x_1 < \ldots < x_r\}$,

$B = \{y_1 < y_2 < \ldots < y_s < y\}$ with $r, s \geq 1$, and the only other relations present in Q are $x < \cdot y$ and relations of the form $x_i > y_j$. (See figure 5.1.)

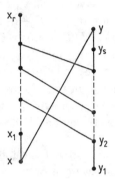

Figure 5.1

Let A be the set of elements $\geq x$ other than y, and B the remaining elements. If any pair in $A - x$ is incomparable, then by Claim 1 one must appear below y, contradicting $x < \cdot y$. Hence A is a chain. Similarly, since any element of $B - y$ is incomparable to x they must all be below y (by Claim 1 again), and we conclude by the reasoning applied to y that B is a chain. If $x_i < y_j$ for any i, j, then $x < \cdot y$ could not hold. Finally, if A or B consists of just the singleton $\{x\}$ or $\{y\}$, respectively, then the inequality v) were trivially true for all k; thus $r, s \geq 1$.

To complete the proof of v) we show that for a poset Q as in Claim 3 the inequalities $e_k(x < y) \leq e_{k-1}(x < y) + e_{k+1}(x < y)$ hold after all. Suppose first $k < n - 1$. We construct an injection $f : E_k(x < y) \longrightarrow E_{k-1}(x < y) \cup E_{k+1}(x < y)$ as follows. If $\sigma \in E_k(x < y)$ and $\sigma(x) \geq 2$, then x being minimal cannot be related to the element below it, so f interchanges them. If $\sigma(x) = 1$ and x is not related to the element immediately above it, then f again switches them. If, finally, x is related to the element above it, then f switches y with the element z above it which can be done since $\sigma(y) = \sigma(x) + k = k + 1 < n$ and y is maximal and thus unrelated to z. It is easily verified that the linear extensions $f(\sigma) \in E_{k-1}(x < y) \cup E_{k+1}(x < y)$ so generated are pairwise distinct.

It remains to consider the case $k = n - 1$. Here $\sigma(x) = 1$, $\sigma(y) = n$ and $e_{n-1}(x < y; Q) = | L(P) |$ where $P = Q - \{x, y\}$. The extensions σ in $E_{n-2}(x < y; Q)$ are those for which $\sigma(x) = 1$, $\sigma(y) = n - 1$, $\sigma(x_r) = n$ or

$\sigma(x) = 2$, $\sigma(y) = n$, $\sigma(y_1) = 1$. Thus, $e_{n-2}(x < y; Q) =| L(P - x_r) | +$ $| L(P - y_1) |$ and we need to show that this number exceeds $| L(P) |$. Since x_1 or y_1 is minimal in every extension of P, we have $| L(P) |\le| L(P - x_1) | + | L(P - y_1) |$, so we need only verify that $| L(P - x_1) |\le| L(P - x_r) |$. By sending each x_i in an extension $\sigma \in L(P - x_1)$ into x_{i-1} for $2 \le i \le r$, we obtain a valid extension $f(\sigma) \in L(P - x_r)$ (recall that no relations $x_i < y_j$ are present in Q). Since f is clearly injective, our proof of v) is complete. The proof of vi) is at present beyond the scope of this book. It uses some deep results in convex geometry, in particular, the Alexandrov-Fenchel inequality for mixed volumes. The interested reader may consult the paper by Stanley [1981] or the book by Busemann [1958].   □

Kahn and Saks [1984] have now proved the following intricate and difficult result on real sequences, which we can only state.

Lemma 5.3. *Suppose $(a_i : i \ge 1)$ and $(b_i : i \ge 1)$ are sequences of nonnegative real numbers satisfying*

i) $\sum_{i\ge1} a_i + \sum_{i\ge1} b_i = 1$

ii) $a_1 = b_1$

iii) $a_i = 0$ implies $a_{i+1} = 0$, and $b_i = 0$ implies $b_{i+1} = 0$ for $i \ge 1$

iv) $a_2 + b_2 \le a_1 + b_1$

v) $a_k \le a_{k-1} + a_{k+1}, b_k \le b_{k-1} + b_{k+1}$ $(k \ge 2)$

vi) $a_k^2 \ge a_{k-1}a_{k+1}, b_k^2 \ge b_{k-1}b_{k+1}$ $(k \ge 2)$.

If $\sum_{i\ge1} ia_i - \sum_{i\ge1} ib_i < 1$, then $\sum_{i\ge1} a_i < \frac{8}{11}$.

Setting $a_k = p_k$ and $b_k = p_{-k}$ yields then the following result.

Theorem 5.4. *In any poset P (not a chain) there exists a δ-central pair with $\delta > \frac{3}{11}$. Hence $S(P) \le -\frac{1}{\log_2 \frac{8}{11}} \log_2 | L(P) |\sim 2.2\log_2| L(P) |$.*

The last result raises the very interesting question as to the *largest $\delta = \delta(P)$*, $0 < \delta \le \frac{1}{2}$, for which a δ-central pair in P exists. We have seen $\delta(P) \ge \frac{1}{3}$ for posets P of width 2 with equality possible (Theorem 4.5). The following conjectures strengthen this to arbitrary posets.

Conjecture A. *If P is not a chain, then $\delta(P) \geq \frac{1}{3}$.*

Conjecture B. *For $k \geq 2$, let $\delta(k) = \min(\delta(P) : P$ has width $k)$. Then $\lim_{k \to \infty} \delta(k) = \frac{1}{2}$.*

We know that the poset $P = \begin{array}{c} \bullet \\ | \\ \bullet \end{array} \begin{array}{c} \bullet \end{array}$ has $\delta(P) = \frac{1}{3}$, and it is known that,

among the width 2-posets, P is essentially the only one with $\delta(P) = \frac{1}{3}$ (see the remark after Theorem 4.5). In fact, it is widely believed that $\delta(P) > \frac{1}{3}$ for all P of width at least 3. Unfortunately, the method of proof in the preceding theorem will not establish this stronger result as the following poset demonstrates.

Example 5.1. Consider the poset P of figure 5.2. The reader may easily check that we have $h(x) = \frac{17}{13}$, $h(y) = \frac{29}{13}$, hence $h(y) - h(x) = \frac{12}{13} < 1$, and $p(x < y) = \frac{9}{13}$. Hence, although $p(x < y) < \frac{8}{11}$ (as it must by the Theorem), we have $\frac{2}{3} < \frac{9}{13}$ and $\frac{4}{13} < \frac{1}{3}$, so conjecture A cannot, in general, be verified by simply taking any pair x, y with $\mid h(y) - h(x) \mid < 1$.

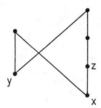

Figure 5.2

Taking, however, y and z, we have $h(z) = \frac{36}{13}$, $h(z) - h(y) = \frac{7}{13} < 1$ and $p(y < z) = \frac{8}{13} < \frac{2}{3}$. Thus while it is quite likely that there always exists a pair x, y with $h(y) - h(x) < 1$ and $p(x < y) < \frac{2}{3}$, the question remains how to find this pair.

Exercises 5.1.

1*. Suppose the poset P has an automorphism $\neq id$. Show that P contains a $\frac{1}{3}$-central pair x, y. (Pouzet)

2. Construct a poset of width 3 with $\delta(P) = \frac{14}{39}$.

3. Consider the following sorting problem. Let P be a poset on n elements $a_1, \ldots, a_n$. At the outset we know that the unknown poset is isomorphic to P. Find P by making comparisons $a_i : a_j$. Let $C^{(s)}(P)$ be the worst-case cost. Find upper and lower bounds for the subset lattice $B(n) \cong \{0 < 1\}^n$.

4*. Let P be a poset on $\{a_1, \ldots, a_n\}$. A set $E = E_1 \cup E_2 \subseteq \{a_1, \ldots, a_n\}^2$ is called *essential* for P if $(a_i, a_j) \in E_1$ implies $a_i < a_j$, $(a_i, a_j) \in E_2$ implies a_i, a_j are incomparable, and P is the only poset consistent with E. Show that there is a unique minimal essential set E where E_1 consists of all covering pairs and E_2 of all incomparable pairs a_i, a_j (called *critical pairs*) such that $x > a_i$ implies $x > a_j$ and $y < a_j$ implies $y < a_i$.

5*. Let P be a poset on $\{a_1, \ldots, a_n\}$ and consider the following recognition problem. By making comparisons we want to find out whether the unknown poset is isomorphic to P or not. Denote by $C^{(r)}(P)$ the worst-case cost. Show $\max(C^{(s)}(P), ess(P)) \leq C^{(r)}(P) \leq C^{(s)}(P) + ess(P)$, where $ess(P)$ is the size of the minimal essential set. (Faigle-Turán).

6. Compute $ess(B_n)$ for the subset lattice.

5.2   Producing Posets

The selection problems treated in the last chapter can be understood as the production of certain partial orders. Consider, e.g., the problem $U_t(n)$ of selecting the top t elements (without regard to order). We can phrase this by saying that we want to "produce" the poset P as in figure 5.3. That is, we require all relations between the top t and the bottom $n - t$ elements. If, in the course of the algorithm, additional relations within the top part or within the bottom part arise, all the better, but we do not really need them.

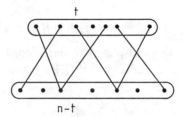

Figure 5.3

To give a clear notion of what we mean by the production of a certain poset P, we give the following definition.

Let $\mathcal{O}(n)$ be the set of all non-isomorphic posets on n elements. As in section 4.2 we define an ordering $\preceq$ on $\mathcal{O}(n)$ by setting $P \preceq Q$ if and only if there exists a monotone embedding f from P to Q, i.e. $a \underset{P}{\leq} b$ implies $f(a) \underset{Q}{\leq} f(b)$, for all a, b. With this ordering, $\mathcal{O}(n)$ becomes a poset in its own right with the antichain as unique minimal element and the chain as unique maximal element. Incidentally, it is an interesting and unsolved problem to determine $|\mathcal{O}(n)|$. The smallest values are $|\mathcal{O}(2)| = 2$, $|\mathcal{O}(3)| = 5$, $|\mathcal{O}(4)| = 16$, and $|\mathcal{O}(5)| = 63$. No non-trivial bounds are known for the growth of $|\mathcal{O}(n)|$ as $n \longrightarrow \infty$.

We now say that an algorithm $\mathcal{A}$ (using comparisons between elements) *produces* the poset P, if for all end-posets Q_i of $\mathcal{A}$ we have $P \preceq Q_i$. As in the previous section let us denote by $e(P)$ the number of linear extensions of P. As remarked before, we have $e(Q) \leq e(P)$ whenever $P \preceq Q$. By $C(P)$ we denote the worst-case cost of producing P. The following result gives the natural information-theoretic lower bound for $C(P)$.

Proposition 5.5. *Let P be any poset on n elements. Then*

$$C(P) \geq \lceil \log_2 \frac{n!}{e(P)} \rceil.$$

Proof. At the beginning we start with the antichain P_0 on n elements, thus $e(P_0) = n!$. Suppose that at some stage of an optimal P-producing algorithm the poset R arises. If $x : y$ is the next comparison, then as noted before

(5.9) $e(R) = e(R; x < y) + e(R; y < x).$

Suppose $Q_1, \ldots, Q_t$ are the end-posets of our algorithm. Then $Q_i \succeq P$ and thus $e(Q_i) \leq e(P)$ for all i, and $t \leq 2^{C(P)}$. By iterating (5.9) we obtain

$$ n! = \sum_{i=1}^{t} e(Q_i), $$

and thus

$$ n! \leq t.e(P) \leq 2^{C(P)} e(P), $$

i.e. $C(P) \geq \lceil \log_2 \frac{n!}{e(P)} \rceil.$ $\square$

5.5 yields for the posets in figure 4.9 the following lower bounds:

$$ U_t(n) \geq \lceil \log_2 (\begin{smallmatrix} n \\ t \end{smallmatrix}) \rceil, V_t(n) \geq \lceil \log_2 t (\begin{smallmatrix} n \\ t \end{smallmatrix}) \rceil, W_t(n) \geq \lceil \log_2 [n]_t \rceil, $$

where $[n]_t = n(n-1) \ldots (n-t+1)$ are the *falling factorials* of n of length t, with the convention $[n]_0 = 1$.

We will now prove a general result suggested by Fussenegger and Gabow [1979] which will improve these bounds and yield some insight on producing "top-posets" in general. First we need some definitions. A *down-set* (or *order ideal*) D in a poset P is a subset of P such that $x \in D$, $y \underset{P}{\leq} x$ implies $y \in D$. Similarly, an *up-set* (or *order filter*) U is a subset such that $x \in U$, $y \geq x$ implies $y \in U$. Observe that when b is a minimal element of P, then $P - b$ is an up-set of cardinality $n - 1$, and conversely. Hence the number of such up-sets equals the number of minimal elements of P. It follows that $e(P) = \sum e(U)$ with the summation extending over all up-sets of cardinality $n - 1$.

Now let T be a poset with t elements. We think of T as the "top-part" of the unknown linear order. We wish to isolate T by a sequence of comparisons meaning that we want to "produce" the following poset P consisting of T at the top and $n - t$ unrelated elements, each one below every element of T (figure 5.4).

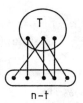

Figure 5.4

The selection problems studied so far correspond to the following tops T (see figure 4.9):

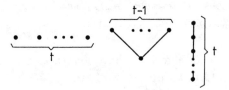

Figure 5.5

Theorem 5.6. *Let P be the poset with top T, $| T |= t$, and $n - t$ unrelated elements below T. Then*

$$C(P) \geq (n - t) + \lceil \log_2 \frac{[n]_{t-1}}{e(T)} \rceil.$$

Proof. For a poset R, let us denote by $\max(R)$ the number of maximal elements in R. We set up the following function

$$f(R) = \sum_{\substack{U \text{ up-set} \\ | U |= t - 1}} e(U) 2^{\max(R-U)-1}.$$

The crux of the proof consists in verifying the recursive inequality

(5.10) $f(R; x < y) + f(R; y < x) \geq f(R).$

We do this by showing that (5.10) holds for every term $e(U)2^{\max(R-U)-1}$.

Case 1. $x, y \in U$. After the comparison $x : y$, U is again an up-set of $(R; x < y)$ and $(R; y < x)$. Since $\max(R - U)$ remains the same and $e(U) = e(U; x < y) + e(U; y < x)$, (5.10) is satisfied with equality.

Case 2. $x \in U$, $y \notin U$. If $x < y$, then U disappears from the sum whereas for $y < x$, U is still an up-set with the same $e(U)$. Since $\max(R - U)$ remains unchanged, (5.10) is again satisfied with equality.

Case 3. $x \notin U$, $y \notin U$. Here $e(U)$ stays the same for either outcome $x < y$ or $y < x$. Since $\max(R - U)$ reduces by at most one in either case we again have

$$e(U)2^{\max(R-U;x<y)-1} + e(U)2^{\max(R-U;y<x)-1} \geq$$
$$e(U)[2^{\max(R-U)-2} + 2^{\max(R-U)-2}] = e(U)2^{\max(R-U)-1}.$$

The rest is easy. Let an algorithm have length ℓ. Since any $t - 1$ elements of the antichain P_0 form an up-set, we have

$$f(P_0) = \binom{n}{t-1}(t-1)!2^{n-t} = [n]_{t-1}2^{n-t}.$$

If $Q \succeq P$ is the poset obtained at the end, with the top part $S \succeq T$, $|S| = t$, then any up-set U of Q with $|U| = t - 1$ is contained in S. Furthermore, since any element of $Q - S$ is below everything in S, we infer that $Q - U$ with $|U| = t - 1$ has precisely one maximal element (the remaining element in S). Hence $\max(Q - U) = 1$ for every such U and we conclude by a previous remark

$$f(Q) = \sum_{\substack{U \subseteq S, U \text{ up-set} \\ |U| = t-1}} e(U) = e(S) \leq e(T).$$

Now if the strategist player B chooses at every stage R with next comparison $x : y$ that outcome whose f-value is at least $\frac{f(R)}{2}$ (which is possible by (5.10)), then

$$e(T) \geq f(Q) \geq \frac{f(P_0)}{2^\ell} = \frac{[n]_{t-1}2^{n-t}}{2^\ell},$$

and thus

$$\ell \geq (n - t) + \lceil \log_2 \frac{[n]_{t-1}}{e(T)} \rceil. \qquad \square$$

As a corollary we obtain for our selection problems $U_t(n)$, $V_t(n)$, and $W_t(n)$ precisely the lower bounds spelled out in **4.13**.

Another selection problem which can be attacked by our method is that of selecting the s-th and t-th element. Let $V_{t,s}(n)$ denote the worst-case cost of this double selection problem. More generally, we take two posets T and B with $|\,T\,|= t$, $|\,B\,|= b$ with $t+b \leq n$ and denote by $P_{T,B}$ the poset which has T as top, B as bottom and $n - (t + b)$ unrelated elements in between (see figure 5.6).

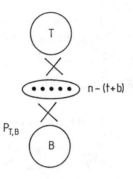

Figure 5.6

Thus our double selection problem corresponds to the top and bottom as in figure 5.7:

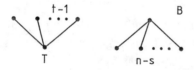

Figure 5.7

For any poset R, let us denote by $\max R$ and $\min R$ the number of maximal elements of R and minimal elements, respectively. Note that $R \preceq Q$ implies $\max R \geq \max Q$, $\min R \geq \min Q$. Let us denote by $V_{T,B}(n)$ the worst-case cost of producing $P_{T,B}$.

Theorem 5.7. *For* $| T |= t,\ | B |= b,\ t + b \le n$, *we have*

$$V_{T,B}(n) \ge (t - \min T) + (b - \max B) + \lceil \log_2(\,^n_b\,)(\,^{n-b}_{\ \ t}\,)\rceil.$$

Proof. The proof is completely analogous to that to the preceding theorem. For any poset R we set up the function

$$f(R) = \sum_{(U,D)} 2^{\min U + \max D}$$

where the summation extends over all pairs (U, D) of up-sets U and down-sets D of R such that $| U |= t$, $| D |= b$ and $U \cap D = \emptyset$. By considering the various cases as in **5.6** it is readily seen that

(5.11) $$f(R; x < y) + f(R; y < x) \ge f(R)$$

for any pair of elements x, y. At the out-set $f(P_0) = (\,^n_b\,)(\,^{n-b}_{\ \ t}\,)2^{t+b}$, whereas for any end-poset $Q \succeq P_{T,B}$ we see $f(Q) \le 2^{\min T + \max B}$, since Q contains precisely one up-set T' with $| T' |= t$ and one down-set B' with $| B' |= b$ and $\min T' \le \min T$, $\max B' \le \max B$ by our remark above. The result follows by iterating (5.11). $\square$

Corollary 5.8. *For the double-selection problem* $V_{t,s}(n)$,

$$V_{t,s}(n) \ge n - (s - t + 1) + \lceil \log_2(\,^{\ \ n}_{s-1}\,)(\,^{s-1}_{\ \ t}\,)\rceil.$$

The bound **5.8** is good for t and s with $s - t \le \frac{n}{2}$, but for $s - t > \frac{n}{2}$ we can do better by a method of Fusenegger and Gabow [1979]. Note, e.g., that $V_{1,n} = \lceil \frac{3n}{2} \rceil - 2$ by **4.16** whereas **5.8** only yields $V_{1,n}(n) \ge \lceil \log_2 n(n - 1)\rceil$ in this case.

Let us call an element of a poset P *isolated* if it is unrelated to any other element of P. In other words, the isolated elements are precisely those which are both maximal and minimal. Let us denote by $is(P)$ the number of isolated elements of P, and by $maxp(P)$ and $minp(P)$ the number of *proper maximal* elements (= maximal, but not isolated) and the number of *proper minimal* elements (= minimal, but not isolated), respectively.

Theorem 5.9. *For* $| T |= t,\ | B |= b,\ t + b \le n$, *we have*

$$V_{T,B}(n) \geq \lceil \frac{3}{2}(n - t - b) + 1 + \log_2 \frac{[n]_{t+b-2}}{e(T)e(B)} \rceil.$$

Proof. For any poset R we set up the function

$$g(R) = \sum_{(U,D)} e(U)e(D)2^{\max p(R-(U \cup D)) + \min p(R-(U \cup D)) + \frac{3}{2}is(R-(U \cup D)) - 2}$$

where the summation extends over all disjoint pairs of up-sets U and down-sets D with $|U| = t - 1$, $|D| = b - 1$. The reader may verify as before that $g(R)$ satisfies again the inequality

(5.12) $$g(R; x < y) + g(R; y < x) \geq g(R).$$

As an example, consider a pair (U, D) appearing in $g(R)$ and suppose that $x, y \in R - (U \cup D)$. The most interesting case arises when one of x or y, say x, is an isolated element of $R - (U \cup D)$ while the other is proper maximal or minimal, say maximal. If $x < y$, then $\frac{3}{2}is(R - (U \cup D))$ goes down by $\frac{3}{2}$, but $\min p(R - (U \cup D))$ goes up by 1, while $\max p(R - (U \cup D))$ stays the same. So the expression for $g(R)$ changes by a factor of $2^{-\frac{1}{2}}$. If, on the other hand $x > y$, then $\frac{3}{2}is(R - (U \cup D))$ goes down by $\frac{3}{2}$, and the other terms remain unchanged, so $g(R)$ changes by a factor of $2^{-\frac{3}{2}}$. Since $2^{-\frac{1}{2}} + 2^{-\frac{3}{2}} = 3.2^{-\frac{3}{2}} = \frac{3}{\sqrt{8}} > 1$ we infer that (5.12) is satisfied. At the start we have

$$g(P_0) = [n]_{t-1}[n - t + 1]_{b-1}2^{\frac{3}{2}(n-t-b)+1} = [n]_{t+b-2}2^{\frac{3}{2}(n-t-b)+1},$$

while for an end-poset Q with top-part $T' \succeq T$ and bottom part $B' \succeq B$ we compute

$$g(Q) = \sum_{(U,D)} e(U)e(D) = \sum_{U \subseteq T'} e(U) \sum_{D \subseteq B'} e(D) = e(T')e(B') \leq e(T)e(B).$$

The result follows by the familiar argument. □

Corollary 5.10. *For $V_{t,s}(n)$, we have*

$$V_{t,s}(n) \geq \lceil \frac{3}{2}(s - t - 1) + 1 + \log_2 \binom{n}{s}\binom{s}{t-1} \rceil.$$

Note that **5.10** yields for $t = 1$, $s = n$ our old result $V_{1,n}(n) \geq \lceil \frac{3n}{2} \rceil - 2$.

Example 5.2. For $s = t+1$, we obtain $V_{t,t+1}(n) \geq (n-2) + \lceil \log_2 (\begin{smallmatrix} n \\ t \end{smallmatrix}) \rceil$ from

5.8 whereas for $s = t+2$, $V_{t,t+2}(n) \geq (n-3) + \lceil \log_2 (\begin{smallmatrix} n \\ t+1 \end{smallmatrix})(t+1) \rceil$ results.
By employing the tournament method used for $V_t(n)$ in **4.11**, the reader may
easily establish $V_{t,s}(n) \leq (n-s) + (t-1)\lceil \log_2(n-t+2) \rceil + \sum_{i=t-1}^{s-2} \lceil \log_2(n-i) \rceil$.
Comparison of the bounds shows that they coincide for $V_{t.t+1}(n)$, $t \leq 3$, when
$n = 2^k$ is large enough.

Analogous to the previous section where it was shown in **5.4** that the sorting
complexity $S(P)$ achieves the lower bound $\log_2 e(P)$ up to a constant factor
for all P, we may ask the corresponding question for the production cost
$C(P)$.

Question. Are there universal constants c_1 and c_2 such that $C(P) \leq$
$c_1 \log_2 \frac{n!}{e(P)} + c_2 n$ for all posets P of size n?

Exercises 5.2.

1. Verify $\mid \mathcal{O}(5) \mid = 63$.

2. Show that $\mathcal{O}(n)$ is a ranked poset, i.e. any longest chain terminating
   in P has the same length. Show that this unique length equals the
   number of relations in P minus 1.

3*. Prove: $C(P) \geq \lceil \frac{3}{2}n \rceil - \max P - \min P$.

4. Complete the proof of **5.9**.

5*. Verify the upper bound in example 5.2.

6. Derive bounds for $U_{t,s}(n)$ and $W_{t,s}(n)$.

7*. Show $\lceil \frac{3n-7}{2} + \log_2 n \rceil \leq V_{2,n}(n) \leq \lceil \frac{3n-10}{2} \rceil + \lceil \log_2(3n-1) \rceil$ $(n \geq 3)$,
    and show equality of the bounds for infinitely many n.

8*. The following generalization of the double selection problem was sug-
    gested by Katona. Show that there is no faster way to select any two
    elements than to select the first two. That is, an algorithm $\mathcal{A}$ is suc-
    cessful in this context if at the end the positions of two elements are

determined whatever they may be. Hence the problem is to show that
$\ell(\mathcal{A}) \geq (n-2) + \lceil \log_2 n \rceil$.

9*. Take two elements a and b. We want to find out whether a is the t-th
largest and b the $(t+1)$-st largest element. Show that this can be done
with $n + t - 2$ comparisons. (Varecza)

10. Given two elements a and b. Show that it takes $2n - 4$ comparisons
to find out whether they are neigbors in the unknown linear order or
not. (Varecza)

5.3 Data Location

In section 7 of chapter 1 we considered the problem of sorting a new element
z into an ordered list $\{y_1 < \ldots < y_n\}$ determining either $z = y_i$ for some i
or the proper position $y_j < z < y_{j+1}$ where z should be sorted in. We called
this the data location problem. In the present section we treat the general
problem when the data is stored at the elements of a poset P in an order
preserving way, and again a new element is to be sorted in.

The set-up of this general data location problem is then as follows: We are
given a poset P together with an order-preserving function $\alpha : P \longrightarrow \mathbb{R}$, i.e.
$x < y$ implies $\alpha(x) < \alpha(y)$; α can thus be viewed as a linear extension of P.
Furthermore, we are given a real number z. By comparing $z : \alpha(x)$ $(x \in P)$
we are asked to find out whether $z = \alpha(x)$ for some $x \in P$ or to determine
the proper position of z among the values $\alpha(x)$. The worst-case cost of this
problem shall be denoted by $DL(P)$.

As in section 1.7 we can view any algorithm as a binary search tree T with
the inner nodes corresponding to $z = \alpha(x)$ and the end-nodes corresponding
to the outcomes $z \neq \alpha(x)$ for all x. How many end-nodes does T have?
Any such node corresponds to a pair P_1, P_2 of subsets of P with $P_1 = \{x :$
$\alpha(x) < z\}$ and $P_2 = \{y : \alpha(y) > z\}$, respectively. A moment's thought
shows that P_1 is a *down-set* of P, whereas P_2 is an *up-set* of P. (In fact, the
set complement of a down-set is always an up-set, and conversely). Since,
clearly, any down-set is possible as the set $\{x : \alpha(x) < z\}$, we conclude that
any search tree will have at least as many end-nodes as there are down-sets
in P. Let us denote the number of down-sets of P by $i(P)$.

Proposition 5.11. *We have*

$$DL(P) \geq \lceil \log_2 i(P) \rceil.$$

Note that in a linear order $\{x_1 < x_2 < \ldots < x_n\}$ the down-sets are precisely the $n + 1$ sets $\emptyset, \{x_1\}, \{x_1 < x_2\}, \ldots, \{x_1 < \ldots < x_n\}$ from which $DL \geq \lceil \log_2(n + 1) \rceil$ results. Since by the usual halving method we have $DL \leq \lceil \log_2(n + 1) \rceil$, we arrive at our result **1.14**, $DL = \lceil \log_2(n + 1) \rceil$.

We have seen that in the worst-case situation our task is to identify the unknown down-set $D^* = \{x : \alpha(x) < z\}$. Hence we may view every comparison $z : \alpha(x)$ as a test: Is $x \in D^*$?, and vice versa. Instead of the data location problem we may therefore (and will from now on) look at the *down-set identification problem*: Given P, by asking questions $x \in D^*$?, determine the unknown down-set D^*!

Example 5.3. Before going further let us look at an example which links up our present situation with the previously discussed merging of chains, Suppose $P_{m,n}$ is the product of two chains $\{1 < \ldots < m\} \times \{1 < \ldots < n\}$, i.e. $P_{m,n}$ consists of all pairs $(i,j), 1 \leq i \leq m, 1 \leq j \leq n$, with $(i,j) \leq (i',j')$ iff $i \leq i'$ and $j \leq j'$. The following figure shows $P_{4,5}$:

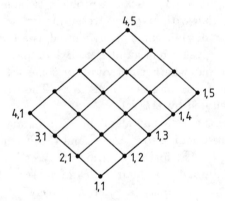

Figure 5.8

The reader may easily prove by induction that $i(P_{m,n}) = \binom{m+n}{n}$. Note that this is also the number of linear extensions of two disjoint chains $S = \{a_1 < \ldots < a_m\}$ and $T = \{b_1 < \ldots < b_n\}$. As observed by Shearer, this is no coincidence. Any down-set D in $P_{m,n}$ corresponds bijectively to a linear extension of $S \cup T$ via the map

$$(i,j) \in D \iff a_i < b_{n+1-j},$$

as is readily verified. Using the correspondence between a test $(i,j) \in D^*?$ for the down-set problem and the comparison $a_i : b_{n+1-j}$, we note that any search tree for $P_{m,n}$ can be transformed into a decision tree for the merging problem on $S \cup T$, and conversely. Thus $DL(P_{m,n})$ is precisely the quantity $M(m,n)$ studied in section 4.2.

We have seen that $M(m,n)$ (and thus $DL(P_{m,n})$) equals the information-theoretic lower bound $\log_2\binom{m+n}{n}$ up to a constant factor. We will now sketch a proof of the deep theorem by Linial and Saks [1985a] that the same holds indeed for every poset P.

We proceed along the lines set out in section 1. At every stage of an algorithm we seek to divide the set of possible down-sets into two parts whose sizes are not too far apart. Denote by $i(P;x)$ the number of down-sets in P which contain x. If we can show that there exists a universal constant $0 < \delta \leq \frac{1}{2}$ such that *every* poset P contains an element x with

(5.13) $$\delta \leq \frac{i(P;x)}{i(P)} \leq 1 - \delta,$$

then by the same reasoning as in section 1, we will be able to conclude that

$$DL(P) \leq \left(-\frac{1}{\log_2(1-\delta)}\right) \log_2 i(P).$$

Let us call an element x satisfying (5.13) a *δ-central element*. Linial and Saks have shown that every poset has a δ_0-central element with $\delta_0 = \frac{3-\log_2 5}{4} \sim 0.1695$. If $\delta(P)$ denotes the largest number $\leq \frac{1}{2}$ such that P contains a $\delta(P)$-central element, then the natural question arises as to what $\min_P \delta(P)$ is.

Example 5.4. Let P be the poset consisting of two antichains A and B with $|A| = |B| = n$ and all elements of A below all elements of B.

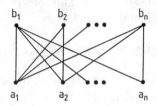

Figure 5.9

It is easily verified that $i(P) = 2^{n+1}-1$, $i(P; a_k) = 3.2^{n-1}-1$, $i(P; b_k) = 2^{n-1}$ for all k. Hence $\delta(P)$ is approximately $\frac{1}{4}$.

Shearer has shown that there are posets P whose $\delta(P)$ is arbitrarily close to the unique root of the equation $\lambda(1-\lambda)^4 - (1-2\lambda)^5 = 0$ between 0 and $\frac{1}{2}$ (approximately 0.197). Hence the universal bound 0.1695 (which has been improved by Shearer to 0.1705) is very good indeed.

Let us return to the proof of the existence of a δ_0-central element in every poset P, where $\delta_0 = \frac{3-\log_2 5}{4}$. The *height* $h(x)$ of an element x is the number of elements minus 1 in a longest chain terminating in x. Thus, the minimal elements in P are precisely those of height 0. We call $h(P) = \max\limits_{x \in P} h(x)$ the *height* of P. Note that the height $h(x)$ differs from the definition given in section 1.

Let us make a few general observations. For $p \in P$, let $D(p)$ and $U(p)$ be the down-set respectively up-set *generated* by p, i.e. $D(p) = \{x \in P : x \le p\}$, $U(p) = \{x \in P : x \ge p\}$. A down-set D contains p iff it contains all of $D(p)$, similarly for up-sets. Thus

$$(5.14) \qquad i(P) = i(P - D(p)) + i(P - U(p)),$$

where $i(P - D(p)) = i(P; p)$.

Suppose p is a maximal element of P. Then $U(p) = \{p\}$ and thus $i(P - U(p)) = i(P-p)$. Any down-set D of P containing p yields a down-set $D-p$ in $P-p$, with $D \ne D'$ implying $D-p \ne D'-p$. Hence $i(P) \le 2i(P-p)$ with equality iff p is an isolated element (since otherwise $D-p = \emptyset$ is not possible). By (5.14) we conclude $i(P; p) = i(P) - i(P - U(p)) = i(P) - i(P - p) \le i(P-p) = i(P-U(p))$, and thus $i(P; p) \le \frac{i(P)}{2}$, with equality iff p is isolated. By symmetry, the analogous statement holds for minimal elements, and we obtain

$$(5.15) \qquad i(P; p) \ge \frac{i(P)}{2} \quad \text{for } p \text{ minimal}$$

$$i(P;p) \;\leq\; \frac{i(P)}{2} \quad \text{for } p \text{ maximal}$$

with equality iff p is isolated.

For $x \in P$, denote by $p(x) = \frac{i(P;x)}{i(P)}$ the proportion of down-sets containing x. We set $J = \{x : p(x) \geq \frac{1}{2}\}$ and $K = P - J = \{x : p(x) < \frac{1}{2}\}$. Let us set

$$p^*(x) = \begin{cases} p(x) & \text{for } p(x) < \frac{1}{2} \\ 1 - p(x) & \text{for } p(x) \geq \frac{1}{2}. \end{cases}$$

Our theorem will be proved if we can show the existence of an element $x \in P$ with $p^*(x) \geq \delta_0$.

In the following we will give a proof when P has heigth 1, and will then outline the general case.

Let P be of height 1, A the elements of heigth 0 and B those of height 1. It follows from (5.15) that $A = J$ in the above notation and $B = K$. Furthermore, we may assume by (5.15) that P has no isolated elements. In an obvious way we can view P as a bipartite graph G on the vertices $A \cup B$ with an edge (a_i, b_j) iff $a_i < b_j$. The down-sets of P have a natural counterpart in G. As in chapter 3 we call a set I of vertices of any graph *stable* if no two vertices of I are joined by an edge. If D is a down-set of P, then the symmetric difference $(D - A) \cup (A - D)$ is a stable set of G (see figure 5.10).

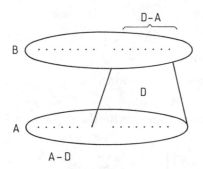

Figure 5.10

Conversely, if I is a stable set of G, then $(I - A) \cup (A - I)$ is a down-set of P. Using this bijection $D \longrightarrow I = (D - A) \cup (A - D)$ it is readily seen that

$p^*(x)$ is precisely the fraction of stable sets in G containing x. Counting the incidences (x, I), $x \in I$, in two ways we conclude

(5.16)
$$\frac{1}{|A \cup B|} \sum_{x \in A \cup B} p^*(x) = \frac{1}{|A \cup B|} \frac{1}{N} \sum_{I \text{ stable}} |I|$$

where $N = i(P)$ is the number of stable sets in G. Since the existence of x with $p^*(x) \geq \delta_0$ is obviously ascertained when the *average* of all $p^*(x)$ is $\geq \delta_0$, it suffices to show by (5.16) that the average size of a stable set in G is at least $\delta_0 |A \cup B|$.

Proposition 5.12. *Let G be a bipartite graph on $A \cup B$ without isolated vertices. The average size of a stable set in G is then at least $\delta_0 |A \cup B|$.*

Proof. Without loss of generality we may assume $|A| \geq |B|$. For $X \subseteq A$, let $R(X) \subseteq B$ denote the set of vertices in B joined to at least one vertex in X, and let N be the total number of stable sets in G. We classify the stable sets according to their intersection with A. Clearly, a set C with $|C \cap A| = X$ is stable iff $C \cap B \subseteq B - R(X)$. In particular, we see that there are precisely $2^{|B - R(X)|}$ stable sets whose intersection with A is X. Using the identity $\sum_{k=0}^{n} k \binom{n}{k} = 2^{n-1} n$ we obtain for the average size of a stable set

(5.17)
$$\frac{1}{N} \sum_{X \subseteq A} [2^{|B-R(X)|} |X| + \sum_{k=0}^{|B-R(X)|} k \binom{|B-R(X)|}{k})]$$
$$= \frac{1}{N} \sum_{X \subseteq A} 2^{|B-R(X)|} (|X| + \frac{1}{2} |B - R(X)|).$$

If we denote by $q(X) = \frac{1}{N} 2^{|B-R(X)|}$ the proportion of stable sets whose intersection with A is X, then $|B - R(X)| = \log_2 N + \log_2 q(X)$ and $\sum_{X \subseteq A} q(X) = 1$. Hence we can rewrite the expression in (5.17) as

$$\sum_{X \subseteq A} q(X) |X| + \frac{1}{2} \sum_{X \subseteq A} q(X) |B - R(X)| =$$
$$\sum_{X \subseteq A} q(X) |X| + \frac{1}{2} \sum_{X \subseteq A} q(X)(\log_2 N + \log_2 q(X)) =$$
$$\frac{\log_2 N}{2} + \frac{1}{2} \sum_{X \subseteq A} q(X)(2|X| + \log_2 q(X)).$$

Since any subset of A is stable we have $N \geq 2^{|A|}$, i.e. $\log_2 N \geq |A|$. By the assumption $|A| \geq |B|$ it therefore suffices to show that

$$(5.18) \quad \sum_{X \subseteq A} q(X)(2\,|\,X\,| + \log_2 q(X)) \; \geq \; |\,A\,|\,(4\delta_0 - 1)$$

$$= \; |\,A\,|\,(2 - \log_2 5) = |\,A\,|\log_2 \frac{4}{5}.$$

Let us look at the summation term in (5.18) setting $n = 2^{|A|}$. Numbering the subsets of A by $X_1, \ldots, X_n$ and setting $x_i = q(X_i)$ we have $\sum_{i=1}^{n} x_i = 1$, $0 \leq x_i \leq 1$. Without the extra complication of the $2\,|\,X_i\,|$'s the term on the left-hand side is precisely the negative of the entropy $H(X)$ for which we know from chapter 1, that $-H(X) \geq -\log_2 n$. Now if the c_i's are any non-negative constants ($i = 1, \ldots, n$), then it is easily seen (exercise 5.3.3), using Lagrange multipliers, that

$$(5.19) \qquad \sum_{i=1}^{n} x_i(c_i + \log_2 x_i) \geq -\log_2\left(\sum_{i=1}^{n} 2^{-c_i}\right).$$

Substituting $c_i = 2\,|\,X_i\,|$ in (5.19) we thus obtain

$$\sum_{X \subseteq A} q(X)(2\,|\,X\,| + \log_2 q(X)) \; \geq \; -\log_2 \sum_{X \subseteq A} 4^{-|X|}$$

$$= \; -\log_2 \sum_{k=0}^{|A|}\binom{|\,A\,|}{k}\left(\frac{1}{4}\right)^k$$

$$= \; -\log_2(1 + \frac{1}{4})^{|A|} = -\log_2\left(\frac{5}{4}\right)^{|A|}$$

$$= \; |\,A\,|\log_2 \frac{4}{5},$$

which is precisely (5.18). $\square$

The proof of the general case proceeds along the same lines. Let J and K be the subposets of P as defined before. Generalizing the notion of a stable set, we call $Q \subseteq P$ *quasi-stable* if $Q = (D - J) \cup (J - D)$ is a down-set of P. The correspondence $D \longrightarrow Q = (D - J) \cup (J - D)$ is a bijection between the down-sets and the quasi-stable sets of P, and $p^*(x)$ is the fraction of quasi-stable sets containing x. Using (5.16) with quasi-stable replacing stable it would be enough to show that the average size of a quasi-stable set is at least

$\delta_0 \mid P \mid$. Unfortunately, this is false in general. However, it is sufficient to find a non-negative weight function $\lambda : P \longrightarrow I\!R^+$ such that the λ-*weighted average* is at least $\delta_0 \lambda(P)$.

Let us make this precise. We extend the definition of λ to all subsets $X \subseteq P$ by setting $\lambda(X) = \sum_{x \in X} \lambda(x)$. If we can show

$$(5.20) \qquad \sum_{x \in P} \lambda(x) p^*(x) \geq \delta_0 \sum_{x \in P} \lambda(x) = \delta_0 \lambda(P),$$

then we must have $p^*(x) \geq \delta_0$ for some x, thus completing the proof. Let N be the number of quasi-stable sets. Then

$$
\begin{aligned}
\sum_{x \in P} \lambda(x) p^*(x) &= \sum_{x \in P} \lambda(x) \frac{1}{N} \sum_{T \; quasi-stable, \, x \in T} 1 \\
&= \frac{1}{N} \sum_{T \; quasi-stable} \sum_{x \in T} \lambda(x) \\
&= \frac{1}{N} \sum_{T \; quasi-stable} \lambda(T).
\end{aligned}
$$

The final (and most difficult) part of the proof consists in the construction of a suitable weight function λ such that $\frac{1}{N} \sum_{T \; quasi-stable} \lambda(T) \geq \delta_0 \lambda(P)$ which by (5.20) finishes the proof. For the details the reader is referred to the paper by Linial and Saks [1985a].

Theorem 5.13. *For every poset* P,

$$DL(P) \leq \frac{1}{2 - \log_2(1 + \log_2 5)} \log_2 i(P) \sim 3.7316 \log_2 i(P).$$

For some classes of posets the general constant 3.73 can be improved. We have already noted that for products of chains, the merging problem results, whence we obtain in this case the constant 1.44 by **4.6**. Another class where the best constant $\frac{3}{\log_2 5} \sim 1.36$ has been obtained (again by Linial and Saks [1985b]), are rooted forests (see exercise 5.3.8). Not surprisingly, virtually nothing is known about the average case except for chains which were discussed in section 1.7.

Exercises 5.3.

1*. Verify directly that $i(P_{m,n}) = \binom{m+n}{n}$ where $P_{m,n}$ is the product of two chains of length m and n, respectively.

2. Verify the numbers $i(P)$, $i(P; a_k)$, $i(P; b_k)$ as in figure 5.10.

3*. Prove (5.19).

4. Suppose P is disjoint union of posets $P_1, \ldots, P_t$. Show $i(P) = \prod_{i=1}^{k} i(P_i)$.

5. Show $DL(P) = 1 + \min_{p} \max\{DL(P - D(p)), DL(P - U(p))\}$.

6. Show that the union and intersection of down-sets is again a down-set.

7*. Call a poset a *rooted forest P* if any non-maximal element covers exactly one element. Thus P is a union of rooted trees where a rooted tree can be pictured as our usual concept looked from bottom down to top. Let $N(p)$ denote the number of down-sets in $U(p)$. Show that for $q < \cdot p$, $(N(p) - 1)i(P; q) = N(p)i(P; p)$, where P is a rooted tree.

8. Show that $DL(P) = \frac{3}{\log_2 5} \log_2 i(P)$ when P is a 4-element chain or the poset $\vee$. (Linial and Saks have shown that for all other rooted forests $DL(P) < \frac{3}{\log_2 5} \log_2 i(P)$.)

5.4   Correlation Among Linear Extensions

Our last topic takes us a little afar from our main theme, search for the unknown linear extension. Instead we want to study in more detail the structure of the set $L(P)$ of all linear extensions and, in particular, of the numbers $p(x < y)$ defined in section 1. As a result some very interesting connections between order-theoretical questions and inequalities for set systems will be established.

Suppose P is a poset on n elements and $L(P)$ is the set of linear extensions. The major problem in section 1 consisted in finding a pair x, y such that $p(x < y) = \frac{|L(P; x < y)|}{|L(P)|}$ is close to $\frac{1}{2}$. In generalization to a single relation $x < y$ let us consider a set A of comparabilities involving elements of P.

We may identify A with the set $L(P; A)$ of linear extensions of P where the relations A are satisfied, and set

$$p(A) = \frac{|L(P; A)|}{|L(P)|}.$$

If Ω is a probability space, then any subset $A \subseteq \Omega$ is called an *event* with $p(A) = \sum_{\omega \in A} Pr(\omega)$. Thus $p(A)$ may be thought of as the probability for the event A in the space $L(P)$ assuming that all linear extensions are equally likely. Let A and B be events where $p(B) \neq 0$. The *conditional probability* for A under the assumption that B holds is defined as $p(A \mid B) := \frac{p(A \cap B)}{p(B)}$. Clearly it makes sense to say that A and B are *independent events* if $p(A \mid B) = p(A)$, i.e. knowledge of B does not alter the probability that A holds. Equivalently, A and B are independent iff $p(A \cap B) = p(A)p(B)$. Now we come to the main topic of this section.

Definition. Two events A and B of a probability space Ω are said to be *positively correlated* (or mutually favorable) if $p(A \mid B) \geq p(A)$, or equivalently if $p(A \cap B) \geq p(A)p(B)$. Notice that by symmetry we also have $p(B \mid A) \geq p(B)$.

Thus, events are positively correlated if the knowledge that one occurs adds to the probability that the other holds. Let us get back to our space $L = L(P)$ of linear extensions. Since we assume uniform distribution, $p(A) = \frac{|A|}{|L|}$, $A \subseteq L$. Thus two sets of relations A and B are positively correlated in P iff $\frac{|A \cap B|}{|L|} \geq \frac{|A|}{|L|} \frac{|B|}{|L|}$, or equivalently iff

$$(5.21) \qquad\qquad |A \,||\, B| \leq |A \cap B \,||\, L|,$$

where we identify A and B with their respective sets of linear extensions. So the question of which of the quantities $p(A)$, $p(B)$ are positively correlated leads directly to an inequality on sets spelled out in (5.21).

Example 5.5. The following inequality, first conjectured by Rival and Sands, called the *xyz-inequality*, served as the prime motivation for our topic. Suppose x, y, z are any three elements in P. Then Rival and Sands conjectured that we always have

$$p(x < y) \mid x < z) \geq p(x < y),$$

or equivalently

$$(5.22) \qquad\qquad p(x < y)p(x < z) \leq p(x < y \wedge x < z).$$

In our terminology, (5.22) states that the events $x < y$ and $x < z$ are positively correlated. Substituting the expressions for $p(x)$, we obtain

$$| L(P; x < y) || L(P; x < z) | \leq | L(P; x < y \wedge x < z) || L(P) |.$$

The reader can easily convince himself that (5.22) certainly holds if one or more relations between x, y, z are already present in P. Thus, the only interesting case arises when x, y and z are pairwise unrelated.

If we interpret the elements as usual as tennis players, the inequality is intuitively obvious: If we know that x is a weaker player than z, then the probability that x is weaker than y should certainly be greater than the probability without this advance knowledge. As an illustration consider the poset of figure 5.11:

Figure 5.11

Here, one computes $|L| = 33$, $|L(x < y)| = 18$, $|L(x < z)| = 24$, $|L(x < y \wedge x < z)| = 16$, and thus $p(x < y \mid x < z) = \frac{2}{3} > p(x < y) = \frac{6}{11}$.

As intuitively clear as (5.22) looks no purely order-theoretical proof is known. The proof of the xyz-inequality by Shepp [1982] which will be presented later on uses a very interesting set inequality which reduces the question to precisely an inequality of the type spelled out in (5.21). Before discussing Shepp's proof let us look at one more example to see that intuition can be wrong.

Example 5.6. Suppose $T = \{a_1, \ldots, a_m\}$ and $U = \{b_1, \ldots, b_n\}$ are two tennis teams where within the teams T and U some relations may already be known. Suppose further that some games C between T and U have already been played where always the players of team U turned out ot be the winner. Let us denote this by $C : T < U$. In poset terms, P is the union of the posets T and U where all relations between T and U are of the form $a_i < b_j$. Now assume that A and B are two other sets of games between T

and U, both of the same type, $A : T < U$, $B : T < U$. Intuition tells us that T generally contains the weaker player, and thus that A and B should be positively correlated. However, as the following example shows, this need not be the case.

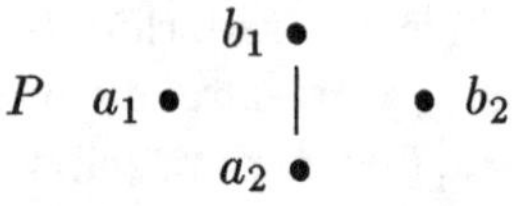

$$P \quad a_1 \bullet \quad \begin{matrix} b_1 \bullet \\ | \\ a_2 \bullet \end{matrix} \quad \bullet\, b_2$$

Figure 5.12

Suppose $A = \{a_2 < b_2\}$, $B = \{a_1 < b_1\}$. Then $\mid L(P) \mid = 12$, $\mid L(P; A) \mid = \mid L(P; B) \mid = 8$, $\mid L(P; A \wedge B) \mid = 5$, and thus $p(A \mid B) = \frac{5}{8} < p(A) = \frac{2}{3}$. Later on we shall show that the inequality $p(A \mid B) \geq p(A)$ does indeed hold when T and U are chains (Proposition 5.18).

Now we turn to a set inequality leading up to formulas of type (5.21). The following fundamental result due to Ahlswede and Daykin [1978] points the way. A few words concerning the terminology first. A poset P is a *lattice* if to any two elements $x, y \in P$ there exists a unique maximal element $x \wedge y$ below x and y, and a unique minimal element $x \vee y$ above x and y. The most familiar example of a lattice is the collection 2^S of all subsets of a set S, ordered by inclusion, where $x \wedge y = x \cap y$ is the intersection of x and y, and $x \vee y = x \cup y$ is the union.

Theorem 5.14. *Let S be a finite set and suppose $\alpha, \beta, \gamma, \delta$ are four functions from 2^S into the non-negative reals $\mathbb{R}^+$. If $\alpha(x)\beta(y) \leq \gamma(x \cup y)\delta(x \cap y)$ holds for all $x, y \in 2^S$, then*

$$\alpha(X)\beta(Y) \leq \gamma(X \vee Y)\delta(X \wedge Y) \ \text{ holds for all } X, Y \subseteq 2^S,$$

where $\alpha(Z) = \sum\limits_{z \in Z} \alpha(z)$ for $Z \subseteq 2^S$, and $X \vee Y = \{x \cup y : x \in X, y \in Y\}$, $X \wedge Y = \{x \cap y : x \in X, y \in Y\}$.

Proof. We use induction on the size n of S. For $n = 0$ there is nothing to prove. Let the ground-set be $S = \{1, 2, \ldots, n\}$ and $S' = S - \{n\}$. Take $X, Y \subseteq 2^S$. We define functions α', β', γ', δ' from $2^{S'}$ into $\mathbb{R}^+$ as follows: For $x', \ldots, w' \in 2^{S'}$ set

$$\alpha'(x') = \sum_{\substack{x \in X \\ x' = x - n}} \alpha(x), \quad \beta'(y') = \sum_{\substack{y \in Y \\ y' = y - n}} \beta(y),$$

$$\gamma'(z') = \sum_{\substack{z \in X \vee Y \\ z' = z - n}} \gamma(z), \quad \delta'(w') = \sum_{\substack{w \in X \wedge Y \\ w' = w - n}} \delta(w).$$

Thus for $x' \in 2^{S'}$, we obtain

$$(5.23) \quad \alpha'(x') = \begin{cases} \alpha(x') + \alpha(x' \cup \{n\}) & \text{if } x' \in X, x' \cup \{n\} \in X \\ \alpha(x') & \text{if } x' \in X, x' \cup \{n\} \notin X \\ \alpha(x' \cup \{n\}) & \text{if } x' \notin X, x' \cup \{n\} \in X \\ 0 & \text{if } x' \notin X, x' \cup \{n\} \notin X. \end{cases}$$

Similarly, for β', γ', δ' with X replaced by Y, $X \vee T$ and $X \wedge Y$, respectively. Note that by (5.23)

$$\alpha'(2^{S'}) = \alpha(X), \qquad \beta'(2^{S'}) = \beta(Y),$$
$$\gamma'(2^{S'}) = \gamma(X \vee Y), \quad \delta'(2^{S'}) = \delta(X \wedge Y).$$

Now if we can show

$$(5.24) \qquad \alpha'(x')\beta'(y') \le \gamma'(x' \cup y')\delta'(x' \cap y') \quad \text{for all } x', y' \in 2^{S'},$$

then it follows by induction with $X' = Y' = 2^{S'}$ that

$$\alpha(X)\beta(Y) = \alpha'(2^{S'})\beta'(2^{S'}) \le \gamma'(2^{S'})\delta'(2^{S'}) = \gamma(X \vee Y)\delta(X \wedge Y),$$

since obviously $2^{S'} \vee 2^{S'} = 2^{S'} \wedge 2^{S'} = 2^{S'}$. Thus it remains to verify (5.24). It is easily seen that (5.24) holds if x' or y' are of type 2, 3 or 4 in (5.23). The only interesting case arises when x' and y' are both of type 1 in (5.23), i.e. when $x', x' \cup \{n\} \in X$, $y', y' \cup \{n\} \in Y$. Let us set $\alpha_0 = \alpha(x')$, $\alpha_1 = \alpha(x' \cup \{n\})$, $\beta_0 = \beta(y')$, $\beta_1 = \beta(y' \cup \{n\})$, and similarly $\gamma_0 = \gamma(x' \cup y')$, $\gamma_1 = \gamma((x' \cup y') \cup \{n\})$, $\delta_0 = \delta(x' \cap y')$, $\delta_1 = \delta((x' \cap y') \cup \{n\})$. With this notation (5.24) becomes

$$(\alpha_0 + \alpha_1)(\beta_0 + \beta_1) \le (\gamma_0 + \gamma_1)(\delta_0 + \delta_1).$$

By the assumption on $\alpha, \dots, \delta$ we have

$$(5.25) \qquad \alpha_0\beta_0 \le \gamma_0\delta_0, \quad \alpha_0\beta_1 \le \gamma_1\delta_0, \quad \alpha_1\beta_0 \le \gamma_1\delta_0, \quad \alpha_1\beta_1 \le \gamma_1\delta_1.$$

Thus it remains to show that

$$\alpha_0\beta_1 + \alpha_1\beta_0 \le \gamma_0\delta_1 + \gamma_1\delta_0.$$

Assume otherwise, $\alpha_0\beta_1 + \alpha_1\beta_0 > \gamma_0\delta_1 + \gamma_1\delta_0$. Then by (5.25), $\alpha_0\beta_1 > \gamma_0\delta_1$, $\alpha_1\beta_0 > \gamma_0\delta_1$ and thus $\alpha_0 \neq 0$, $\alpha_1 \neq 0$, $\beta_0 \neq 0$, $\beta_1 \neq 0$, which in turn, implies by (5.25) that all $\gamma_0, \gamma_1, \delta_0, \delta_1$ are $\neq 0$. Again by (5.25), we have

$$(\gamma_1\delta_0 - \alpha_0\beta_1)(\gamma_1\delta_0 - \alpha_1\beta_0) \geq 0,$$

hence

$$\gamma_1^2\delta_0^2 - \gamma_1\delta_0\alpha_0\beta_1 - \gamma_1\delta_0\alpha_1\beta_0 + \alpha_0\beta_0\alpha_1\beta_1 \geq 0,$$

$$\gamma_1\delta_0^2 - \alpha_0\delta_0\beta_1 - \beta_0\delta_0\alpha_1 + \alpha_0\beta_0\frac{\alpha_1\beta_1}{\gamma_1} \geq 0,$$

and thus

$$\gamma_1\delta_0^2 - \alpha_0\delta_0\beta_1 - \beta_0\delta_0\alpha_1 + \alpha_0\beta_0\delta_1 \geq 0.$$

This, finally, implies

$$\gamma_1\delta_0^2 + \alpha_0\beta_0\delta_1 \geq \delta_0(\alpha_0\beta_1 + \alpha_1\beta_0) > \delta_0(\gamma_0\delta_1 + \gamma_1\delta_0),$$

i.e.

$$\alpha_0\beta_0\delta_1 > \gamma_0\delta_0\delta_1$$

and thus

$$\alpha_0\beta_0 > \gamma_0\delta_0,$$

in contradiction to (5.25).   □

Setting $\alpha = \beta = \gamma = \delta \equiv 1$ we obtain the following corollary due to Daykin [1977].

Corollary 5.15. *Let S be a finite set, then*

$$\mid X \mid\mid Y \mid \; \leq \; \mid X \vee Y \mid\mid X \wedge Y \mid \quad for \quad any \quad X, Y \subseteq 2^S.$$

Corollary 5.15, in turn, immediately implies the following result first obtained by Seymour [1973] which is the starting point for our further discussion.

Corollary 5.16. *Let U_1, U_2 be two up-sets in the lattice 2^S, $\mid S \mid = n$. Then*

$$\mid U_1 \mid\mid U_2 \mid \; \leq \; \mid U_1 \cap U_2 \mid 2^n.$$

Similarly, for two down-sets D_1, D_2 we have

$$\mid D_1 \mid\mid D_2 \mid \; \leq \; \mid D_1 \cap D_2 \mid 2^n.$$

Proof. We have $U_1 \vee U_2 \subseteq U_1 \cap U_2$ (in fact, $U_1 \vee U_2 = U_1 \cap U_2$) since U_1, U_2 are up-sets, and trivially $U_1 \wedge U_2 \subseteq 2^S$. The dual argument applies to down-sets. $\square$

The formulas in our last result look very much like the defining inequality (5.21) for positively correlated events. Before applying **5.16** to posets, let us note that the Ahlswede-Daykin inequality together with its corollaries hold more generally for all *sublattices* of 2^S. By a sublattice L of 2^S we mean, of course, a collection L of subsets of S which is closed under $\cup$ and $\cap$, i.e. $x, y \in L$ imply $x \cup y, x \cap y \in L$. Indeed, we may extend any function $f : L \longrightarrow \mathbb{R}^+$ to all of 2^S by simply stipulating $f(x) \equiv 0$ whenever $x \notin L$. Hence if $\alpha(x)\beta(y) \leq \gamma(x \cup y)\delta(x \cap y)$ holds for all $x, y \in L$, then it will clearly hold for all $x, y \in 2^S$. We may thus deduce the implications of **5.14**, since L is a sublattice. Now it is a well-known (and easily proved) fact in order theory that sublattices of 2^S are characterized by the *distributive property* (exercise 5.4.5).

Definition. A lattice L with $\wedge$ and $\vee$ is called *distributive*, if for any $x, y, z \in L$

$$(5.26) \qquad \begin{aligned} x \wedge (y \vee z) &= (x \wedge y) \vee (x \wedge z) \\ x \vee (y \wedge z) &= (x \vee y) \wedge (x \vee z). \end{aligned}$$

The reader may prove that either one of the identies in (5.26) implies the other. Note that any sublattice of a distributive lattice is again distributive. Let us state **5.16** in this general setting.

Corollary 5.17. *Let L be a finite distributive lattice, and let U_1, U_2 be two up-sets in L, and D_1, D_2 be two down-sets. Then*

$$(5.27) \qquad \begin{aligned} |\, U_1\,||\, U_2\,| &\leq |\, U_1 \cap U_2\,||\, L\,| \\ |\, D_1\,||\, D_2\,| &\leq |\, D_1 \cap D_2\,||\, L\,|. \end{aligned}$$

A comparison of (5.21) and (5.27) now suggests our method of proof. In order to prove the positive correlation of two events A and B we impose an order on $L(P)$ which makes the set of linear extensions into a distributive lattice and prove then that A and B are both two up-sets or both two down-sets.

We first give a proof (due to Shepp [1980]) of the result of Graham, Yao and Yao [1980] that our intuition in example 5.6 is right if T and U are chains.

Proposition 5.18. *Let $T = \{a_1 < \ldots < a_m\}$, $U = \{b_1 < \ldots < b_n\}$ be two chains, and let P be a poset on $\{a_1, \ldots, a_m, b_1, \ldots, b_n\}$ consisting of the chains T and U together with (possibly) some relations between T and U. (In other words, P is poset of width 2.) Let $L = L(P)$ be the set of linear extensions, and $A, B \subseteq L$ be two subsets of L, both of the form $A : T < U$, $B : T < U$. Then A and B are positively correlated, i.e.*

$$p(A \cap B) \geq p(A)p(B).$$

Proof. We have to prove $|\,A \parallel B\,| \leq |\,A \cap B \parallel L\,|$. Consider the set E of all bijections of $\{a_1, \ldots, a_m, b_1, \ldots, b_n\}$ into the chain $\{1, 2, \ldots, m + n\}$, which respect the order on T and U. Any mapping $\lambda \in E$ is thus determined by its images on T. Let us set

$$\lambda(a_i) = x_i, \quad \lambda(b_j) = y_j \quad (i = 1, \ldots, m; j = 1, \ldots, n),$$

where $1 \leq x_1 < x_2 \ldots < x_m \leq m + n$, $1 \leq y_1 < y_2 \ldots < y_n \leq m + n$. Since the y_j's are determined by the x_i's we write shortly $\lambda = (x_i)$. Now we define an order on E by setting

$$\lambda \leq \lambda' :\Longleftrightarrow x_i \leq x_i' \text{ for all } i,$$

when $\lambda(a_i) = x_i$, $\lambda'(a_i) = x_i'$. $E_\leq$ is clearly a poset and indeed a lattice by observing that

(5.28) $$\lambda \vee \lambda' = (\max(x_i, x_{i'})), \lambda \wedge \lambda' = (\min(x_i, x_i')).$$

It follows immediately from (5.28) that E is, in fact, a distributive lattice. Next we claim that the set L of linear extensions is a sublattice of E and thus also distributive by our remark above. We have to show that $\lambda, \lambda' \in L$ imply $\lambda \vee \lambda'$, $\lambda \wedge \lambda' \in L$. Let us just verify $\lambda \vee \lambda' \in L$, the other case being analogous.

Suppose $\lambda = (x_i)$, $\lambda' = (x_i')$ are in L, with y_j, y_j' denoting the images of b_j, $j = 1, \ldots, n$. Suppose $a_i < b_j$ is a relation that holds in P. We have to show that $a_i < b_j$ is respected in $\lambda \vee \lambda'$. Since $\lambda, \lambda' \in L$ we must have $x_i < y_j$, $x_i' < y_j'$ and thus $x_i \leq i + j - 1$, $x_i' \leq i + j - 1$, hence $\max(x_i, x_i') \leq i + j - 1$. It follows from (5.28) that $(\lambda \vee \lambda')(a_i) \leq i + j - 1 < (\lambda \vee \lambda')(b_j)$. If, on the other hand, $a_i > b_j$ holds in P, then $x_i \geq i + j$, $x_i' \geq i + j$, and thus $(\lambda \vee \lambda')(a_i) \geq i + j > (\lambda \vee \lambda')(b_j)$. Now let $A \subseteq L$ be the set of linear extensions compatible with relations of the form $a_{i_1} < b_{j_1}, a_{i_2} < b_{j_2}, \ldots$. We claim that A is a down-set in L, which by (5.27) will finish the proof. Let $\lambda \in A$ and $\lambda' \leq \lambda$. We have to show that λ' respects a relation $a_i < b_j$ if λ does. Since $a_i < b_j$, we have $x_i < y_j$, i.e. $x_i \leq i + j - 1$, and $x'_i \leq x_i$ since $\lambda' \leq \lambda$. From $x'_i \leq i + j - 1$, it follows that $x'_i < y'_j$, and the proof is complete. $\square$

Let us now tackle the xyz-inequality. The proof proceeds along the same lines, but the ordering on L has to be defined in a different way.

Lemma 5.19. *Let $E_N = \{1, \ldots, N\}^n$ be the set of all n-tuples $x = (x_1 \ldots, x_n)$ with $x_i \in \{1, \ldots, N\}$. With the ordering $x \leq y$ iff $x_1 \geq y_1$, $x_i - x_1 \leq y_i - y_1$ $(i = 1, \ldots, n)$, E_N becomes a distributive lattice.*

Proof. E_N is clearly a lattice under $\leq$ with

$$
\begin{aligned}
(x \vee y)_i &= \max(x_i - x_1, y_i - y_1) + \min(x_1, y_1) \\
(x \wedge y)_i &= \min(x_i - x_1, y_i - y_1) + \max(x_1, y_1).
\end{aligned}
$$

Let us verify the first identity in (5.26). Set $w = y \vee z$. Then $w_i - w_1 = \max(y_i - y_1, z_i - z_1)$, and thus

$$
\begin{aligned}
(5.29) \quad (x \wedge (y \vee z))_i &= \min(x_i - x_1, w_i - w_1) + \max(x_1, w_1) \\
&= \min(x_i - x_1, \max(y_i - y_1, z_i - z_1) \\
&\quad + \max(x_1, \min(y_1, z_1)).
\end{aligned}
$$

From $(x \wedge y)_i - (x \wedge y)_1 = \min(x_i - x_1, y_i - y_1)$, we infer for the right-hand side in (5.26)

$$
\begin{aligned}
(5.30) \quad ((x \wedge y) \vee (x \wedge z))_i &= \max(\min(x_i - x_1, y_i - y_1), \\
&\quad \min(x_i - x_1, z_i - z_1)) \\
&\quad + \min(\max(x_1, y_1), \max(x_1, z_1)).
\end{aligned}
$$

Now note that $\mathbb{R}$ is a chain with the usual ordering $<$, and thus a distributive lattice, where $a \vee b = \max(a, b), a \wedge b = \min(a, b)$. This means that

(5.31) $\max(a, \min(b, c))\ =\ \min(\max(a, b), \max(a, c))$

              $\min(a, \max(b, c))\ =\ \max(\min(a, b), \min(a, c)).$

Applying (5.31) to the right-hand sides of (5.29) and (5.30) we see that $(x \wedge (y \vee z))_i = ((x \wedge y) \vee (x \wedge z))_i$ holds for all i.   □

Theorem 5.20. *Let P be a poset and x, y, z three elements of P. The events $A = \{x < y\}$ and $B = \{x < z\}$ are then positively correlated, i.e.*

$$p(x < y \wedge x < z) \geq p(x < y)p(x < z).$$

Proof. Let $\{a_1, \ldots, a_n\}$ be the elements of P and let us set $x = a_1$, $y = a_2$, $z = a_3$. We choose an integer $N \geq n$ and consider the distributive lattice E_N as in the lemma. Let L_N be the set of strict monotone mappings of P into $\{1, \ldots, N\}$, i.e. the set of all $x \in E_N$ such that $a_i \underset{P}{<} a_j$ implies $x_i < x_j$. Note, however, that the mapping need not be injective, unrelated elements in P may have the same image. We prove that L_N is a sublattice of E_N and hence distributive. Suppose $u, v \in L_N$ and $a_i < a_j$ holds in P. Then $u_i < u_j$, $v_i < v_j$ and thus clearly $(u \vee v)_i = \max(u_i - u_1, v_i - v_1) + \min(u_1, v_1) < \max(u_j - u_1, v_j - v_1) + \min(u_1, v_1) = (u \vee v)_j$. Similarly, we have $(u \wedge v)_i < (u \wedge v)_j$, hence $u \vee v, u \wedge v \in L_N$.

Next we show that any subset $A_N \subseteq L_N$ respecting a relation $a_1 < a_k$ (in addition to P) is an up-set in L_N. Indeed, let $u \in A_N$ and $v \in L_N$, $v \geq u$. Then $u_1 < u_k$, and by the definition of the order on E_N, $v_k - v_1 \geq u_k - u_1 > 0$, i.e. $v_1 < v_k$. Hence if A_N and B_N are the two subsets of L_N respecting $a_1 < a_2$ and $a_1 < a_3$, respectively, then by Corollary 5.17

(5.32) $| A_N | | B_N |\ \leq\ | (A \cap B)_N | | L_N |.$

Now what we are really interested in are linear extensions, i.e. injective mappings of P into $\{1, \ldots, N\}$. Denote by $\overline{L}_N$ the subset of all injective mappings in L_N, and similarly define $\overline{A}_N$, $\overline{B}_N$, $(\overline{A \cap B})_N$. Let us compare the sizes of L_N and $\overline{L}_N$. If e_k denotes the number of *surjective* strict monotone mappings of P into the chain of k elements, then clearly

$$| L_N | = \sum_{k=1}^{n} e_k \binom{N}{k}, \quad | \overline{L}_N | = e_n \binom{N}{n}.$$

Note that the expressions for $|L_N|$ and $|\overline{L}_N|$ are both polynomials in N of degree n with leading coefficient e_n (which is clearly equal to $|L|$). Hence we conclude

$$\lim_{N\to\infty} \frac{|\overline{L}_N|}{|L_N|} = 1.$$

The same holds for A_N, B_N and $(A\cap B)_N$, so we summarize:

$$(5.33)\quad \lim \frac{|\overline{L}_N|}{|L_N|} = \lim \frac{|\overline{A}_N|}{|A_N|} = \lim \frac{|\overline{B}_N|}{|B_N|} = \lim \frac{|(\overline{A\cap B})_N|}{|(A\cap B)_N|} = 1.$$

The rest is easy. We have already noted $|\overline{L}_N| = \binom{N}{n}|L|$. Similarly, we have $|\overline{A}_N| = \binom{N}{n}|A|$, and analogously for B and $A\cap B$. We conclude

$$\frac{|A|}{|L|} = \frac{|\overline{A}_N|}{|\overline{L}_N|}, \frac{|B|}{|L|} = \frac{|\overline{B}_N|}{|\overline{L}_N|}, \frac{|A\cap B|}{|L|} = \frac{|(\overline{A\cap B})_N|}{|\overline{L}_N|} \quad \text{for all } N \geq n,$$

and hence

$$(5.34)\frac{|A|}{|L|} = \lim \frac{|\overline{A}_N|}{|\overline{L}_N|}, \frac{|B|}{|L|} = \lim \frac{|\overline{B}_N|}{|\overline{L}_N|}, \frac{|A\cap B|}{|L|} = \lim \frac{|(\overline{A\cap B})_N|}{|\overline{L}_N|}.$$

Now by (5.33),

$$\lim \frac{|\overline{A}_N|/|\overline{L}_N|}{|A_N|/|L_N|} = \lim \frac{|\overline{A}_N|/|A_N|}{|\overline{L}_N|/|L_N|} = 1,$$

and thus by (5.34)

$$\lim \frac{|A_N|}{|L_N|} = \lim \frac{|\overline{A}_N|}{|\overline{L}_N|} = \frac{|A|}{|L|},$$

and similarly for B and $A\cap B$. Since we know from (5.32) that

$$(5.35)\qquad \frac{|A_N||B_N|}{|L_N||L_N|} \leq \frac{|(A\cap B)_N|}{|L_N|} \quad (N \geq n),$$

we arrive at our desired conclusion $\mid A \parallel B \mid \leq \mid A \cap B \parallel L \mid$ by letting N go to infinity in (5.35).   □

Remark. The reader may have wondered why we took the trouble of considering arbitrary order-preserving mappings first instead of linear extensions right away as in the proof of **5.18**. The reason is simple. The set S_n of all permutations endowed with the ordering $\leq$ is not distributive (nor is any other reasonable ordering), so the technique of **5.17** could not have been applied.

Example 5.7. It is tempting to surmise that some "longer" events may also be positively correlated in any poset P. For example, it certainly seems reasonable to assume that

$$p(x < y \wedge x < u < v) \geq p(x < y)p(x < u < v).$$

However, this need not be the case as the following poset of figure 5.13 demonstrates.

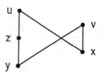

Figure 5.13

Here $p(x < y) = p(x < u < v) = \frac{3}{8}$, $p(x < y \wedge x < u < v) = \frac{1}{8}$, i.e. $p(x < y \mid x < u < v) = \frac{1}{3} < p(x < y) = \frac{3}{8}$.

Note that the proof actually furnishes the more general result spelled out in the following statement.

Corollary 5.21. *Let P be a poset, and x a fixed element. If A and B are both events of the form $\{x < y_1, x < y_2, \ldots\}$, then A and B are positively correlated.*

The reader will have noticed that **5.18** and **5.20** differ in the sense that the first result singles out a specific instance of positively correlated pairs present in posets of width 2 while **5.20** or **5.21** hold universally in *any* poset. Hence the interesting question arises as to which pairs of posets A and B are *always* positively correlated whenever the relations of A and B are contained in a poset P. A characterization of these "universally" positively correlated pairs was obtained by Winkler [1983] who showed that all pairs can be essentially deduced from the xyz-inequality **5.20** (see exercise 5.4.9). One additional remark: As conjectured by Rival and Sands and proved by Fishburn [1984], the xyz-inequality is actually a strict inequality whenever x, y, z are pairwise unrelated.

Let us close with some further comments on the quantities $p(x < y)$. Let P be a poset. We say that y *dominates* x, in symbols $x \ll y$, if there are more linear extensions that put y above x than the other way around. Thus $x \ll y$ if and only if $p(x < y) > \frac{1}{2}$. Clearly, the relation $\ll$ extends the ordering $<$ of P, but it need not be transitive anymore. The following example due to Ganter, Häfner and Poguntke [1987] gives a poset P where a cycle $x \ll y \ll z \ll x$ occurs.

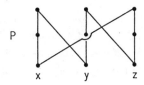

Figure 5.14

The reader may verify that $|L(P)| = 1431$ and $p(x < y) = p(y < z) = p(z < x) = \frac{720}{1431} > \frac{1}{2}$, thus $x \ll y \ll z \ll x$.

Exercises 5.4.

1. Show that the xyz-inequality is trivially true when one or more relations hold between x, y and z.

2*. Deduce from **5.14** the so-called FKG-inequality: Let $B(S)$ be the lattice of all subsets of a finite set S, and let $f : B(S) \longrightarrow \mathbb{R}^+$, $g : B(S) \longrightarrow \mathbb{R}^+$ be two monotone (both increasing or both decreasing) functions, and $\mu : B(S) \longrightarrow \mathbb{R}^+$ a function satisfying $\mu(x)\mu(y) \leq \mu(x \cap y)\mu(x \cup y)$ for $x, y \in B(S)$. Then

$$\frac{\sum f(x)g(x)\mu(x)}{\sum \mu(x)} \geq \frac{\sum f(x)\mu(x)}{\sum \mu(x)} \cdot \frac{\sum g(x)\mu(x)}{\sum \mu(x)}.$$

(Fortuin-Kasteleyn-Ginibre). Note that the FKG-inequality holds in general for finite distributive lattices.

3. Prove that $\mid U \cap D \parallel B(S) \mid \leq \mid U \parallel D \mid$ for any up-set U and down-set D of the subset lattice $B(S)$. (Kleitman)

4*. Show that $\mid A \mid \leq \mid A \backslash A \mid$ for all $A \subseteq B(S)$, where $A \backslash A = \{x - y : x \in A, y \in A\}$. (Marica-Schönheim)

5. Show that any finite distributive lattice can be embedded as a sublattice into a lattice 2^S.

6*. Prove that either inequality in (5.26) for all x, y, z implies the other for all x, y, z.

7*. Let $P = T \,\dot{\cup}\, U$ be the union of two disjoint finite posets (with no relations between T and U). Show by a similar argument as in the proof of **5.20** that $p(A \mid B) \geq p(A)$ where A and B are both sets of comparabilities of the form $\{t_{i_1} < u_{j_1}, t_{i_2} < u_{j_2}, \ldots\}$, $t_i \in T$, $u_j \in U$. (Shepp)

8. Let Ω be a finite probability space with distribution $Pr(\omega)$, $\omega \in \Omega$. As usual we call subsets A of Ω an *event*. If $A \subseteq B$, then we say A *induces* B, and use the symbol $A \longrightarrow B$. Show: a. Suppose A, B, C are events with $Pr(A \cap B \mid C) \geq Pr(A \mid C)Pr(B \mid C)$ and $A \longrightarrow C$, $B \longrightarrow C$, then $Pr(A \cap B) \geq Pr(A)Pr(B)$, b. If $Pr(A \cap B) \geq Pr(A)Pr(B)$ and $(A \cap B) \longrightarrow C \longrightarrow B$, then $Pr(A \cap C) \geq Pr(A)Pr(C)$, c. If $Pr(A \cap B) \geq Pr(A)Pr(B)$ and $Pr(A \cap C \mid B) \geq Pr(A \mid B)Pr(C \mid B)$, then $Pr(A \cap (B \cap C)) \geq Pr(A)Pr(B \cap C)$.

9. Using the previous exercise, prove one half of Winkler's characterization of universally correlated pairs: Let A and B be two consistent comparabilities in a poset P, and let A' and B' be the coverings pairs in A and B, respectively. A and B are then positively correlated, if either one of the four cases holds:

   i) A' or B' is empty,

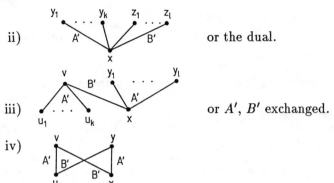

ii)   or the dual.

iii)   or A', B' exchanged.

iv)

10*. Construct suitable examples (as in figure 5.14) to show that for any pair A, B other than the ones in exercise 9, there exists a poset P where A and B are negatively correlated, thus completing the characterization of universal pairs. (Winkler)

11. Verify the relevant numbers of extensions in figure 5.15.

12*. Let $h(x)$ be the expected height of x as in section 1. Prove that $h(x \mid x > y) \geq 1 + h(x \mid x < y)$ for any two unrelated elements x, y and conclude that $h(x \mid x < y) < h(x) < h(x \mid x > y)$. (Winkler)

Problems

1. Prove that $\delta(P) \geq \frac{1}{3}$ for posets P of width 3, or in general, for all posets which are not chains. (5.1)

2. Prove that $\delta(P) > \frac{1}{3}$ for any poset P of width 3, or in general. (5.1)

3. Let $\delta(k) = \min(\delta(P) : P$ has width $k)$. Prove that $\lim_{k \to \infty} \delta(k) = \frac{1}{2}$. (5.1)

4. Improve the bound in **5.4**. (5.1)

5. Are there constants c_1, c_2 such that $C(P) \leq c_1 \log_2 \frac{n!}{e(P)} + c_2 n$ for all posets P of size n? (5.2)

6. Generalize the results of section 2 to the k-fold selection problem. (5.2)

7. Improve the constant in **5.13**. (5.3)

8. Prove exact results for the data location problem of other interesting classes of posets. (5.3)

9. Find the universally positively correlated pairs in posets of width 2. (5.4)

10. Is the example in figure 5.15 the smallest instance when a cycle with respect to $\ll$ occurs? (5.4)

11. Define $x \ll y$ whenever $p(x < y) > \alpha p(x > y)$ for a given $\alpha \geq \frac{1}{2}$. What is the largest α for which a cycle with respect to $\ll$ can occur? (5.4)

Notes and References

The problems of sorting and producing posets were first treated in some depth by Fredman [1976] and Schönhage [1976], see also Aigner [1981]. Saks [1985] gives a magnificent survey of these and related results. Linial-Saks [1985a] and Kahn-Saks [1984] can be considered landmarks on the sorting and the data location problem. Many beautiful ramifications of the FKG-inequality, first proved in Fortuin-Kasteleyn-Ginibre [1970], can be found in Graham [1982]. The remarkable generalization of the FKG-inequality is due to Ahlswede-Daykin [1978/9]. Shepp [1980, 1982] was the first to apply this method to poset problems.

Ahlswede R., Daykin D. [1978], An inequality for the weights of two families of sets, their unions and intersections. Z. Wahrscheinlichkeits-theorie u. verw. Gebiete 43, 183-185.

Ahlswede R., Daykin D. [1979], Inequalities for a pair of maps $S \times S \longrightarrow S$ with S a finite set. Math. Zeitschrift 165, 267-289.

Aigner M. * [1979], Combinatorial Theory. Springer-Verlag, New York.

Aigner M. [1981], Producing posets. Discrete Math. 35, 1-15.

Aigner M. [1988], The double selection problem. Discrete Math. To appear

Bonneson T., Fenchel W. * [1934], Theorie der konvexen Körper. Springer, Berlin.

Busemann H. * [1958], Convex Surfaces. Interscience, New York.

Chung F.R.K., Fishburn P.C., Graham R.L. [1980], On unimodality for linear extensions of partial orders. SIAM J. Alg. Discrete Methods 1, 405-410.

Daykin D. [1977], A lattice is distributive iff $|A\|B| \leq |A \vee B\|A \wedge B|$. Nanta Math. 10, 58-60.

Faigle U., Lovász L., Schrader R., Turán G. [1986], Searching in trees, series-parallel and interval orders. SIAM J. Computing 15, 1075-1084.

Faigle U., Sands B. [1986], A size-width inequality for distributive lattices. Combinatorica 6, 29-33.

Faigle U., Turán G. [1985], Sorting and recognition problems for ordered sets. Lecture Notes Computer Science 182, Springer.

Fishburn P.C. [1974], On the family of linear extensions of a partial order. J. Combinatorial Theory B 17, 240-243.

Fishburn P. [1984], A correlational inequality for linear extensions of a poset. Order 1, 127-137.

Fortuin C.M., Kasteleyn P.W., Ginibre J. [1970], Correlation inequalities on some partially ordered sets. Comm. Math. Phys. 22, 89-103.

Fredman M. [1976], How good is the information theory bound in sorting? Theoretical Computer Sci. 1, 355-361.

Fussenegger F., Gabow H. [1979], A counting approach to lower bounds for selection problems. J. Ass. Comp. Mach. 26, 227-238.

Ganter B., Häfner G., Poguntke W. [1987], On linear extensions of ordered sets with a symmetry. Discrete Math. 63, 153-156.

Graham R.L. [1982], Linear extensions of partial orders and the FKG inequality. In: Ordered Sets, Reidel, 213-236.

Graham R.L., Yao A.C., Yao F.F. [1980], Some monotonicity properties of partial orders. SIAM J. Alg. Discrete Methods 1, 251-258.

Kahn J., Saks M. [1984], Balancing poset extensions. Order 1, 113-126.

Kahn J., Saks M. [1987], On the widths of distributive lattices. Discrete Math. 63, 183-195.

Kleitman D. [1966], Families of non-disjoint sets. J. Combinatorial Theory 1, 153-155.

Kleitman D., Shearer J.B. [1981], A monotonicity property of partial orders. Studies in Appl. Math. 65, 81-83.

Knuth D. * [1973], The Art of Computer Programming, vol. 3, Sorting and Searching. Addison-Wesley, Reading.

Linial N. [1984], The information-theoretic bound is good for merging. SIAM J. Computing 13, 795-801.

Linial N., Saks M. [1985a], Every poset has a central element. J. Combinatorial Theory A 40, 195-210.

Linial N., Saks M. [1985b], Searching ordered structures. J. Algorithms 6, 86-103.

Marica J., Schönheim J. [1969], Differences of sets and a problem of Graham. Canad. Math. Bull. 12, 635-637.

Saks M. [1985], The information theoretic bound for problems on ordered sets and graphs. In: Graphs and Orders, Reidel, 137-168.

Sands B. [1981], Counting antichains in finite partially ordered sets. Discrete Math. 35, 213-228.

Schönhage A. [1976], The production of partial orders. Asterisque 38, 229-246.

Seymour J. [1973], On incomparable selections of sets. Mathematika 20, 208-209.

Seymour J., Welsh D.J.A. [1975], Combinatorial applications of an inequality from statistical mechanics. Math. Proc. Cambridge Phil. Soc. 77, 485-495.

Shepp L. [1980], The FKG inequality and some monotonicity properties of partial orders. SIAM J. Alg. Discrete Methods 1, 295-299.

Shepp L. [1982], The XYZ conjecture and the FKG inequality. Annals Probability 10, 824-827.

Stanley R.P. [1981], Two combinatorial applications of the Alexander-Fenchel inequality. J. Combinatorial Theory A 31, 56-65.

Winkler P. [1982], Average heigth in a partially ordered set. Discrete Math. 39, 337-341.

Winkler P. [1983], Correlation among partial orders. SIAM J. Alg. Discrete Methods 4, 1-7.

Chapter 6

Some More Problems

In the final chapter we present some topics that received much attention in recent years. In particular, we want to connect search problems with notions from algebra and geometry. Quite often, a computational problem can be stated in the following form: Given n real numbers $x_1, \ldots, x_n$, determine whether they satisfy some fixed set of linear inequalities. For example, the problem of verifying whether $x_1, \ldots, x_n$ appear in non-decreasing order can be stated as: Given $x_1, \ldots, x_n$; are the inequalities $x_1 \leq x_2, x_2 \leq x_3, \ldots, x_{n-1} \leq x_n$ satisfied?

Geometrically, a set of linear inequalities involving $x_1, \ldots, x_n$ determines a polyhedron P in the n-dimensional space $I\!R^n$, and our question can be formulated as the decision problem: Is $\underline{x} = (x_1, \ldots, x_n) \in P$?

We shall discuss several noteworthy instances of this problem later on. To begin, let us collect some basic facts about polyhedra.

6.1 Notions From Convex Geometry

Consider the vector space $I\!R^n$ of dimension n. We know from Linear Algebra that any *affine* $(n-1)$-dimensional subspace H, usually called a *hyperplane*, is determined by a linear equation $a_1 x_1 + \ldots + a_n x_n = b$, $\underline{a} = (a_1, \ldots, a_n) \neq \underline{0}$, i.e. $H = \{\underline{x} : \ell(\underline{x}) = 0\}$ where $\ell(\underline{x}) = \sum_{i=1}^{n} a_i x_i - b = \underline{a}.\underline{x} - b$ is a linear form. The *half-spaces* corresponding to H are the sets $H^+ = \{\underline{x} : \ell(\underline{x}) > 0\}$ and $H^- = \{\underline{x} : \ell(\underline{x}) < 0\}$. Thus any linear equation partitions the space $I\!R^n$ into the hyperplane and its two associated half-spaces. More precisely, we call H^+ and H^- *open* half-spaces, and we speak of *closed* half-spaces when considering $\{x : \ell(x) \geq 0\}$ or $\{x : \ell(x) \leq 0\}$.

Definition. A *polyhedron P* in $\mathbb{R}^n$ is the intersection of a finite number of half-spaces (open or closed).

Polyhedra are thus sets of points in $\mathbb{R}^n$ which satisfy a finite set of linear inequalities where we may always assume $\leq$ by changing $\underline{a}$ and b to $-\underline{a}$ and $-b$ if necessary.

Example 6.1. Consider the inequalities $-x_1 \leq 0$, $-x_2 \leq 0$, $x_1 - x_2 \leq 3$, $4x_1 + 3x_2 \leq 19$, $-2x_1 + x_2 \leq 3$ in $\mathbb{R}^2$. Figure 6.1 shows the corresponding polyhedron.

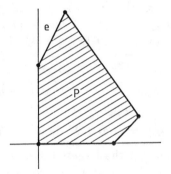

Figure 6.1

We notice that P is a *bounded* set in $\mathbb{R}^2$, i.e. there is an upper bound on the distances from the origin to any point in P. If we only consider the first three inequalities, then the corresponding polyhedron would be unbounded. Another immediate observation is that P is convex.

Definition. A set $S \subseteq \mathbb{R}^n$ is called *convex*, if to any points $\underline{x} \neq \underline{y}$ in S, the whole segment $[\underline{x}, \underline{y}]$ is in S.

Convexity is one of the fundamental notions in geometry, based on the following natural aesthetic principle. A person situated at any point is able to see any other point of the convex set. Obviously, any hyperplane or half-space is convex and equally obviously, any intersection of convex sets is

again convex. So, in particular, any polyhedron is a convex set. The reader
may easily prove for himself that each closed convex set in $I\!R^n$ (i.e. a convex set containing its boundary) is the intersection of all closed half-spaces
containing it; similarly for open convex sets. Note, however, that not every
convex set is a polyhedron. A closed disk in $I\!R^2$ (= a circle plus its interior)
is certainly convex, but is not a polyhedron.

There are two more notions that we need at present: *face* and *dimension*.
Consider the polyhedron P of figure 6.1. Its boundary consists of five line
segments (called *edges*) which are themselves convex (of dimension 1), and
there are five distinguished points, called the *vertices* of P. Look at the edge
e in figure 6.1. We see that e is precisely the set of points in $I\!R^2$ which satisfy
the first four inequalities and the last one with equality, $-2x_1 + x_2 - 3 = 0$.
We generalize this observation in a natural way.

Definition. Let $P = \{\underline{x} : \ell_i(\underline{x}) < 0, i = 1, \dots, r, \ell_i(\underline{x}) \le 0, i = r + 1, \dots, s\}$
be a polyhedron. Take $J \subseteq \{1, \dots, s\}$. A *face* $F_J(P)$ of P is a set $F_J(P) =$
$\{\underline{x} : \ell_i(\underline{x}) < 0$ for $i \in J \cap \{1 \dots, r\}, \ell_i(\underline{x}) \le 0$ for $i \in J \cap \{r + 1, \dots, s\}$ and
$\ell_i(\underline{x}) = 0$ for $i \notin J\}$.

The notion of dimension that we use is that of *affine dimension*. A set
$\{\underline{x}_1, \dots, \underline{x}_s\} \subseteq I\!R^n$ is called *affinely dependent* if there are reals $a_1, \dots, a_s$,
not all 0, such that $\sum_{i=1}^{s} a_i \underline{x}_i = \underline{0}$ and $\sum_{i=1}^{s} a_i = 0$. A set $A \subseteq I\!R^n$ is said
to have (affine) dimension d if the largest (affinely) independent set in A
has size $d + 1$. Thus $\dim I\!R^n = n$, and by convention $\dim \emptyset = -1$. The
points of $I\!R^n$ have dimension 0 and the usual (affine) lines have dimension
1. The hyperplanes are the largest sets of dimension $n - 1$, and intersections
of hyperplanes are called (affine) *subspaces*. Any subspace of dimension d is
the intersection of $n - d$ hyperplanes, for any $d = 0, \dots, n$. It is readily seen
that $A \subseteq I\!R^n$ has dimension d if A is contained in a subspace of dimension
d, but not in one of lower dimension. In particular, a face F of a polyhedron
has dimension d if the smallest subspace (determined by the linear forms of
P) containing F has dimension d. Faces of dimension 1 are called *edges* of
P, and those of dimension 0 *vertices*.

Figure 6.2 displays two polyhedra in $I\!R^3$, the octahedron and the triangular
prism. The first has 8 faces of dimension 2, 12 edges and 6 vertices, while
for the prism the numbers are 5, 9 and 6.

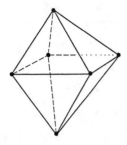
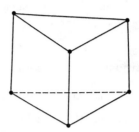

Figure 6.2

We say that $P \subseteq \mathbb{R}^n$ is a *full-dimensional* polyhedron if $\dim P = n$, or equivalently, if P is not contained in a hyperplane. For more information on polyhedra and convex sets, in general, the reader may consult the book by Grünbaum [1967].

Exercises 6.1.

1. Let $A \subseteq \mathbb{R}^n$. Since the intersection of convex sets is convex, we may define the *convex hull conv A* of A as the smallest convex set containing A. Show that *conv A* consists of precisely the convex combinations of points of A, i.e., $conv\,A = \left\{ \sum\limits_{i=0}^{t} a_i \underline{x}_i : \underline{x}_i \in A, \sum\limits_{i=0}^{t} a_i = 1, a_i \geq 0 \right\}$.

2*. Prove Caratheodory's theorem: If $A \subseteq \mathbb{R}^n$, then every $\underline{x} \in conv\,A$ is expressible as a convex combination of at most $n + 1$ points of A.

3. A point $\underline{x}$ of a convex set is called an *extreme point* of A if $A - \underline{x}$ is still convex. Show: If A is closed convex set of $\mathbb{R}^n$ which contains no lines, than A has extreme points.

4*. A convex *polytope* in $\mathbb{R}^n$ is the convex hull of a finite number of points. Consider full-dimensional polytopes in $\mathbb{R}^3$, and let f_i be the number of i-dimensional faces, $i = 0, 1, 2$. Euler's relation states $f_0 - f_1 + f_2 = 2$ for these polytopes. Call the polytope P *regular* if every vertex is incident with the same number p of edges, and every side ($= 2$-dimensional face) is incident with the same number q of edges. Show that there are 5 possible combinations (p, q) and construct a model for each.

5*. Suppose we want to cover the plane with regular convex polygons containing p vertices such that every corner is contained in q such polygons. Determine the possible (p, q)-patterns.

6. Determine the maximal number f_n of regions into which $\mathbb{R}^2$ can be partitioned by n straight lines. Thus, e.g., $f_0 = 1$, $f_1 = 2$, $f_2 = 4$.

7. Let P be a convex polygon in $\mathbb{R}^2$ with the vertices $x_1, \ldots, x_n$, and let L be the length of the boundary of P, i.e. $L = \sum_{i=1}^{n-1} d(x_{i,i+1}) + d(x_n, x_1)$, where $d(x_i, x_j)$ is the Euclidian distance. Show that the total length of any other straight line cycle of the vertices is at least L, i.e. $L \leq \sum_{i=1}^{n-1} d(x_{\sigma i}, x_{\sigma(i+1)}) + d(x_{\sigma n}, x_{\sigma 1})$ where σ is any permutation.

8*. Puzzle: In a forest there are trees with heights $h(x)$ between m and M. Suppose $d(x, y) < | h(x) - h(y) |$ for any two trees x, y. Show that we can run a fence around the forest with length $< 2(M - m)$.

6.2   Polyhedral Membership Problem

In the previous section we have introduced the concept of a polyhedron. For most applications we need a slightly more general notion. First of all, we say that $P \subseteq \mathbb{R}^n$ is an *open* polyhedron if P is an open set in the usual topological sense. In particular, an open polyhedron is always full-dimensional, and in all results to follow we will always be dealing with full-dimensional polyhedra. The general statement will then follow without difficulty.

Definition. A *polyhedral set* $S \subseteq \mathbb{R}^n$ is a union of disjoint open polyhedra.

Example 6.2. The set $S = \{\underline{x} = (x_1, \ldots, x_n) : x_i \neq x_j\}$ is a polyhedral set consisting of the two half-spaces $H^+ \cup H^-$ (which are open half-spaces), where $H = \{\underline{x} : x_i = x_j\}$.

The main question we want to address is the following *polyhedral membership problem (PMP)*: Given the polyhedral set $S \subseteq \mathbb{R}^n$ and an unknown point $\underline{x} \in \mathbb{R}^n$. Decide whether $\underline{x} \in S$ by using as few linear comparisons ℓ as possible, i.e. questions of the form: Is $\ell(\underline{x}) < 0$, $\ell(\underline{x}) = 0$ or $\ell(\underline{x}) > 0$? Let us denote the worst-case cost by $C(S)$.

Since there are only two answers to our problem, $\underline{x} \in S$ or $\underline{x} \notin S$, the usual information-theoretic bound is worthless. However, there is a natural lower bound due to Dobkin and Lipton [1979] which we now discuss.

Let S be a polyhedral set. By $comp(S)$ we denote the number of (topologically) connected components of S. Recall from Analysis that a set $S \subseteq I\!R^n$ is connected if and only if it cannot be separated by open sets A and B, i.e. there are no disjoint open sets A and B with $S = (S \cap A) \cup (S \cap B)$. Equivalently, S is connected iff any two points of S can be joined by a Jordan curve lying entirely in S. In our example 6.2 we clearly have $comp(S) = 2$.

Theorem 6.1. *We have* $C(S) \geq \lceil \log_2 comp(S) \rceil$ *for any polyhedral set* S.

Proof. Let T be a decision tree solving the PMP for S. By the setup of our problem, T is a ternary tree. Each leaf D_i corresponds to a sequence of linear inequalities or equalities leading up to it, and is thus convex. The D_i's are pairwise disjoint and their union is $I\!R^n$. Furthermore, since T solves the PMP, each D_i is either wholly contained in S or disjoint from it. Let $S_1, \ldots, S_m$ be the components of S. By the convexity of the leaves we infer that any leaf D_i contained in S is entirely contained in some component of S. Thus T has at least m leaves, from which we immediately infer $C(S) \geq \lceil \log_3 comp(S) \rceil$. We can, however, improve this bound to $\log_2 comp(S)$ right away. Let T' be the binary tree obtained after deleting all branches from T which correspond to answers $\ell(\underline{x}) = 0$. Then the union of all leaves in T' is equal to $I\!R^n$ minus a finite number of hyperplanes. Since such a union of hyperplanes (which is closed) can never fully cover an (open) component S_j, we conclude that the leaves of T' must still intersect all S_j, from which our result immediately follows. $\square$

Consider again the examples in figure 6.1 and 6.2. Since they are all connected, our bound of the previous theorem is no good. Yao and Rivest [1980] have, however, found a way to relate the cost $C(S)$ to the number of faces of S. For simplicity, let us treat a single (connected) polyhedron $P = \{\underline{x} : \ell_i(\underline{x}) \leq 0\}$ first. The corresponding result for arbitrary polyhedral sets will follow without difficulty.

Let $P \subseteq I\!R^n$ be a full-dimensional polyhedron. We denote by $\mathcal{F}_d(P)$ the set of d-dimensional faces of P with $f_d(P) = |\mathcal{F}_d(P)|$, $d = 0, \ldots, n$. Thus for the prism of figure 6.2 we have $f_0 = 6$, $f_1 = 9$, $f_2 = 5$, $f_3 = 1$. We view the polyhedral membership problem as the usual game between players A and

B. Player B adapts the following strategy. He chooses a fixed dimension d between 0 and $n - 1$, and provides his answers in such a way that f_d is as large as possible as the game proceeds. The following result is the key to this strategy.

Lemma 6.2. *Let P be a full-dimensional open polyhedron, $P = \{\underline{x} : \underline{\ell}_i(x) < 0,\ i = 1,\dots,t\}$, and let $g(\underline{x}) = \sum\limits_{i=1}^{n} a_i x_i - b$ be a linear form. Denote by P^-, P^+ the polyhedra $P^- = P \cap \{\underline{x} : g(\underline{x}) < 0\}$ and $P^+ = P \cap \{\underline{x} : g(\underline{x}) > 0\}$, respectively. Then $f_d(P^-) + f_d(P^+) \geq f_d(P)$ for any d.*

Proof. If one of P^- or P^+, say P^+, is empty, then $P \subseteq P^- \cup \{\underline{x} : g(\underline{x}) \leq 0\}$ and thus $P = P^-$, since P is an open set. Hence in this case $f_d(P^-) = f_d(P)$, and there is nothing to prove.

Now suppose $P^- \neq \emptyset$ and $P^+ \neq \emptyset$, or in other words, P has non-empty intersection with both half-spaces determined by $g(\underline{x})$. We shall prove our claim by constructing an injective map $\varphi : \mathcal{F}_d(P) \longrightarrow \mathcal{F}_d(P^-) \cup \mathcal{F}_d(P^+)$. Let $F_J(P) \in \mathcal{F}_d(P)$, i.e. $F_J(P) = \{\underline{x} : \ell_i(\underline{x}) < 0$ for $i \in J$, $\ell_i(\underline{x}) = 0$ for $i \notin J\}$. Denote by A, A^- and A^+ the sets

$$
\begin{aligned}
A &= F_J(P) \cap \{\underline{x} : g(\underline{x}) = 0\} \\
A^- &= F_J(P) \cap \{\underline{x} : g(\underline{x}) < 0\} \\
A^+ &= F_J(P) \cap \{\underline{x} : g(\underline{x}) > 0\}.
\end{aligned}
$$

Case 1. $A^- \cup A^+ = \emptyset$. Here we have $F_J(P) \subseteq \{\underline{x} : g(\underline{x}) = 0\}$. Writing $P^- = \{\underline{x} : \ell_i(\underline{x}) < 0, i = 1,\dots,t+1\}$ with $\ell_{t+1}(\underline{x}) = g(\underline{x})$, we infer for the d-dimensional face $F_J(P^-)$ of P^-, $F_J(P^-) = F_J(P) \cap \{\underline{x} : g(\underline{x}) = 0\} = F_J(P)$. Accordingly, we define $\varphi(F_J(P)) = F_J(P^-)$.

Case 2. $A^- \cup A^+ \neq \emptyset$. Assume $A^- \neq \emptyset$ (the case $A^+ \neq \emptyset$ being analogous). Again we write $P^- = \{\underline{x} : \ell_i(\underline{x}) < 0, i = 1,\dots,t+1\}$ with $\ell_{t+1} = g$ and set $J' = J \cup \{t+1\}$. The face $F_{J'}(P^-) = F_J(P) \cap \{\underline{x} : g(\underline{x}) < 0\}$ of P^- is clearly d-dimensional, and we set $\varphi(F_J(P)) = F_{J'}(P)$.

It remains to show that φ is injective. Note that in all cases $\varphi(F_J(P)) \subseteq F_J(P)$. Since the d-dimensional faces of P are pairwise disjoint (P is open!), the injectivity follows immediately. $\square$

Example 6.3. Consider the open polyhedron in figure 6.1, i.e. all inequalities are strict. Suppose $g(x)$ is the linear form $g(x) = -3x_1 + 2x_2 - 2$. The map φ keeps an edge which is not cut by g unchanged, and carries an edge which is cut by g (like edge e) onto one of the sub-edges created by the cut.

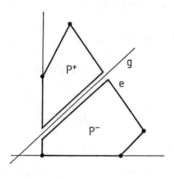

Figure 6.3

Theorem 6.3. *Let P be a polyhedron in $\mathbb{R}^n$. Then*

$$2^{C(P)} \binom{C(P)}{n-d} \geq f_d(P) \quad \text{for any } d = 0, \dots, n.$$

In particular,

$$C(P) \geq \lceil \tfrac{1}{2} \log_2 f_d(P) \rceil \quad \text{for any } d.$$

Proof. Let $P = \{x : \ell_i(x) < 0, i = 1, \dots, r, \ell_i(x) \leq 0, i = r+1, \dots, s\}$, where we may assume P to be full-dimensional. Suppose T is an optimal decision tree solving the PMP for P. Player B adopts the following strategy. He only considers the subtree T' as in the proof of Theorem 6.1 and keeps a list of open polyhedra $Q_0, Q_1, \dots$ as the algorithm proceeds. Suppose T' has length t, thus $C(P) \geq t$. Initially, $Q_0 = \{x : \ell_i(x) < 0, i = 1, \dots, s\}$, thus $f_d(P) = f_d(Q_0)$ for all d. Suppose Q_{j-1} is the polyhedron before the j-th query $g_j(x)$. By the lemma we know that $f_d(Q_{j-1}^-) + f_d(Q_{j-1}^+) \geq f_d(Q_{j-1})$. Changing the sign in $g_j(x)$ if necessary we may assume $f_d(Q_{j-1}^-) \geq \frac{1}{2} f_d(Q_{j-1})$. Player B now chooses the answer $g_j(x) < 0$ and sets $Q_j = Q_{j-1}^-$. Proceeding in this manner we see that after t tests the polyhedron Q_t satisfies

(6.1) $$f_d(Q_t) \geq \frac{1}{2^t} f_d(Q_0) = \frac{1}{2^t} f_d(P).$$

Note that $P \supseteq Q_0 \supseteq Q_1 \supseteq \ldots \supseteq Q_t$. Hence to any $\underline{x} \in Q_t$ the eventual answer must be "yes". It follows that any $\underline{x} \in \mathbb{R}^n$ which is consistent with all answers $g_j(\underline{x}) < 0$ must also be in P, thus

$$E = \{\underline{x} : g_j(\underline{x}) < 0, \quad j = 1, \ldots, t\} \subseteq P.$$

As Q_0 is the largest open set contained in P we must, in fact, have $E \subseteq Q_0$, and hence

$$Q_t = E \cap Q_0 = E = \{\underline{x} : g_j(\underline{x}) < 0, \quad j = 1, \ldots, t\}.$$

Since Q_t is determined by t linear forms it is clear from our discussion at the end of section 1 that Q_t has at most $\binom{t}{n-d}$ d-dimensional faces. Together with (6.1) and $C(P) \geq t$ this implies

$$2^{C(P)} \binom{C(P)}{n-d} \geq 2^t \binom{t}{n-d} \geq f_d(P).$$

Since $\binom{C(P)}{n-d} \leq 2^{C(P)}$, the last claim follows immediately.   □

The reader may easily generalize the lemma and the proof of the theorem to arbitrary polyhedral sets.

Corollary 6.4. *For any polyhedral set $S \subseteq \mathbb{R}^n$,*

$$2^{C(S)} \binom{C(S)}{n-d} \geq f_d(S), \quad d = 0, \ldots, n,$$

where $f_d(S)$ is the total number of d-dimensional faces among all components of S. In particular,

$$C(S) \geq \lceil \frac{1}{2} \log_2 f_d(S) \rceil \quad \text{for any } d.$$

What about upper bounds? Let us just look at convex polygons P in $\mathbb{R}^2$. A convex m-gon P_m is determined by m linear forms with $f_0(P_m) = f_1(P_m) = m$. Theorem 6.3 says in this case $C(P_m) \geq \lceil \frac{1}{2} \log_2 m \rceil$. By examining **6.2** more closely the reader will find that, in fact, $\lceil \log_2 m \rceil + 1$ tests are necessary (see exercise 6.2.2). Now we show, conversely, that $\lceil \log_2 m \rceil + 1$ queries also suffice. First we choose a point $\underline{w}$ in the interior of P_m, e.g. the midpoint of any diagonal of P_m. Let $\{\underline{v}_1, \ldots, \underline{v}_m\}$ be the vertices of P_m arranged in clockwise fashion. Any two successive vertices $\underline{v}_i$, $\underline{v}_{i+1}$ together with $\underline{w}$ determine a *wedge* $W_{i,i+1}$ of the polygon (see figure 6.4).

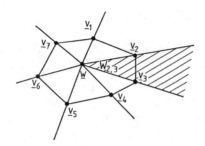

Figure 6.4

By the way the wedges are arranged it is clear that we can determine a wedge $W_{i,i+1}$ containing the unknown point $\underline{x}$ with at most $\lceil \log_2 m \rceil$ tests. Probing the line through $\underline{v}_i, \underline{v}_{i+1}$ will now tell us whether $\underline{x}$ is in P_m or not. Thus $C(P_m) = \lceil \log_2 m \rceil + 1$.

Exercises 6.2.

1. Generalize Lemma 6.2 to arbitrary polyhedral sets.

2*. Show $C(P_m) = \lceil \log_2 m \rceil + 1 \ (m \geq 3)$.

3. The n-dimensional simplex $\Delta_n \subseteq I\!\!R^n$ is the convex set spanned by the $n + 1$ points $\underline{0} = (0, 0, \ldots, 0)$ and $\underline{e}_1 = (1, 0, \ldots, 0)$, $\underline{e}_2 = (0, 1, \ldots, 0)$, $\ldots, \underline{e}_n = (0, 0, \ldots, 1)$. That is, $\Delta_n = \{\sum_{i=1}^{n} \lambda_i \underline{e}_i : \sum_{i=1}^{n} \lambda_i \leq 1, \lambda_i \geq 0$ for all $i\}$. Prove $C(\Delta_n) = n + 1 \ (n \geq 2)$.

4. Determine $C(Q)$ for the 3-dimensional cube Q.

5*. Denote by Q_n the n-dimensional cube, spanned by the 2^n points $(a_1, \ldots, a_n)$, $a_i = 0$ or 1. Show $C(Q_n) + 1 \leq C(Q_{n+1}) \leq C(Q_n) + 2$ $(n \geq 2)$ and conclude $C(Q_n) \leq 2n - 1$.

6. Compute $C(O)$ for the octahedron in $\mathbb{R}^3$, and in general, for any double pyramid erected over a convex m-gon.

7. Let S be a polynomial in $\mathbb{R}^n$ defined by s essential inequalities. Prove that $f_d(S) \leq s^{\frac{n}{2}}$ for all dimensions d.

6.3   Colorings of Graphs

Consider the following problem first investigated by Dobkin and Lipton [1979]. We are given n reals $x_1, \ldots, x_n$. Decide whether they are pairwise distinct by using comparisons $x_i : x_j$ where the answer may be $x_i < x_j$, $x_i = x_j$ or $x_i > x_j$. How many tests are necessary?

We can readily rephrase this question as a polyhedral membership problem. Interpret the n reals as an unknown point $\underline{x} = (x_1, \ldots, x_n) \in \mathbb{R}^n$, and let $S(n)$ be the polyhedral set $S(n) = \{\underline{x} : x_i \neq x_j, 1 \leq i < j \leq n\}$. Then our problem reduces precisely to the PMP for $S(n)$: Is $\underline{x} \in S(n)$? Well not precisely, since in the PMP we are allowed any linear form $\ell(\underline{x})$ as test function whereas in our present situation we only use queries of the form $x_i - x_j$. But at any rate, the lower bound of Theorem 6.1 will also apply to this situation. Thus the number of tests necessary is at least $\log_2 c(n)$ where $c(n)$ is the number of components of $S(n)$. We will see in a moment that $c(n) = n!$ whence $\log_2 n! \sim n \log_2 n$ tests are necessary. As a matter of fact it is easy to see that in the worst case we are required to sort the n numbers $x_1, \ldots, x_n$, so the sorting cost of section 4.1, also denoted by $S(n)$, applies in this situation.

Manber and Tompa [1984] have generalized the foregoing question to a very interesting type of problems for graphs. First we need some definitions.

Definition. Let $G(V, E)$ be a graph. A mapping $f : V \longrightarrow \mathbb{R}$ is called a (vertex-) *coloring* of G if $v_i v_j \in E$ implies $f(v_i) \neq f(v_j)$; f is called an *r-coloring* if the mapping f assumes r distinct values.

Coloring problems count among the most widely studied questions in graph theory. The smallest r for which there exists an r-coloring of G is called the *chromatic number* of G. Trivially, G has chromatic number 1 if and only if the edge-set is empty. There is one more characterization (see exercise 6.3.2): A graph G with non-empty edge-set has chromatic number 2 iff G contains no cycle of odd length. The origin of graph colorings is, of course, the famous 4-*color problem*: Is every planar graph 4-colorable? already mentioned in section 3.2.

Let us get back to our theme. We are given a (known) graph $G(V, E)$ with $V = \{v_1, \ldots, v_n\}$ and an (unknown) function $f : V \longrightarrow \mathbb{R}$. Our task is to decide whether f is a coloring by asking questions of the type: Is $f(v_i) = f(v_j)$ for an edge $v_i v_j$, or more generally, by testing any linear function involving the $f(v_i)$'s. Let $C(G)$ be the worst-case cost of this coloring recognition problem. Clearly, our starting example refers to the case when G is the complete graph K_n on n vertices.

Let us interpret the mapping f as a vector $\underline{x} = (x_1, \ldots, x_n) \in \mathbb{R}^n$, with $x_i = f(v_i)$, and let $S(G)$ be the polyhedral set $S(G) = \{\underline{x} : x_i \neq x_j$ for $v_i v_j \in E\}$. Then our problem reduces to the PMP for $S(G)$. To apply **6.1** we have to estimate the number $c(G)$ of components of $S(G)$. Clearly, two points $\underline{u}$, $\underline{w}$ lie in the same component if and only if they lie in the same half-space of each of the hyperplanes $H_{ij} = \{\underline{x} : x_i = x_j, v_i v_j \in E\}$. In other words, $u_i < u_j$ iff $w_i < w_j$ for any edge $v_i v_j \in E$. This observation suggests the following equivalent formulation of our problem.

An *orientation* $\mathcal{O}$ of G assigns a sense of traversal to each edge $v_i v_j$, and we write $v_i \longrightarrow v_j$ if the orientation goes from v_i to v_j. $\mathcal{O}$ is called *acyclic* if the directed graph $\vec{G}$ (oriented according to $\mathcal{O}$) has no directed cycle $v_{i_1} \longrightarrow v_{i_2} \longrightarrow \ldots \longrightarrow v_{i_s} \longrightarrow v_{i_1}$. Now let S_h be a component of $S(G)$. Our observation above implies that S_h induces a unique orientation $\mathcal{O}_h$ of G by directing $v_i \longrightarrow v_j$ iff $u_i < u_j$ for some $\underline{u} \in S_h$ (and hence for all points of S_h). Clearly, $\mathcal{O}_h$ is acyclic. Moreover, any acyclic orientation specifies a unique component of S. We conclude that $c(G)$ equals precisely the number $a(G)$ of acyclic orientations of G.

Examples 6.4. Consider the graph G of figure 6.5. Obviously, the number of acyclic orientations with $v_1 \longrightarrow v_4$ is the same as for the reverse orientation $v_4 \longrightarrow v_1$. Suppose $v_1 \longrightarrow v_4$. Among v_1, v_2, v_4,

Figure 6.5

the only forbidden combination is $v_4 \longrightarrow v_2 \longrightarrow v_1$ which would together with $v_1 \longrightarrow v_4$ create a directed cycle. Hence we may assign arrows to $v_1 v_2$ and $v_2 v_4$ in 3 ways, and the same holds for $v_1 v_3$ and $v_3 v_4$. Since orientations of the upper and lower half never yield a directed cycle, we compute $a(G) = 2.3.3 = 18$.

As a further example consider the complete graph K_n with vertex-set $V = \{1, \ldots, n\}$. Any permutation $\sigma(1), \ldots, \sigma(n)$ of V yields an acyclic orientation by setting $i \longrightarrow j$ iff $\sigma(i) < \sigma(j)$. Suppose, conversely, that $\mathcal{O}$ is an acyclic orientation. There must be a vertex i from which all arrows point away since otherwise we would obtain a directed cycle. Set $\sigma(i) = 1$. Continuing in this fashion we obtain a unique permutation σ with $i \longrightarrow j$ iff $\sigma(i) < \sigma(j)$. Hence $a(K_n) = n!$ which proves our previous claim $S(n) \geq \lceil \log_2 n! \rceil$.

Our main task consists thus in estimating the number $a(G)$ for a graph G. We digress for a moment to discuss an interesting connection of $a(G)$ with the chromatic polynomial of G pointed out by Stanley [1973]. Let us denote by $p(G; \lambda)$ the chromatic function of G in the variable λ where $p(G; \lambda)$ counts the number of different λ-colorings of G for positive integers λ. We shall see shortly that $p(G; \lambda)$ is a polynomial in λ so that the term *chromatic polynomial* is justified.

As an example, note that $p(K_n; \lambda) = \lambda(\lambda - 1) \ldots (\lambda - n + 1)$. Indeed, for the first vertex v_1 we have λ colors available. Having chosen a fixed color for v_1 there remain $\lambda - 1$ colors for v_2, and so on. At the other extreme, when G is a graph on n vertices with no edges at all, then $p(G; \lambda) = \lambda^n$. To derive a formula for arbitrary graphs G, let $e = uv$ be an edge of G. We denote by $G \backslash e$ the graph which results upon deletion of e, and by G/e the graph on $n - 1$ vertices where we have contracted edge e to a single vertex uv, and where we keep an edge (uv, w) if u or v is adjacent to w in G. If u and v were both adjacent to w, then we keep just one edge. All other edges in G/e remain unchanged.

Example 6.5. Consider the graph G of example 6.4 and choose $e = v_1 v_4$. The resulting graphs $G \backslash e$ and G/e are shown in figure 6.6.

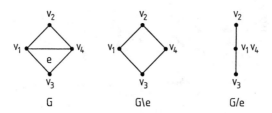

Figure 6.6

Now take any λ-coloring f of $G\backslash e$, $e = uv \in E(G)$. There are two cases: The vertices u and v receive different colors in f or the same color. In the first case, f is also a λ-coloring for G, while in the second case we can use f as a λ-coloring for G/e. Since any λ-coloring of G and G/e is obtained precisely once in this way, we have proved the following basic recursion for the function $p(G; \lambda)$:

(6.2) $$p(G; \lambda) = p(G\backslash e; \lambda) - p(G/e; \lambda).$$

Many consequences on the nature of $p(G; \lambda)$ can be derived from (6.2). For $n = 1$, we know that $p(K_1; \lambda)$ is a polynomial in λ of degree 1. Using induction on n, and within a given number of vertices on the number of edges, we infer from (6.2) that $p(G; \lambda)$ is a polynomial in λ of degree n with leading coefficient 1. As a matter of fact, it can be easily deduced from (6.2) that $p(G; \lambda) = \sum_{i=0}^{n} a_i \lambda^{n-i}$ is a polynomial whose coefficients a_i are precisely 0 for $i > n - t$, $t =$ number of connected components of G, with $a_0, a_1, \ldots, a_{n-t}$ having alternating signs.

Example 6.6. Let us again consider the graph of example 6.4. We write the recursion relation in obvious symbolic notation, designating each time the edge e.

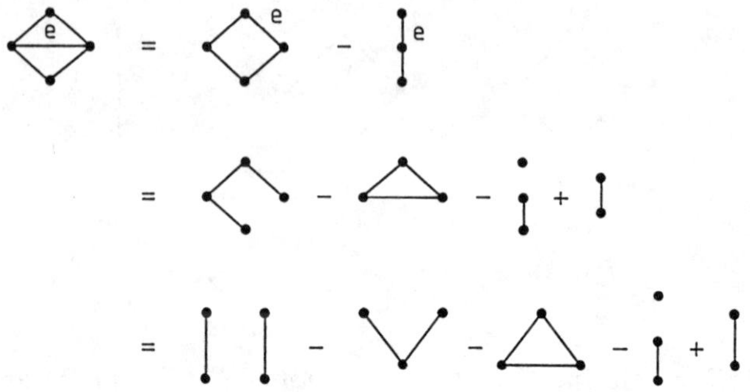

Figure 6.7

The chromatic polynomials of the last 5 graphs are trivial and we obtain

$$
\begin{aligned}
p(G;\lambda) &= \lambda^2(\lambda-1)^2 - \lambda(\lambda-1)^2 - \lambda(\lambda-1)(\lambda-2) - \lambda^2(\lambda-1) + \\
&\quad \lambda(\lambda-1) \\
&= \lambda(\lambda-1)(\lambda-2)^2.
\end{aligned}
$$

Thus, G has 6 colorings with 3 colors and 48 colorings with 4 colors.

Now what is the connection of the chromatic polynomial to our parameter $a(G)$? We are going to show that $a(G) = (-1)^n p(G;-1)$ where n is the number of vertices of G. To prove this we set $a(G) = 1$ if G has empty edge-set and verify then that the numbers $a(G)$ satisfy precisely the recursion (6.2) for $(-1)^n p(G;-1)$.

Setting $\lambda = -1$ in (6.2) yields

$$(-1)^n p(G;-1) = (-1)^n p(G\backslash e;-1) + (-1)^{n-1} p(G/e;-1).$$

Hence we have to prove

(6.3) $a(G) = a(G\backslash e) + a(G/e).$

Consider an arbitrary acyclic orientation $\mathcal{O}$ of $G\backslash e$, $e = uv$. There is always one direction $u \longrightarrow v$ or $v \longrightarrow u$ such that $\mathcal{O}$ can be extended to an acyclic orientation of G. Indeed, if both directions were forbidden, then we would have a directed path in $\overrightarrow{G\backslash e}$ from u to v and one from v to u which would yield a directed cycle in $\overrightarrow{G\backslash e}$. Hence those orientations which permit exactly one direction on e result in different orientations of G by assigning the proper direction to e. Now suppose tht $\mathcal{O}$ allows both directions. Those orientations have been counted only once in $\vec{G}$ so far. But now it is clear that $\mathcal{O}$ induces also an orientation on G/e by noting that in this case no directed paths exist from u to v nor from v to u in $G\backslash e$. In particular, this implies that any two edges uw, vw must receive the same orientation in $G\backslash e$ and thus can be safely identified. Since all orientations of G are obtained in this way exactly once, (6.3) follows immediately.

Proposition 6.5. *Let $a(G)$ be the number of acyclic orientations of a graph G, and $p(G; \lambda)$ its chromatic polynomial. Then*

$$a(G) = (-1)^n p(G; -1) = | \, p(G; -1) \, | \, .$$

Example 6.7. Returning once more to our graph G of example 6.5, we again compute $a(G) = | \, p(G; -1) \, | = 18$. For complete graphs K_n we deduce from $p(K_n; \lambda) = \lambda(\lambda - 1) \ldots (\lambda - n + 1)$ again the formula $a(K_n) = n!$.

The following result due to Linial [1983] completes our analysis by providing a lower bound for $a(G)$ in terms of the number of edges.

Proposition 6.6. *Let $\mathcal{G}(n, m)$ be the class of graphs on n vertices with m edges. Denote by k and ℓ the unique integers with $m = \binom{k}{2} + \ell$, $0 \le \ell < k$. Then*

$$a(G) \ge (\ell + 1)k! \; for \; G \in \mathcal{G}(n, m),$$

and the bound is attained for any n and $m \le \binom{n}{2}$.

Proof. Let $m = \binom{k}{2} + \ell \le \binom{n}{2}$, and consider the following graph $B_{n,m} \in \mathcal{G}(n, m)$. $B_{n,m}$ contains a complete subgraph A on k vertices. Of the remaining $n - k$ vertices, one is joined to ℓ vertices of A while the others are isolated. The chromatic polynomial is easily computed to $p(B_{n,m}; \lambda) = \lambda(\lambda - 1) \ldots (\lambda - k + 1)(\lambda - \ell)\lambda^{n-k-1}$, whence $a(B_{n,m}) = (\ell + 1)k!$ by **6.5**. The proof of the inequality is established by induction on n. For $n = 1$, there is nothing to prove. Let $G \in \mathcal{G}(n, m)$. We denote by $G - v$ the graph on $n - 1$

vertices where vertex v and all its incident edges have been removed. $G - v$ has thus $m - d$ edges where $d = d(v)$.

Suppose $\mathcal{O}$ is an acyclic orientation of $G - v$ and let $u_1, \ldots, u_d$ be the neighbors of v in G. Since $\mathcal{O}$ is acyclic we can order the u_h's in such away that $i < j$ whenever there is a directed path from u_i to u_j in $G - v$. Pick a number $s \in \{0, 1, \ldots, d\}$ and extend $\mathcal{O}$ to all of G by directing $u_i \longrightarrow v$ for $i \leq s$ and $v \longrightarrow u_i$ for $s < i$. Clearly, this creates no directed cycle in G and we conclude

$$(6.4) \qquad\qquad a(G) \geq (d+1)a(G-v), \quad d = d(v).$$

If $k = n$, then $\ell = 0$ and $m = \binom{n}{2}$, i.e. G is complete. In this case our claim is true by example 6.7. If $k \leq n - 1$, then $\frac{nk}{2} \geq \frac{k(k+1)}{2} > m$ by the choice of k, and we infer from **3.1** that the average degree $\overline{d} = \frac{2m}{n}$ in G satisfies $\overline{d} < k$. Hence there exists a vertex v of degree $d \leq k - 1$. Now we proceed by induction.

Case 1. $d \leq \ell$. The graph $G - v$ has $m - d = \binom{k}{2} + (\ell - d)$ edges. By (6.4) and induction we infer

$$a(G) \geq (d+1)a(G-v) \geq (d+1)(\ell - d + 1)k!.$$

Since $1, \ell + 1$ and $d + 1, \ell - d + 1$ both sum to $\ell + 2$ with $1 \leq d + 1$, $\ell - d + 1 \leq \ell + 1$, we have $(d+1)(\ell - d + 1)k! \geq (\ell + 1)k!$.

Case 2. $\ell < d$. The graph $G - v$ has $m - d = \binom{k-1}{2} + (k - 1 + \ell - d)$ edges, and we obtain as before

$$a(G) \geq (d+1)a(G-v) \geq (d+1)(k + \ell - d)(k-1)!.$$

Since $\ell + 1, k$ and $d + 1, k + \ell - d$ both sum to $\ell + k + 1$ with $\ell + 1 \leq d+1, k+\ell-d \leq k$, we infer $(d+1)(k+\ell-d)(k-1)! \geq (\ell+1)k(k-1)! = (\ell+1)k!$, thus completing the proof.   □

Let us use this last result to estimate $a(G)$ via the number m of edges. From $\binom{k}{2} \leq m < \binom{k+1}{2}$ one readily deduces $k = \lfloor \sqrt{2m} \rfloor$ or $k = \lceil \sqrt{2m} \rceil$. Using **6.1** and $a(G) = c(G)$ the following result is established.

Corollary 6.7. *Let G be a graph with m edges. Then*

$$C(G) \geq \log_2 \lfloor \sqrt{2m} \rfloor! \sim \sqrt{\frac{m}{2}} \log_2 m + \sqrt{\frac{m}{2}}.$$

We have seen that for $G = K_n$ this lower bound is asymptotically the correct answer for $C(G)$. Whether this is also true for arbitrary graphs with m edges is a very interesting and unsolved problem.

Note that there is a natural *identification problem* corresponding to the recognition question just discussed. Take a graph G and suppose we know that there is an unknown acyclic orientation $\mathcal{O}^*$ imposed on G. What is the minimum number of queries necessary to determine $\mathcal{O}^*$ when the tests ask for the direction of individual edges $uv \in E(G)$? For complete graphs this corresponds precisely to the general sorting problem. For arbitrary graphs we have again the lower bound $\lceil \log_2 a(G) \rceil$. In fact, it is easy to see that the two costs of the recognition and the identification problem are the same for any graph G (see exercise 6.3.7). Thus coloring problems or orientation identification problems provide a natural generalization of sorting questions.

Example 6.8. The maximum problem for ordered sets rephrased in the language of graphs calls for determining the unique vertex v which has all incident edges directed towards it. In general, we call a vertex v a *sink* of the directed graph $\vec{G}$ if all incident edges lead into v. Now suppose there is an unknown acyclic orientation $\mathcal{O}^*$ on G. Determine a sink (there is at least one since $\mathcal{O}^*$ is acyclic) with as few questions as possible! Let us denote by $Max(G)$ the worst-case cost of this problem, where we may obviously assume G to be connected. It is easy to see that $n - 1$ tests will always suffice (exercise 6.3.8). If G contains an edge e whose removal splits G into two non-trivial components, then we have $Max(G) \leq n - 2$ by testing e first. But even if G contains no such edge, $Max(G)$ may be less than $n - 1$. Figure 6.8 shows the smallest such example.

Figure 6.8

Starting with edge e, a sink is readily located with 3 more queries.

Exercises 6.3.

1. Verify that to decide whether n given reals are distinct we need to sort the n numbers in the worst case.

2*. Let $G(V, E)$ be a graph with $E \neq \emptyset$. Show that G has chromatic number 2 iff G contains no cycle of odd length.

3. Let $p(G; \lambda) = \sum_{i=0}^{n} a_i \lambda^{n-i}$ be the chromatic polynomial of G. Show: i) $a_0 = 1$, $a_1 = -|E|$, ii) $a_i = 0$ for $i > n - t$, where t is the number of connected components of G, iii) $a_0, a_1, \ldots, a_{n-t}$ are all $\neq 0$ with alternating sign.

4*. Compute the chromatic polynomial and $a(K_{m,n})$ for the complete bipartite graphs $K_{m,n}$.

5. Use recursion (6.3) to show $a(G) \leq \prod_{u \in V} \max(2, d(u))$ for any graph G, where $d(u)$ is the degree of u. (Linial)

6. Generalize **6.5**: Let $p(G; \lambda)$ be the chromatic polynomial of G. Then $|p(G; -r)|$ equals the number of pairs $(f, \mathcal{O})$ where $f : V \longrightarrow \{1, \ldots, r\}$ and $\mathcal{O}$ is an acyclic orientation such that $u \xrightarrow{\mathcal{O}} v$ implies $f(u) \leq f(v)$.

7*. Show that the coloring recognition problem of G and the orientation identification problem have the same worst-case cost.

8*. Prove that $Max(G) \leq n - 1$ for any graph G, n=number of vertices.

9. Show that $Max(T) \leq n - 2$ for any tree on n vertices except for the star when $Max(T) = n - 1$.

10*. Let P_n and C_n be the path and cycle on n vertices, respectively. Verify $Max(P_n) = \lceil \log_2 n \rceil$, $Max(C_n) = n - 1$.

6.4 Longest Increasing Subsequences

In our final topic we return once more to sorting questions. Suppose we are given a sequence $x_1, \ldots, x_n$ of distinct elements which are ordered according to an unknown linear ordering. We say that $x_{i_1}, x_{i_2}, \ldots, x_{i_k}$ is an *increasing subsequence of length* k if $i_1 < i_2 < \ldots < i_k$, and $x_{i_1} < x_{i_2} < \ldots < x_{i_k}$ in the linear ordering. In the present situation we are not required to fully sort the given sequence, instead we are only asked to determine the length L of a *longest* increasing subsequence, i.e. $L = \max\{k : 1 \le i_1 < \ldots < i_k \le n, x_{i_1} < \ldots < x_{i_k}\}$. As in previous chapters the tests at our disposal are comparisons $x_i : x_j$ between individual elements. Since L may be any number between 1 and n, our information-theoretic bound yields $C(n) \ge \lceil \log_2 n \rceil$, where $C(n)$ is the worst-case cost of our problem.

Example 6.9. Consider $n = 3$ where we take a, b, c as our given sequence. The following decision tree shows that $C(3) = 2$.

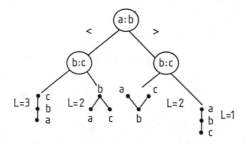

Figure 6.9

Notice that the leaves correspond to posets determined by the previous outcomes. For an algorithm to be successful, all linear extensions associated with a leaf-poset must define the same value L. Hence our task consists in partitioning the $n!$ linear orderings as economically as possible into sets with the same value of L within each set. Since there is only one linear ordering with $L = n$, namely $x_1 < x_2 < \ldots < x_n$, and only one with $L = 1$, $x_n < x_{n-1} < \ldots < x_1$, we conclude that these orderings must constitute leaves of any successful decision tree. As it takes at least $n - 1$ comparisons to establish the outcome $x_1 < x_2 < \ldots < x_n$ with certainty, we obtain the trivial bound $C(n) \ge n - 1$. For $n = 3$ this is exact, but already for $n = 4$ it is easily seen that 3 tests do not suffice (see exercises 6.4.4-6). However, 4 comparisons will do as the following figure demonstrates. The given sequence is a, b, c, d.

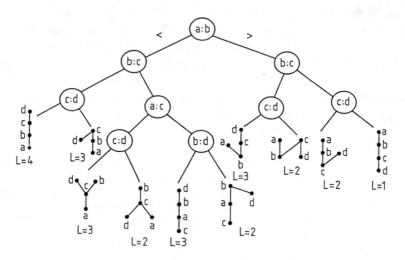

Figure 6.10

Exact values of $C(n)$ seem to be extremely hard to come by, so we content ourselves with asymptotic values. For this, we need the widely used O-notation. Let $f(n)$ and $g(n)$ be functions on the set $I\!N$ of natural numbers. We write $f(n) = O(g(n))$ if and only if $\mid \frac{f(n)}{g(n)} \mid \leq C$ for all $n \geq n_0$ and some constant C. In other words, $f(n)$ grows approximately as fast as $g(n)$ when n goes to infinity. We set $f(n) \sim g(n)$ if $\lim_{n \to \infty} \frac{f(n)}{g(n)} = 1$. As an example, it follows from (4.1) that the cost $S(n)$ of sorting n elements is bounded above by $n \log_2 n + O(n)$. Since we certainly know L once we have completely sorted the given sequence, $n \log_2 n + O(n)$ is also an upper bound for the cost $C(n)$. The following analysis due to Fredman [1979] demonstrates we can actually lower this bound in our present situation.

To the given sequence $x_1, \ldots, x_n$ we associate a table $T(1), T(2), \ldots$ as follows. At the start $T(1) = x_1$ with all other positions of the table being empty. Suppose we are processing x_j where $T(1), \ldots, T(m)$ are the current non-empty positions of the table. We compare the content of $T(m)$ with x_j. If $T(m) < x_j$, then we set $T(m + 1) = x_j$ keeping the other positions unchanged, and go on to x_{j+1}. If $T(m) > x_j$, then we find the least k such that $x_j < T(k)$, replace the content of $T(k)$ by x_j, and proceed to x_{j+1}. The reader may easily verify by induction that at each stage, $T(k)$ contains the smallest (already processed) x_i which is the last term of an increasing subsequence of length k. If follows, in particular, that at each stage

$T(1) < T(2) < \ldots < T(m)$, whence we can insert x_j into its proper place using binary insertion. At the end, our analysis implies that the number of non-empty positions in our table is precisely L.

Example 6.10. Consider the sequence 3 4 1 8 6 5 2 9 7 in their natural ordering. Our algorithm runs as follows: $3 \longrightarrow 3\ 4 \longrightarrow 1\ 4 \longrightarrow 1\ 4\ 8 \longrightarrow 1$ $4\ 6 \longrightarrow 1\ 4\ 5 \longrightarrow 1\ 2\ 5 \longrightarrow 1\ 2\ 5\ 9 \longrightarrow 1\ 2\ 5\ 7$, hence $L = 4$. Note that 1 2 5 7 is not a subsequence, but there must be an increasing subsequence of length 4 ending in 7, e.g. 3 4 6 7.

Let us now count the number of comparisons used by this method. Assume that m positions of the table are non-empty when x_j is processed. If $T(m) < x_j$, then a new position $T(m+1)$ is filled. If $T(m) > x_j$, then it takes at most $\lceil \log_2 m \rceil$ further comparisons to put x_j into its proper place. Since a new position is created $L - 1$ times (after the initial position $T(1) = x_1$) we conclude that at most

$$(6.5) \qquad (n - L)\lceil \log_2 L \rceil + (n - 1) = (n - L)\log_2 L + O(n)$$

comparisons are required when L is the final length. By elementary analysis it follows that the worst value for L is approximately $\frac{n}{\log_2 n}$. Hence we obtain the following upper bound for $C(n)$

$$C(n) \leq n \log_2 n - n \log_2 \log_2 n + O(n).$$

We turn to lower bounds for $C(n)$. The idea is the following: We know that any leaf of a decision tree corresponds to a poset whose linear extensions all have the same value of L, say $L = k$. We are going to show that there are k^{n-2k} linear orderings with $L = k$ which must correspond to *different* leaves of any valid decision tree, where k may be any number $\leq \frac{n}{2}$. Hence any such tree must have at least k^{n-2k} leaves, implying $C(n) \geq (n - 2k)\log_2 k$. Choosing $k = \lfloor \frac{n}{\log_2 n} \rfloor$ we thus obtain

$$
\begin{aligned}
C(n) &\geq \left(n - 2\frac{n}{\log_2 n} \right)(\log_2 n - \log_2 \log_2 n) - (n - 2k) \\
&= n \log_2 n - n \log_2 \log_2 n + O(n).
\end{aligned}
$$

To find these k^{n-2k} orderings we need a combinatorial lemma which is interesting in its own right.

Lemma 6.8. *Let P be a poset on $\{x_1,\ldots,x_n\}$. The maximum value of L (with respect to the numbering $x_1,\ldots,x_n$) of any linear extension of P equals the minimal number of decreasing chains (again with respect to $x_1,\ldots,x_n$) into which P can be decomposed.*

Before proving the lemma let us look at an example. Consider the poset P of figure 6.11 where we set $x_i = i$.

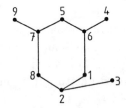

Figure 6.11

We can partition P into 5 decreasing chains $\{2 < 1\}$, $\{3\}$, $\{6 < 4\}$, $\{8 < 7 < 5\}$, $\{9\}$; hence $L \leq 5$ by the Lemma. The extension $\{2 < 1 < 3 < 8 < 7 < 6 < 4 < 5 < 9\}$ shows that indeed $L = 5$.

Proof of the Lemma. One half of the assertion is trivial. If P can be partitioned into k decreasing chains, then in any linear extension of P, L cannot be greater than k since any increasing subsequence can pick only one element from each chain. Hence max $\leq$ min certainly holds in our statement. To prove equality, we make use of a theorem of Dilworth (see exercise 4.2.1): The largest size of an antichain in P equals the minimal number of chains into which P can be decomposed. Consider now the following poset Q on $\{x_1,\ldots,x_n\}$. We set $x_i \underset{Q}{\leq} x_j$ iff $x_i \underset{P}{\leq} x_j$ and $j \leq i$. Clearly, Q is a sub-poset of P, and chains in Q correspond precisely to *decreasing* chains in P. Hence, if k is the minimal number of decreasing chains into which P can be partitioned, then k is the minimal number of chains into which Q can be partitioned (called the *width* of Q in chapter 4). By Dilworth's theorem, there exist k pairwise unrelated elements in Q, say $x_{i_1},\ldots,x_{i_k}$ with $i_1 < \ldots < i_k$. If $i_r < i_s$, then because x_{i_r} and x_{i_s} are unrelated in Q, either $x_{i_r} < x_{i_s}$ in P or x_{i_r}, x_{i_s} are unrelated in P. It follows that any linear extension of P which stipulates $x_{i_1} < x_{i_2} < \ldots < x_{i_k}$ (which is possible by what we have just noted) satisfies $L \geq k$. Hence we also have max $\geq$ min, and the lemma is proved. $\square$

Let us return to the proof of the lower bound for $C(n)$. We are given $x_1, \ldots, x_n$ and a fixed $k \leq \frac{n}{2}$. We define the following set E of linear extensions. Each extension in E partitions $\{x_1, \ldots, x_n\}$ into k decreasing subsequences $S_1, \ldots, S_k$ such that $x_i, x_{n-k+i} \in S_i$, $i = 1, \ldots, k$, and each element in S_i is below each element in S_{i+1}, $i = 1, \ldots, k-1$. Thus for an extension in E we have

$$x_{n-k+1} < x_1 < x_{n-k+2} < x_2 < \ldots < x_n < x_k.$$

A particular extension in E is therefore completely determined by stating to which set S_i an element x_j, $k < j \leq n-k$, belongs. The elements x_j belonging to S_i must then be uniquely placed such that S_i is a decreasing subsequence. We conclude $| E |= k^{n-2k}$.

As an example, consider $n = 6$, $k = 2$. The four extensions in E are

$$x_5 < x_1 < x_6 < x_4 < x_3 < x_2 \qquad x_5 < x_4 < x_1 < x_6 < x_3 < x_2$$
$$x_5 < x_3 < x_1 < x_6 < x_4 < x_2 \qquad x_5 < x_4 < x_3 < x_1 < x_6 < x_2.$$

By our lemma, $L = k$ for any such extension. Now comes the crucial observation. Any extension in E can be decomposed in only *one* way into k decreasing subsequences, namely the sets $S_1, \ldots, S_k$ we started from. Indeed, partitioning the subset $\{x_1, \ldots, x_k, x_{n-k+1}, \ldots, x_n\}$ into k decreasing subsequences forces us to use $\{x_{n-k+1} < x_1\}, \{x_{n-k+2} < x_2\}, \ldots, \{x_n < x_k\}$, and this, in turn, determines the placement of the remaining elements. (See exercise 6.4.4 for a generalization of this idea.)

Now let T be a decision tree which computes L. It remains to prove that all extensions in E must be associated with different leaves of T. Let Q be an extension in E belonging to the leaf v. Since $L = k$ for Q, any other extension Q' associated with v must also satisfy $L = k$. By our lemma, Q' can be decomposed into k decreasing subsequences. Since there is only such partitioning for the extensions in E we conclude that $Q' \in E$ implies in fact $Q' = Q$, and our proof is complete.

Theorem 6.9. *The worst-case cost $C(n)$ for computing the length of a longest increasing subsequence in a sequence of n elements is asymptotically*

$$C(n) = n \log_2 n - n \log_2 \log_2 n + O(n).$$

Having come this far in the book, the reader will not be surprised to learn that little is known about the average cost $\overline{C}(n)$. So let us close this book of problems with this challenging question: What is the growth of $\overline{C}(n)$?

Exercises 6.4.

1. Prove the validity of the statements concerning the table $T(1), \ldots$ used in the algorithm for determining the length L of a largest increasing subsequence. In particular, show that at any stage, $T(k)$ contains the smallest element already processed which is the last term of an increasing subsequence of length k. Infer from this that $T(1) < T(2) < T(3) < \ldots$ at any stage of the algorithm.

2*. Determine the number of permutations of $\{1, \ldots, n\}$ which have a longest subsequence of length $n - 1$.

3. Verify that (6.5) assumes its maximum value at roughly $\frac{n}{\log_2 n}$.

4*. Suppose $\pi = i_1 \ldots i_n$ is a permutation of $\{1, \ldots, n\}$ which splits into a minimal number of k consecutive decreasing subsequences, $\pi = Z_1 \mid Z_2 \mid \ldots \mid Z_k$, all Z_i decreasing. Call π *uniquely recoverable* if there is no other way to decompose π into k decreasing subsequences. The extensions used in the proof of **6.9** are of this form as is e.g. $31 \mid 542 \mid 6 \mid 7$. Let f_i, ℓ_i be the first and last number in the block Z_i where $f_i = \ell_i$ may happen. Show that π is uniquely recoverable iff $f_1 < f_2 < \ldots < f_k$ and $\ell_1 < \ell_2 < \ldots < \ell_k$.

5*. Let $R_k(n)$ be the number of uniquely recoverable permutations with k blocks. Prove: $R_1(n) = 1$, $R_2(n) = 2^{n-2}$ $(n \geq 2)$, $R_3(n) = \frac{3^{n-2} + 2n - 5}{4}$ $(n \geq 3)$, $R_{n-1}(n) = n - 1$, $R_n(n) = 1$.

6. Infer from the previous exercise that $C(4) = 4$. What is $C(5)$?

7*. Show $C(n) \leq S(n-k) + (2k-1)$, where $S(n)$ is the sorting complexity on n elements, $1 \leq k \leq n - 1$.

8. Show that $C(n) = \min_{1 \leq k \leq n-1} (S(n-k) + (2k-1))$ for $n \leq 6$. What about $n = 7$ or 8?

Problems

1. It follows from exercise 6.2.7 that **6.4** can provide no better bound than $O(n \log_2 s)$ when the polyhedron S in $\mathbb{R}^n$ is defined by s essential

inequalities. Is $C(S) = O(n \log_2 s)$ the correct answer? Note that this is true for $n = 2$. (6.2)

2. Compute $C(Q_n)$ for the n-dimensional cube. (6.2)

3. Find algorithms which asymptotically achieve the lower bound of **6.7** or prove that they do not exist. (6.3)

4. Find good estimates for $Max(G)$ when G is an arbitrary graph. (6.3)

5. Investigate the maximum value of $a(G)$ for graphs G with n vertices and m edges. (6.3)

6. Estimate the number of permutations which have a longest subsequence of length L. (6.4)

7. Compute the number $R_k(n)$ of uniquely recoverable permutations with k blocks (see exercise 6.4.5). (6.4)

8. Does the table method of proof for the upper bound in **6.9** give the correct value of $C(n)$ for infinitely many n? (6.4)

9. What is the growth of the average cost $\overline{C}(n)$? (6.4)

Notes and References

Dobkin-Lipton [1979] were probably the first to consider the point-location problem in depth. Since then algorithmic geometry has witnessed an astounding growth. We have just barely touched upon this fascinating subject. The interested reader may consult the books by Preparata-Shamos [1985] and Edelsbrunner [1987] for a wealth of information. Saks [1985] is a beautiful survey of most of the material treated in this chapter.

Aigner M. * [1987], Graph Theory, a Development From the 4-Color Problem. BCS Associates, Moscow. (Translation of the German book: Graphentheorie, eine Entwicklung aus dem 4-Farben Problem, Teubner, Stuttgart. 1983.)

Dilworth R.P. [1950], A decomposition theorem for partially ordered sets. Annals Math. 51, 161-166.

Dobkin D., Lipton R.J. [1974], On some generalizations of binary search. In: ACM Symposium on the Theory of Computing.

Dobkin D., Lipton R.J. [1979], On the complexity of computations under varying sets of primitives. J. Computer Systems Sci. 18, 86-91.

Edelsbrunner H. * [1987], Algorithms in Combinatorial Geometry. Springer-Verlag, Berlin.

Fredman M. [1979], On computing the length of the longest increasing subsequence. Discrete Math. 11, 29-35.

Grünbaum B. * [1967], Convex Polytopes. Wiley, London.

Knuth D. [1970], Permutations, matrices and generalized Young Tableaux. Pac. J. Math. 34, 709-727.

Linial N. [1983], Legal colorings of graphs. In: Proc. 24th Symposium on Foundations of Computer Science, 470-472.

Manber U., Tompa M. [1984]. The effect of number of Hamiltonian paths on the complexity of a vertex coloring problem. In: Proc. 22nd Symposium on Foundations of Computer Science, Nashville, 220-227.

Preparata F.P., Shamos M.I. * [1985], Computational Geometry, an Introduction. Springer-Verlag, New York.

Saks M. [1985], The information theoretic bound for problems on ordered sets and graphs. In: Graphs and Order, Reidel, 137-168.

Spira P.M. [1972], Complete linear proofs of systems of linear inequalities. J. Computer Systems Sci. 6, 205-216.

Stanley R.P. [1973],Acyclic orientations of graphs. Discrete Math. 5, 171-178.

Yao A.C. [1975], On the complexity of comparison problems using linear functions. In: Proc. 16th IEEE Symposium on Switching and Automata Theory, 85-99.

Yao A.C., Rivest R.L. [1980], On the polyhedral decision problem. SIAM J. Computing 9, 343-347.

Answers to Recommended Exercises

Section 1.1

1. Suppose $n = 3^k$. Weigh 3^{k-1} coins against 3^{k-1} others. After the weighing, it is known in which of the three subsets (each containing 3^{k-1} coins) the fake coin lies. Now use induction.

3. Number the coins 1, 2, 3, 4. The sequences of comparisons $1 : 2$, $3 : 4$, $\max(1,2) : \max(3,4), \min(1,2) : \min(3,4)$, $\min(\max(1,2), \max(3,4)) : \max(\min(1,2), \min(3,4))$ will do.

5. No. Let's show it for general n. Suppose ℓ sets $A_1, \ldots, A_\ell \subseteq S$, $\ell \leq n - 1$, suffice to isolate the sick. If there is $x \in S - \cup A_i$, then the status of x is not determined. If $S = \cup A_i$, then there exists y with $A_i \neq \{y\}$ for all i (since $\ell \leq n - 1$). Hence if the answer to all tests is "yes", then both outcomes "all are sick" and "all but y are sick" are possible, contradiction.

8. If $m = 1$, then $n - 1 = m + n - 2$ questions are needed. Now show by induction that $m + n - 2$ is the answer for arbitrary m and n.

Section 1.2

3. Let $f(n)$ be the worst-case cost for $(S, \mathfrak{A}_{\leq 2})$, $|S| = n \geq 2$. Then $f(2) = 1$, $f(3) = 2$ and clearly $f(n) \geq f(n-1)$. Since the first test-set may contain one or two elements, we have $f(n) = 1 + \min\{\max(f(n-1), 0), \max(f(n-2), 1)\} = 1 + f(n-2)$ for $n \geq 4$. It follows that

333

$L(S, \mathfrak{A}_{\leq 2}) = 2 + f(3) = 4$ for $|S| = 7$. By an analogous argument, $\overline{L}(S, \mathfrak{A}_{\leq 2}) = 3$.

4. $S = \{1, 2, \ldots, 7\}$. The four sets $A_1 = \{1, 2\}$, $A_2 = \{2, 3\}$, $A_3 = \{4, 5\}$, $A_4 = \{5, 6\}$ prove $L_{pre}(S, \mathfrak{A}_{\leq 2}) = 4$.

7. Suppose the left subtree at the root has i end-nodes. We can pick the labels in $\binom{n}{i}$ ways. We may pair all labelings of the two subtrees. By summing over all i we obtain $2t_n = \sum_{i=0}^{n} \binom{n}{i} t_i t_{n-i}$ $(n \geq 2)$ where the factor 2 results from interchanging the two subtrees. With $t_0 = 0$, $t_1 = 1$, we conclude for the generating function $y = y(x) = \sum_{n \geq 0} \frac{t_n}{n!} x^n$ that $2y = y^2 + 2x$. Differentiating we obtain $y'(1 - y) = 1$ or $y'(1 - 2x) = 1 - y$. Taking the $(n-1)$-st derivative of both sides yields $(1 - 2x)y^{(n)} - 2(n-1)y^{(n-1)} = -y^{(n-1)}$ and the result is obtained by setting $x = 0$.

Section 1.3

3. Write $w \in C$ as $w = w'iw''$. By regularity there exists $v \in C$ with $v = w'v''$ where v'' is initial segment of w'' or w'' is initial segment of v''. Hence v is prefix of $w - i$ or $w - i$ is prefix of v. The converse is just as easy. The code $C = \{00, 01, 1, 2, \ldots, q - 1\}$ is not regular for $q \geq 3$, but loses the prefix property whenever a letter is removed.

6. Let C be an $(\overline{L})$-optimal code and $v = u0$, $w = u1$ be codewords of maximal length ℓ. If $x \in C$ has $\ell(x) = m \leq \ell - 2$, then by replacing x by u, and v, w by $x0, x1$, respectively, we obtain a prefix code C' with $\overline{L}(C') < \overline{L}(C)$.

8. Let $C = \kappa(S)$ be a prefix code. Suppose $v_1 v_2 \ldots v_s = w_1 w_2 \ldots w_t$ with $v_i, w_j \in C$, then by the prefix property $v_1 = w_1$. Deleting $v_1 = w_1$, we conclude $v_2 = w_2$, and finally $v_s = w_s$, $s = t$. The last property clearly holds. Conversely, let v be a prefix of w, $v \neq w \in C$. If the last property holds, then $w = vv'$, $v' \in C^*$, i.e. $v' = v_1 \ldots v_s$, $v_i \in C$. Hence C is not uniquely decodable. Note that $C = \{0, 01\}$ is not a prefix code, but uniquely decodable.

Section 1.4

1. For $n = 1$, we have $e(T) = i(T) = 0$. Replace an end-configuration as in the proof of **1.1** and use induction.

4. The information-theoretic bound is $\lceil \log_2 mn \rceil = \lceil \log_2 m + \log_2 n \rceil$. Using Theorem 1.2 on the rows and then on the columns, we can determine X^* with $\lceil \log_2 m \rceil + \lceil \log_2 n \rceil \leq \lceil \log_2 mn \rceil + 1$ tests.

6. Weigh in the first test two sets containing $\lfloor \frac{n}{3} \rfloor$ coins, and proceed by induction.

Section 1.5

1. Follows from Lemma 1.5.

3. Set $\lfloor \log_2 n \rfloor = k$. Then

$$\overline{L} = (k+2) + \begin{cases} \binom{n+1}{2}(3.2^{2k-3} - 3.2^{k-2}(2n+1)) & 2^k \leq n < 3.2^{k-1} \\ \binom{n+1}{2}(3.2^{2k-1} - 3.2^{k-1}(2n+1)) & 3.2^{k-1} \leq n < 2^{k+1}. \end{cases}$$

5. By deleting an end-node of length $\ell = \lceil \log_q n \rceil$ in a complete tree $T \in \mathcal{T}(n+1, q)$, we obtain $h(n,q) \leq \frac{1}{n}(e(n+1,q) - \ell) = h(n+1,q) - \frac{1}{n}(\ell - h(n+1,q)) \leq h(n+1,q)$. For $q = 2$, we make a replacement of an end-configuration as in the proof of **1.1.** and obtain $h(n+1,2) \geq h(n,2) + \frac{1}{n} + \frac{1}{n}(\ell - h(n+1,2))$. Hence equality is attained when $n + 1 = 2^k$ for some k.

7. It follows from $p_{n-1} + p_n \geq p_1$ that we may assume $\ell_n - \ell_1 \leq 1$ in an optimal tree T, i.e. T is complete.

9. Let us first prove the following result: Suppose $x_1, \ldots, x_n, y_1, \ldots, y_n \in \mathbb{R}^+$ with $\sum y_i = 1$. Then $\sum y_i \log_a x_i \leq \log_a(\sum y_i x_i)$. To see this, set $s_i = \frac{y_i x_i}{\sum y_i x_i}$ and apply **1.5**. Note that this result is equivalent to $\prod x_i^{y_i} \leq \sum y_i x_i$ whence by setting $y_i = \frac{1}{n}$ for all i, we obtain the inequality of the geometric and arithmetic mean. Suppose $\underline{q} = M\underline{p}$ where M is doubly-stochastic. Since all rows of M sum to 1,

the vector $(\sum_i m_{ij}q_i)_{j=1}^n$ is a distribution. Hence by exercise 1 and the result just proved, we obtain $H(\underline{p}) \leq -\sum_j p_j \log_2(\sum_i m_{ij}q_i) \leq$

$$-\sum_j p_j \sum_i m_{ij} \log_2 q_i = -\sum_i (\sum_j m_{ij}p_j) \log_2 q_i = H(\underline{q}).$$

10. Consider the distribution $p_1 = p_2 = \frac{1}{4} + \varepsilon$, $p_3 = p_4 = \frac{1}{4} - \varepsilon$ with $0 < \varepsilon \leq \frac{1}{12}$, $q = 2$.

Section 1.6

2. Let $L = \max \ell_i$. By assumption, $q \sum q^{L-\ell_i} \leq q^L$. Consider the complete (q^L, q)-tree. We construct C (and its corresponding decision tree) inductively from 1 to n. Our induction hypothesis is: There exists an alphabetic code C_i with word lengths $\ell_1, \ldots, \ell_i$ such that the end-nodes of T which are below the codewords $c_1, \ldots, c_i$ appear among the left-most $q \sum_{j=1}^{i} q^{L-\ell_j}$ end-nodes. As start, we take $c_1 = (0, \ldots, 0)$ of length ℓ_1. Since $q \sum_{j=1}^{i-1} q^{L-\ell_j} \leq q^L - q \cdot q^{L-\ell_i}$, the right-most $q \cdot q^{L-\ell_i}$ end-nodes are still free. The induction step from C_i to C_{i+1} is now easily completed.

5. Let $\underline{p}$ be any distribution, and consider a complete tree $T \in \mathcal{T}(n, 2)$. By example 1.12, T has a leaves on level S_{L-1} and $n - a$ leaves on level S_L, $L = \lceil \log_2 n \rceil$. Suppose n is even, then a is even. Set $s_k = p_{2k-1} + p_{2k}$ $(k = 1, \ldots, \frac{n}{2})$ and pick $K \subseteq \{1, \ldots, \frac{n}{2}\}$ with $|K| = \frac{a}{2}$ such that $s_k \geq s_\ell$ for all $k \in K$, $\ell \notin K$. Choose T in such a way that precisely the end-nodes with indices $2\ell - 1, 2\ell$ $(\ell \notin K)$ have length L. Since $\sum_{k \in K} s_k \geq \frac{a}{2}(\frac{n}{2})^{-1}$ (see the proof of 1.10), $\overline{L}(n, \mathcal{F}_{mon}, \underline{p}) \leq \overline{L}(T; \underline{p}) = \lceil \log_2 n \rceil - \sum_{k \in K} s_k \leq \lceil \log_2 n \rceil - \frac{a}{2}(\frac{n}{2})^{-1}$. The case when n is odd is settled in an analogous way. If $\underline{p}^*$ is the distribution with $p_k^* = 0$ $(k$ odd$)$, $p_k^* = \lfloor \frac{n}{2} \rfloor^{-1}$ $(k$ even$)$, then $\overline{L}(T; \underline{p}^*) = \lceil \log_2 n \rceil - \lfloor \frac{a}{2} \rfloor \lfloor \frac{n}{2} \rfloor^{-1}$ for any complete tree. Hence it remains to prove no non-complete tree can do better for $\underline{p}^*$, and this follows easily by induction.

6.

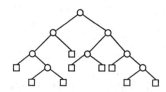

8. $\overline{L}(6;\underline{p}) = \frac{30}{12}$, $\overline{L}_{mon}(6;\underline{p}) = \frac{31}{12}$.

Section 1.7

2. We prove that for a bound of the kind mentioned, $a \geq 1$, $b \geq 2$, $c \geq 1$ must hold. Suppose $q_j = 0$ for all j, and $p_i = \frac{1}{n+1}$ for all i. By **1.7**, $\overline{DL}(n;p) \geq H(\underline{p}) = \log_2(n+1)$. Hence $aH(\underline{p}) + b \sum_{i=0}^{n} p_k = a\log_2(n+1) + b \geq \log_2(n+1)$, i.e. $a \geq 1 - \frac{b}{\log_2(n+1)}$. Since n can be any number, $a \geq 1$. The bounds $b \geq 2$, $c \geq 1$ are established by considering small examples.

4. Let $c = \overline{DL}(n;\underline{p})$ and $c' = \overline{DL}(n-1;\underline{p}')$ where $\underline{p}' = (p_0,\ldots,p_{n-1};q_1, \ldots, q_{n-1})$. If T is an optimal search tree for $\underline{p}$ and T' the tree obtained by the replacement mentioned, then $c' \leq \overline{DL}(T') \leq c - p_{n-1}$. On the other hand, $c \leq c' + p_{n-1}$ by the reverse replacement.

6. Take $n = 3$, $p_k = 0$ for all k, $q_1 = \frac{1}{2} + 2\varepsilon$, $q_2 = q_3 = \frac{1}{4} - \varepsilon$ with $0 < \varepsilon < \frac{1}{4}$. Then y_2 is the root of any balanced search tree. Hence the cost is $\frac{7}{4} + \varepsilon$. By **1.16**, however, $\overline{DL} = \frac{7}{4} - 3\varepsilon$.

7. Obviously, $\max_{\underline{p}} \overline{L}_{mon}(n+1,2;\underline{p}) \leq \sup_{\underline{p}} \overline{DL}(n;\underline{p})$. For $\underline{p} = (p_0,\ldots,q_n)$ define $\underline{p}^* = (p_0^*,\ldots,p_n^*)$ by $p_0^* = p_0$, $p_k^* = p_k + q_k$ $(1 \leq k \leq n)$. Let T be an optimal tree for $\underline{p}^*$, i.e. $\overline{L}(T) = \sum_{k=0}^{n} p_k^*\ell(x_k) = \overline{L}_{mon}(n + 1,2;\underline{p}^*)$. View T as binary search tree by filling in the y_k's in alphabetic fashion. Clearly, $\ell(y_k) + 1 \leq \ell(x_k)$ $(1 \leq k \leq n)$, hence $\overline{DL}(n;\underline{p}) \leq \overline{DL}(T) = \sum_{k=0}^{n} \ell(x_k)p_k + \sum_{k=1}^{n} (\ell(y_k) + 1)q_k \leq \sum_{k=0}^{n} \ell(x_k)p_k + \sum_{k=1}^{n} \ell(x_k)q_k = \sum_{k=1}^{n} \ell(x_k)p_k^* = \overline{L}_{mon}(n + 1,2;p^*)$.

8. Take $n = 3$, $\underline{p} = \frac{1}{24}(4, 0, 3, 10; 4, 3, 0)$. There is a unique min $-$ max tree with cost $\frac{45}{24}$ whereas $\overline{DL} = \frac{44}{24}$.

Section 1.8

2. In a sequential algorithm test row 1 and column 1 first. If "no", then the problem is reduced to a 4 $\times$ 2-grid which can be searched with $\log_2 4 + \log_2 2 = 3$ more tests. The "yes"-part is equally easy. Clearly $L_{pre}(5, 3) \leq \lceil \log_2 5 \rceil + \lceil \log_2 3 \rceil = 5$ since we may search rows and columns independently. A predetermined algorithm of length 4 can be viewed as a 4 $\times$ 8-matrix M over $\{0, 1\}$ with the columns indexed by $1_R, \ldots, 5_R; 1_L, 2_L, 3_L$. M is a successful search matrix iff all 15 unions $i_R \cup j_C$ are distinct, where we identify a column with a subset of $\{r_1, \ldots, r_4\}$ via the characteristic vector. If $|j_C| \geq 2$, say $r_1, r_2 \in j_C$, then $\{r_1, r_2\} \subseteq i_R \cup j_C$ for all i, which implies that all 5 sets $i_R \cap \{r_3, r_4\}$ must be distinct, which is plainly impossible. If $|j_C| \leq 1$ for $j = 1, 2, 3$, then a contradiction is readily derived by considering the element $r_k \notin \bigcup_{j=1}^{3} j_C$.

3. See Theorem **2.1**.

5. For odd n, consider $\underline{p}^*$ of exercise 1.7.7. For even n, a small change has to be made.

Section 1.9

1. If $|A| = k$, then the probability that $A = X^*$ is $p(A) = p^k(1 - p)^{n-k}$. Hence we obtain what is called the binomial distribution on 2^S. Element-for-element search yields $L \leq n$ and thus $L = n$ by **1.3**. By **1.6**, $\overline{L} \geq - \sum_{k=0}^{n} [\binom{n}{k} p^k(1 - p)^{n-k} \cdot \log_2 p^k(1 - p)^{n-k}]$ which is easily seen to be $nH(p)$.

2. The only alternative to element-for-element search is to test $S = \{a, b\}$ first. We receive $S \cap X^* = \emptyset$ with probability $(1 - p)^2$ and $S \cap X^* \neq \emptyset$ with probability $1 - (1 - p)^2$. In the first case we are finished, in the second case we test $a \in S$ and receive $X^* \cap \{a\} = \emptyset$ with probability $p(1 - p)$. If $X^* \cap \{a\} \neq \emptyset$, then test b. Hence with probability $1 - (1 - p)^2 - p(1 - p) = p$ we need 3 tests. Altogether, $\overline{L} = (1 - p)^2 + 2p(1 - p) + 3p = -p^2 + 3p + 1$ which is ≥ 2 for $p \geq \frac{3 - \sqrt{5}}{2}$.

5. Set $T = 2^{\mathfrak{A}}$ and define $\varphi : S \longrightarrow T$ by $\varphi x = \mathfrak{A}_x = \{A \in \mathfrak{A} : x \in A\}$. Since $\mathfrak{A}$ is completely separating we have $\mathfrak{A}_x \not\subseteq \mathfrak{A}_y$ for any x, y, i.e. $\{\mathfrak{A}_x : x \in S\}$ forms an antichain in the poset T. By a well-known theorem in combinatorics (see Aigner [1979], chapter VIII.3) the size of an antichain in 2^m is bounded above by $\binom{m}{\lceil m/2 \rceil}$.

6. For $n \leq 2k$, we have $\overline{L}(S, \mathfrak{A}_{\leq k}) = \overline{L}(n, 2)$, so assume $n > 2k$. Suppose the first test probes an i-set, $i \leq k$. The right subtree T' is then a complete $(i, 2)$-tree, and hence has length $\lceil \log_2 i \rceil$. Suppose $i < k$. Since $n - i > i$, the left subtree T'' has length $m \geq \lceil \log_2 i \rceil$. If i is not a power of 2, then we could move an end-node of T'' over to T' without increasing the external length. If $i = 2^j$, then $n - i > 2^j$ and thus $\lceil \log_2(n - i) \rceil \geq \lceil \log_2 i \rceil + 1$ and we can move an end-node from T'' to T'. Thus we may assume that T splits off k-sets until the "no"-subtree has $n - tk \leq 2k$ end-nodes from which point on we take a complete $(n - tk, 2)$-tree. Using **1.8** and writing $e(s) = e(s, 2)$, we obtain $\overline{L} = t + \frac{1}{n}[te(k) - k\binom{t}{2} + e(n - tk)]$ where $t = \lceil \frac{n}{k} \rceil - 2$. It is easily seen that $\overline{L} \leq \frac{n}{2k} + (\lceil \log_2 k \rceil + 1) + \frac{k}{n}(\lceil \log_2 k \rceil + \frac{3}{2})$, so for fixed k and $n \longrightarrow \infty$, $\overline{L} \leq \frac{n}{2k} + (\lceil \log_2 k \rceil + 1)$. Thus, $\overline{L}$ uses roughly half the number of tests as in the worst case.

8. Clearly, $f(1) = 0$, $f(2) = 2$, $f(3) = 5$. Let us slightly generalize our problem. We consider partial search matrices M consisting of a block of n columns and r blocks of 2 columns each such that any row of M contains at most two 1's and M satisfies the prefix property on the columns within each block. Let $g(n, r)$ be the minimal number of entries in such a matrix M. Thus $f(n) = g(n, 0)$, and we set $g(n, r) = \infty$ for $n < 0$ or $r < 0$. Looking at the 1st row we deduce $g(n, r) = n + g(n-2, 1) = (n+2r) + \min\{(g(n-2, r+1), g(n-1, r-1), g(n, r-2)\}$ (observe that $g(n, r)$ is monotone in n and r). Hence $f(n) = 2n + \min\{g(n-4, 2), g(n-3, 0)\} = 2n + \min\{g(n-4, 2), f(n-3)\}$. Now it is easily seen that $g(n-4, 2) \geq f(n-3)$, whence $f(n) = f(n-3) + 2n$. Solving this recursion yields $f(n) = \frac{n^2 + 3n - 3}{3}$ for $n \equiv 0 \pmod 3$, $f(n) = \frac{n^2 + 3n - 4}{3}$ for $n \equiv 1, 2 \pmod 3$.

Section 1.10

2. Suppose S_0 consists of k-sets. Player B uses the following strategy. He picks a set $C \in S_0$ and answer "yes" whenever an element of C is probed, and "no" otherwise. With this strategy player A cannot be certain about the outcome before he has tested all elements.

3. $T = \{a, b\}$, $S_0 = \{\{a\}, \{a, b\}\}$. A probes a first.

Section 2.1

2. Consider $L_{pre}(n)$, $n = 3^{L-1} + r$, $1 \le r \le 2.3^{L-1}$. M is a search matrix iff M is admissible and has the 0-property. Hence $L_{pre}(n) \le \lceil \log_3 n \rceil$ for $n \ne 3^L, 3^L - 2$ by **2.1**, i.e. $L_{pre}(n) \le \lceil \log_3(n+1) \rceil$ for $n \ne 3^L - 2$. In the latter case, a search matrix does not exist (**2.1**), whence $L_{pre}(n) = \lceil \log_3(n+1) \rceil + 1$ for $n = 3^L - 2$. It remains to show that $L(3^L - 2) = L$, $L \ge 2$, and this is easy by first weighing $A : B$ with $|A| = |B| = 3^{L-1}$.

5. Set $f_k(n) = L_{\le k}(S, W)$. For $n \le 3k$, there are no restrictions, hence $f_k(n) = \lceil \log_3 n \rceil$. For $n > 3k$, proceed as in the proof of **1.25**.

6. Set $g_k(n) = L_{pre, \le k}(S, W)$ and apply the argument of the previous exercise. In particular, for $k = 1$, $g_1(3) = 2$, $g_1(4) = 3$ by **2.3** and thus $g_1(n) = \frac{n-3}{2} + g_1(3) = \frac{n+1}{2}$ for odd n, and $g_1(n) = \frac{n-4}{2} + g_1(4) = \frac{n}{2} + 1$ for even n.

8. Let $L(S, W)$ and $\overline{L}(S, W)$ denote the respective costs. Clearly, $L(S, W) = \lceil \log_3 n \rceil$ by weighing $\lfloor \frac{n'}{3} \rfloor$ against $\lfloor \frac{n'}{3} \rfloor$ coins if n' is the current number of doubtful coins. The lower bound $\overline{L}$ in **2.2** cannot be achieved if $3^{\lceil \log_3 n \rceil} - n \equiv 3 \pmod 4$, in the other cases it is correct.

11. $L(n) = \lceil \log_{r+1} n \rceil$ is shown by testing r sets of size $\lfloor \frac{n}{r} \rfloor$ each, and applying induction. Consider $L_{pre}(n)$ and set $q = r + 1$. Suppose $q^{L-1} < n \le q^L$, and denote by B_L the full $L \times q^L$-matrix over $\{0, 1, \ldots, r\}$. B_L and $B_L - \{\underline{0}\}$ are search matrices for $n = q^L$ and $n = q^L - 1$, respectively. For $n \le q^L - 2$, the set of columns removed must contain at least one non-zero entry in some row, hence we must remove at least r columns. So, for $q^L - r + 1 \le n \le q^L - 2$ a search matrix with L rows is not possible, and it is easily seen that we need one more row. For $n < q^L - r + 1$ a search matrix with L rows is readily constructed.

Section 2.2

1. If $=$ results after the 1st test, weigh $1,2,3 : 8,9,10$. The resulting configurations for $>, =, <$ are:

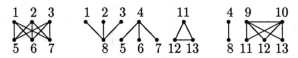

| 1 2 3 | 1 2 3 4 | 11 | 4 9 10 |
| 5 6 7 | 8 5 6 7 12 13 | | 8 11 12 13 |

In each case two more weighings suffice.

3. $L^{(3)}(3) = 0 = \lceil \log_3(\begin{smallmatrix} 3 \\ 3 \end{smallmatrix}) \rceil$ is trivial. We proceed by induction on L.

Note that $\lceil \log_3(\begin{smallmatrix} 3^L \\ 3 \end{smallmatrix}) \rceil = 3L - 1$ $(L \geq 2)$. Split S into 3 parts A, B, C of size 3^{L-1}, and weigh $A : B$. If $A = B$, then weigh $A : C$, and if $A \neq B$, weigh C against the lighter of A and B. Let $w(X)$ be the number of defective elements in $X, X \subseteq S$.

Case 1. $A = B$. Then $w(A) = w(B) = 0$ or 1, $w(C) = 3$ or 1. Hence if $C > A$, then $w(C) = 3$, thus $L \leq 2+(3L-4) = 3L-2$ by induction. If $C = A$, then $w(A) = w(B) = w(C) = 1$ and $L \leq 2+3(L-1) = 3L-1$ by **2.1**. $C < A$ cannot occur.

Case 2. W.l.o.g. $A > B$. Then $(w(A), w(B), w(C)) \in \{(3,0,0), (2,0,1), (2,1,0), (1,0,2)\}$. If $B > C$, then $w(A) = 2$, $w(B) = 1$, $w(C) = 0$, and $L \leq 2+(2L-2)+(L-1) = 3L-1$ by **2.5(ii')** and **2.1**. If $B = C$, then $w(A) = 3$ and $L \leq 3L - 2$ by induction. If $B < C$, then $w(B) = 0$, and $(w(A), w(C)) \in \{(2,1), (1,2)\}$, and it is easily shown that again $3L - 3$ more weighings suffice. The other two claims are established by similar arguments.

5. Let $3^{L-1} < n \leq 3^L$. We know by exercise 3 that $3^{3L-2} < (\begin{smallmatrix} 3^L \\ 3 \end{smallmatrix}) \leq 3^{3L-1}$. If $(\begin{smallmatrix} n \\ 3 \end{smallmatrix}) > 3^{3L-4}$, enlarge S to a set T containing 3^L coins by adding good coins. By exercise 3, $L_g^{(3)}(S) \leq L^{(3)}(T) = 3L - 1 \leq \lceil \log_3(\begin{smallmatrix} n \\ 3 \end{smallmatrix}) \rceil + 2$. If $(\begin{smallmatrix} n \\ 3 \end{smallmatrix}) \leq 3^{3L-4}$, then $n \leq 3^{L-1} + 3^{L-2}$. Enlarge S to a set T with $|T| = 3^{L-1} + 3^{L-2}$. Since $(\begin{smallmatrix} 3^{L-1} + 3^{L-2} \\ 3 \end{smallmatrix}) \leq 3^{3L-3}$, we

have by exercise 3 again $L_g^{(3)}(S) \leq L^{(3)}(T) \leq 3L - 2 \leq \lceil \log_3(\begin{array}{c} n \\ 3 \end{array})\rceil + 2$.

7. Suppose M_k is a $(2^{k-1} - 1) \times (2^k - 1)$-search matrix. Let $\underline{a}_1, \ldots, \underline{a}_{2^k-1}$ be the columns, $\ell = 2^k - 1$. The matrix $M_{k+1} =$

$$
\begin{array}{cccccccccc}
1 & 1 & \ldots & 1 & -1 & -1 & \ldots & -1 & 0 \\
\underline{a}_1 & \underline{a}_2 & & \underline{a}_\ell & \underline{a}_1 & \underline{a}_2 & & \underline{a}_\ell & 0 \\
\underline{a}_2 & \underline{a}_3 & \ldots & \underline{a}_1 & -\underline{a}_2 & -\underline{a}_3 & \ldots & -\underline{a}_1 & 0
\end{array}
$$ is then a search matrix.

Section 2.3

2. Use the analogous decompositions as in the proofs of **2.8** and **2.9**.

7. The lower bound is the information-theoretic bound. By determining each defective element separately in T and U, we obtain $M_{pre}^{(2)}(m, n) \leq \lceil \log_2 m \rceil + \lceil \log_2 n \rceil \leq \lceil \log_2 mn \rceil + 1$. (See exercise 1.4.4).

8. $M = (A \mid B)$ where A has 2 columns and B has n columns is a search matrix iff $\underline{a}_i + \underline{b}_j \neq \underline{a}_k + \underline{b}_\ell$ for all $\{i, j\} \neq \{k, \ell\}$. If $2^{\ell-1} \leq n < 2^\ell$, we choose $\underline{a}_1 = \underline{1}$, $\underline{a}_2 = \underline{0}$, and n different columns $\neq \underline{0}$ in B. If $n = 2^\ell$, then an ℓ-rowed matrix would have to contain all 0,1-columns of length ℓ in B whence $\underline{b}_j = \underline{a}_2$, $\underline{b}_k = \underline{a}_1$ for some j, k, and thus $\underline{a}_1 + \underline{b}_j = \underline{a}_2 + \underline{b}_k$.

Section 2.4

3. In the last part of the proof of **2.16** assume inductively $\frac{r}{2} \log_2 r - r + \frac{\log_2 3}{2} r < N(r)$. Let $m = 2^\ell + r$. Then we have by the proof in **2.16** with $a = \frac{3}{4}$, $b = \frac{1}{4}$, $\frac{m}{2} \log_2 m \leq \ell 2^{\ell-1} + \frac{r}{2} \log_2 r - 2^{\ell-1} \log_2 3 + 2^\ell + r = N(m) - N(r) + \frac{r}{2} \log_2 r - 2^\ell \frac{\log_2 3}{2} + 2^\ell < N(m) + r - \frac{\log_2 3}{2} r - \frac{\log_2 3}{2} 2^\ell + 2^\ell = N(m) + m - \frac{\log_2 3}{2} m$. For the upper bound note that $N(m) = \sum_{i=0}^{m-1} \alpha(i)$ where $\alpha(i)$ is the number of 1's in the binary expansion of i. Set $\alpha(i, j) =$ number of common 1's in the expansions of i and j, where $1 \leq i, j \leq m - 1$, and $\alpha(0, j) = \alpha(i, 0) = 0$, for all $i \leq m - 1$. Consider the $m \times m$-matrix $M(m) = (a_{ij})$ where $a_{ij} = (-1)^{\alpha(i,j)}$. It is not hard to obtain the formula $\det M(m) = \det M(2^\ell) \cdot (-2)^r \cdot \det(M(r))$. The function $D(m) = \log_2 |\det M(m)|$ thus satisfies the recursion $D(2^\ell + r) = D(2^\ell) + r + D(r)$ which is just the recursion for $N(m)$. It follows easily that, in fact, $N(m) = D(m)$, i.e. $|\det M(m)| = 2^{N(m)}$. By Hadamard's inequality, any $+1, -1$-matrix M of order m satisfies $|\det M| \leq m^{\frac{m}{2}}$, whence $N(m) \leq \frac{m}{2} \log_2 m$.

5. Let $(a_1, \ldots, a_m)$ be a solution. The vector $(b_1, \ldots, b_m)$ with $b_i = \sum_{j=1}^{i} a_j + (i-1)$ satisfies $0 \le b_1 < b_2 < \ldots < b_m \le m+h-1$. The mapping $\underline{a} \longrightarrow \underline{b}$ is a bijection between all solution vectors $\underline{a}$ and all m-sized subsets of $\{0, 1, \ldots, m+h-1\}$. Thus the number of solutions is $\binom{m+h}{h}$.

7. Let A be a 0,1-matrix detecting all defectives in a d-set, and set $B = B_\ell$ where B_ℓ is the $\ell \times 2^\ell$-matrix containing all 0,1-columns of length ℓ. Set $C = B \times A$ where $B \times A$ is the Kronecker product, i.e. every 1 in B is replaced by A, and every 0 by $0.A$. It is readily seen that C is a search matrix for our problem. Since the number of rows in C is ℓ times the number of rows of A, the result follows from **2.18**. In fact, it is known that $\lim\limits_{d \to \infty} M_{pre}(2^\ell, d) \frac{\log_2 d}{d} = 2\ell$.

Section 3.1

2. If G is without cycles, then it contains a forest. Any non-trivial component (which is a tree) has at least two vertices of degree 1 (see the remark after **3.2**).

4. Proposition 3.2 proves a) $\Rightarrow$ b). If c) is false, then G has a cycle C. Denote by G' the subgraph obtained after removing some edge e of C. Since G' is still connected, it contains a spanning tree whence $|E(G)| > |E(G')| \ge |V| - 1$. This proves c) $\Rightarrow$ b). The implication c) $\Rightarrow$ a) is obvious.

6. If G is not connected, then $|E(G)| \le \binom{i}{2} + \binom{n-i}{2}$ for some $1 \le i \le \frac{n}{2}$. Since $\binom{i}{2} + \binom{n-i}{2} \le \binom{n-1}{2}$, the assertion is correct. The bound is best possible, as seen from the graph consisting of K_{n-1} and a single isolated vertex.

Section 3.2

3. Suppose $\binom{n}{2} < 2^k$, where we may assume $n = \lfloor 2^{\frac{k+1}{2}} + \frac{1}{2} \rfloor$ by **3.4**. Set $i = \lfloor 2^{\frac{k}{2}} + \frac{1}{2} \rfloor$, then $\binom{i}{2} < 2^{k-1}$ by **3.4**, and $n - i < 2^{\frac{k+1}{2}} + \frac{1}{2} - 2^{\frac{k}{2}} + \frac{1}{2} =$

$2^{\frac{k}{2}}(\sqrt{2}-1)+1 < 2^{\frac{k-1}{2}}+\frac{1}{2}$. Thus $\binom{n-i}{2} < 2^{k-2}$ by **3.4**. The small cases can be checked directly, so assume $k \geq 8$. Then $3i \geq 2n+1$, and thus $i(n-i) \leq \binom{i}{2} < 2^{k-1}$. Test K_i first. If "yes", then apply induction. If "no", then test the complementary complete subgraph K_{n-i}. If "yes", we are done by induction, while in case of "no" we are left with $K_{i,n-i}$ which can now be settled by **3.14**.

7. Let k be the smallest number such that G is k-degenerate. Set $m = |E(G)|$, $U = \{u \in V(G) : d(u) \geq k\}$. Note $|U| \geq k+1$ by the choice of k. Hence $m \geq \binom{k+1}{2} \geq 5k$ for $k \geq 9$, and thus $m-k \geq \frac{4m}{5}$, $m+k \leq \frac{6m}{5}$ for $k \geq 9$. Now apply inequality (3.8). The small cases can be checked directly.

9. Denote by $\oplus$ the addition in $GF(2)$, and extend this to vectors over $GF(2)$. In our algorithm we first take a 0,1-matrix M of size $\lceil \log_2 n \rceil \times n$ with all columns distinct. If $\underline{b}$ is the outcome vector and $\underline{a}, \underline{a}'$ are the columns corresponding to the end-vertices of e^*, then $\underline{b} = \underline{a} \oplus \underline{a}'$. If $\underline{a} \oplus \underline{a}' = \underline{a} \oplus \underline{a}''$, then $\underline{a}' = \underline{a}''$. Hence after these $\lceil \log_2 n \rceil$ tests the set E_0 of possible edges equals $\{a_1 b_1, a_2 b_2 \ldots, a_t b_t\}$ with all a_i, b_j distinct. Set $A = \{a_1, \ldots, a_t\}$, $B = \{b_1, \ldots, b_t\}$. By the usual halving procedure on, say, B we conclude $P(n) \leq \lceil \log_2 n \rceil + \lceil \log_2 \frac{n}{2} \rceil \leq \lceil \log_2 \binom{n}{2} \rceil + 1$.

For $n = 91$, we have $\binom{91}{2} = 4095 = 2^{12}-1$. Hence if $P(91) = 12$, then we should be able to find i with $i(n-i) = 2^{11}$ or $2^{11}-1$. But this is not possible.

10. $P_{pre}(n)$ is non-decreasing in n, so it suffices to show $P_{pre}(2^k) \leq 2k$. We proceed as in the proof of **2.11**. Consider $GF(2^k)$ and let α be a generating element. We consider the elements of $GF(2^k)$ as vectors of length k over $GF(2)$. Let M be the following matrix: Let us number the columns $0, 1, \ldots, 2^k-1$. The column $\underline{c}_0$ has all 0's, and the column $\underline{c}_i = \binom{\alpha^i}{\alpha^{3i}}$, $i \geq 1$, i.e. the first k entries correspond to α^i and the bottom half to α^{3i}. Now verify $\underline{c}_i \oplus \underline{c}_j \neq \underline{c}_k \oplus \underline{c}_\ell$ for $\{i,j\} \neq \{k,\ell\}$ as in the proof of **2.11**.

Section 3.3

1. Consider $K_{3,2^k-k}$ $(k \geq 2)$. Let the first test be of type $(2, 2^{k-1} - k + 1)$. Then $G_2, G_0 \subseteq G_1$ where $G_1 = K_{2,2^{k-1}-1} + K_{1,2^{k-1}-k+1}$. For G_1 we choose a test of type $(1, 2^{k-2}) + (0, 2^{k-2} - k + 1)$. For the resulting graphs we have $G_{1,2}, G_{1,0} \subseteq G_{1,1}$ where $G_{1,1} = K_{1,2^{k-2}} + K_{1,2^{k-2}-1} + K_{1,2^{k-2}-k+1}$. Hence $G_{1,1}$ is a star forest and as such is a subgraph of $N(k-2)$ in the notation of **3.25**. Hence $M(K_{3,2^k-k}) \leq k$ by **3.24**. Now consider $K_{3,2^k-k+1}$. For $k = 2$, it is easily seen that $M(K_{3,3}) = 3$. Let $k > 2$. By symmetry, we have two cases: a. The first test is of type $(3, j)$, b. the first test is of type $(2, j)$. Case a. is easily disposed of as is case b. with $j = 0$ or $j = 2^k - k + 1$. So assume $0 < j < 2^k - k + 1$. Then $G_1 = K_{2,2^k-k+1-j} + K_{1,j}$. The result will thus follow from the inequality $M(K_{2,i} + K_{1,j}) \geq k$ whenever $i + j \geq 2^k - k + 1$ $(k \geq 2)$. This latter claim is now readily proved using **3.25**.

4. The assertion is trivial when any of the t_i's satisfies $t_i \leq \frac{1}{9}$ or $t_i \geq \frac{4}{9}$. Hence assume $\frac{1}{9} < t_2 < \frac{4}{9}$. Consider the function $g(t_2) = 2(\sqrt{t_2} - t_2)$. We have $g(\frac{1}{9}) = g(\frac{4}{9}) = \frac{4}{9}$ and thus $g(t_2) > \frac{4}{9}$, i.e. $t_1 > \frac{4}{9}$ by **3.27**. To see that $\frac{4}{9}$ cannot be improved decompose $K_{9,9}$ into $K_{6,6}, K_{6,3} + K_{3,6}$, and $K_{3,3}$.

5. The numbers $n = 3^k + 3^{k-1}$ satisfy $\lambda . 3^{2k-1} < \binom{n}{2} < 3^{2k}$ for $k \geq 2$, with λ as in **3.29**.

7. The lower bound is clear. For the upper bound, consider the star $K_{1,2^t+1}$.

9. For brevity, set $M(n) = M_{pre}(K_n, K_n)$. We first prove that $\lim_{n\to\infty} \frac{M(n)}{\log_2 n}$ exists. It suffices to show this for $n = 2^\ell$, i.e. $\lim_{\ell\to\infty} \frac{M(2^\ell)}{\ell}$ exists. Let $A = (A_1 \mid A_2)$ be a search matrix for $n = 2^s$, thus A has $M(2^s)$ rows and each A_i has 2^s columns. Similarly let $B = (B_1 \mid B_2)$ be a search matrix for 2^t. Then as in the proof of **3.30**, $C = \begin{pmatrix} A_1 & A_2 \\ \times & \times \\ B_1 & B_2 \end{pmatrix}$ is a search matrix for $n = 2^{s+t}$. Hence $M(2^{s+t}) \leq M(2^s) + M(2^t)$, and by a well-known theorem of Analysis, $\lim_{\ell\to\infty} \frac{M(2^\ell)}{\ell}$ exists, and thus also $\lim_{\ell\to\infty} \frac{M(n)}{\log_2 n}$. Setting $n = m(k)$, we conclude that $\lim_{\ell\to\infty} \frac{k}{\log_2 m(k)}$

exists, and thus also $\lim_{k\to\infty}[m(k)]^{\frac{1}{k}}$. Now apply **3.30** to the sequence $(2^{\ell} : \ell = 0, 1, 2, \ldots)$.

Section 3.4

2. Consider the proof of **3.36**.

4. Suppose $v_1, \ldots, v_{\ell}$ is the sequence of vertices tested when player B always says "no". The remaining subgraph $G - \{v_1, \ldots, v_{\ell}\}$ must then be either complete or contain no edges. Hence $n - \ell \leq \omega(G)$ or $n - \ell \leq \alpha(G)$ which proves the lower bound. To prove the upper bound, it suffices to show $L^{(r)}(G) \leq n - \frac{\alpha(G)}{2}$ since $\alpha(\overline{G}) = \omega(G)$. Let U be a set of vertices with no edges of maximal size, $|U| = \alpha(G)$. Player A tests the vertices $v_1, \ldots, v_{n-\alpha}$ of $G - U$. Denote by d_i the degree of v_i in the subgraph $G - \{v_1, \ldots, v_{i-1}\}$. If B always says "no", then A is finished after $n - \alpha$ queries. If B says "yes" for the 1st time at the i-th test, then A needs $\min(d_i, n - i - d_i) \leq \frac{n-i}{2}$ tests thereafter. Hence $L^{(r)}(G) \leq \max(1 + \frac{n-1}{2}, 2 + \frac{n-2}{2}, \ldots, (n - \alpha) + \frac{\alpha}{2}, n - \alpha) = n - \frac{\alpha}{2}$.

5. Suppose v is the first vertex to be tested, and let $v_1, \ldots, v_d$ be the neighbors of v, $d = d(v)$. The "yes"-subtree splits off the edges one by one and hence has external length $\sum_{i=1}^{d-1} i + (d - 1) = \binom{d+1}{2} - 1$.

Thus $\overline{L}_1(G) = 1 + \frac{1}{m}(\binom{d+1}{2} - 1) + (1 - \frac{d}{m})\overline{L}_1(G - v)$, where $m = |E|$.
We use induction on n. For $n = 2$, the claim is trivial. As first vertex choose v with $d = d(v) \geq \overline{d} = \frac{2m}{n}$. Then $\overline{L}_1(G) \leq 1 + \frac{1}{m}(\binom{d+1}{2} - 1) + (1 - \frac{d}{m})(\frac{2}{3}n - \frac{2}{\overline{d}_1})$, where $\overline{d}_1 = \frac{2(m-d)}{n-1}$ is the average degree of $G - v$. Hence $\overline{L}_1(G) \leq 1 + \frac{3d(d+1-n)}{6m} - \frac{dn}{6m} + \frac{2}{3}n - \frac{2}{d}$, and the result follows from $d + 1 \leq n$ and $dn \geq 2m$.

7. $L_1(S) = \min_{A \subseteq V}(|A| : G - A \text{ contains a single edge})$.

Section 3.5

3. We have to exhibit an algorithm of length $\leq \binom{n}{2} - 1$. Let the vertices be $1, 2, \ldots, n$. Choose vertex 1 and ask all edges $1i$. If there are two

"yes", say $1k, 1\ell \in E$, then $k\ell \notin E$ dand hence $k\ell$ need not be asked. Hence we may assume that 12 is the only edge in E. Now test all edges $2i, i \geq 3$. Continuing in this way, we may assume that the path $(1, 2, \ldots . n - 1)$ is in G while all edges $ij, 1 \leq i < j \leq n$, are not in G. But then the edge $n - 1, n$ must be in G and hence need not be probed.

4. Let $P = (v_1, v_2, \ldots, v_n)$ be the unique Hamiltonian path. Then $d(v_1) = d(v_n) = 1$, since if $v_1 v_i \in E, i \geq 3$, then $(v_{i-1}, v_{i-2}, \ldots, v_1, v_i, v_{i+1}, \ldots, v_n)$ is another Hamiltonian path. Suppose $n \equiv 0 \pmod 2$. If v_3 is adjacent to $v_j, j \geq 5$, then v_2 is not adjacent to v_{j-1} since otherwise we obtain the path $(v_1, v_2, v_{j-1}, v_{j-2}, \ldots, v_3, v_j, v_{j+1}, \ldots, v_n)$. Hence if v_3 is adjacent to ℓ vertices with index ≥ 5, then v_2 is adjacent to at most $n - 4 - \ell$ vertices with index ≥ 4. Thus v_2, v_3 are adjacent between them to at most $n - 4$ vertices outside P. Similarly, v_4, v_5 are adjacent to at most $n-6$ vertices to the right outside P, and so on. We conclude $|E| \leq (n - 1) + (n - 4) + (n - 6) + \ldots + 2 = (\frac{n-1}{2})^2 + \frac{3}{4} = \lfloor (\frac{n-1}{2})^2 \rfloor + 1$. The same reasoning applies to $n \equiv 1 \pmod 2$. Extremal graphs are easily constructed.

6. Pick a vertex u. After at most $n - 2$ tests the neighbors v and w of u in the Hamiltonian cycle are determined. Now apply an optimal algorithm to find the unique path P connecting the remaining $n - 3$ vertices, and use one more query to see how P is connected to (v, u, w).

8. Let $t(m, \ell)$ be the maximal number of edges in a graph on m vertices without a K_ℓ. Suppose G has a unique subgraph $\cong K_\ell$ and let $G' = G - K_\ell$. G' contains no K_ℓ and every vertex of G' is joined to at most $\ell - 2$ vertices of K_ℓ. Hence $m(K_\ell) \leq \binom{\ell}{2} + t(n - \ell, \ell) + (\ell - 2)(n - \ell)$. This bound can easily be realized by using a theorem of Turán in graph theory (see Aigner [1987, p.140]).

Section 3.6

2. For $n \leq 3$, **3.45** or **3.51** applies. For $n = 4$, there are 11 non-isomorphic graphs displayed in the figure. The number below each graph indicates the number of isomorphic copies. On the right, there is a table of the isomorphism types arranged according to even and odd cardinality.

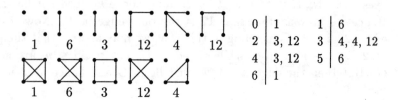

0	1	1	6
2	3, 12	3	4, 4, 12
4	3, 12	5	6
6	1		

Case 1. $\emptyset, K_4 \in \mathcal{P}$. By exercise 1, we may assume that all single edges and all graphs $K_4 - e$ are in $\mathcal{P}$. Looking at the table we conclude that the number p_{odd} of graphs with odd size is ≥ 12 and $\equiv 0$ (mod 4). Using **3.51(i)** we may assume $p_{odd} = p_{even} = 20$. By the table, $o(\mathcal{P}) = 9$ and thus $o(\mathcal{P}^c) = 2$ which implies elusiveness by **3.45**.

Case 2. $\emptyset \in \mathcal{P}$, $K_4 \notin \mathcal{P}$ (or $\emptyset \notin \mathcal{P}$, $K_4 \in \mathcal{P}$). By exercise 1, we may assume that all single edges are in $\mathcal{P}$, whereas $K_4 - e$ is not. From the table we see $p_{even} \equiv 1$ (mod 3), $6 \leq p_{odd} \leq 26$ and $p_{odd} \equiv 2$ (mod 4). The table implies $p_{even} \neq p_{odd}$.

Case 3. $\emptyset, K_4 \notin \mathcal{P}$. By exercise 1, single edges and $K_4 - e$ are not in $\mathcal{P}$. By the table, $p_{even} \equiv 0$ (mod 3), $p_{odd} \equiv 0$ (mod 4). Hence for $p_{even} = p_{odd}$ only 12 is possible, implying $o(\mathcal{P}) = 2$.

4. Proceed as in figure 3.18. First we pick an arbitrary vertex v_1 and test all its incident edges. Next we choose a neighbor v_2 of v_1 and test all its incident edges. Repeating, we arrive after at most $\frac{n}{2} + 1$ iterations at the situation where we either know $X \notin \mathcal{P}$ or where we have isolated a, b, A and B. It is now easily seen that either no edge in A or no edge in B need be tested, whence $C(\mathcal{P}) \leq \binom{n}{2} - \frac{1}{2}(\frac{n}{2}-1)(\frac{n}{2}-2) = \frac{3}{8}n^2 + \frac{n}{4} - 1$.

7. By the transitivity of $\Gamma(\mathfrak{C})$, every element $x \in T$ is contained in the same number a'_i of i-sets of $\mathfrak{C}$. Let $\mathfrak{C}'_x = \{X \in \mathfrak{C} : x \in X\}$, $\mathfrak{C}_x{''} = \mathfrak{C} - \mathfrak{C}'_x$. Set $p(\mathfrak{C}; z) = \sum a_i z^i$, $p(\mathfrak{C}'_x; z) = \sum a'_i z^i$, $p(\mathfrak{C}_x{''}; z) = \sum a_i{''} z^i$. Thus $a'_i = \frac{ia_i}{t}$, $a_i{''} = (1 - \frac{i}{t})a_i$. Suppose $\mathfrak{C}$ is not elusive, and assume A probes x first. By the transitivity of $\Gamma(\mathfrak{C})$, it is immaterial which x is tested first. If B answer "yes", then the problem is reduced to $\mathfrak{C}' = \{X - x : X \in \mathfrak{C}'_x\} \subseteq 2^{T-x}$, which must be non-elusive whence $(1 + z) \mid p(\mathfrak{C}'; z)$. Since $p(\mathfrak{C}'; z) = \sum a'_i z^{i-1} = \frac{1}{t} \frac{dp(\mathfrak{C}; z)}{dz}$, we conclude

$(1+z) \mid \frac{dp(\mathfrak{C};z)}{dz}$, and thus $(1+z)^2 \mid p(\mathfrak{C};z)$. An analogous argument applies to the answer "no". The remaining claim is now obvious.

9. Suppose $V(G) = \{u_1, \ldots, u_n\}$, $V(H) = \{v_1, \ldots, v_n\}$ is any representation of G and H where u_i and v_i are identified, and where the number m of common edges is minimal. Suppose $m > 0$, $u_1 u_2 \in E(G)$, $v_1 v_2 \in E(H)$. Let L be the index-set of vertices with index > 2 which can be reached from $u_2 = v_2$ by either an edge in G followed by an edge in H, or the other way around. Starting with edges in G we see that we can reach at most $\Delta(G)\Delta(H) - 1$ vertices (note that v_2 cannot be reached), and similarly when we start with H. Hence $|L| \leq 2\Delta(G)\Delta(H) - 2 < n - 2$. Thus there is an index $\ell \notin L$, $\ell \geq 3$. Interchanging the indices 2 and ℓ in $V(G)$, it is readily seen that fewer than m common edges result in this new representation, contradiction. An example for the last claim is $G = H = K_3 + K_3 + K_1$ with $\Delta(G) = \Delta(H) = 2$, $n = 7$. This can easily be generalized.

10. Since $\Delta(T_i) < n - 1$, there exist end-vertices u_1, u_2 in T_1 (and T_2) whose neighbors v_1, v_2 are distinct. Suppose we can pick such a pair such that $\Delta(T_1') < n-3$ where $T_1' = T_1 - \{u_1, u_2\}$, and similarly for T_2. By induction, we may pack T_1' and T_2' on $n - 2$ vertices and complete the packing to all of T_1 and T_2. If, say, in T_1 no such pair u_1, u_2 exists, then $\Delta(T_1) = n - 2$ in which case the packing can be readily achieved directly.

Section 4.1

1. We have $M(2) = B(2) = 1$, $M(3) = B(3) = 3$. Suppose $n \geq 4$. We know the recursion $M(n) = M(\lfloor \frac{n}{2} \rfloor) + M(\lceil \frac{n}{2} \rceil) + (n-1)$ and from (4.2) it is easy to derive the same recursion for $B(n)$.

6. Clearly, $S'(n) \geq S(n)$ since the keys may be distinct. On the other hand, if $\mathcal{A}$ is an algorithm of length $S(n)$ for distinct keys, then we can easily modify it to one for equal keys by identifying $=$ with $<$.

7. The worst-case cost is $n - 1$. We can achieve this by comparing the first key to all other keys, and when all keys are equal we certainly need $n - 1$ comparisons to discover this. Let $f(n)$ be the average cost, and let $g(n)$ be the average cost when we already know k values (equal to 0 or 1) among $n + k$ keys. Then $f(0) = f(1) = g(0) = 0$,

$g(1) = 1$, and $f(n) = 1 + \frac{1}{2}f(n-1) + \frac{1}{2}g(n-2)$, $g(n) = 1 + \min\{g(n-1), \frac{1}{2}(g(n-1) + g(n-2))\} = 1 + \frac{1}{2}(g(n-1) + g(n-2))$. It follows that $f(n) - g(n) = \frac{1}{2}(f(n-1) - g(n-1))$. Solving the recursion for $g(n)$ yields $g(n) = \frac{2}{3}(n + \frac{1}{3}(1 - (-\frac{1}{2})^n)$, and thus $f(n) = \frac{2}{3}n + \frac{2}{9} - \frac{2}{9}(-\frac{1}{2})^n - (\frac{1}{2})^{n-1} \sim \frac{2}{3}n$.

8. Set $d(n) = F(n) - \log_2 n! = \sum_{i=2}^{n} \left(\lceil \log_2 \frac{3i}{4} \rceil - \log_2 i \right)$. We show $d(n) > 1$ for $n \geq 22$. For $22 \leq n \leq 128$ this can be checked directly, e.g. we obtain $d(128) > 13$. Set $a_i = \lceil \log_2 \frac{3i}{4} \rceil - \log_2 i$, thus $d(n) = \sum_{i=2}^{n} a_i$.

Suppose $2^k \leq i < 2^{k+1}$. Then $a_i = \lceil \log_2 i - \log_2 \frac{4}{3} \rceil - \log_2 i = \lceil \log_2 2^k \frac{i}{2^k} - \log_2 \frac{4}{3} \rceil - \log_2 2^k \frac{i}{2^k} = \lceil \log_2 \frac{i}{2^k} - \log_2 \frac{4}{3} \rceil - \log_2 \frac{i}{2^k}$. It follows that $a_i = 0$ for $i = 2^k$, $a_i < 0$ for $2^k < i < \frac{4}{3}2^k$, $a_i > 0$ for $\frac{4}{3}2^k < i < 2^{k+1}$. Hence $\min(d(i) : 2^k < i \leq 2^{k+1}) = d(\lfloor \frac{4}{3}2^k \rfloor)$, and it suffices to show that $d(\lfloor \frac{4}{3}2^k \rfloor) > 1$ for $k \geq 7$. We have

$$d(2^{k+1}) - d(2^k) = \sum_{i=2^k+1}^{2^{k+1}} (2^{k+1} - \lfloor \frac{4}{3}2^k \rfloor) - \sum_{i=2^k+1}^{2^{k+1}} \log_2 \frac{i}{2^k} \geq \frac{2}{3}2^k + k2^k -$$

$\sum_{i=2^k+1}^{2^{k+1}} \log_2 i$. Since $\sum_{i=2^k+1}^{2^{k+1}} \log_2 i = 1 + \sum_{i=2^k}^{2^{k+1}-1} \log_2 i \leq 1 + \int_{2^k}^{2^{k+1}} \log_2 t\, dt = 1 + (2k+2)2^k - \frac{2}{\ell n 2}2^k - k2^k + \frac{1}{\ell n 2}2^k \leq 2^k(\frac{1}{128} + k + 2 - \frac{1}{\ell n 2})$, we infer $d(2^{k+1}) - d(2^k) \geq 2^k(\frac{2}{3} + k - \frac{1}{128} - k - 2 + \frac{1}{\ell n 2}) = 2^k \cdot (\frac{1}{\ell n 2} - \frac{4}{3} - \frac{1}{128}) = c_0 2^k$ with $0.10154 < c_0 < 0.10155$. Since $d(2^7) > 13 > 128 c_0$ we have $d(2^{k+1}) \geq d(2^k) + 2^k c_0 \geq 2^{k+1} c_0$ by induction. Using integrals it is easy to see that $d(\lfloor \frac{4}{3}2^k \rfloor) - d(2^k) > -0.07836.2^k$ for $k \geq 7$ whence finally $d(\lfloor \frac{4}{3}2^k \rfloor) > d(2^k) - 0.07836.2^k \geq (c_0 - 0.07836)2^k > 0.02318.2^k \geq (0.02318).128 \geq 2.967 > 1$.

9. The external length for the comparison tree using the Ford-Johnson algorithm for $n = 6$ is 6912. We show that $\overline{S}(6)$ actually attains the lower bound given by Theorem 1.8 by exhibiting an algorithm all of whose end-nodes have length 9 or $10 = \lceil \log_2 6! \rceil$. Take 5 elements and perform the first 5 steps as in figure 4.1 and 4.2. It is then an easy matter to insert the 6th element such that our claim is true.

Section 4.2

1. Set $d(P)$ equal to the minimal number of chains into which P can be decomposed, and let $s(P)$ be the size of a maximal antichain. Clearly,

$d(P) \geq s(P)$. To show $d(P) \leq s(P)$, we use induction on $|P|$. For $|P| = 1$ there is nothing to prove.

Case 1. There exists an antichain $A \subseteq P$ with $|A| = s = s(P)$ which contains neither all maximal nor all minimal elements of P. Set $P^+ = \{p \in P : p \geq a$ for some $a \in A\}$, $P^- = \{p \in P : p \leq a$ for some $a \in A\}$. By the hypothesis on A we have $P^+ \neq P$, $P^- \neq P$, $P = P^+ \cup P^-$, $A = P^+ \cap P^-$. By induction, P^+ and P^- can be decomposed into s chains and we can now glue the chains together.

Case 2. Each antichain of size s contains either all maximal or all minimal elements. This is easy.

4. Suppose n is even. We have $|L(P_n)| = |L(P_n; a_1 < b_1)| + |L(P_n; a_1 > b_1)|$. In the first case a_1, b_1 are the two smallest elements, and the remaining poset is P_{n-2}. In the second case b_1 is the minimal element, and the remaining poset is P_{n-1}. The same argument applies to odd n. Hence $|L(P_n)| = |L(P_{n-1})| + |L(P_{n-2})|$, and with the initial values $|L(P_2)| = 2$, $|L(P_3)| = 3$, we infer $|L(P_n)| = F_n$, the n-th Fibonacci number. The last claim is easily proved.

6. Merge $\{a_1 < \ldots < a_m\}$ with $\{b_2 < b_4 < \ldots < b_{2\lfloor \frac{n}{2} \rfloor}\}$. Now insert the odd-numbered elements $b_1, b_3, \ldots$ into the holes between the neighboring even-numbered b_j's. Clearly, this takes m comparisons at the most.

7. Compare $a_1 : b_k$. If $a_1 > b_k$, then the $M(m, n - k)$-problem results. If $a_1 < b_k$, insert a_1. In the worst case, the $M(m - 1, n)$-problem remains.

9. The claim is obvious for $n - m \leq 2$. For $n - m = 3$, the only case to be checked is $M(3, 6) \leq 7$. For $n - m = 4$, the cases to be checked are $M(3, 7) \leq 8$, $M(4, 8) \leq 10$, $M(5, 9) \leq 12$. By exercise 5, $M(3, 7) \leq M(3, 3) + 3 = 8$. By exercise 6, $M(4, 8) \leq 1 + \max(M(4, 6), M(3, 8) + 1) = \max(10, M(3, 8) + 2)$. Again by exercise 6, $M(3, 8) \leq 1 + \max(M(3, 6), M(2, 8) + 1) \leq \max(8, M(2, 8) + 2) = 8$ by **4.7** and $M(3, 6) \leq 7$. So it remains to verify $M(3, 6) \leq 7$ and $M(5, 9) \leq 12$, and this can be done directly.

10. Let $H(m, n)$ be the length of the algorithm. It is straightforward that $H(m, n) \leq H(m, n + 1)$. Suppose $2^t m \leq n < 2^{t+1} m$. Thus $H(m, n) = 1 + \max(H(m, n - 2^t), H(m - 1, n) + t)$. Replace n by $2n + \varepsilon$,

$\varepsilon = 0$ or 1, then $H(m, 2n + \varepsilon) = 1 + \max(H(m, 2n + \varepsilon - 2^{t+1}), H(m - 1, 2n + \varepsilon) + t + 1)$. It is easy to see that $H(m, n) = m + n - 1$ for $m \le n < 2m$. Now prove by induction $H(m, 2n + \varepsilon) = H(m, n) + m$ for $1 \le m \le n$. Hence if $2^t m \le n < 2^{t+1} m$, then by repeatedly dividing by 2, we obtain $H(m, n) = m + \lfloor \frac{n}{2^t} \rfloor - 1 + tm$. Set $\Theta = \log_2 \frac{n}{m} - t$. Then $0 \le \Theta < 1$ and $2^\Theta m = \frac{n}{2^t}$, i.e. $\lfloor 2^\Theta m \rfloor = \lfloor \frac{n}{2^t} \rfloor$. Furthermore, $2^\Theta \le 1 + \Theta$. Finally, $m! \le \frac{m^m}{2^{m-1}}$ since $i(m - i) \le (\frac{m}{2})^2$. Thus we obtain

$$\log_2 \binom{m + n}{n} > \log_2 n^m - \log_2 m! \ge m \log_2 n - m \log_2 m + m - 1 =$$
$$m \log_2 \frac{n}{m} + m - 1 = m(\Theta + t) + m - 1 = H(m, n) + m\Theta - \lfloor \frac{n}{2^t} \rfloor \ge$$
$$H(m, n) + m(\Theta - 2^\Theta) \ge H(m, n) - m.$$

Section 4.3

1. If v is the t-th largest element, and $w_1, \ldots, w_h$ are unrelated to v, then either less than $t - 1$ elements are above v or less than $n - t$ elements are below v in the end-poset. Assume w.l.o.g. the former. Then there is a linear extension with all w_i below v whence v would not be the t-th largest.

3. Let $\mathcal{A}$ be an algorithm of length ℓ. We may assume $n \ge 4$. To each stage i ($i = 0, \ldots, \ell$) we associate a pair (T_i, f_i), where $T_i \subseteq S = $ set of players, $f_i : S \longrightarrow \mathbb{N}_0$. At the start $T_0 = \emptyset$, $f_0 \equiv 1$. If $x : y$ is the $(i+1)$-st game, then the strategy stipulates: i) if $x, y \in T_i$, then $x > y$ if x entered T before y, ii) if $x \in T_i$, $y \notin T_i$, then $x > y$, iii) if $x, y \notin T_i$, then $x > y$ if $f_i(x) > f_i(y)$ with an arbitrary choice if $f_i(x) = f_i(y)$. After game $i + 1$ we set in cases i) and ii), $T_{i+1} = T_i$, $f_{i+1} = f_i$, in case iii) $T_{i+1} = T_i \cup \{x\}$, $f_{i+1} = f_i$ if $f_i(x) + f_i(y) \ge n - 1$ and $T_{i+1} = T_i$, $f_{i+1}(x) = f_i(x) + f_i(y)$, $f_{i+1}(y) = 0$, $f_{i+1}(z) = f_i(z)$ for $z \ne x, y$ if $f_i(x) + f_i(y) < n - 1$. With this strategy it is not hard to show that $\ell \ge (n - 2) + \lceil \log_2(n - 1) \rceil$ by considering the number $v_i(x)$ of victories as in the proof of **4.12**.

5. We proceed as in the proof of **4.12**. Denote by $\{x_1, \ldots, x_s\}$ the maximal elements of P. If x_h is the eventual top element, then every x_i, $i \ne h$, must have lost at least once. Suppose x_h played against p of the x_i's. Then everyone of these players (except possibly the second best) must have lost a second time, and further everyone of the a_h elements covered by x_h in P (except possibly the 2nd best) must lose at least

once. Hence the length of the algorithm is at least $(s - 2) + (p + a_h)$, and it remains to show that $2^{p+a_h} \geq \sum_{i=1}^{s} 2^{a_i}$. By setting $f_0(x_i) = 2^{a_i}$ $(i = 1, \ldots, s)$, $f_0(z) = 0$ for $z \notin \{x_1, \ldots, x_s\}$, the proof goes through as in **4.12**.

6. Comparing the bounds in **4.13**(i) for $t = 3$ with **4.14** and using the monotonicity (see exercise 2), it suffices to prove $W_3(n) \leq (n - 3) + (2k + 1)$ for $n = 2^k + 2^{k-2}$. Split S into two disjoint sets S_1 and S_2, containing 2^k and 2^{k-2} elements, respectively. Set up tournaments to determine the top element a of S_1 and v of S_2. This takes $n - 2$ comparisons. The element a covers k elements in S_1, let b be the one compared last to a (covering $k - 1$ elements). Now compare $b : v$. If $b > v$, then a is the maximum, and we can determine the 2nd and 3rd (using the previous exercise) with $(k - 2) + \lceil \log_2(\sum_{i=0}^{k-2} 2^i + 2^k) \rceil = 2k - 1$ more comparisons. If $b < v$, then compare $a : v$. If $a > v$, then a is the top element. Using exercise 5 we can now determine the 2nd and 3rd with $(k - 2) + \lceil \log_2(\sum_{i=0}^{k-1} 2^i) \rceil = 2k - 2$ comparisons. If $a < v$, then v is the largest element, and again $2k - 2$ more comparisons suffice by exercise 5. Thus in all cases $\ell \leq (n - 3) + (2k + 1)$.

11. Set up the tournament. This takes $n - 1$ comparisons. To determine the 2nd best, we need k games if the top element w was among the $2r$ elements on the last level, and $k - 1$ games otherwise. The formula follows immediately.

12. Split S into 5 disjoint subsets $S_0, S_1, \ldots, S_4$ with $| S_0 | = 2^{k-1}$, $| S_i | = 2^{k-3}$, $i = 1, \ldots, 4$, and set up a knock-out tournament for each S_i. This takes $2^k - 5$ comparisons. Let a be the maximum of S_0, b its last opponent, called the submaximum, and let c_i be the maximum of S_i. We call S_0 the main set. We now insert the c_i's one by one observing the following rule. If the main set has a unique maximum, then compare c_i to the current submaximum b'. If $c_i < b'$, the main set is enlarged by S_i and b' remains the submaximum. If $c_i > b'$, compare c_i to the current maximum. The winner is the maximum and the loser the new submaximum. It is not hard to see that this procedure takes $2^k + k - 2 - \frac{1}{10}$ comparisons on the average. Note that this is not the best procedure, as Matula has shown that $\overline{V}_t(n) \leq n + t \lceil \log_2 t \rceil (11 + \ln \ln n)$.

Section 4.4

2. As in the proof of **4.27**, there must exist a line j leading up to the top line which contains at least $\lceil \log_2 n \rceil$ comparisons.

6. Consider the vectors $\underline{a}_1, \ldots, \underline{a}_m$ as before **4.20**. In any of the $\underline{a}_i$'s $(1 \le i \le m-1)$ the top element is already in its correct position whereas the top element in $\underline{a}_m$ $(=0)$ is not. Hence there must be a comparison which changes only the vector $\underline{a}_m$.

8. Consider the network $[1:2][3:4][1:3][3:5][2:4][2:3][3:5]$.

9. Define $x_j = 1$ iff $p_j \ge k$ and $y_j = 1$ iff $p_j > k$. The mappings $p \longrightarrow x$, $p \longrightarrow y$ are monotone. Hence $(\pi p)_i = k$ implies $(\pi x)_i = 1$ and $(\pi y)_i = 0$. Clearly, x covers y, and y has k 0's. The converse is just as easy.

10. For notational reasons it is convenient to consider networks which select the smallest t elements in the top t lines, moving at each comparison $i:j$ $(i < j)$ the smaller element into line i. After each test we compute the vector $\ell = (\ell_1, \ldots, \ell_n)$ where ℓ_i denotes the smallest possible number that can appear in line i considering all possible inputs. Thus at the start $\ell = (1, 1, \ldots, 1)$. Suppose ℓ is the current vector, and $i:j$ is the next comparison. Let ℓ' be the new vector. Obviously, $\ell'_k = \ell_k$ for $k \ne i, j$, and $\ell'_i = \min(\ell_i, \ell_j)$. We claim that $\ell'_j \le \ell_i + \ell_j$. Denote by π the network up to ℓ. By the previous exercise there exist $x, y \in \{0, 1\}^n$ where $(\pi x)_i = 0$, x has ℓ_i 0's, and $(\pi y)_j = 0$ and y has ℓ_j 0's. Consider $x \wedge y$. Since $x \wedge y \le y$, we have $(x \wedge y)_i$ and $(x \wedge y)_j = 0$, and thus $(x \wedge y)'_j = 0$. Furthermore $x \wedge y$ has at most $\ell_i + \ell_j$ 0's. By adding 1's to $x \wedge y$, we deduce from exercise 9 the existence of a permutation p with $(\pi' p)_j = k \le \ell_i + \ell_j$, where π' is the network up to ℓ'. Now associate to each comparison the following vector $m = (m_1, \ldots, m_n)$. At the start $m = (0, 0, \ldots, 0)$. After $i:j$, we set $m'_k = m_k$ for $k \ne i, j$, and $m'_i = \min(m_i, m_j)$, $m'_j = \max(m_i, m_j) + 1$. By our results on the vector ℓ, we have $2^{m_i} \ge \ell_i$ at each stage. At the end, $\sum m_i$ is the number of comparisons. Now if the network selects the t smallest elements, then $n - t$ of the numbers ℓ_i must be $\ge t + 1$, whence $n - t$ of the m_j's are $\ge \lceil \log_2(t+1) \rceil$. The result follows.

12. Let $p = (p_1, \ldots, p_n)$ be a permutation of $\{1, \ldots, n\}$. By $i(p)$ we denote the number of pairs $i < j$ with $p_i < p_j$. Clearly, any comparison

between adjacent slots reduces this number by at most 1. Hence if $p = (1, 2, \ldots, n)$, then $i(p) = \binom{n}{2}$, and we need at least $\binom{n}{2}$ comparisons. On the other hand, if we first use the $n - 1$ comparisons $[1:2][2:3]\ldots[n-1:n]$, then 1 moves to the bottom, and we obtain $\hat{S}(n) \le \binom{n}{2}$ by induction. By the argument before **4.25**, the values of $\hat{V}_1(n)$, $\hat{V}_2(n)$ and $\hat{U}_2(n)$ stay the same.

Section 4.5

3. Use the 0,1-principle as in the proof of the correctness of Batcher's odd-even merge.

7. The inequality is easily checked for $n \le 8$. The general result will follow from $S^{(p)}(n) \ge S^{(p)}(\lceil \frac{n}{2} \rceil) + 2$. Let us verify this for even $n = 2m$, the odd case being analogous. After the 1st round we obtain m relations $a_1 < b_1, a_2 < b_2, \ldots, a_m < b_m$. Now show that no matter how round 2 is played, there is a possible outcome P such that P contains an antichain of size m. From this the result follows immediately.

10. Suppose $\ell \ge 2$. From $c_{i+1} \ge \frac{c_i^2}{2n+c_i}$ we obtain the sharper inequality $c_i \ge n(3^{2^i - 2^{i-2} - 1})^{-1}$. Hence the length of the algorithm will exceed i as long as $n > 3^{2^i - 2^{i-2}}$. Since $n = 2^{2^\ell} > 3^{2^{\ell-1} - 2^{\ell-3}}$ (proof by induction) we see that indeed ℓ comparisons are required.

12. If i and j are not compared, then all elements $\ne i, j$ may be smaller than i and j whence we would have no information on the ranking of i and j.

13. For one round, $\binom{n}{2}$ comparisons are required. For two rounds, our analysis yields that k comparisons per round are needed such that $\binom{\alpha}{2} \le k$ and $(\lceil \frac{n}{\alpha} \rceil - 1)(2n - \alpha \lceil \frac{n}{\alpha} \rceil) \le 2k$ and k is minimal. Solving these inequalities yields $k \sim n^{\frac{4}{3}}$.

14. Let $S = \{a_1 < \ldots < a_n\}$ and $T = \{b_1 < \ldots < b_n\}$ be the chains. We mark the elements indexed by $i\lceil \sqrt{n} \rceil$ in S and T, $i = 1, 2, \ldots$. In the first round we compare all marked elements, using one round.

This round determines for each element of S a segment in T of length $\leq \lceil \sqrt{n} \rceil$ into which it needs to be inserted. Hence insertion of all marked elements of S takes at most $\lfloor \sqrt{n} \rfloor (\lceil \sqrt{n} \rceil - 1) \leq n$ comparisons. Thus it can be done in round 2. It remains to merge the segments between marked elements of S and T where each segment has length $\leq \lfloor \sqrt{n} \rfloor$. Now apply induction.

Section 5.1

1. Let $\alpha \neq id$ be an automorphism, then $p(x < y) = p(\alpha x < \alpha y)$. Assume there is no $\frac{1}{3}$-central pair. We define a new relation $\ll$ on P by setting $u \ll v$ iff $p(u < v) > \frac{2}{3}$. Suppose $u \ll v$, $v \ll w$. Then $|L(u < v)| + |L(v < w)| > \frac{4}{3}|L|$. Since $|L(u < v < w)| + |L(v < w < u)| + |L(w < u < v)| \leq |L|$, we infer $|L(u < v < w)| + |L(u < w < v)| + |L(v < u < w)| = |L(u < w)| > \frac{1}{3}|L|$, thus $|L(u < w)| > \frac{2}{3}|L|$, i.e. $u \ll w$. Hence $\ll$ is transitive and thus a linear order by the definition of $\ll$. Sind α respects the ordering $\ll$, we conclude that α must be the identity.

4. The covering pairs and critical pairs cannot be implied by other relations. Conversely, the covering pairs determine all comparabilities in P, and the critical pairs are incomparabilites.

5. Apply a recognition algorithm to P. If the unknown poset is isomorphic to P, then it must be determined at the end; hence $C^{(s)}(P) \leq C^{(r)}(P)$. Since P is determined, all pairs of an essential set must have been probed, i.e. $ess(P) \leq C^{(r)}(P)$. To obtain a recognition algorithm we proceed as follows. We assume that P is the unknown order. After $C^{(s)}(P)$ steps we have arrived at the situation where either a unique poset P is possible or none. Hence it suffices to check an essential set to see which case applies.

Section 5.2

3. Use the same strategy as in the proof of **4.16**.

5. Pick any subset A of $n - t + 2$ elements and set up a tournament to determine the top element w of A. This takes $n - t + 1$ comparisons. Since w is above $n - t + 1$ elements, it is above the t-th largest. Now insert the remaining $t - 2$ elements as in the proof of **4.11**(ii). After

these $(t-2)\lceil\log_2(n-t+2)\rceil$ comparisons we have isolated all elements above the t-th largest. Now use the method of **4.11**(ii) to determine the t-th,$(t+1)$-st,...,s-th element.

7. The lower bound is that of **5.10**. For the upper bound we distinguish 4 cases depending on n mod 4. As an example, consider $n = 4k+3$. Split S into k groups S_i with $|S_i| = 4$ each and one group T with $|T| = 3$. In each group S_i we make two disjoint comparisons and compare then the two losers. In T we make one comparison, and compare then the loser to the third element. This takes $3k + 2$ comparisons. The minimal element can now be determined with k further tests, and the top two elements with $\lceil 2k + \log_2(3k + 2)\rceil$ comparisons by exercise 4.3.5. The bounds are never more than 1 apart and coincide for $2^{\lceil\log_2 n\rceil} \geq \frac{3}{2}n$ (n odd) and $2^{\lceil\log_2 n\rceil} \geq \frac{3n}{2}$ or $2^{\lceil\log_2 n\rceil} < \sqrt{2}n$ (n even).

8. Suppose $1 \leq t < s \leq n$ with $t \leq \frac{n}{2}$. Define the functions $\tilde{f}_{t,s}(n) = \binom{n}{s-1}\binom{s-1}{t}2^{n-(s-t+1)}$ and $\tilde{g}_{t,s}(n) = \binom{n}{s}\binom{s}{t-1}2^{\frac{3}{2}(s-t-1)+1}$.
It is an easy exercise on binomial coefficients that $\tilde{f}_{s,t}(n) \geq n2^{n-2}$ for $s - t \leq \frac{n}{2}$ while $\tilde{g}_{t,s}(n) \geq n2^{n-2}$ for $s - t \geq \frac{n}{2}$. Given an algorithm $\mathcal{A}$ we associate with a poset R all functions $f_{t,s}(R)$ as in **5.7** and all $g_{t,s}(R)$ as in **5.9**. At the end, a pair of positions is determined, and our familiar argument together with $\max(\tilde{f}_{t,s}(n), \tilde{g}_{t,s}(n)) \geq n2^{n-2}$ yields the result.

9. Compare $a : b$ first. If $a < b$, we are done. Otherwise, compare b to the remaining $n - 2$ elements. Unless there are precisely $n - t - 1$ elements below b, we are again finished. In the latter case we compare a to the $t - 1$ elements above b. It can be shown that $n + t - 2$ is optimal for $t + 1 \leq \lceil\frac{n}{2}\rceil$.

Section 5.3

1. Proof by induction.

3. Consider the extremal problem $\sum_{i=1}^{n} x_i(c_i + \log_2 x_i) = \min$ under the condition $\sum_{i=1}^{n} x_i = 1$. We have $(x \log_2 x)' = \log_2 x + \log_2 e$. Using the Lagrange multiplier λ we infer $c_i + \log_2 x_i + \log_2 e + \lambda = 0$, and thus

$c_i + \log_2 x_i = C =$ constant as necessary condition. It is easy to see that this condition actually yields the minimum, whence $\sum x_i . C = C$ is the extreme value. Now $c_i + \log_2 x_i = c_1 + \log_2 x_1$ implies $x_i = 2^{c_1 - c_i} x_1$ and thus $1 = (\sum 2^{c_1 - c_i}) x_1$. From this we infer $C = c_1 + \log_2 x_1 = c_1 - \log_2(\sum 2^{c_1 - c_i}) = -\log_2(\sum 2^{-c_i})$.

7. Note that any down-set containing q but not p can be extended to a down-set containing p by adding any non-empty down-set in $U(p)$. Since any down-set containing p is thus obtained in a unique way we have $(N(p) - 1)(i(P; q) - i(P; p)) = i(P; p)$.

Section 5.4

2. Assume f, g are both increasing, and set $\alpha = \beta = \gamma = \delta = \mu$. Denote by $I_A(x)$ the indicator function of $A \subseteq S$, i.e. $I_A(x) = 1$ or 0 according to $x \in A$ or $x \notin A$. It is immediate that $f = \sum \lambda_i I_{A_i}$ for suitable up-sets A_i and $\lambda_i \geq 0$; similarly $g = \sum \rho_j I_{B_j}$. Furthermore, we have $A \vee B = A \cap B$ for any two up-sets. Now,
$$\sum_{x \in 2^S} f(x)\mu(x) = \sum_x \mu(x) \sum_x \lambda_i I_{A_i}(x) = \sum_x \mu(x) \sum_{x \in A_i} \lambda_i = \sum_i \lambda_i \mu(A_i),$$
and similarly $\sum_x g(x)\mu(x) = \sum_j \rho_j \mu(B_j)$. Also, $\sum_x f(x)g(x)\mu(x) =$
$$\sum_x \mu(x) \sum_x \lambda_i I_{A_i}(x) \sum_x \rho_j I_{B_j}(x) = \sum_x \mu(x) \sum_{x \in A_i} \lambda_i \sum_{x \in B_j} \rho_j = \sum_x \mu(x)$$
$$\sum_{i,j : x \in A_i \cap B_j} \lambda_i \rho_j = \sum_{i,j} \lambda_i \rho_j \mu(A_i \cap B_j) = \sum_{i,j} \lambda_i \rho_j \mu(A_i \vee B_j). \text{ By } \textbf{5.14}, \text{ we}$$
conclude $\sum_x f(x)\mu(x) \sum_x g(x)\mu(x) \leq \sum_i \lambda_i \mu(A_i) \sum_j \rho_j \mu(B_j) =$
$$\sum_{i,j} \lambda_i \rho_j \mu(A_i)\mu(B_j) \leq \sum_{i,j} \lambda_i \rho_j \mu_j(A_i \vee B_j)\mu(A_i \wedge B_j) \leq \sum_{i,j} \lambda_i \rho_j \mu(A_i \vee$$
$$B_j)\mu(2^S) = \sum_x f(x)g(x)\mu(x) \cdot \sum_{x \in 2^S} \mu(x).$$

4. Set $X = A$, $Y = \{S - z : z \in X\}$, then $|X| = |Y| = |A|$. Let $x \in A$, $y \in Y$. Then $y = S - z$, $z \in A$, and thus $x \cap y = x \cap (S - z) = x - (x \cap z) = x - z \in A \backslash A$, i.e. $X \wedge Y \subseteq A \backslash A$. Similarly, $X \vee Y \subseteq \{S - w : w \in A \backslash A\}$. Hence $|X \wedge Y| \leq |A \backslash A|$, $|X \vee Y| \leq |A \backslash A|$, and the result follows from **5.15**.

6. Assume $x \wedge (y \vee z) = (x \wedge y) \vee (x \wedge z)$ holds. Then $(x \vee y) \wedge (x \vee z) = x \vee ((x \vee y) \wedge z) = x \vee ((x \wedge z) \vee (y \wedge z)) = x \vee (y \wedge z)$. The reverse implication follows upon interchanging $\wedge$ and $\vee$.

7. Set $N = m + n$, and let $E_N = (x_1, \ldots, x_m; y_1, \ldots, y_n)$ bet the set of all sequences with $1 \leq x_i, y_j \leq N$. Ordering E_N by setting $(x_i; y_j) \leq (x'_i; y'_j)$ iff $x_i \leq x'_i$ for all i and $y_j \geq y'_j$ for all j, E_N becomes a distributive lattice. Let L_N be the set of strict monotone mappings of P into the chain $\{1 < 2 < \ldots < N\}$. Then L_N is a sublattice of E_N and thus distributive. The rest of the proof is as in **5.20**.

10. For the conditions of the previous exercise to fail we must have one of two cases: a. There are distinct elements x, y, u, v such that $x < y$ in A' and $u < v$ in B', b. there are distinct elements x, y, z such that $x < y$ in A' and $y < z$ in B' (or with A', B' interchanged). The general case is easily reduced to the situation when $A = A'$, $B = B'$ and P contains all relations except A', B'. In case a. example 5.7 will do, in

case b. consider the poset $y \bullet \quad \begin{matrix} z \bullet \\ | \\ x \bullet \end{matrix}$. Here $p(x < y \mid y < z) = \frac{1}{3} <$

$p(x < y) = \frac{2}{3}$.

12. We have $h(x) = \frac{1}{|L|} \sum_{\sigma \in L} \sigma(x) = \frac{1}{|L|}(|\{(x, z) : x > z\}| + |L|) = \sum_{z \neq x} p(x > z) + 1$. Similarly, $h(x \mid x < y) = \sum_{z \neq x} p(x > z \mid x < y) + 1$, $h(x \mid x > y) = \sum_{z \neq x} p(x > z \mid x > y) + 1$. If A and B are positively correlated events, then $p(A \cap B) \geq p(A \mid B)$ and thus $p(A \cap \text{non } B) = p(A) - p(A \cap B) \leq p(A)p(\text{non } B)$. Hence $p(A \mid \text{non } B) \leq p(A) \leq p(A \mid B)$. Setting $A = \{x > z\}$, $B = \{x > y\}$, we obtain by the (dual) xyz-inequality, $p(x > z \mid x < y) \leq p(x > z) \leq p(x > z \mid x > y)$ for all $z \neq x$. For $z = y$, we have $p(x > y \mid x < y) = 0$, $p(x > y \mid x > y) = 1$ and $0 < p(x > y) < 1$. Summing over the terms yields $h(x \mid x < y) \leq 1 + h(x \mid x > y)$, and also $h(x \mid x < y) < h(x) < h(x \mid x > y)$.

Section 6.1

2. Let $\underline{x} = \sum_{i=0}^{p} a_i \underline{x}_i$, $\underline{x}_i \in A$ be a convex combination with p minimal.

If $p > n$, then $\underline{x}_0, \ldots, \underline{x}_p$ are affinely dependent, hence $\sum_{i=0}^{p} b_i \underline{x}_i = \underline{0}$,

$\sum_{i=0}^{n} b_i = 0$. Choose the numbering so that $b_p > 0$, $a_p b_p^{-1} \leq a_i b_i^{-1}$ for

all i with $b_i > 0$. Set $c_i = a_i - (a_p b_p^{-1}) b_i$, then $\sum_{i=0}^{p} c_i = \sum_{i=0}^{p} a_i -$

$(a_p b_p^{-1}) \sum\limits_{i=0}^{p} b_i = 1$. Furthermore, $c_i \geq 0$ for all i, and thus $\underline{x} =$
$$\sum_{i=0}^{p} a_i \underline{x}_i = \sum_{i=0}^{p-1} (a_i - (a_p b_p^{-1}) b_i) \underline{x}_i = \sum_{i=0}^{p-1} c_i x_i, \text{ i.e. } p \text{ was not minimal.}$$

4. We have $p f_0 = 2 f_1 = q f_2$ since every edge touches on precisely two vertices and two sides. By Euler's relation, $f_0(1 - \frac{p}{2} + \frac{p}{q}) = 2$, and thus $p f_0 = 2(\frac{1}{p} - \frac{1}{2} + \frac{1}{q})^{-1} = 4pq(2(p+q) - pq)^{-1}$. Since $2(p+q) - pq > 0$ we infer $(p-2)(q-2) < 4$. The possible pairs (p,q) are therefore $(3,3), (4,3), (3,4), (5,3), (3,5)$. These pairs are realized by the platonic solids: tetrahedron, octahedron, cube, icosahedron, dodecahedron.

5. Let v be an arbitrary corner of a regular (p,q)-pattern, and α be the angle between two neighboring edges, hence $\alpha = \frac{2\pi}{q}$. Since the angle-sum of a p-gon is $(p-2)\pi$, we have $\alpha = (1 - \frac{2}{p})\pi$. This implies $\frac{1}{p} + \frac{1}{q} = \frac{1}{2}$, or $(p-2)(q-2) = 4$. Hence the possible pairs (p,q) are $(3,6), (4,4), (6,3)$. These are realized by the hexogonal, square and triangular patterns.

8. From $d(x,y) < |h(x) - h(y)|$ follows that all trees have different heights. Let the vertices of the convex hull be $x_1, \ldots, x_n$ where we order the $x_i's$ in increasing height. By our hypothesis $\sum\limits_{i=1}^{n-1} d(x_i, x_{i+1}) < \sum\limits_{i=1}^{n-1} (h(x_{i+1}) - h(x_i)) = h(x_n) - h(x_1) < M - m$, and also $d(x_1, x_n) < M - m$. Hence the total length is $< 2(M-m)$, and the result follows from the previous exercise.

Section 6.2

2. Consider the following inductive hypothesis: Let $n \geq 1$, and suppose in a convex m-gon P, $m \geq n$, exactly $m - n$ edges of P have been probed (i.e. we know that the unknown point lies in the half-plane containing the interior of P) and n edges are undecided. Then it takes $\lceil \log_2 n \rceil + 1$ tests to solve the PMP. Take any line g. Clearly, one of the polygons created by g has at least $\frac{n}{2}$ undecided edges.

5. To prove $C(Q_{n+1}) \leq C(Q_n) + 2$, test first two parallel hyperplanes cutting Q_{n+1} in $(n-1)$-dimensional faces, say the hyperplanes $H_0 = \{\underline{x} : x_1 = 0\}$ and $H_1 = \{\underline{x} : x_1 = 1\}$. Either $x^* \notin Q_{n+1}$ or x^* lies between H_0 and H_1, and the PMP is now essentially that for Q_n. For

the lower bound, observe that any hyperplane leaves a Q_n undecided in one of the half-hyperplanes.

Section 6.3

2. Let C_n be a cycle of odd length $n \geq 3$. Since in a 2-coloring of C_n, the vertices must be colored alternately, we conclude that the first and last vertex must receive the same color. So, a 2-coloring is not possible. Assume, conversely, that G is connected and has no odd cycle. Pick a vertex v_0 and color it red. The *distance* $d(v_0, w)$ is the length of a shortest path from v_0 to w. Color $w \neq v_0$ red if $d(v_0, w)$ is even and blue if $d(v_0, w)$ is odd. It is easy to see that this provides an admissible 2-coloring of G.

4. Let the defining vertex-sets of $K_{m,n}$ be S and T, $|S| = m$, $|T| = n$. Since S is stable, any mapping $f : S \longrightarrow \{1, \ldots, \lambda\}$ is a λ-coloring. Suppose f assumes i different values, then f can be extended to a λ-coloring of $K_{m,n}$ in $(\lambda - i)^n$ ways. By a well-known formula in combinatorics, the number of mappings $S \longrightarrow \{1, \ldots, \lambda\}$ with i different values is $\binom{\lambda}{i} \sum_{j=1}^{m} (-1)^{i+j} \binom{i}{j} j^m$. Hence $p(K_{m,n}; \lambda) =$

$$\sum_{i=1}^{m} \sum_{j=1}^{m} (-1)^{i+j} \binom{i}{j} j^m \binom{\lambda}{i} (\lambda - i)^n. \text{ By } 6.5, a(K_{m,n}) = (-1)^m \sum_{i,j=1}^{m} (-1)^j$$

$$\binom{i}{j} j^m (i+1)^n.$$

7. Any coloring $f : V \longrightarrow \mathbb{R}$ is associated with an acyclic orientation $\mathcal{O}_f$, $u \longrightarrow v$ iff $f(u) < f(v)$, and any acyclic orientation arises in this way. Suppose we want to solve the coloring problem. In the worst case we have to produce the whole orientation, since as long as an edge $uv \in E$ has no direction assigned to we could still not decide whether $f(u) = f(v)$ or $f(u) \neq f(v)$. Thus the cost c_i of the identification problem is no greater than the cost c_r of the coloring problem. The converse $c_r \leq c_i$ is obvious.

8. We may assume G to be connected. After some tests we have assigned directions to certain edges. Let us say v *dominates* u if there is a directed path from u to v. Suppose inductively that after k tests either a sink is found or there exists a vertex v dominating at least k vertices and v is not dominated by any other vertex. Suppose that

after $k < n - 1$ tests no sink has been found and that v is a vertex with the stated property. Since v is not a sink there must be an edge $vw \in E$ with no direction assigned yet. Now test vw and proceed by induction.

10. We have $Max(P_n) \geq \lceil \log_2 n \rceil$. Suppose $n = 2k$ is even, and let the edges along the path be numbered $e_1, \ldots, e_{n-1}$. As 1st test we pick the middle edge $e_k = u_k u_{k+1}$. W.l.o.g. we receive the answer $u_k \longrightarrow u_{k+1}$. Hence there is a sink among the $\frac{n}{2}$ vertices on the path $u_{k+1}, u_{k+2}, \ldots, u_n$, which can be found inductively with $\lceil \log_2 n \rceil - 1$ tests. The case of odd n is settled in analogous fashion. For C_n we know $Max(C_n) \leq n - 1$ by exercise 8. To prove the lower bound, the strategist player chooses a fixed orientation around the cycle and answers accordingly. It is then immediately clear that $n - 1$ questions need to be asked before the sink is found.

Section 6.4

2. Let this number be $f(n)$. Thus $f(1) = 0$, $f(2) = 1$. If a permutation starts with $i \geq 3$, then the rest must be sorted. If it starts with 2, then apart from 1, which may be anywhere, the rest must be sorted. Finally, there are $f(n-1)$ permutations starting with 1. Summing, we obtain $f(n) = f(n-1) + 2n - 3$, and thus $f(n) = (n-1)^2$.

4. If, say, $f_i > f_{i+1}$, then $\pi = Z_1 | Z_2 | \ldots | Z_k$ could also be decomposed into $Z_1 | \ldots | Z_{i-1} | Z_i - \{f_i\} | \{f_i\} \cup Z_{i+1} | \ldots | Z_k$; similarly for $\ell_i > \ell_{i+1}$. Suppose the conditions are satisfied. Since $f_1 < f_2 < \ldots, < f_k = n$ form an increasing subsequence they must be in different subsequences; similarly for $1 = \ell_1 < \ell_2 < \ldots < \ell_k$. Let $S_1, \ldots, S_k$ be the decreasing subsequences. Then it follows as in the proof of **6.9** that f_i, ℓ_i are in the same subsequence, whence we may assume $f_i, \ell_i \in S_i$ for all i. But then any $a \in Z_1$ is smaller than f_2 and hence must be in S_1. Similarly, any $b \in Z_i$ $(i \geq 2)$ is greater than ℓ_1 and hence cannot be in S_1. Thus $S_1 = Z_1$. Now continue in this way.

5. $R_1(n) = R_n(n) = 1$ are obvious. Let $\pi = A | B$ be a permutation with two blocks. By the previous exercise, π is uniquely recoverable iff $1 \in A$, $n \in B$. Since the other elements may be placed arbitrarily in decreasing fashion, we have $R_2(n) = 2^{n-2}$. $R_3(n)$ and $R_{n-1}(n)$ also follow from exercise 4.

7. Sort the first $n - k$ numbers. Suppose that x is the smallest number which is the end of a longest increasing subsequence of length L among $\{x_1, \ldots, x_{n-k}\}$. Compare $x : x_{n-k+1}$. If $x_{n-k+1} > x$, then x_{n-k+1} is the smallest element of a longest increasing subsequence of length $L+1$, and we proceed by induction. If $x_{n-k+1} < x$, then compare x_{n-k+1} to the element y which is the smallest element of an increasing subsequence of length $L - 1$. Whatever the outcome, we have determined the smallest element at the end of an increasing subsequence of length L in $\{x_1, \ldots, x_{n-k+1}\}$. Clearly, for the final element x_n we need only one comparison.

Index